In the Cauldron

IN THE CAULDRON

Terror, Tension, and the American Ambassador's Struggle to Avoid Pearl Harbor

LEW PAPER

REGNERY
HISTORY

Also by Lew Paper

John F. Kennedy: The Promise and the Performance

Brandeis: An Intimate Biography

Empire: William S. Paley and the Making of CBS

Deadly Risks (a novel)

Perfect: Don Larsen's Miraculous World Series Game and the Men Who Made It Happen

Regnery History™ is a trademark of Salem Communications Holding Corporation
Regnery® is a registered trademark of Salem Communications Holding Corporation

Cataloging-in-Publication data on file with the Library of Congress

ISBN 978-1-62157-631-0
ebook ISBN 978-1-62157-897-0

Published in the United States by
Regnery History
An imprint of Regnery Publishing
A Division of Salem Media Group
300 New Jersey Ave NW
Washington, DC 20001
www.Regnery.com

Manufactured in the United States of America

10 9 8 7 6 5 4 3 2 1

Books are available in quantity for promotional or premium use. For information on discounts and terms, please visit our website: www.Regnery.com.

For Ellie and Charlie
May they prosper in a world without war.

Contents

Characters and Conventions

The list below identifies the key people in this story and the positions they held prior to December 7, 1941. Japanese names follow the Japanese convention of surname first and given name second. In some cases, there is more than one spelling in the English translation of a Japanese name. In each case like that, I have used the name used by Joseph Grew. As an example, Konoye Fumimaro's name is sometimes spelled Konoe. However, Grew always referred to him as Konoye, and that is the spelling I have used. In other situations, the spelling of a place has changed. As one example, Nanking is now Nanjing. In each case like that, I have used the spelling that Grew used.

Joseph W. Ballantine	Head of Japan Desk, Far Eastern Division, Department of State
Sir Robert Craigie	Great Britain's ambassador to Japan
Edward (Ned) S. Crocker	First Secretary, United States Embassy in Tokyo
Eugene H. Dooman	Counselor, United States Embassy in Tokyo
James Drought	Father and Vicar General of the Catholic Foreign Mission Society of America in Maryknoll, New York
John K. Emmerson	Third Secretary, United States Embassy in Tokyo (and, beginning in October 1941, staff, Far Eastern Division, State Department)
Anita Grew English	Daughter of Joseph C. Grew
Robert Fearey	Private Secretary to Joseph C. Grew (April 1941–)
Marshall Green	Private Secretary to Joseph C. Grew (October 1939–March 1941)
Alice Perry Grew	Wife of Joseph C. Grew
Maxwell M. Hamilton	Chief, Far Eastern Division, State Department
Hara Yoshimichi	President, Privy Council, Japan
Waldo Heinrichs	Author, *United States Ambassador: Joseph C. Grew and the Development of the United States Diplomatic Tradition*

Hiranuma Kiichiro	Home Minister, Japan (July 1940-July 1941) and then Minister without Portfolio (July 1941–)
Hirohito Michinomiya	Emperor, Japan (and often referred to only as Hirohito)
Stanley K. Hornbeck	Political Relations Adviser, State Department
Cordell Hull	Secretary of State
Harold L. Ickes	Secretary of the Interior
Iwakuro Hideo	Special Envoy of Japanese Army
Kase Toshikazu	Secretary to Foreign Minister Matsuoka and then Secretary to Foreign Minister Togo (and Chief of the First Section in the American Bureau)
Kido Koichi	Lord Keeper of the Privy Seal, Japan
Frank Knox	Secretary of the Navy
Konoye Fumimaro	Prime Minister of Japan (June 1937-January 1939, July 1940–October 1941)
Lord Halifax	Edward Frederick Lindley Wood, Great Britain's ambassador to the United States
Elsie Grew Lyon	Daughter of Joseph C. Grew
George Marshall	Chief of Staff, United States Army
Matsuoka Yosuke	Foreign Minister, Japan (July 1940–July 1941)
Lilla Grew Moffat	Daughter of Joseph C. Grew
Nagano Osami	Chief of General Staff, Japanese Navy
Oikawa Koshiro	Minister of Navy, Japan (July 1940–October 1941)
Nomura Kichisaburo	Japan's Ambassador to the United States
Kurusu Saburo	Japan's Special Envoy to the United States
Max Waldo Schmidt (Bishop)	Third Secretary, United States Embassy in Tokyo, then staff, Far Eastern Division, State Department (July 1941–)
Ricardo Rivera Schreiber	Peruvian Minister to Japan and China
Shimada Shigetaro	Navy Minister, Japan (October 1941–)

Henri Smith-Hutton	Naval Attaché, United States Embassy in Tokyo
Harold Stark	Chief of Operations, United States Navy
Henry L. Stimson	Secretary of State under President Hoover and Secretary of War under President Roosevelt (July 1940–)
Sugiyama Hajime	Chief of General Staff, Japanese Army
Togo Shigineori	Foreign Minister, Japan (October 1941–)
Tojo Hidecki	Minister of War (July 1940–October 1941) and Prime Minister of Japan (October 1941–)
Toyama Mitsuru	Head of Black Dragon Society
Toyoda Teijiro	Foreign Minister, Japan (July 1941–October 1941)
Ushiba Tomohiko	Private Secretary to Prime Minister Konoye
Wakasugi Kaname	Minister-Counselor, Japanese Embassy in Washington, DC
James Walsh	Bishop and Superior General of the Catholic Foreign Mission Society of America in Maryknoll, New York
Wikawa Tadao	Former Japanese bank official and unofficial Japanese representative in Washington, DC
Summer Welles	Under Secretary of State
Yamamoto Isoroku	Admiral, Japanese Navy

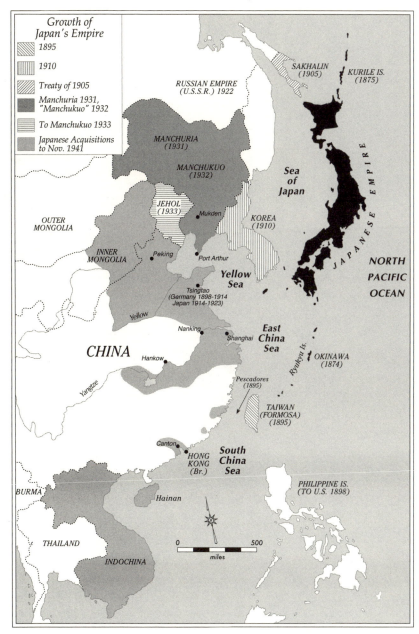

Map by Dick Gilbreath, University of Kentucky Cartography Lab.

Source: Sidney Pash, *The Currents of War: A New History of American-Japanese Relations*, 1899-1941 (University Press of Kentucky: Lexington, KY 2014)

CHAPTER 1

Anticipation

I t was, in many ways, a typical Sunday afternoon at the White House. The President, dressed casually in flannel slacks and a gray pullover sweater that once belonged to his eldest son, Jimmy, was working on his stamp collection—a lifelong passion—behind the small wooden desk in the second-floor Oval Study. The President loved that room. The high ceilings, the assorted knick-knacks on the desk and tables, the lion skin on the floor, and the built-in bookshelves conveyed a warmth missing in the larger and more formal rooms of the mansion. Model ships were displayed on various tables, and scattered on the tan colored walls were oil paintings and other art depicting sailing vessels from long ago, all reflecting another passion of the President's: the sea. In earlier times, he had loved the exhilaration of sailing and was in fact struck down by polio in August 1921 while on a family vacation at Campobello, Maine, where sailing was a principal activity. That love of the sea was not confined to leisure activities. He had treasured his service as Assistant Secretary of the Navy in President Woodrow Wilson's administration more than twenty years earlier. It was probably no small coincidence that the leather sofa and chairs in the study were once used on the USS *Mayflower*, which had served as a presidential yacht during the tenure of his cousin Theodore Roosevelt (who had been Assistant Secretary of the Navy in President William McKinley's administration).

The appeal of the Oval Study was enhanced by its proximity to his bedroom. The bedroom—which he did not share with his wife Eleanor—was next to the study, a point of particular importance for a man who had to rely on a wheelchair for mobility. Arthur Prettyman, a large black man and a retired Navy Chief Petty Officer, had served as the President's valet since 1939, and he probably would have entered the bedroom sometime shortly after 8 a.m. on that Sunday morning. Prettyman would generally stay with the President as he sat up in the narrow bed and went through his morning ritual—eating breakfast (typically orange juice, eggs, bacon, and toast along with coffee that he made himself) while poring over a stream of newspapers (usually the *New York Times*, the *New York Herald Tribune*, the *Washington Post*, the *Baltimore Sun*, and others).

In these private moments with his valet, the President almost always displayed an "amiable, sweet disposition" that made him seem immune to the burdens of the office. He was very fond of Prettyman, and the two would often engage in light banter as the morning progressed. The President liked to tease Prettyman about his good looks and would invariably refer to him as a "lady killer," which prompted the valet to respond that "one does not refute the Chief Executive, Mr. President." It is doubtful that anyone had a more intimate relationship with Franklin D. Roosevelt at the time than Prettyman. He assisted the President with dressing, using the bathroom, and bathing (although Roosevelt liked to shave himself), and the valet performed those chores wherever the President went. But the valet was a master of discretion, and rarely would he disclose details about the man he served. Later, after he and Roosevelt had died, Prettyman's widow would answer inquiries about what her husband knew by saying that he "didn't talk to us about anything."

However much he may have appreciated Prettyman's company and the unobstructed view of the Washington Monument outside his bedroom window, Roosevelt's thoughts on that first Sunday morning in December 1941 surely drifted to the expected armed conflict with Japan. Sometime around 9:30 p.m. on the prior Saturday evening, Lieutenant Lester Schulz, an aide to Roosevelt's naval attaché, had given him the first thirteen parts of a highly confidential fourteen-part memorandum that had been transmitted by the Japanese Government to its ambassador in Washington. The Ambassador would later be instructed to give the entire memorandum to

Secretary of State Cordell Hull at 1 p.m. on that first Sunday in December, but American intelligence sources had intercepted the first thirteen parts of the memorandum on Saturday after it was transmitted to the Japanese Embassy (and they would soon intercept the last part).

The memorandum was an ostensible reply to a prior proposal of the United States in the ongoing discussions that Hull and Roosevelt had been having with Japan's representatives. Roosevelt already suspected that the Japanese would make a surprise attack somewhere, and now, after a scan of this new document, he knew that a diplomatic resolution of America's disagreements with Japan was indeed unreachable. He handed the document to Harry Hopkins, a longtime associate who was with him in the Oval Study, and said, as Schulz later recalled, words to this effect, "This means war."

Despite that perspective, the President had no suspicion that Japan would attack the United States. As he later explained on Sunday morning to Ross McIntire, his personal physician, he did not think that "even the madness of Japan's military masters" would lead them to directly attack the United States—a country with far greater resources. No, he assumed that the Japanese would focus on some distant point in the Far East—such as British-controlled Singapore or perhaps Thailand (and the *New York Times* did in fact report on Sunday morning that the Japanese crisis was "more acute than ever" because of an anticipated "Japanese invasion of Thailand").

Still, Roosevelt knew that any aggression by Japan—even in the Far East—would raise the prospect of war with the United States, and he had to be prepared to move quickly after the Japanese ambassador presented the memorandum to Hull on Sunday afternoon. So when Henrietta Nesbitt, the White House housekeeper, telephoned Hopkins in the morning to ask about plans for the day, Hopkins replied that he would be having lunch with the President at 1 p.m. in the Oval Study and that the President would not attend the luncheon that Eleanor had scheduled for about thirty-two guests that afternoon.

There was nothing unusual in Hopkins getting that telephone call from Nesbitt. He was living in the White House in a suite that had once been Abraham Lincoln's study and that was down the hall from the Oval Study and the President's bedroom. The White House staff was now accustomed to his presence and, more than that, to his ability to speak for the President on schedules and other matters that were part of the White House routine.

Hopkins' presence at the White House was a matter of happenstance. A native of Sioux City, Iowa, with thinning hair combed straight back, the fifty-one-year-old, frail-looking Hopkins had been a social worker in New York City in 1928 when he first met Roosevelt, who was then campaigning to be New York's Governor. In time, Hopkins was asked to head the new Governor's Temporary Emergency Relief Administration to help address the problems of the Depression. When Roosevelt moved to the White House in March 1933, he asked Hopkins to join his administration.

Harry Hopkins was a tireless advocate for the poor, the displaced, and others in need, and the new president appointed him to head the Federal Emergency Relief Administration and then the Civil Works Administration. The appointments were well suited to Hopkins' interests and talents. He used those positions to distribute millions of dollars of assistance—whether in the form of direct grants or jobs—for citizens still suffering from the effects of the Depression. In fulfilling his responsibilities, Hopkins did not dwell on procedural propriety—he cared only about getting immediate results. (When someone approached Hopkins about a project that would "work out in the long run," the new federal administrator responded, "People don't eat in the long run—they eat every day.")

Hopkins' tenacity no doubt endeared him to a president who was equally interested in results. But their relationship also reflected a compatibility that extended beyond the younger man's drive to succeed. The intense, chain-smoking Hopkins was an impressive raconteur with considerable charm—and he had a selfless devotion to Roosevelt. There was the time in January 1941 when Hopkins was on an overseas presidential assignment and Roosevelt famously told Wendell Willkie, his Republican opponent in the 1940 presidential election, "[S]omeday you may well be sitting here where I am now as President of the United States. And when you are, you'll be looking at that door over there and knowing that practically everybody who walks through it wants something out of you. You'll learn what a lonely job this is, and you'll discover the need for somebody like Harry Hopkins, who asks for nothing except to serve you."

In May 1940, Roosevelt had asked Hopkins—then the Secretary of Commerce—to stay for dinner after an afternoon cabinet meeting. When dinner was over, the President—sensing that Harry was not feeling well (perhaps a product of his prior treatment for stomach cancer)—asked him to stay the night, which Hopkins did. He did not leave until more than three years later.

Despite his proximity to the President's bedroom, Hopkins would probably not have disturbed Roosevelt's early morning routine on that Sunday in December. The same could not be said about McIntire. A balding, congenial, fifty-two-year-old Rear Admiral (and also Surgeon General of the Navy), the President's physician had a practice of checking on Roosevelt every morning as well as every evening. He entered the President's bedroom around 10 a.m. Captain John Beardall, Roosevelt's naval attaché, arrived about the same time with the last part of the Japanese memorandum. The last part did not declare war or say anything about any military moves planned by the Japanese Government. It simply concluded that "it is impossible to reach an agreement through further negotiations." The President looked up at Beardall with his blue eyes after reading the last part and said, in effect, "It looks like the Japanese are going to break off negotiations." Roosevelt was not surprised. It undoubtedly confirmed his assumption that something momentous was about to happen.

Still, he saw no need to do anything, and he passed the rest of that Sunday morning talking with McIntire and going through the newspapers. Prettyman probably began the process of dressing the President sometime around noon. Although Roosevelt prided himself on being able to handle certain matters without assistance, the valet was an indispensable part of the process. While he laid flat on his back on the bed, Prettyman would have removed the President's pajama pants, and then (depending on Roosevelt's schedule for the day) he may have strapped a brace (weighing about five pounds and painted black to camouflage it from outsiders) on each of the President's lifeless legs. Prettyman would have then helped Roosevelt pull on his pants and secure shoes on his feet. After putting on his sweater, Roosevelt would have slipped into his wheelchair (a homemade contraption built around a wooden kitchen chair), wheeled himself into the Oval Study, and then, using his massive upper body muscles, maneuvered himself into the chair behind the desk.

It was there that he welcomed Dr. Hu Shih, the Chinese ambassador to the United States, at 12:30 p.m. A principal focus of Hull and Roosevelt's discussions with Japan's representatives had been the fate of China. In a contrived effort to safeguard Japan's interest in a railway in Manchuria, some soldiers with Japan's Kwantung Army had engineered an attack on Chinese forces in 1931 near the capital of Mukden. A seemingly minor incident (and one that had not been sanctioned by the government in Tokyo) then mushroomed into Japan's occupation of that northern Chinese territory and the eventual establishment of a puppet regime under Japanese control. The Mukden Incident (or Manchurian Incident, as it was called) was compounded in 1937 by another seemingly minor skirmish (later known as the "Marco Polo Bridge Incident"), where Japanese forces from the Kwantung Army attacked Chinese troops near the Marco Polo Bridge located southwest of Peiping. The encounter spiraled out of control, and Japan soon became locked with Chiang Kai-Shek's National Revolutionary Army in a full-scale military struggle which the Japanese euphemistically referred to as the "China Incident."

China in general and Chiang Kai-shek in particular had many ardent supporters in the United States, including in Congress, and China had come to place considerable reliance on American assistance—both financial and strategic. China was therefore more than a little interested in making sure that the United States did not enter into any agreement with Japan that might undermine China's status or Chiang Kai-shek's leadership. Roosevelt was obviously aware of that interest, and he wanted Hu Shih to know that on Saturday (before the President had received the first thirteen parts of the Japanese memorandum), he had sent a telegram to Hirohito, the Japanese Emperor, requesting a withdrawal of the substantial Japanese military forces in Indochina that could be used to launch an attack on other points in Southeast Asia. Despite his hopes for a favorable response, Roosevelt recognized that the odds were against him, and he told Hu Shih that something "nasty" was likely to happen in the Far East.

Hu Shih left around 1:10 p.m., and lunch was brought in for Hopkins and the President, who remained seated at his desk. The two men had discussed the situation with Japan on many prior occasions, but on this afternoon the conversation ranged far and wide on other matters. After eating, Roosevelt picked up one of his treasured stamp albums.

■ ■ ■

As Roosevelt was concluding his meeting with Hu Shih, Fuchida Mitsuo, a small man with a toothbrush moustache (a reflection of his admiration for Adolf Hitler) was sitting in his single-engine bomber at an altitude of approximately 9,800 feet over the churning seas of the North Pacific, peering through binoculars to look for some sign of Oahu. As General Commander of Japan's Air Attack Squadron, Fuchida had the responsibility to signal the attack by the other 182 planes under his command (consisting of horizontal bombers like his plane, which carried a single bomb weighing almost a ton, as well as dive bombers, torpedo bombers, and Zero fighters). If he determined that the Americans would be surprised, he would open the canopy of his plane and fire a single flare from his rocket pistol. In that case, the torpedo bombers would dive toward the targets and release their payload close to the water's surface while the fighter planes tried to control the airspace above them. If it appeared that the Americans were not surprised, then Fuchida would fire two flares from his rocket pistol. In that event, the horizontal and dive bombers would make the initial foray under the protection of the fighter planes, and the torpedo bombers would wait before descending to the lower elevations to release their payload. In either event, Fuchida obviously could not issue that signal until he knew they had reached their destination.

Finding Oahu had proved to be more challenging than Fuchida had expected. He and the other planes had been catapulted in the pre-dawn darkness from six aircraft carriers in stormy weather, with high waves splashing over the flight decks, about 220 miles north of Oahu around six o'clock that morning Hawaiian time (which was five hours and thirty minutes behind Washington time). The bearings were easy to plot, but sightings of their targets were compromised by the heavy clouds below them.

Fuchida was proud to be leading the aviation assault team. It was a responsibility he accepted with a cool composure. True, he had donned red long underwear and a red flying shirt to mask any blood if he was shot over Pearl Harbor because he did not want to demoralize the crew upon his return. But there was a serenity about him that defied the tension of the moment. He had slept soundly, awoke around 5 a.m., ate a good breakfast, and went about his preparations without fear. "There is no need to worry now," he had told a fellow officer the night before. "We are right in the theater of operation. The die is cast."

As Fuchida was preparing to climb into his plane on *Akagi*, the lead aircraft carrier, the senior maintenance officer approached him with a white scarf, or *hachimaki*. "All of the maintenance crew members would like to go along to Pearl Harbor," he said. "But since we cannot, please take this *hachimaki* from us as a symbol of our being with you." Touched by the gesture, Fuchida took the *hachimaki*, tied it around his flight cap, and climbed into the middle seat of his plane (with the front seat occupied by the pilot and the rear seat occupied by the radio operator, who would communicate information about the attack to the naval command on the *Akagi*). The planes then began their launch, leaving to cheers of crew members yelling "Banzai" and waving their caps and handkerchiefs with great energy and high expectations.

The thirty-nine-year-old commander had come a long way from his small village near the base of Mt. Nijyo in southeastern Japan. Ever since childhood, Mitsuo had aspired to be an admiral in Japan's navy, but he was a shy boy, and his parents tried to dissuade him from pursuing a career in the military. "Your nature is so gentle," his mother said, "and the best suited job for you is a doctor." Even his classmates noticed Mitsuo's social reticence. They called him "Octopus" because, when teachers called on him to speak, he turned red from embarrassment and thus had the coloring of a boiled octopus. But Mitsuo's ambition could not be turned aside, and in due course, he was able to engineer an appointment to Japan's Naval Academy in Etajima on August 26, 1921.

Mitsuo's gravitation toward a career in aviation was fortuitous. In an effort to overcome his shyness, he would raise his hand quickly whenever a teacher asked a question—regardless of whether he knew the answer. He was equally quick in raising his hand if the teacher or anyone else asked for volunteers—regardless of the task at hand. Not surprisingly, he was the first to raise his hand during his third year at the Naval Academy when the commander of a sea plane squadron asked if anyone in the class aspired to be an aviation officer, bearing in mind that only six could be admitted to the program.

Mitsuo's decision did not sit well with his parents. His father had warned him "not to volunteer in the future for anything having to do with planes or submarines." Later, as his mother lay dying from uterine cancer, she reminded Mitsuo that his father was worried "because you want to be a flier," and she implored her son to set his father "free from any worries." But Mitsuo was exhilarated to be part of a program that was sure to be a critical component of Japan's military arsenal. So, however much he loved his father, he could not abandon his ambition of becoming an aviator.

Fuchida's advancement in the navy's aviation program was rapid: specialized training in horizontal bombing at the Yokosuka Air Corps in 1933; admission to the Naval Staff College in 1936; appointment as the aviation leader of the *Ryujyo*, a medium-sized aircraft carrier in 1937; and then appointment as a flight commander on *Akagi* in November 1939. It was there that he met Admiral Yamamoto Isoroku, the Commander of the Combined Fleet and the one who later crafted and relentlessly pursued the strategy of attacking the American fleet at Pearl Harbor. But no personal relationship proved to be more fateful than the one Fuchida had established at the Naval Academy.

Genda Minoru was in the same class as Fuchida, but he was two years younger. The two became close friends and would find themselves on remarkably similar career paths. Like his academy classmate, Genda worked with the Yokosuka Air Corps, was admitted to the Navy Staff College, and served on the *Ryujyo*. But unlike Fuchida, Genda was appointed as an Air Staff Officer in the First Air Fleet, a position of considerable stature. It was in that capacity that the intense naval officer with the oval face, glaring eyes, and close-cropped hair received an invitation in February 1941 to meet with Rear Admiral Onishi Takijiro, Chief of Staff of the Navy's Eleventh Air Fleet, on the aircraft carrier *Kaga*.

Onishi handed Genda a highly confidential letter written by Admiral Yamamoto in early January (the second of two written by Yamamoto) that described the proposed attack on the American fleet in Pearl Harbor. A proposed attack on the United States was no surprise to Genda. From their earliest days at the Naval Academy, Genda and his classmates had been taught to regard the United States as Japan's principal enemy. "What I always heard," Fuchida later explained, "was, 'Your enemy is the United States.'"

That perspective reflected the widespread resentment of America in Japan. To some extent, that resentment evolved from President Theodore

Roosevelt's mediation in ending the Russo-Japanese War in 1905. The resulting Treaty of Portsmouth left Japan with little to show for her successful military campaigns and generated "hostile riots"before the American embassy in Tokyo. Japanese hostility intensified after the negotiation of the Versailles Treaty in 1919 because the United States refused to support the proposal of Japan (which had opposed Germany during World War I) that would entitle all countries in the soon-to-be-formed League of Nations to equal treatment without regard to race.

Japanese antipathy toward the United States was further exacerbated by the Immigration Act of 1924, which foreclosed immigration to the United States from all Asian countries, including Japan. Adoption of that law drew heated criticism in Japan and was not soon forgotten. "The Japanese people were always indignant whenever the subject came up," remembered Henri Smith-Hutton, who served as Naval Attaché in the American embassy in Tokyo. It was a view shared by Joseph C. Grew, who served as America's ambassador to Japan between 1932 and 1942. That act, said Grew, "cast a dark shadow" over Japanese-American relations.

The Japanese believed—correctly—that these and other actions reflected widespread American prejudice against the Japanese people. That perspective was perhaps exemplified by the testimony of Virgil S. McClatchy, owner of the *Sacramento Bee* and president of the Oriental Exclusion League of California, before the United States Senate in 1924. "The yellow and brown races do not intermarry with the white race," said McClatchy, "and their heredity, standard of livings, ideas, psychology all combine to make them unassimilable with the white race."

For many in Japan, that racial prejudice was reflected in treaties promoted by the United States in 1922 and 1930 that limited the construction of ships in the country's Navy. The United States and Great Britain agreed to limitations as well, but the comparative ratios appeared to place Japan at a disadvantage—a point of particular bitterness to officers in the Japanese Navy. So, to Genda, there could be nothing new about a Japanese plan to do harm to the United States.

Nor was there anything new to the notion of a surprise air attack on the American naval base in Pearl Harbor. In 1925 (when Yamamoto was the naval attaché in the Japanese embassy in Washington), the *New York Times Sunday Book Review* had a first-page review of a novel by Hector

C. Bywater, the *London Daily Telegraph*'s naval correspondent, that described a surprise attack by the Japanese on the American fleet in Pearl Harbor. But that was fiction. Reality was a different story. The risks were almost beyond comprehension. A large task force of Japanese ships would have to cross about 3,500 miles of open water in the North Pacific without being detected. And then—after their planes were launched from aircraft carriers—Japanese pilots would have to hope that their approach was not detected by American radar or by American airplanes conducting patrols around the perimeter of Pearl Harbor.

Still, Yamamoto could not resist the appeal of such an attack. The U.S. Pacific Fleet—which consisted of three aircraft carriers, nine battleships, twelve heavy cruisers, and an assortment of other vessels—had been based in San Diego but periodically used Pearl Harbor for exercises in the Western Pacific. In May 1940, Roosevelt decided to leave the fleet stationed there indefinitely. He was convinced that the continued presence of the fleet in Pearl Harbor would deter further Japanese aggression in Southeast Asia. But where the American president saw a deterrent, the Japanese admiral saw an opportunity. If a surprise attack on the American fleet succeeded, Yamamoto told colleagues, Japan could "decide the fate of the war on the very first day."

Yamamoto recognized the hazards. As he later explained to a Navy colleague, the attack on Pearl Harbor would be "so difficult and so dangerous that we must be prepared to risk complete annihilation." But to Yamamoto, the risks warranted the benefits. With a much smaller population and far fewer resources, Japan could not hope to win a war against the United States that dragged on for years. It was therefore necessary to deliver a crippling blow to the Americans at the very outset of any armed hostilities. Only in that way could Japan have any hope of being victorious. The planned attack on Pearl Harbor was, in effect, nothing more than a gamble of monumental proportions. While such a gamble might—and did—discourage others, Yamamoto embraced the challenge. As one friend later said of Yamamoto, "He had a gambler's heart."

Genda's perspective was not very different from Yamamoto's. "Genda was sometimes too willing, too risky in his judgment when he should have been more careful," Fuchida later remarked. "Genda was like a daring quarterback who would risk the game on one turn of pitch and toss." So

Genda read Yamamoto's letter with growing excitement on that cold day in February 1941, and, as he handed it back to Onishi, the junior commander commented, "The plan is difficult but not impossible."

The letter was known only to a very few of Japan's other naval officers in the early months of 1941, and almost all of them opposed the plan. But as relations with the United States deteriorated, Yamamoto's proposal gained new adherents, and Genda soon became involved in the planning. That responsibility in turn required him to find an aviator who could lead the air attack. Genda knew the perfect candidate for that role, and he did not waste time in making the selection. On a muggy day in September 1941—while relaxing after a drill flight at the Kagoshima command center in southwestern Japan—Fuchida was told that Staff Officer Genda had come to see him. "The fact is," Genda quickly advised his friend, "you have been assigned at this time as the General Commander of the air attack squadron for the Pearl Harbor air raid."

Now, as he searched for the Oahu coastline on that Sunday morning in December, Fuchida hoped, almost expected, that the attack on Pearl Harbor would transform Japan's future. His confidence in the outcome was reinforced by the sunrise he had witnessed that morning shortly after takeoff from the aircraft carrier. A huge crimson ball appeared through breaking clouds, and the brilliant rays of sunshine created an image remarkably similar to Japan's naval flag. As he watched the unfolding radiance, Fuchida said softly to himself, "Glorious dawn"—in English (a language he had studied in preparation for the inevitable conflict with the United States). He pulled back the canopy of his plane and stood up for a few minutes to absorb the stirring sight, and, as he did so, aviators in the other planes started waving to him.

Fuchida then returned to the middle seat of his plane. Shortly before 7:30 a.m. Hawaiian time (1 p.m. in Washington), Fuchida picked up the voice pipe and directed the pilot to descend. Through scattered clouds, Fuchida eventually saw the white lines of a beach, and, by checking a map, determined that it was Kahuku Point on the northern tip of Oahu. Fuchida had put receivers on his ears and could hear music coming from an Oahu radio station. To Fuchida, that was sign that the attack would be a surprise. If the Japanese planes had been detected, he assumed that the Hawaiian radio stations would be broadcasting an alert. That impression was reinforced when Fuchida scanned the skies as they traveled along Oahu's west coast—there was no sign of enemy aircraft approaching them.

As the Japanese planes descended toward Pearl Harbor, Fuchida picked up his rocket gun and prepared to open the canopy to convey the signal to his compatriots (who could easily see his plane because the tail had a yellow background with three red stripes). The time for decision was at hand.

■ ■ ■

As Fuchida prepared for the assault on the American fleet in Pearl Harbor, it was about 3:10 a.m. on Monday, December 8, in Tokyo, and Joe Grew was asleep with his wife Alice in the Ambassador's sumptuous residence in the Embassy's two-acre compound. The residence—an L-shaped building on the top of a hill—epitomized the elegance that Grew treasured in his long diplomatic career. The prior Embassy buildings had been destroyed in an earthquake in 1923, and the United States Government seemingly spared no expense in replacing them. In 1934—three years after the new Embassy was completed—*Time* magazine called the Embassy "one of the finest in the US Foreign Service" (although the extravagance led some to call the Embassy "Hoover's Folly"). White stucco walls were complemented by large front doors cast in bronze. The spacious foyer featured a polished teak staircase leading to the second floor. It boasted a walnut-paneled study, a large ballroom, a banquet hall, and a salon with thick oriental carpets and large comfortable chairs. The residence overlooked an abundance of trees, azalea bushes, broad lawns, and an outdoor pool made of marble. A series of stepping stones led down to the Chancery, which housed offices for the Embassy staff (including one on the second floor for Grew). The entire grounds were surrounded by high walls that preserved the park-like setting of the compound.

A lean, tall, distinguished-looking man with silver hair combed straight back, bushy eyebrows, and a full gray moustache, the sixty-one-year-old Grew had used the residence on many occasions to entertain government officials, military officers, business leaders, and other members of the diplomatic community throughout his almost ten years of service in Tokyo. He had developed close relations with Japanese men (almost no women) in the highest echelons of Japanese government and society—but he did not know about the impending attack on the American fleet in Pearl Harbor.

Not that he would have been surprised. He had seen the writing on the wall for months and had tried—repeatedly—to have the State Department take actions that he believed would avert an almost certain armed conflict. He had even written "Dear Frank" letters to the President to convey his views about the impending doom and his recommendations to facilitate amicable relations with Japan. The letters reflected, in part at least, a personal relationship with the President dating back to when they both attended Groton, the famed Episcopalian preparatory school in Groton, Massachusetts, and Harvard College (although Roosevelt was two years behind Grew).

For all his effort, Grew was now imbued with frustration and bitterness. Very few of his recommendations in the preceding months had been acknowledged—let alone accepted—by the President or the Secretary of State. Grew would later say that "reporting to our Government was like throwing pebbles into a lake at night" and that he "could only assume that our recommendations were not welcome." It was especially debilitating to Grew because he had fervently tried—and no doubt hoped—to shepherd an agreement between the United States and Japan that would avoid war and be the crowning achievement of his long diplomatic career.

It had not been an easy task. Japan was not a democracy, and trying to pinpoint the locus of government decision-making was often difficult. That difficulty was heightened by the growing inability of Grew and his staff to communicate in the last few months with informed Japanese. People were afraid to be seen with Americans. The United States was a well-known adversary. Those who consorted with Americans were routinely watched and later interrogated by the Special Higher Police, often referred to as the "thought police," or the Kempeitai, the secret military police whose penchant for brutality was well-known.

Beyond that, Japanese citizens were fearful of expressing views that might be regarded as unacceptable by the Japanese Government. There was little tolerance for dissent. As early as 1900, the Public Peace Police Law gave the Home Minister the power to disband any organization that he believed constituted a danger to Japanese society (a power that Home Ministers did not hesitate to invoke). If a Japanese citizen expressed views critical of the government or belonged to an organization that advocated positions at odds with government policies, he or she could be arrested, confined to prison for an indeterminate period, and, if necessary to cleanse the person of troublesome thoughts, subjected to unbearable torture (a favorite technique being to "pull their finger and toenails out as a gentle way of creating the right attitude"). As Grew himself later said of his time in Tokyo, "Many a Japanese finds himself in a solitary prison cell, undergoing long months of intensive investigation, on the basis of a mere indiscreet word uttered in the hearing of some stranger or even friend."

Despite those obstacles, Grew saw considerable progress toward a solution that could avoid armed conflict between the two countries. Central to that progress was a proposed meeting between the Japanese Prime Minister and President Roosevelt. The Prime Minister had proposed the meeting in August 1941, and Grew had urged Roosevelt and Hull to accept the invitation. Grew was hopeful that the meeting would generate some movement toward a mutually-satisfactory agreement. He knew, of course, that there was no guarantee the meeting would be productive. "Nobody can answer that question," Grew told a congressional committee which investigated the Pearl Harbor attack after the war. "It is not susceptible to proof." But he thought the meeting was a risk worth taking to reach an agreement and thus avoid a war that would otherwise be inevitable. But Washington was not really interested. Instead, Grew found that the Roosevelt administration "was almost completely inflexible" and unwilling to simplify the Prime Minister's task "or to meet him even part way." The Prime Minister eventually resigned in October 1941 without the benefit of any meeting.

There was a certain irony to the situation. While he was struggling to foster harmonious relations and an eventual agreement with Japan, Grew did not fully appreciate the contrary perspective of the State Department. Although Cordell Hull repeatedly stated that he was interested in reaching an agreement with Japan, and although he and his staff (as well as President Roosevelt), spent untold hours meeting with Japanese representatives in an apparent effort to reach an agreement, as a practical matter the Secretary of State had no real intention of entering into an agreement with Japan. To be sure, Hull could have fashioned an agreement that *he* would have found acceptable. But he knew, or had to know, that there was no agreement that would be acceptable to both him and Japan. For his part, Roosevelt was prepared to accept his Secretary of State's approach—as long as Hull could keep the discussions with the Japanese alive and thereby extend the time that the United States needed to bolster its resources for the anticipated war with Germany (and perhaps Japan as well).

It was an irony that Joe Grew grasped after the Pearl Harbor attack. Still, the story of Grew's final months in Japan is one worth telling. It is a story filled with hope and exasperation, with complex and fascinating people, and with a drama befitting the momentous decisions at stake.

And like all stories, this one must begin at the beginning.

CHAPTER 2

The Diplomat

A twenty-three-year-old hunter with dark hair and an equally dark moustache crawled through a cave of large boulders, his way barely illuminated by torches that the huntsmen from the village had placed in the crevices of the rocks. He was tracking a tiger with his powerful double-barreled .450 Holland & Holland cordite powder express. But the hole through which he was crawling was barely large enough to accommodate his six foot, two inch frame, and so he had to drag the rifle behind him.

The experience was unlike any other he had previously encountered, and he had many to use as comparison. Despite his youth, he could think back to elks he had hunted in Jackson Hole, Wyoming, and the moose he had taken down in New Brunswick, Canada, not to mention the black bears he had shot in Kashmir at an earlier point on this trip. He was hoping, however, that this last hunt would be the most rewarding. The killing of a tiger in the foothills of Amoy in southeastern China (across the water from Formosa) would put him on a new plateau.

As he squinted in the dark for a sign of the tiger on that fall day in 1903, Joe Grew was focused on the drama unfolding before him and unlikely to be thinking of his good fortune. Here he was, only fifteen months after graduation from Harvard College, enjoying an eighteen-month trip around the world to indulge his passion for travel and hunting. True, the trip was not a luxurious one at every turn. He had endured elephant leeches while tramping through the Malay jungles, suffered the bites of swamp mosquitoes that resulted in a bout of malaria, and slept on a makeshift bed outdoors in the snow and freezing temperatures of the Kashmir mountains because the only alternative was the smoke and filth of the natives' tents. But he was never at a loss for money or for support. At one point, he had eighteen ponies and ten coolies to carry baggage and equipment, and at another point, he had been accompanied by "forty-odd villagers" who "composed the rank and file" of his "diminutive army." It was clearly an adventure that only a privileged few could afford.

The considerable wealth of Joe Grew's family found its roots in revolutionary times. His great-grandfather—the descendent of an Englishman—had been born in Boston a century before Joe entered the world. The family had prospered in New England business, and his father had amassed a fortune as a wool merchant by the time Joe was born on Marlborough Street in Boston's Back Bay section on May 27, 1880 (a date that carried special meaning for Joe, who always regarded twenty-seven as his lucky number). Joe romped in the streets of Back Bay with his two older brothers and sister, visited their family's estate in nearby Hyde Park, and spent summers sailing and pursuing other activities at the family's seaside home in Manchester. It was a happy childhood. But Joe's father was a hard taskmaster—so much so that he required his young son, who was naturally left-handed, to learn to write with his right hand.

In 1892, twelve-year-old Joe was enrolled in the Groton School. It was there that the teenager learned the importance of public service, and there too that he became acquainted with another youth two years behind him—Franklin D. Roosevelt. Groton held other advantages that would also last a lifetime. Public speaking was certainly one. From his very first classes in Latin, Joe was taught to speak "smoothly" and "without hitches or 'ers' while searching for the next phrase." It was a point of pride Grew would remember decades later when, as the American ambassador to Japan, he listened to a speech by Sir Robert Craigie, Great Britain's ambassador to Japan, who "hesitates and stammers."

Still, the early experience at Groton was not an idyllic one. Joe was prone to daydreaming and had difficulty with his studies, and his teachers were "freely predicting that he would never pass the college examinations."

The frustrations extended to athletic activities, and one day in his junior year Joe was thrown off the crew team for reasons that he thought were "wholly unfair." The incident inexplicably provided the spark Joe needed. On a spring morning shortly afterwards, he awakened at dawn—which was unusual in itself—and took a walk in the hills surrounding the school. More than fifty years later, he could vividly recall that morning—"the freshness of the dawn breeze and the all-pervading smell of the fields and flowers." It was then that the struggling Groton student decided that he had to take charge of his life. From that point forward, he would rise early and study, as he knew he should. As he later remembered, "I don't believe that the astonished headmaster and the faculty ever really understood just what happened."

Harvard was the appropriate choice to complete his education, but Joe never lost his fondness for Groton. Years later, after he became the American ambassador to Japan, Grew would always turn to the Groton headmaster to recommend a Groton alumnus who was about to graduate from college to be his private secretary. As Grew explained in one letter to the Groton headmaster, the request for recommendations reflected his "devotion to the School and all it stands for...."

Grew developed similar feelings for Harvard (and would in time became a member of the Harvard Board of Overseers and be known at the Metropolitan Club of Washington—a private club where he often dined—as "Mr. John Harvard," a reference to the school's founder). His academic career was undistinguished, and he failed to earn a varsity letter despite forays into football, crew, and track. But he did find success on the literary front, ultimately becoming a senior editor on the *Crimson*, whose staff included Frank Roosevelt. He was also accepted as a member of the Fly Club, an exclusive male "final club" (so named because its members had to be in or near their final year of school).

All of that was now behind Joe Grew as he closed in on the tiger in the darkened cave in Amoy. He did not know exactly where in the cave the tiger was located, but the village huntsmen had already warned him that the cat was "very large." And then Joe heard a deep-throated growl that seemed to confirm the huntsmen's assessment. He inched towards the sound and finally caught a glimpse of the tiger in another cavern just beyond the young hunter's position. "He lay on a ledge of rock," Grew later remembered, "his green eyes shining and blinking up and down as he panted from fright and anger." With the tiger roaring and snarling at him, Grew brought up his gun and fired. The explosion immediately extinguished the torches that provided some light, and in the darkness, Joe heard the tiger roaring and thrashing about. He fired at the noise, and the ensuing silence convinced him that the tiger was now dead. When the huntsmen later brought the slain animal out in the open, their earlier assessment was confirmed—the tiger measured ten feet, six inches from the tip of his nose to the tip of his tail, which the huntsmen said was a record.

The killing of the tiger would provide an incidental benefit that the young hunter could never have anticipated: the start of a long diplomatic career. His father hoped that Joe would return from the post-graduation trip with his restless spirit in check and his desire for a conventional job in Boston intact. But it was not to be. As Grew later said, the trip inspired a spirit of "'wanderlust,'" and "there was no settling down thereafter." He thought a career in the Diplomatic Service would satisfy that spirit. His father thought the choice was "crazy," but Joe could not be turned aside.

Settling on a career path was easy, but securing a job was not. A position in the Diplomatic Service required a presidential appointment, and they were few and far between—in part because most of the administrative functions of the country's embassies were handled by a separate Consular Service, which would later be merged with the Diplomatic Service into a unified Foreign Service through the Rogers Act of 1924. The first opportunity came through the American ambassador in Korea shortly after Joe's graduation from Harvard. But that opportunity evaporated when one of Joe's Harvard professors advised the Ambassador that the recent graduate was deaf.

In fact, that was not so. A childhood bout with scarlet fever had impaired Joe's hearing (especially in his left ear), but he could converse with people in close quarters (especially if they were located on his right side). The professor's mistake was corrected, and shortly thereafter, Grew was able to engineer a clerkship in the Consular Service with the American embassy in Cairo. While it was not on the diplomatic track, the position was a step in the right direction. Grew arrived in Cairo on July 19, 1904—with the temperature reported to be 118 degrees in the shade.

Fate then intervened. Alfred Cooley, a close friend of Grew's older brother and an Assistant Attorney General, mentioned the younger Grew's encounter with the tiger one day in March 1906 while on a hike with Theodore Roosevelt. The President, more than most, appreciated the value of men who had the courage to stare down big game. It was a trait he believed to be lacking in diplomats, whom he generally regarded as "stuffed dolls." Roosevelt had recently signed an executive order requiring examinations for those entering the Diplomatic Service (other than ambassadors and ministers). The President nonetheless arranged for Joe to become the Third Secretary in the Embassy in Mexico City without the need for any examination because Grew's appointment was deemed to be a transfer.

Roosevelt never forgot that appointment. He later visited with Grew in April 1910 at the young diplomat's new post in Berlin (Roosevelt later saying, "I never had a pleasanter experience"). More than that, he gave Grew a letter to be used as a Foreword to *Sport and Travel in the Far East*, Grew's book about his experiences on the post-graduation trip. "I cannot imagine a more thrilling or thoroughly sportsmanlike experience," said the former president, "than that of your crawling through the narrow rock passages and shooting the tiger in its cavern lair not four feet from you." (Years later, when addressing Foreign Service candidates after his retirement, Grew would often remark, "You young men, you don't know how fortunate you are. All you have to do to get into the Foreign Service is to answer a few questions. I had to shoot a tiger.")

After Mexico City, Grew was relocated to the St. Petersburg embassy in Czarist Russia as Third Secretary. There, he enjoyed the pomp and ceremony of diplomatic life, including the wearing of a uniform that boasted a sword. That experience was followed by an appointment in 1908 as Second Secretary in Berlin. Aside from service as Counselor in the Vienna embassy in Austria-Hungary between 1911 and 1912, he would remain in Berlin until shortly before the United States declared war against Germany in April 1917. In time, Grew received Senate confirmation as the First Secretary, which authorized him to supervise the Berlin embassy when the Ambassador was absent—which occurred when Ambassador James W. Gerard returned to the United States in September 1916 for a three-month period.

It was a tense time for the young diplomat, especially after war erupted in the summer of 1914. Grew's initial sympathies were with the German military because, as he wrote his mother in September 1914, he admired "their marvelous organization and the fact that they are fighting against enormous odds...." Those sympathies faded quickly in the face of Germany's brutality, especially the unrestricted submarine campaign which resulted in the sinking of the *Lusitania* in May 1915 (Grew saying that "the dreadfulness of the calamity struck us with full force at once").

Relations between the United States and Germany continued to spiral downwards, and in February 1917, about two months before the United States formally entered the war, diplomatic relations between the two countries were severed. Grew returned to the United States in April 1917 after a brief service as Counselor in the Vienna embassy. He was then appointed Chief of the Western European Division in the State Department, but by October 1918, he was on his way back to Europe. He was now the diplomatic secretary to Colonel Edward House, the intimate adviser of Woodrow Wilson who was charged with negotiating the peace treaty at Versailles. That appointment morphed into Grew being chosen as Secretary of the United States Commission to the Peace Conference, which required him to oversee administrative matters for the American delegation and included the rank of Envoy Extraordinary and Minister Plenipotentiary.

It was a prestigious position, but, as Grew later commented, the time in Versailles proved to be "the most discouraging, unsatisfactory and regrettable experience of his career" to date. Part of that frustration reflected the bureaucratic struggle between Colonel House and Robert Lansing, who believed that, as Secretary of State, he should manage the United States' participation. The other part was the President himself. Wilson was dissatisfied with the American delegation's performance and proposed to dismiss all of its members shortly after he arrived in Paris in December 1918. House persuaded the President to retain Grew. He is a "gentleman" and "honest and trustworthy," House told Wilson. In due course, Grew became the member of the delegation who affixed the President's signature to the "molten wax of the peace parchment" (which was never ratified by the United States Senate).

Despite the frustrations, Grew's work at Versailles did help to advance his diplomatic career. He received appointments as Minister to Denmark in 1920 and then as Minister to Switzerland in 1921. A principal responsibility in Switzerland was to be the United States' representative at the Lausanne Conference, which was held between 1922 and 1923 and was charged with resolving post-war issues related to Turkey, which had been formed from the Ottoman Empire, a German ally. Although a treaty was signed in July 1923, it was never ratified by the United States Senate.

Grew's foreign assignments precluded any participation in the presidential campaigns of 1920 or 1924 (although he did tell a friend that Frank Roosevelt, the Democratic Vice Presidential nominee in 1920, "got right down in the gutter and trotted out all the usual catch phrases, mud-slinging and campaign slogans that one associates with the lowest form of ward politics"). But his work in Lausanne did earn him the respect of colleagues in the State Department, most especially Charles Evan Hughes, the Secretary of State. On March 1, 1924, William Phillips—who had grown up in the same Back Bay neighborhood as Grew and had preceded him by two years at Harvard—advised the forty-three-year-old minster that he had been selected to succeed Phillips as Under Secretary of State.

To some, the appointment might have been a welcome recognition of past achievements. But not to Joe Grew. "I am rather appalled at the prospect of the responsibility and difficult work ahead," he confided to his diary. "It's about the last post I ever expected to be called upon to fill." But he understood what lay behind the appointment and added that "it's gratifying."

For his part, the regal-looking Hughes (who had been the Republican presidential nominee in 1916 and would soon became the Chief Justice of the United States Supreme Court) was delighted to have Grew share his suite of offices on the second floor of the State, War, and Navy Building on 17th Street in Washington. And so, when Grew asked his new boss whether he should come into Hughes' office "informally when [he] had something to take up," the Secretary of State answered in the affirmative, telling Grew that the two men had to be "thick as two thieves."

That perspective proved to be a blessing as well as a curse. The two men conversed on matters large and small, day and night, but Grew soon became weary of hearing the buzzer in his office to signal that the Secretary demanded his presence. Still, when Hughes resigned his position in January 1925, he did not hesitate to recommend Grew to the new Secretary of State, Frank B. Kellogg, saying of Grew that he was "not only a man of great ability but one who has had extended experience."

Although the sixty-eight-year-old Kellogg was quick to accept the recommendation, relations between the new Secretary of State and his Under Secretary did not fare as well as either man would have liked. Part of the problem was the criticism leveled at Kellogg's Under Secretary. Grew had been charged with implementing the Rogers Act. But merging the Diplomatic and Consular Services into the new unified Foreign Service proved to be a demanding task. There were many in Congress and in the press who thought that the system of merit envisioned by the Rogers Act was not being honored and that ambassadorships and other high posts were too freely given to men of influence rather than to those whose credentials warranted an appointment. The criticism did not sit well with Kellogg. For his part, Grew found that Kellogg could be cantankerous in the face of controversy, saying that the Secretary often behaved "like a petulant child, and in those moods it was quite useless to try to argue or talk with him"—although Grew did add that "no man could be more kindly or charming in his gentler moods."

The solution to the discord was an overseas appointment, and in May 1927, Grew was named ambassador to Turkey. The *New York Times* hailed the appointment, saying that it "returns to the field a professional diplomat who has had wide experience" and who "is particularly well versed in the complicated questions involved in Turkey's new international status." Those high expectations were soon fulfilled. Grew negotiated several treaties with Turkey that were ratified by the Senate, and Grew was later recognized as "[o]ne of the most popular foreigners in Turkey."

Not surprisingly, new frontiers beckoned. In November 1931, Bill Castle, who had attended Harvard with Grew and had worked with him in the Berlin embassy and later in the State Department, contacted his friend to see if he might be interested in becoming the ambassador to Japan. Castle himself had occupied that position for five months in 1930 to represent the United States in the London Naval Conference, which was designed to establish limits on the naval capacity for the United States, Japan, and other major powers. Castle had returned to the State Department, ultimately becoming Under Secretary of State. The position in Tokyo needed to be filled with someone who had the experience to handle a situation that was becoming explosive. By January 1932, the appointment was confirmed.

Grew was sad to leave Turkey, where he had been "unusually happy." Although he had expended considerable effort in negotiating treaties and fulfilling other diplomatic responsibilities, the Ambassador found much to enjoy in other activities. He played the piano as much as two hours a day. Gambling was another favorite pastime. He made numerous trips to the casinos in Monaco to play poker, a passion that did not subside when he went to Japan. (During more than six months of internment in Tokyo after the Pearl Harbor attack, Grew and other members of the Embassy staff would play poker almost every night, and, as Henri Smith-Hutton later remembered, players "won or lost two or three thousand dollars" during that time.) Grew also prided himself on being physically active—whether it be tennis, golf, or swimming—and it showed in his appearance. *Time* magazine said of him in 1928 that he was "John Pierpont Morgan's lithe, athletic and slightly deaf cousin." His lean physique, coupled with a full moustache and graying hair combed straight back, gave him the appearance of the polished diplomat he was.

Despite the pleasures of life in Turkey, the fifty-one-year-old diplomat could not turn down the appointment in Tokyo. As he himself acknowledged, it represented "the opportunity of a lifetime."

There was no mystery behind Grew's enthusiasm for the position. About a year before the ascension of Adolf Hitler in Germany, the embassy in Tokyo probably represented the most difficult diplomatic post in the Foreign Service. It was not merely a reflection of the vast differences between American and Japanese cultures. The new ambassador would also have to find creative ways to resolve simmering disputes between the two countries.

One dispute of paramount importance concerned the London Naval Conference, which had concluded in April 1930. It was one of several conferences designed to promote international cooperation and disarmament in the wake of World War I. The first conference in Washington—which was initiated by the United States and terminated in 1922—resulted in several treaties, one of which (the Five Power Treaty) established a 5:5:3 ratio for the United States, Great Britain, and Japan in terms of tonnage for battleships and other major vessels (called "capital ships"). The formula recognized that, unlike the United States and Great Britain (whose navies operated in both the Atlantic and Pacific Oceans), Japan's navy only operated in one ocean. Despite that rationale, there was considerable resentment in Japan—especially in military circles—because Japan was not given parity with the United States and Great Britain. The London conference—which was also largely driven by the United States—applied the same ratio to heavy cruisers but did give Japan a slight increase (10:10:7) for light cruisers and other auxiliary vessels.

The Japanese government's agreement to those ratios was not well-received in certain quarters in Japan (especially right-wing groups and certain military factions), and the Japanese Prime Minister—Hamaguchi Osachi—paid with his life. He was walking on the platform at the Tokyo Railway Station on November 14, 1930 when a member of a right-wing group emerged from the crowd, pointed a pistol at Hamaguchi from a distance of about six feet, and felled him with one shot (although Hamaguchi did not die from his wound until August 1931). The incident helped to energize groups in Japan who bristled at the seeming refusal of the United States to treat Japan as an equal.

Japanese animosity toward the United States was compounded by the Manchurian Incident of September 1931. Japan had long coveted Manchuria as a territory that could supply the country with access to vital resources to accommodate Japan's growing population. The Treaty of Portsmouth, which concluded the Russo-Japanese War in 1905, enabled Japan to take control of the South Manchurian Railway. The railway became the vehicle for the relocation of thousands of Japanese citizens to establish farms and businesses near the railway—not to mention the thousands of Japanese troops positioned along the railway route (known as the Kwantung Army because of Japan's occupation of the Kwantung Peninsula in the eastern part of Manchuria).

Long desirous of occupying all of Manchuria (an area larger than California, Oregon, and Washington State combined), the Kwantung Army staged an incident that would provide an excuse to achieve that goal. Japanese soldiers exploded dynamite on a portion of the railway near Mukden, the Manchurian capital, and then claimed that the explosion was triggered by nearby Chinese troops. The Kwantung Army immediately moved on those Chinese troops, who were ordered to avoid any resistance to the Japanese troops because Chiang Kai-shek was more interested in fighting the communists in China. The Japanese troops continued to fan out, overpowering Chinese militias, until all of Manchuria was under Japanese control by early 1932. By March of that year, the Japanese had established a puppet regime in Manchuria called Manchukuo.

The Japanese claim that the Kwantung Army had acted in self-defense was not accepted blindly by the international community. Secretary of State Henry L. Stimson, for one, believed that Japan's actions violated the

Nine-Power Treaty (another treaty produced through the 1922 Washington Conference), which recognized Japan's special interests in Manchuria but also required the signatories (including Japan) to accept the territorial integrity of China. The question was what, if anything, Stimson could do about it. President Herbert Hoover was opposed to military action, and other signatories to the Nine-Power Treaty did not seem inclined to do anything. Frustrated but not defeated, Stimson was reduced to sending notes to Japan and China on January 7, 1932, which said that the United States would not "recognize any treaty or agreement" that impaired "the sovereignty, the independence, or the territorial and administrative integrity of the Republic of China." And so never would the United States recognize the puppet regime of Manchukuo.

Stimson's notes—later referred to as the Stimson Doctrine—would remain a bitter source of dispute between the United States and Japan until December 7, 1941. Joe Grew could not have known that when he accepted the ambassadorship to Japan in January 1932. But he knew enough to know that the Manchurian matter—as well as other issues—would require full application of the diplomatic skills he had nurtured in his prior positions. It was a challenge that Grew welcomed.

That self-confidence was born not only from Grew's prior diplomatic service. He also had the personality to make it work. He was smooth, ingratiating, and, when appropriate, full of life. "He has the most saint-like character," said Lipsen Crocker, wife of First Secretary Ned Crocker, in a 1936 letter to her mother, "as well as being a very keen and brilliant statesman and wonderful looking. We all adore him and would do anything in our power for him." It was a presence that even captured the imagination of the Embassy staff's children. Decades later, Henri Smith-Hutton's daughter remembered that "his eyes sort of twinkled when he smiled and spoke."

Another part of Grew's appeal was the way he interacted with people. He could be intense, standing or sitting with his ever-present pipe, listening, absorbing whatever was said, and deciding how to respond. He could be firm in his comments, whether conversational or formal, but rarely would they would be harsh or openly critical of any person. (Although he developed a deep dislike for Cordell Hull and was not afraid to express his differences on policy choices, one can scour Grew's private diaries and letters during the period before and immediately after Pearl Harbor without finding any personal criticism of the aging Secretary of State.)

Even those who found fault with Grew's performance could not resist the pull of his personality. "Joe hasn't much executive ability," said one State Department official who worked with Grew during the Paris peace conference, "but he is a terribly nice fellow."

These traits were complemented by an ability to make others feel comfortable—whatever their station in life. Waldo Heinrichs, a young Harvard Ph.D. whose biography of Grew was published in 1966, remembered going to visit the retired ambassador at his Manchester home shortly before he died. Grew made a point to come out to see the author's young son, who was sitting in the car. "That was quite memorable," said Heinrichs.

All of this made Joe Grew a welcome presence in almost any situation. There was perhaps no better example than the speech he gave before about two hundred people at the American-Japan Society in Tokyo in October 1939. Many of the society's members belonged to the elite of Japanese business and government. Grew had just returned from a few months' stay in the United States and had been surprised to find that American public opinion was "steadily hardening against Japan." He and President Roosevelt agreed that he should inform the Japanese about that public opinion. But it had to be the right tone. "To threaten the Japanese," Grew advised the Embassy staff, "is merely to increase their own determination. The attitude of the American Government and people must be presented merely as a patent fact which exists and should therefore be given full weight in formulating Japanese policy."

The ensuing speech was blunt, matter-of-fact, and without rancor. "What I shall say in Japan in the ensuing months," the Ambassador began, "comes 'straight from the horse's mouth' in that it will accurately represent and interpret some of the current thoughts of the American Government and people with regard to Japan and the Far East." The Japanese in attendance seemed very attentive, but not in any way disturbed. That reaction did not surprise Henri Smith-Hutton, who was in the audience. "[T]his was a remarkable speech," the Naval Attaché remembered, "because of the way the Ambassador delivered it....He was well liked, and he did it in such a courteous, friendly way that even the Japanese couldn't very well take offense."

That same grace served Grew well in social situations as well—even when he committed a faux pas. There was the time in 1949 after he had retired when Grew attended a farewell dinner for George Marshall, the distinguished Army general who was retiring as Secretary of State. Those in attendance included General Dwight D. Eisenhower and his wife Mamie. Grew stood up to give a toast and concluded his homage to Marshall by saying, "All he wants to do is retire to his farm in Leesburg with Mrs. Eisenhower." The guests immediately erupted in laughter, and Grew, realizing his mistake, quickly and coolly said, "My apologies to the General." To which Eisenhower retorted, "Which General?"

Those skills in dealing with people would surely be tested in trying to maneuver the United States and Japan toward a harmonious relationship. But Joe Grew would not be making that effort by himself.

CHAPTER 3

Alice

I t was a chance encounter he would treasure for the rest of his life and a date he would long remember: January 4, 1904. He had recently returned from a month-long stay in Japan to conclude his eighteen-month travel and decided to attend a dance at the Hotel Somerset in Boston. It was there that he saw "a lovely creature" who, he was told, had also just returned from Japan. He knew that could be a point of common interest and asked a friend to introduce him to the young lady. But his friend became preoccupied, and so Joe Grew turned to another friend and asked him to make the introduction.

To his surprise, the friend brought him to a different woman: Alice de Vermandois Perry, a tall, vivacious twenty-year-old beauty with long dark hair. As it turned out, Alice too had just returned from Japan. Not yet endowed with diplomatic skills, the twenty-three-year-old Harvard graduate blurted out, "I didn't intend to meet *you*!" Quick-witted and assertive, Alice responded in kind, but the two nonetheless agreed to dance. The other woman (Maya Lindsley) was quickly forgotten, and for young Joe, the chase was on. There were further dates as well as notes and flowers delivered by Suzuki, Joe's Japanese valet, and it appeared that the couple was moving toward marriage.

It would be a union well suited to Joe's background. Alice possessed impeccable family credentials. Her father was Thomas Sergeant Perry. He was not only an educator and prolific writer in his own right; he was also the grandson of Commodore Oliver Hazard Perry, the famous naval commander of the early nineteenth century whose brother was Commodore Matthew C. Perry, the naval commander who engineered the 1854 treaty that opened Japan to trade with the West. Alice's mother was Lilla Cabot Perry, the renowned impressionist painter whose friendship with Claude Monet had been spawned by the many summers that Lilla and her family had spent in Giverny, France, as Monet's neighbor.

Joe was living with a family in Tours, France, some months after meeting Alice when he learned that he had gotten the job as a clerk in the Cairo embassy. He returned immediately to Boston and proposed to Alice before making the trip to Cairo. He returned to Boston later in the year, and they were married on October 7, 1905.

Joe and Alice's life together had an inauspicious start when the ship carrying their wedding presents to Cairo was lost in a storm off the Barbary Coast. Matters took another, more serious turn for the worse shortly after Joe and Alice arrived in Mexico City in September 1906. Alice had just given birth to their daughter Edith in Giverny, where Alice was staying with her parents. Before too long, Alice was stricken with a near fatal condition that defied diagnosis but that left her partially paralyzed and required that she be immediately transported to Boston for treatment. She eventually recovered most but not all of her physical functions. There was nothing that could be done to restore the dexterity in her hands, and Alice was forced to abandon any hope of continuing to play the piano, one of her many passions.

The source of Alice's condition was never determined, but it was the impetus for Joe receiving a new assignment. It was apparently believed that the high altitude of Mexico City contributed to Alice's condition (and in later years she was diagnosed with Meniere's Disease, which can cause a person to lose his or her balance, especially at high altitudes). Whatever the cause of Alice's condition, the Grews were relocated to St. Petersburg in May 1907. Their daughter Lilla was born there in November 1907, followed by Anita in Berlin in 1909, and then Elsie in Vienna in 1912.

Joe and Alice formed a tight-knit circle with their children, giving them nicknames and lavishing time on their development and activities.

For her part, Alice would read them stories in French from the time they were little girls. Joe encouraged their involvement in sports and would later follow Anita in a rowboat in 1931 when she swam nineteen miles from the mouth of the Black Sea through the Bosporus, which separates the Asian portion of Turkey from the European portion of Turkey. In time, the family circle included Maria Langer—whom the family called "Mizzie"—a short, slightly plump girl whom Alice originally hired as a seamstress in Vienna but who soon assumed many other roles, including help with the children. Mizzie would remain with the Grews for the rest of her life, and, in later years she would tell the children and grandchildren how touched she was by the many courtesies the Ambassador showed her—opening the door for her, carrying her luggage, and otherwise treating her like a daughter.

Alice was devoted to the children, but Joe remained her first priority. When war came to Europe in 1914, she rented a house in Boston and sometimes left the children there with Mizzie and a governess to visit Joe in Berlin (meaning that Alice would have to sail through the submarine-infested waters of the North Atlantic).

In later years, the family would spend time in Hancock, a quaint community in southern New Hampshire. The Perry family had purchased land there to build homes for family members. Joe and Alice were given a particular plot that they used to build a home they affectionately called the "cottage." Before the Pearl Harbor attack, the Grews would often return there when Joe was granted leave. But the bond among family members remained strong wherever they were. Joe referenced that bond in a 1941 letter to Tippy, their nickname for Lilla, who was then living with her husband Jay Pierrepont Moffat in Canada, where he was the American minister. "[W]e are so blessed in our family closeness," said the doting father, "and so much more than the often more or less conventional love that exists between members of some families that we can be happy even in absence."

It was a way of life that seemed to give them all untold pleasure. But none of that could forestall tragedy. Edith (nicknamed "Didi") died at the age of seventeen in the spring of 1924 after contracting scarlet fever during a school trip to Venice. Joe was in Boston (on his way to Washington to become Under Secretary of State). The event hit him hard, but Alice was particularly devastated. Years later, one family member would say that Alice never "really recovered" and that, to offset the pain, she "very much spoiled" Elsie, the youngest daughter.

Despite that loss, Alice remained a vital part of Joe's professional life. Although she had little formal education because of her parents' travels, Alice was a well-informed woman of many strong opinions that she was willing, if not eager, to share with her husband. And he was willing to listen. "I am so built," Joe explained in a letter to Elsie a few months before the Pearl Harbor attack (when she was living in Chile with her husband Cecil Lyon, a Foreign Service officer), "that I like to discuss such problems with Mummy, and she often gives me very sound advice on which I often act. I very seldom send an important letter or telegram without consulting her...."

On occasion, Alice could take undue advantage of her husband's deference. There was the time in the summer of 1939 when Grew was interviewing Marshall Green, a Groton alumnus and recent Yale graduate, about becoming the Ambassador's next private secretary. The two men were sitting in the library of the Grew home on Woodland Drive in the Northwest section of Washington. Grew was on leave from the Embassy, and he and Alice were spending part of the summer in the nation's capital. At one point in the conversation, a woman's voice penetrated the wall, saying, "Whom are you speaking to, Joe dear?"

"I'm speaking to Marshall Green."

"Who is he, for heaven's sake?"

"He's interested in being my private secretary," Joe replied.

"Oh."

Grew resumed the conversation but was soon interrupted again by the woman's voice.

"Ask him, Joe, if he plays bridge."

The question may have startled Green, but it did not surprise Grew. He knew that bridge was one of his wife's passions. Grew asked the question, and Green responded, "I'm crazy about bridge, Mr. Ambassador."

Joe turned to the wall and said, "He's crazy about bridge, Alice."

That brought an immediate response from beyond the wall. "Well, take him, Joe," said Alice. "Take him, and let's get it over with."

So Marshall Green traveled to Tokyo in October to become the Ambassador's private secretary, where he often played bridge with Alice. But Green proved to be invaluable to Grew as well. When the young man left Tokyo in April 1941, the Ambassador praised Green as "a splendid type of virile young American, energetic, wry, graceful in movement and direct in manner, sometimes to the extent of bluntness, with curly red hair and a profile like a classic Greek, keen minded and thoroughly intelligent."

Joe may have accepted Alice's role in his decision-making process, but her involvement drew criticism from others. "Grew is a nice fellow," James Gerard, the American ambassador to Germany, wrote to Colonel House in May 1916, "but he is entirely under his wife's influence, and she affects his judgment." But Joe's reliance on Alice did have limits. He wanted to hear her opinions, but he also wanted his decisions to be based on fact rather than emotion. As he explained in a 1941 letter to his friend and colleague Bill Castle, "[O]ne of the things I most abhor in life is a heated argument when any and every argument can and ought to be conducted with pure objectivity. It has taken me the better part of forty years to get that point across to my dear wife, but I've succeeded at last."

Still, there was no denying that, whatever the circumstance, Alice was a lively figure. As one relative observed, "She knew how to do a good conversation and keep the balls up in the air." Bob Fearey, Marshall Green's successor as Grew's private secretary in the months before the Pearl Harbor attack, remembered that she was also "a formidable adversary in repartee." One incident in particular remained clear in Fearey's recollection. The Grews were entertaining Sir Robert Craigie, the British ambassador, and his wife, Lady Craigie, at the Embassy residence. Neither of the Grews liked Lady Craigie (Joe saying in his diary in May 1941 that Lady Craigie is "utterly nasty" and that Alice "simply shudders to come into contact with the woman"). But Craigie and Grew were confidants and often shared information, especially as Japan's relations with the United States and Great Britain deteriorated in the final months of 1941. Given that relationship, the two couples often socialized together. On this particular occasion, the Grews decided to show a movie after dinner. But the projector (being operated by Fearey) broke down in the middle of a reel. "Isn't it unfortunate, my dear," said Lady Craigie to Alice, "that that machine of yours is always breaking down?" Without skipping a beat, Alice responded, "Yes, my dear, but isn't it fortunate that we have no important guests tonight?"

That quickness, that ability to seize the initiative when necessary, was evidenced elsewhere, and on one occasion, it resulted in the arrest of a

German spy during World War II. On a spring day in 1944, Alice was on a train traveling from New York City to Washington and sitting at a table in the dining car with some strangers. When the train made an unexpected lurch, the coffee cup of a man wearing a British uniform tipped over and spilled coffee on Alice. The man cried out in German, "Ach! Mein Gott!" Alice spoke German and was immediately suspicious that a British soldier would make a spontaneous exclamation in German. She made her suspicions known to the conductor, and, when the train arrived in Union Station, FBI agents took the British "soldier" into custody and later advised Alice that the man "was one of the most dangerous of German spies."

Alice's assertive personality served her well in the Embassy. Joe could oversee the professional staff, but Alice was there to make sure the Embassy functioned well. Dress codes, compliance with protocol, and other routine matters generally fell within her jurisdiction, and she did not hesitate to exercise the authority that came with that responsibility. "She was one of the Foreign Service's difficult wives," said one family member. "She was a little bit dictatorial in that role" and "was sometimes hard on the wives, particularly of other Foreign Service people." Lispen Crocker agreed, telling her mother in one letter that Alice had a "ferocious reputation on three continents." Cynthia Bowers, Henri Smith-Hutton's daughter, shared that view. "She wasn't as likeable or as charming as Mr. Grew," said Bowers. "And she and my mother didn't hit it off, only because my mother was also very opinionated."

Still, Alice could be very gracious and forgiving. Bob Fearey saw evidence of that when the Embassy personnel were interned on the Embassy compound after the Pearl Harbor attack. All sixty-five members of the staff (many of whom previously lived outside the Embassy compound) were crowded into the residence and the Chancery, with offices being used as bedrooms. Cleaning clothes was a challenge because the Embassy did not have a washing machine—or so everyone thought. But then Fearey found an old machine in the residence attic, brought it down to the Chancery basement, and advised everyone to bring their laundry down at nine o'clock each morning. One day, Alice brought down her treasured white silk curtains. Fearey placed them in the machine, not realizing that one staff member's black socks were still inside. Alice handled the mishap with cool composure.

"[A]fter recovering from the shock," said Fearey, "[she] was kind enough to say that grey had always been her favorite color."

In all of this, Alice appears to have had few bad habits, but one of them was certainly cigarettes. Even in her later years, relatives would say they could not remember a time when she was not carrying a long cigarette holder in her hand with a lit cigarette. But Alice paid the price for that indulgence. The smoking darkened her teeth and probably contributed to the several heart attacks she experienced, including some before the Pearl Harbor attack. She ultimately succumbed to a heart attack in 1959.

Long before then, she had agreed to return to Tokyo with her husband for a new and hopefully fulfilling experience. They left Ankara on March 3, 1932, for Istanbul and the cruise to the United States. After a short visit at home, they traveled to Chicago, where they boarded the *Overland Limited* on May 14, 1932, for the train ride to San Francisco. They then journeyed to Japan on the SS *President Coolidge.*

CHAPTER 4

Japan

A s the Grews were getting ready to board the train to San Francisco, it was already May 15 in Japan (because Japan was thirteen hours ahead of Chicago time). Prime Minister Inukai Tsuyoshi was no doubt hoping to spend a quiet Sunday at his Tokyo residence with his daughter-in-law, who had just given birth. It had started out as a pleasant spring morning, and the diminutive seventy-five-year-old leader with closely-cropped hair and a full gray moustache surely thought he would have a day without disruption. It was not to be.

Around five o'clock that evening, two cabs pulled up in front of the Prime Minister's expansive two-story stone residence. Construction had been completed in 1929, and the Art Deco style of the residence appeared to mimic the motif of the nearby Imperial Hotel designed by Frank Lloyd Wright. Nine men, aged between twenty-four and twenty-eight, emerged from the two cabs. All were wearing military uniforms, and they were armed with revolvers and daggers. They broke up into two groups, with one group approaching the front gate and the other group going to the rear gate.

The men approaching the front gate expected resistance, but the guards with the regalia of the Emperor allowed the men to enter the building without objection or inquiry. The uniforms worn by the group surely assuaged any concern the guards might have had. Once inside, the young officers assumed they would find Inukai in the private quarters of the building, but they had no idea where those quarters were located. They eventually wandered upstairs and heard a key turning in a lock. The group assumed that it was the Prime Minister and rushed the door.

Inukai had to know why they were there. Although he had been in office only since December 1931, he had already incurred the wrath of many in the armed forces, primarily because he had criticized the Kwantung Army's action in Manchuria and had refused to recognize the puppet regime of Manchukuo as an independent nation. Many in the Navy and the Army—especially the extremists recruited from the farms and small towns of rural Japan—saw him as an impediment to a glorious future for Japan.

Whatever concerns he may have had for his life, Inukai displayed a calm demeanor, which impressed the young officers. He led them to an interior room and asked them to remove their shoes. Inukai's daughter-in-law was there with her baby. The men, "knowing what would happen in a few minutes," suggested that she leave, but the young woman refused. Inukai lit a cigarette and appeared eager to engage the group in conversation. But that opportunity soon evaporated. The other group of officers burst into the room, and the leader, carrying a dagger in one hand, yelled, "No use in talking. Fire!" The officers immediately commenced firing, and Inukai quickly slumped to the matted floor.

The conspirators included two other officers who had thrown grenades at the offices of the Bank of Japan and the offices of Inukai's political party. All of the conspirators surrendered almost immediately to the military police and were soon put on trial for murder. Much of the trial was devoted to statements by the defendants explaining their patriotic motivations. "The Japanese, for some curious reason," Henri Smith-Hutton later observed, "have felt that if someone is serious enough to attack and kill a political enemy, he is showing what they call 'great sincerity,' and his ideas merit considerable attention." One of the judges failed to appreciate that perspective, and he was removed from the case because "his attention had wandered" during one of the defendant's speeches.

In the course of their testimony, the defendants explained that their original plans had included the assassination of Charlie Chaplin, who had arrived for a visit in Japan the previous day and was watching a sumo wrestling match with Inukai's son on that fateful Sunday. There was no mystery behind that plan. The conspirators assumed that the actor's demise would trigger a war for the United States. For the same reason, they had also considered assassinating the new American ambassador, who was due to arrive in Tokyo within the month.

Despite the heinous nature of the crime, there was broad sympathy throughout Japan for the defendants. A petition with about 350,000 signatures in blood was delivered to the court seeking leniency. Eleven youths from the countryside advised the court that they were prepared to take the position of the eleven defendants and, as proof of their sincerity, included eleven severed fingers in the package. Those and similar public sentiments appeared to have an impact. None of the defendants received a severe punishment from the court.

Grew knew nothing of the assassins' motivations—or their plan to assassinate him—as he began his train trip to San Francisco, but a correspondent from the *Chicago Herald-Examiner* did hand him a newspaper which blared the headline, "Japanese Premier Slain." Although the new ambassador was very much aware of Japan's proclivity to political assassinations, he could not help thinking, "There must be something wrong here." He knew he was entering a political cauldron. But he remained hopeful that his mission could help turn things around.

The SS *President Coolidge* arrived in Yokohama in the early morning hours of June 6, 1932, and as the dawn lifted, Joe and Alice could see the relatively new docks and wide streets, all a product of the reconstruction undertaken throughout the Tokyo area after the earthquake of September 1923. Within a short time, he and Alice were in the Embassy car, taking the bumpy eighteen-mile drive in a drizzling rain to the American Embassy in the Akasaka neighborhood, the location of many government buildings, including the Prime Minister's residence. They passed narrow, crowded streets that had no names and were lined with small shops, shanty homes, and newly-constructed office buildings, some of which were eight or ten stories high. Although engaged in conversation with the Embassy's counselor, Grew remembered the "ugliness of the route" and how the Embassy seemed like "a real oasis in the more or less ugly surroundings of the new-grown city."

From the start, Grew wanted to create a cooperative atmosphere in the Embassy. Within a week after his arrival, he convened a meeting with the professional staff to convey his perspective. He said that he "wanted them to drop in whenever they had any information, views, or suggestions which they thought would be helpful." He also wanted them to send him "confidential memorandums whenever they picked up any significant opinions or information, especially of a political nature...." But the ability to work with others was paramount. As Grew explained in one of his letters to Groton describing the requirements for his private secretary, the candidate had to "be personally qualified to fit harmoniously into our closely-knit and intimate official family where the factor of congenial teamwork, both in work and play, is important." In keeping with the aura of informality, the Ambassador was prone to call staff members on the phone himself and, when the staff member answered, simply say, "Grew speaking."

For his part, Grew adopted a schedule that varied with the time and circumstance but usually resulted in him getting up around 6:30 a.m. and getting to his Chancery office by 7:15. There was almost always an endless number of communications coming in and going out of the Embassy. Sometimes Grew drafted the important telegrams and other outgoing communications himself and then shared drafts with the senior staff; at other times, he would edit the drafts of his staff. But rarely would he let any significant matter escape his attention. As Marshall Green later commented, the Ambassador "had an infinite capacity for detail."

Developing and maintaining relationships with Japanese government officials, representatives from other embassies, journalists, and members of Japanese society occupied a good portion of Grew's time. That preoccupation required attendance at meetings and other functions inside and outside the Embassy that might occur during the day or evening. As Grew later commented, the evening affairs were "generally a great deal less amusing than sitting at one's desk watching the hands of the clock get around to six." Many of the outside meetings and functions were at the nearby Tokyo Club, an upscale venue for prominent foreigners and Japanese. As explained by Gene Dooman, who was born in Japan and would become the Embassy's Counselor in 1937, the club "promoted an aura of intimacy and personal intercourse which existed nowhere else in Japan."

Never, however, would Grew try to speak to members of the Japanese community in their native language. He had a flair for foreign languages and spoke fluent French as well as German. But he knew that learning

Japanese far exceeded the demands of any other language he had studied. The Japanese language consisted of thousands of characters, and each year the State Department would appoint individuals (usually recent college graduates) to become language officers. They would endure two or three years of intensive study to learn the language. Dooman, for one, remembered that his final examination as a language officer required him to know 6,000 characters. Smith-Hutton, a graduate of the Naval Academy in Annapolis (who spoke fluent French), was assigned by the Navy to the American Embassy in Tokyo in 1926 to learn Japanese. After completing the required program of instruction, he concluded that "Japanese is perhaps the most complicated and difficult language of any of the world's great languages" and that "it is capable of being interpreted in several different ways, particularly if you try to hide your real thoughts or your real intentions." It was a telling point that would have serious repercussions in the months before the Pearl Harbor attack when American intelligence officers incorrectly translated secret Japanese cables.

Grew intuitively understood the challenges of mastering Japanese. As he told John Emmerson, a young language officer in the Embassy, he "feared that the dangerous hazards of ludicrous wrong usages would impair the dignity and esteem of the president's representative." It was a judgment Emmerson shared, later saying, at most, Grew would have had time only to learn "a collection of polite phrases that might have amused the Japanese he met, but would not truly have won him respect." And so at the beginning of each day, the Ambassador would usually have one of the Embassy's language officers read to him relevant sections from the many periodicals which populated Tokyo in those years.

Although she had learned a few phrases when she visited Japan in her early years—before she met Joe—Alice too was unable to speak or read Japanese. On one occasion, it resulted in some embarrassment to the Ambassador's wife. She had purchased a bowl in a Tokyo market and placed it on a table in the foyer of the Embassy, only to see it disappear the next day. When she inquired about the missing bowl to the Japanese butler, he said it was in the pantry. Alice said she wanted it returned to the foyer, and the butler dutifully complied. But after another day, it disappeared again, and again the butler said he had placed it in the pantry. Alice was not one to keep her silence, and she took the butler to task for ignoring her instructions. He then explained that the writing on the bowl advertised it as an artifact for a Geisha house and made it inappropriate for the Embassy.

Joe and Alice's inability to speak Japanese did not impede their ability to socialize with the Japanese community. Dinners at the Embassy were a frequent occurrence. They would sometimes be small affairs, but they would sometimes involve dozens of guests. Whatever the number of guests, the event almost always provided an occasion for the Ambassador to enjoy a Johnnie Walker Red Label Scotch whiskey cocktail before dinner and to serve wine from the extensive collection he had brought with him from the United States.

Grew also had to be available at hours when others might be sleeping because, given the time difference between Tokyo and Washington, he would often be awakened by the Embassy's night clerk about a telegram or other communication from the State Department that required his immediate attention. He was never one to shirk any of these responsibilities, but, as he told his daughter Anita at one point, it was important to maintain "a reasonable sense of balance and proportion"—so he found time to indulge interests outside work.

He loved tennis, but as his age advanced, he found it more and more difficult to pursue that sport. He had an unremitting devotion to golf (playing left-handed with an unusual croquet style of putting, which seldom enabled him to break 100) and would play as often as he could—a fact well known in the diplomatic community. Grew became aware of that notoriety in the fall of 1941 when tensions between Japan and the United States were escalating. Grew casually asked a member of the French embassy at a diplomatic function why people would always ask him about his golf game. "Why, Mr. Ambassador," the French official responded, "your golf is the thermometer which measures the temperature in the Diplomatic Corps. If a week goes by without your playing golf, the fact is cabled to every chancellery in the world over, for the situation is then indeed critical!"

Grew was also a voracious reader, usually favoring biography and history but occasionally reaching for a detective story. Music was another passion. The demands of the Tokyo position precluded him from practicing the piano as much as he had in earlier years, but music never lost its appeal. It became a refuge for him as the Pearl Harbor attack neared, and the tension mounted. At one point in October 1941, he remarked in his diary that, after attending church on one Sunday morning, he worked all day and "that evening enjoyed what is to me the most perfect form of relaxation—a comfortable chair, the lights out, and that glorious violin concerto of Brahms coming over the radio."

Throughout all of this, Grew continued to maintain the diary he had started at the beginning of his diplomatic career. On many evenings and sometimes on weekends, he would sit at his desk, his pipe clenched between his teeth, and peck out the words on his seemingly ageless Smith-Corona typewriter. He placed great stock in that diary and would share copies of certain sections with his daughters (when they were older and living away from home) as well as friends and State Department colleagues, hoping that his contemporaneous comments would be interesting and, in the case of the State Department, useful in formulating policy.

In the meantime, one of Grew's first obligations as ambassador was to present his credentials to the Emperor of Japan. On the morning of June 14, 1932, imperial coaches pulled up in front of the Chancery with Japanese cavalry flanked in the front and rear. Grew, dressed in formal wear with a top hat, entered the lead coach by himself (which already included a representative of the Emperor). The procession of cavalry and coaches (which carried Alice and the Embassy staff as well) then proceeded through the rain to the Imperial Palace, an imposing structure of high stone walls surrounded by a moat of greenish water. The Imperial Palace grounds encompassed almost one and a half square miles of land with numerous buildings, gardens, and ponds.

After passing over the moat through the main gate, the procession pulled in front of the main palace, a large, austere building reflecting traditional Japanese architecture. Grew and the rest of the party entered the palace and ascended the red-carpeted stairs through a large hall emblazoned with gold screens and ceilings. In due course, they proceeded to an interior room where Hirohito, Japan's 124th emperor, dressed in full military regalia, was waiting for them.

The thirty-one-year-old monarch was an unimposing man of medium build and height (for Japanese) with a small moustache on an oval face, sloping shoulders, dark hair parted on the side, horn-rimmed glasses, and a modest countenance. Ned Crocker wrote his mother that Hirohito "was the most unimpressive monarch" he had ever seen—"[s]mall, pasty-faced, soft, and he holds himself terribly badly...." In other circumstances and dressed in other clothes, the Emperor could have easily passed for an aspiring marine biologist—which did indeed reflect one of his passions (one of his favorite pastimes being the study of marine life, whether on the Palace grounds or at his vacation resort at Hayama on the Japanese coast).

His reign officially began on December 25, 1926, when his father, the Emperor Taisho, succumbed at the age of forty-seven to a long-standing illness that was probably precipitated by meningitis. Hirohito, as the Emperor's first son, had already been acting as his father's regent since November 1921 because Taisho's physical and psychological deterioration had already left him largely incapacitated—a condition exemplified by Taisho's inability to read a statement of five sentences at the opening of the Diet, Japan's legislative body, in December 1919.

Hirohito was a soft-spoken man with a high-pitched voice who never smoked, preferred carbonated water, and had a passion for discipline and frugality. He would, for example, wear nondescript clothes inside the Palace until they wore out and use pencils until they were worn down to the stub. He maintained a rigid schedule for his work and hobbies, rising around 6 a.m. (in the summer) or 7 a.m. (in the winter) and going to the Palace study (which included busts of Charles Darwin, Abraham Lincoln, and Napoleon) to dispose of whatever papers or meetings were required. His outdoor activities included golf and riding (usually a white Arabian stallion or gelding). If he had to travel locally, it would be in a maroon automobile—the Emperor being the only Japanese allowed a car of that color. He did not travel outside of Japan; his only visit beyond Japan's borders was a trip he had taken in 1921 to Western Europe, where he visited heads of state and royalty. He had led a sheltered life, being raised in isolation from his parents to prepare him for the role he would ultimately assume, and the exposure to Western European societies made him realize that he had been living "like a bird in a cage."

Hirohito's mild manner concealed a quick mind and deep-seated convictions which would periodically surface in the months before the Pearl Harbor attack. These traits were in evidence long before he became Emperor. In 1918, the Palace elders had selected three princesses as suitable brides for the Crown Prince. Hirohito chose Princess Nagako, and he persisted in that choice despite the elders' effort to recant her selection because they had discovered color blindness in her family history.

Whatever his preferences, Hirohito recognized the need to preserve the Emperor's status in Japanese life. The line of his predecessors—so the Japanese believed—began in 660 BC. According to Japanese mythology, the first Emperor was the descendent of the Sun Goddess Amaterasu Omikami, which, to most Japanese, made the Emperor the divine representative of their country. "His Majesty is not human," said Tojo Hideki, Japan's Prime Minister in the months before the Pearl Harbor attack. "He is God." The veneration for the Emperor was so entrenched that, when Japan celebrated the 2,600th birthday of the empire outside the Palace grounds in November 1940, no one was allowed to witness the festivities from the windows and rooftops of nearby office buildings because it was forbidden to look down on the Emperor.

The reverence for the Emperor was a critical component of Japan's military strength. He was the inspiration, the rallying point, that made sacrifice by the country's soldiers not only possible but also honorable. "[T]o die for the Emperor," said *New York Times* correspondent Otto Tolischus, was the soldier's "greatest glory, to surrender his greatest disgrace." Grew himself saw evidence of that perspective in 1941 before the Pearl Harbor attack. He received word from the Chinese government of a Japanese soldier who had been taken prisoner and who wanted his family to know that he was still alive. Grew passed the information on to the Japanese Government, but he soon received a reply that the Japanese Government was not interested in receiving such information. So far as the Government and the man's family were concerned, "that man was officially dead" because "[t]he man who allows himself to be captured has disgraced himself and his country."

The Imperial Household Law stipulated that the Emperor was a living god, and that divine status was recognized in the Japanese Constitution promulgated in 1889. The Emperor was identified as "sacred and inviolable" and the "head of the Empire." In accordance with that elevated status, the Emperor was endowed with all powers of sovereignty, including the right to "supreme command of the Army and Navy," the right to appoint and dismiss ministers, the right to convoke and dismiss the Diet, and the right to issue all other orders necessary for the governance of the country, including any ordinances of "urgent necessity" required when the Diet was not sitting. Many of these imperial orders were called "Rescripts." (Japan's declaration of war on the United States on December 7, 1941, was identified as an Imperial Rescript.)

Although it was seemingly based on the political systems of Western European countries—primarily Germany and Great Britain—the Japanese Constitution, as implemented, resulted in an unusual form of governing that could be easily distinguished from the political systems of those other countries. The Japanese people had virtually no direct role in the selection of their government's leaders or in the shaping of its policies, especially in the years before the Pearl Harbor attack. They only elected members of the House of Representatives of the Diet. The other chamber, the House of Peers, consisted of members of the Imperial family, members of nobility, and other persons appointed by the Emperor. Although it could adopt budgets and enact certain laws with the concurrence of the Emperor, the Diet rarely formulated national policy. Rather, the Diet—which was in session for only limited time periods—generally responded to the initiatives of the civilian and military leaders.

As Dooman later explained, "What the ordinary person—the man in the street—thought about important events was really of little moment.... National policies were not the formulation of the hopes and aspirations of the masses, but rather what a small group of people considered in the interests of the nation." It was a critical point that Cordell Hull often disregarded when discussing a possible agreement with Japanese representatives in the months before the Pearl Harbor attack. The Secretary of State repeatedly told those representatives that the negotiations would have a better chance of success if only Japanese leaders could educate the Japanese people about the benefits of policies that were not dependent on military aggression.

The public's lack of involvement in public affairs was reflected in the selection and retention of the Prime Minister, the chief executive of the civilian government and the one who chose the other ministers of the cabinet (other than the Navy Minister and War Minister, who had to be approved by the Navy and Army, respectively). The Prime Minister was selected by the Emperor, who generally relied only on the recommendation of the *Genro*, or elder statesmen. When the last *Genro* died in 1940, the Emperor then relied on the *jushin*, a group composed of former Prime Ministers. The Prime Minister's tenure could be terminated at any time—not by an upheaval of criticism from the public, but usually because he lost the confidence of the Army and the Navy and, to a lesser extent, other individuals who exercised influence over government policy.

Unlike in Great Britain or Germany, the Prime Minister of Japan had no direct control over the Army or the Navy. Each of those branches reported directly to the Emperor. As Dooman later observed, this structure constituted "a two-headed monstrosity" because the civilian government "was not cloaked with authority over the Armed Forces." That separation was exemplified by the Japanese Navy's attack on Pearl Harbor: although the Prime Minister and the ministers in his cabinet ultimately approved (with the concurrence of the Army and Navy) the decision to go to war with the United States, the civilian members of the government knew nothing of the planned attack on Pearl Harbor until after it had commenced.

Beyond all these divisions of responsibility in the government, Hirohito was imbued with the notion that the Emperor should never be placed in the position of being blamed for an erroneous government decision. It was his responsibility, or so he was taught, to appear infallible. That point was drilled into his thinking in 1928 by Prince Saionji, the last remaining *Genro*, when the Kwantung Army assassinated Marshal Chang Tso-lin, the aging Chinese warlord of Manchuria. The army had blown up the train in which Chang was riding because they thought he was contemplating a pact with Chiang Kai-shek. The young emperor was furious that the Army had allowed the Kwantung Army to engage in such nefarious action and contemplated what he could do. Saionji disabused Hirohito of any such thoughts, telling him that his obligation was to "reign, not rule." And so, as Hirohito later told an aide, he believed that the emperor had to accept any decision which reflected a consensus of the civilian government and military command "even if he personally does not agree with it." Otherwise, said Hirohito, the emperor would not be acting like a "constitutional monarch" but as "an absolute monarch."

That limited perspective of his prerogatives did not prevent Hirohito from trying to influence the consensus in government decision-making. He would convey his views in private meetings with cabinet ministers as well as the leaders of the Army and Navy. He would probe, push, and pull in whatever direction he thought would best serve the country. Sometimes— but especially after the death of Prince Saionji in 1940—he would exert his influence indirectly through the Lord Keeper of the Privy Seal, his principal aide (and the one who impressed the Imperial seal on all ordinances, orders, and other documents). At other times, especially in formal conferences, he would rely on the President of the Privy Council, the constitutional advisory arm of the emperor. For their part, the cabinet ministers as well as the members of the Army and Navy command were generally eager to accommodate the Emperor, believing that his sanction was a prerequisite to any action they might take—although there were occasions, especially with respect to the Kwantung Army and the other military forces in China, where the Emperor's wishes were ignored.

All of this often made it difficult for Grew to pinpoint the locus of governmental decision-making or to nail down the direction of government policy. His principal government contacts were almost entirely within the civilian cabinet and its ministries. His naval and military attachés did have some contacts in the Army and Navy, but, as subordinate officers, they did not have comparable contacts in the highest levels of the armed forces. And so, in trying to assess Japan's intentions or actions from a military perspective, Grew was often reduced to communicating with civilian leaders who had no direct control over the Army or Navy and frequently had no information on what the Army and Navy had done or what they were planning.

None of those limitations prevented Grew from drawing general conclusions about the Japanese people. He found that they were almost always unfailingly polite, smiling and bowing at the commencement of a meeting and during the course of conversation. But it was a trait that, at least to the Ambassador, could not be taken at face value. "Their traditional politeness," he confided to his diary at one point, "is generally but a veneer, save in the case of well-bred families" and "does not comprise thoughtful consideration of others in any degree."

Discipline was another hallmark of the Japanese personality. They rigidly adhered to patterns of life, regardless of any change in circumstance. Bob Fearey, Grew's private secretary, well remembered the scene when he was allowed to leave the Embassy for a doctor's appointment in 1942 while the Embassy staff was interned after the Pearl Harbor attack. Petroleum products were reserved almost exclusively for military purposes, and "the streets were almost barren of cars...." said Fearey. But "when the traffic light was against them, the crowds, without a car in sight in either direction, would pile up en masse on the sidewalk corners until the light turned green." For his part, Grew recognized that the Japanese discipline would be an advantage to the country in any armed conflict. In contrast to the German citizenry he had observed while stationed at the Berlin embassy during World War I, said Grew, the Japanese "will not crack morally or psychologically or economically, even when eventual defeat stares them in the face. They will pull in their belts another notch, reduce their rations from a bowl to a half bowl of rice, and fight to the bitter end."

There were, however, moments of kindness, and in the first years of Grew's tenure in Tokyo, none was more endearing—or more notorious—than the fate of Sambo, the Grews' black cocker spaniel. The dog initially belonged to Cecil Lyon, the twenty-nine-year-old Third Secretary in the Embassy, who was ardently pursuing Grew's twenty-one-year-old daughter Elsie. After they became engaged, Lyon had planned to visit Elsie during the summer of 1933 at the house her parents had rented in Karuizawa, a wooded mountainside resort about an hour outside of Tokyo. Cecil passed word that he was bringing Sambo with him, but he soon received some discouragement through the Embassy staff: "Mrs. Grew says not to bring Sambo. You've got to choose between Elsie and Sambo." Being a headstrong diplomat, Lyon disregarded the Embassy warning and traveled to Karuizawa with Sambo, who jumped out of the car on arrival, ran up the stairs to the Grews' bedroom, and jumped into bed with Alice. "And," as Lyon later recalled, "I never got him back."

Cecil did receive a compensating benefit a few months later. He and Elsie planned to take a honeymoon after their marriage in October, but State Department regulations said a Foreign Service officer could receive leave only if he had been employed for one year, and Lyon had not been in the service that long. He discussed the matter with Grew, who pulled out the regulations and saw that leave could be granted in an emergency. The Ambassador looked up at his future son-in-law and said, "This is certainly an emergency."

Cecil and Elsie proceeded with their marriage, but Sambo remained the Grews' dog. The following January, Elsie was taking a walk with Sambo and her father near the Palace grounds on a cold, wintry day when they realized that Sambo was nowhere to be found. They soon saw that Sambo had fallen into the moat surrounding the Palace and, as Grew remembered, the dog was "struggling in the ice and water with only his head showing, like a drowned rat." The wall surrounding the moat was a steep vertical drop, and neither Grew nor Elsie could reach the hapless dog. Joe ran to the guardhouse to see if there might be a rowboat which he could maneuver into the moat, but the guard said no such vessel was available. The dejected Ambassador returned to where Elsie was, assuming that they had seen the last of Sambo. But when he reached Elsie, he saw a crowd surrounding the shivering dog. Elsie explained that a passing taxi driver, along with a nearby delivery boy and the Grews' chauffer, had worked together to use a rope to descend the vertical moat wall and retrieve the dog.

Grew never saw the taxi driver, who had already left the scene without giving Elsie his name. Upon hearing the story, one of Grew's Japanese friends thought it warranted publication, and he arranged to have Grew interviewed by the press. In the ensuing articles, Grew mentioned his desire to know the name of the taxi driver so that he could be given an appropriate reward—a watch that Alice had purchased. A few days later, a man arrived at the Chancery, saying he was the taxi driver who had rescued Sambo. Before Alice could come down to the Chancery to give him the watch, the alleged rescuer was assaulted by another taxi driver, who said that the purported hero had stolen his taxi in an effort to claim the reward. A few days later, the real savior showed up at the Embassy to receive the watch from Alice. By then, the tale of Sambo was well known in Tokyo circles. So Grew could not have been entirely surprised when the Emperor asked him at a Palace function, "How is Sambo?"

Long before then, Grew was more worried about his continued status as the American ambassador to Japan than the fate of a dog. Franklin D. Roosevelt had been elected president in November 1932. Grew sent the president-elect a "Dear Frank" letter, saying that "Groton, Harvard, and the Fly are immensely proud"—although Grew confided to his diary that they were now entering a period of "watchful waiting" because he had "very little knowledge of Frank Roosevelt's potential capabilities." Despite the personal connection with the President-elect, Grew followed protocol and submitted his resignation—even though he hoped to remain in Tokyo. He made his interest known to well-connected intimates, including John W. Davis (the 1924 Democratic presidential nominee), Colonel Edward House (for whom Grew had worked during the Versailles Treaty negotiations), and Mrs. Woodrow Wilson (whom he and Alice had entertained in Tokyo the previous October). His efforts paid dividends. In March 1933, Grew received word that the newly-elected president wished him to remain at his post.

Even before he received word of his retention, Grew had seen the hand of the Japanese military—whose influence had expanded after the assassination of Prime Minister Inukai—in preparing the nation for war. The press was replete with articles and speeches attacking foreign powers, especially the United States, who were critical of Japanese actions in Manchuria and elsewhere. "This situation reminds me strongly of the efforts of the German Government...to build up a public war psychology in 1914," Grew had written Hoover's Secretary of State, Henry L. Stimson, on August 13, 1932. "The German military machine, supported by a carefully nurtured public war psychology, took the bit in its teeth and overrode all restraining influences in 1914. The Japanese military machine is not dissimilar. It has been built for war, feels prepared for war, and would welcome war."

His assessment was shared by Stanley K. Hornbeck, Chief of the State Department's Division of Far Eastern Affairs. Hornbeck held that position when Grew had arrived in Tokyo in June 1932, and he would hold that position until 1937. He then became the Secretary of State's Adviser on Political Relations and Hull's principal aide on matters relating to Japan, a job he would retain up to and even after the Pearl Harbor attack. Like Grew, Hornbeck recognized the dominant influence of the military, especially in foreign affairs. Japan's foreign policy, said Hornbeck in a 1933 memo, constituted a "two-faced policy." To the West, Japan presented a diplomatic, "smiling, refined face." To its neighbors, Japan presented the face of "Attila," the notoriously violent leader of the Huns. Behind the diplomatic façade, said Hornbeck, the United States and its allies were really "dealing with a military and militant state."

The Ambassador's and Hornbeck's agreement at this early stage of Grew's tenure would not stand the test of time. Although they would always maintain cordial relations and would communicate frequently (with Grew sometimes sending Hornbeck excerpts of his diary entries), the two men had diametrically different views on how to handle Japan. The divergence was reflected in Hornbeck's propensity to write critical comments with a red pencil on the diary entries which Grew sent to him. Years after the war,

Dooman—who served on the Embassy staff between 1937 and 1942—acknowledged that he and Grew realized "that we were dealing in Washington with a person—I am here referring to Stanley Hornbeck—who was on the opposite side of the fence, who was being extremely busy negating, as it were, the purport of our reports from Tokyo." Rarely, if ever, would that personal frustration with Hornbeck—who almost always had the upper hand in shaping American policy—surface in any document or written communication Grew generated before the Pearl Harbor attack. Instead, the frustration would almost always emerge when Grew expressed disappointment with the policies and decisions of the Roosevelt administration.

Hornbeck was fifty years old when he wrote that 1933 memo on the two-faced Japanese foreign policy. A lean, intense, chain-smoking man with a balding head, an angular and often unsmiling face, dark eyes, a sharp nose, and large ears, Hornbeck's interest in China and Japan took root when he traveled to China in 1909 at the age of twenty-six. He had been an instructor at the University of Wisconsin (where he would later earn his doctorate), having graduated from the University of Denver and then having spent three years in Oxford, England, as a Rhodes Scholar. One day when he was at Wisconsin, Stanley saw an article in a school newspaper which said that a provincial college in Hangchow, China, was looking for professors. Then and there, the young scholar decided that he was going to China.

Hornbeck's four years in China proved to be an indelible experience. He met many interesting and important Chinese, including the Manchurian warlord Chang Tso-lin, whom Hornbeck later described as "a courteous, soft-spoken Chinese gentleman" who was "small in stature but large in capabilities and in vision." (Years later, after Chang had been assassinated by the Kwantung Army, Hornbeck would remember with fondness a visit in Washington from "a bright-eyed and charming Chinese girl" who told Hornbeck that Chang was her grandfather.) Those treasured memories of the Chinese were counterbalanced by stories he had heard from a British citizen about boys at one of the many Japanese schools who "talked most" about the "war which Japan was going to have with the United States" and how "Japan would defeat the United States."

All of these early experiences in China no doubt played a large role in Hornbeck's later perspective on American policy toward Japan. Dooman, who worked with Hornbeck in the Far Eastern Division of the State

Department between 1933 and 1937, remembered that it was "a very unpleasant experience" because, as the Embassy Counselor said, "I did not feel I could deal with Dr. Hornbeck as a person with a completely objective mind. I discovered that he had two supreme passions. One was a feeling of affection and sympathy for China. And the second was a pathological hatred of Japan and the Japanese."

For those who worked with him, Hornbeck's firm views on China and Japan were complemented by an unyielding perspective. He was "very dictatorial," said Dooman, and those who worked in the Far Eastern Division were "terrified by him." That dogmatic demeanor was particularly pronounced when it came to writing memos and other communications. Hornbeck was an unforgiving taskmaster. The sentence structure had to be precise, the grammar impeccable, and the word selection flawless. One staff member recalled Hornbeck telling a subordinate to spend a few hours studying the difference between "in regard to" and "with respect to."

"For an officer assigned to Far Eastern affairs," remembered John Emmerson, who worked in the Far Eastern Division in the months before Pearl Harbor, "getting a piece of paper as far as Hornbeck, let alone beyond, was a moment of minor triumph." The roadblock was Max Hamilton, who had assumed Hornbeck's position as Chief of the Far Eastern Division in 1937. Although he had been elevated to the status of Adviser on Political Relations, Hornbeck exercised supervisory control over his former division. "Fearful of his chief's eagle eye for error," said Emmerson, "Max Hamilton would fix on every phrase, every word, and every comma to achieve the perfection that would pass the Hornbeckian judgment."

Despite these demands, there were those who respected the long-time State Department employee. Joe Ballantine, who had worked in the Embassy with Grew and then returned to Washington in 1937 to the take over the Japan Desk in the Far Eastern Division, said of Hornbeck and Hamilton, "I never could have worked with two more selfless persons."

Long before Ballantine began to work with Hornbeck, the Japanese military experienced a transformation that was to affect the dynamics of Japanese policy in the months before the Pearl Harbor attack. The precipitating event was brutal, and it was one that Joe Grew would long remember.

CHAPTER 5

Turmoil

It was the kind of evening Joe Grew cherished: thirty-four guests assembled at the Embassy for dinner and the showing of a recent movie. Tokyo had experienced a record snowfall of more than ten inches at the beginning of the month, and now, on this Tuesday, the twenty-fifth day of February, 1936, snow was falling again. But the weather was not an impediment to the evening's activities. When dinner was finished, the guests gathered in the salon to watch *Naughty Marietta*. The MGM movie featured a princess (Jeannette MacDonald) who avoids an arranged marriage to a Spanish duke by fleeing on a ship that is later captured by pirates. The pirates are then overtaken by a group of mercenaries whose captain (Nelson Eddy) falls for the princess. The movie was nominated for Best Picture and was one the Ambassador thought would be appropriate for his guests because "it was full of lovely old Victor Herbert music, beautiful scenes, a pretty, romantic story and no vulgarity whatever.... "

Grew was an attentive host who catered to his guests, but he was especially concerned about the comfort of one person—Viscount Admiral Saito Makoto. Saito had succeeded Inukai as Prime Minister in 1932 and was now the Lord Keeper of the Privy Seal. The seventy-seven-year-old, white-haired statesman was generally not one to stay at a social event past ten o'clock, and so, after dinner (where Saito had sat next to Alice), Grew sequestered him in a comfortable chair so that he could sleep if he became bored. But Saito surprised him, staying awake throughout the movie and later telling his wife that he "had loved the picture." When Saito and his wife left the Embassy around half past eleven, Grew could not know that he would never see the aging politician again—alive.

While the Grews and their guests were enjoying the evening at the Embassy, about 1,400 soldiers from the Army's First Division were getting ready to fan out to assassinate many of Japan's political leaders. The Emperor was not among the targets. Quite the contrary. The soldiers believed that they were acting to protect Hirohito from people who were leading him astray. The soldiers would soon distribute a Manifesto on Tokyo's streets which said that the Emperor's reign was essential to Japan's "national glory" but that there were "[m]any troublesome issues now confronting our country" and that it was the soldiers' "duty to take proper steps to safeguard our fatherland by killing those responsible."

The underpinnings of the soldiers' complaints, although never clearly articulated, seemed to evolve from the growing conflict between two factions of the Army. The Imperial Way faction believed that the Emperor embodied Japan's sovereignty, that Japan should restore its former traditions and practices in government and business, and that Japan's glory would be served by a war against the Soviet Union, Japan's traditional nemesis. In contrast, the Control faction accepted the Emperor's role within the Constitution's framework, did not want to undo the country's industrial progress, and believed that Japan would be better served by controlling all of China and expanding in Southeast Asia rather than pursuing war against the Soviet Union.

The Imperial Way appeared to gain ground in 1935 when it orchestrated the persecution of Minobe Tatsukichi, one of Japan's foremost constitutional scholars and a member of the House of Peers. He had written several scholarly books that said that the Emperor controls Japan "as the head of state, or its highest organ." The notion that the Emperor was merely an "organ," or instrumentality of government, rather than the embodiment of Japan's sovereignty, offended many in the Imperial Way faction. Minobe was subjected to intense investigation by local prosecutors (called "procurators") in response to a complaint filed by a disgruntled general. The procurators agreed that Minobe's books could be regarded as "disturbing peace and order" but abandoned the inquiry, in part because Minobe's books had been published decades earlier. That did not end the matter. Under pressure from the Army, the cabinet ordered that Minobe's books be suppressed, and in some instances, public gatherings were convened for the burning of his books. The strain on the elderly professor was considerable, and he eventually felt forced to withdraw from the House of Peers.

Minobe's persecution was compounded by the assassination of Major General Nagata Tetsuzan, Chief of the Army's Military Affairs Bureau, in August 1935. The assassin—Lieutenant Colonel Aizawa Saburo—had received orders to be transferred with his unit to Formosa. As the time for his unit's transfer approached, Aizawa said he had received "an impulse from on high" that Nagata had to be removed from office, in part because he was deemed to be part of a clique that had forced the dismissal of another colonel who was part of the Imperial Way faction. Aizawa walked into Nagata's office in the dilapidated War Office Building on August 12 and used his sword to kill Nagata, with one thrust pinning Nagata to the door as he tried to flee. (When later asked by the military police what he planned to do after the assassination, Aizawa replied that he had some shopping to do and would then return to his barracks, pack his things, and travel to Formosa with his unit.)

Aizawa's trial, like those of earlier assassins, became a showcase for vague grievances about the existing political structure and the need to take corrective action. "I assassinated Major General Nagata," Aizawa testified, "to save the nation from a crisis." But as the trial meandered over many weeks into February 1936, it became clear that there would be no immediate implementation of Aizawa's ideas. Many of the captains and younger officers of the First Division—who had received orders for transfer to Manchukuo—believed that further action was necessary to rescue the Emperor from misguided advisors.

Saito was among those at the top of the list of advisors to be eliminated. As the Lord Keeper of the Privy Seal, he was one of Hirohito's most trusted advisors. Not surprisingly, Aizawa's attorney had expressly cited the former Prime Minister in his court arguments as one of the "outside influences" who were allegedly corrupting the country. Before Saito left the American Embassy on that snowy evening on February 25, the Embassy received a call from someone who asked that he be informed when Saito was leaving.

Grew later traced the call to the local police station but could not help but wonder whether the caller was indeed a policeman concerned with Saito's safety or one of the rebellious soldiers planning an assassination.

A group of the First Division soldiers burst into Saito's home around 5 a.m. and rushed into the small room where Saito and his wife had placed themselves. Saito's wife tried to shield her husband from the soldiers, saying, "You shall not kill Saito. He still has work to do for the country." Her pleas fell on deaf ears. As they made ready to fire their weapons, she placed herself in front of her husband to protect him, but the soldiers pushed her aside and began to pump bullets into the former Prime Minister. Saito's wife threw herself on top of her husband after he slumped to the floor. "Since we had no intention of injuring anyone but her husband," one of the soldiers later testified, "we had to shove her aside and thrust our weapons under her body. We fired again and again until we were sure that there was no more life left in the old man." The soldier added that they also wanted to cut Saito's throat but gave up on that idea "because the woman refused to leave the body." The soldiers then left the Saito household "and gave three *Banzais* for the Emperor."

Ed Neville, the Embassy Counselor, called Grew later that morning to tell him about the assassinations of Saito and other prominent leaders. (Prime Minister Okada was spared because his brother-in-law had rushed out of the Prime Minister's residence to stop the intruding soldiers, who then shot him on the mistaken belief that he was the Prime Minister. Okada later made his escape by pretending to be one of the mourners as his brother-in-law's body was carried away.) On Thursday, February 27, Grew had his chauffeur drive him to the Saito home, where he was taken upstairs to the room that Grew believed to be the scene of the assassination. Saito's body was still lying on the floor under a sheet. His wife assumed that the Ambassador wanted one last look and removed the sheet from Saito's face. The elderly gentleman "looked peaceful enough," but Grew could see one of the thirty-six bullet wounds the former Prime Minister had endured. It was, said the Ambassador, "a harrowing experience."

Grew returned to the Embassy where the fear created by the rebellion endured. Alice, for one, wondered whether the soldiers would scale the walls to break into the compound. The Japanese Foreign Office advised the Ambassador to relocate the Embassy staff "to the military barracks on the outskirts of Tokyo where the government could afford them protection." Although he and Alice were taking care of Elsie's baby, Grew decided that they should remain in the Embassy compound.

The revolting soldiers had assumed that the Emperor would support their deadly mission on his behalf. They were sorely mistaken. Hirohito was furious when Chamberlain Kanroji awakened him with a report of the early morning's events. "[N]ever have I seen the emperor," said Kanroji, "a peaceful man who rarely loses his temper, as angry as he was when he learned of the assassinations." Hirohito did not waste time pondering his next move. He immediately instructed the War Minister, "I will give you one hour to suppress the rebels."

The War Minister no doubt wanted to comply with that imperial command, but he understood the risks of armed action against rebellious soldiers who had been motivated by patriotic ideals, who now occupied many government buildings in central Tokyo, and who had created an aura of suspenseful silence. ("The city," recalled New York Times correspondent Hugh Byas, "was lifeless under grimy snow.") Still, the Army accepted the need to do something. For its part, the Navy assembled war ships in the harbor and made clear its intention to take action against the rebels if the Army did not.

Instead of armed force, the War Minister decided to employ more subtle means to end the mutiny. Handbills were distributed, balloons with messages were floated, and radio broadcasts were aired—all in an effort to persuade the rebellious soldiers to lay down their arms and return to their barracks. "The Emperor himself has ordered you to return to your regiments," said an Army General in one broadcast. "It is not too late. Cease your resistance and go home in order that your sins may be forgiven. Your fathers, your mothers, and the whole nation are praying for you."

The appeals succeeded. The soldiers slowly began to withdraw from the buildings they had occupied. The leaders surrendered (except for one who committed suicide), but, contrary to their hopes, the officers were not provided a public forum to air their grievances. They were tried in secret, and fifteen of them (along with Aizawa) were executed.

Not surprisingly, the February 26 Incident—as it was later called—precipitated a change in the government. No longer would Army leaders—principally those in the Control faction—tolerate dissident factions that might derail the Army's policies or create public dissension. In response to Army pressure, Hirota Koki, who succeeded Okada as Prime Minister in March 1936, agreed to restore an earlier practice that required the War Minister to be an active duty officer with a rank no lower than lieutenant general (in the case of the Army) and the Navy Minister to be an active duty officer of no lesser rank than rear admiral (in the case of the Navy). In effect, the change gave the Army and Navy veto power over the formation of a cabinet because either service could refuse to appoint one of its officers to join the cabinet as a minister.

That point was driven home when Hirohito asked Ugaki Kazushige to become Prime Minister in February 1937. Ugaki tried to form a cabinet, but the Army, which had reservations about Ugaki, refused to accede to the appointment of an officer from their ranks as War Minister. And so Ugaki had to report to the Emperor that he could not form a cabinet and that, accordingly, someone else would have to succeed Hirota as Prime Minister.

The significance of these developments did not escape Grew. The Ambassador lamented in his diary that the "military are too firmly in the saddle and will continue to remain there." Part of that lament no doubt reflected the end of free elections, the last one having been held on February 20, 1936, only days before the February 26 Incident. "One feels a little like living on a volcano here," Grew continued in that same diary entry, "never knowing when an explosion is going to occur, and I am quite sure that the day of possible explosions is by no means past."

He did not have long to wait for the next "explosion." It emerged from the 1901 Boxer Protocol, an agreement among China and the nations who had helped to quell the rebellion by right-wing militia, called "Boxers," against foreigners and Christian missionaries who had settled in China. The protocol entitled those nations—including Japan—to station troops at certain locations in China. In accordance with that right, Japan placed troops near the Marco Polo Bridge, which provided a direct route to Peiping and was a matter of vital importance to the Chinese. The so-called Marco Polo Bridge Incident began with a missing Japanese soldier on the evening of July 7, 1937 while Japanese troops were conducting night-time maneuvers near the bridge. The Japanese initially assumed that the soldier had been captured by Chinese troops, which turned out not to be the case. But no matter. Accusations were exchanged, bullets were soon fired, and by August the

two countries were engulfed in full-scale war. Although it had not sanctioned the conflict at the start, the Japanese government soon sent reinforce-
ments to the area from the Kwantung Army in Manchukuo and additional
troops from Japan itself.

Grew was prompt in feeding the State Department reports on the
"China Incident" and recommendations for American policy in dealing with
it. And in doing all that, he had the benefit of a new Embassy Counselor:
Eugene H. Dooman, who had joined the staff in May 1937.

The forty-seven-year-old Counselor was, in many respects, the antith-
esis of Grew. Standing about five feet eleven inches, Dooman was balding
and slightly overweight. "[S]warthy, pudgy," is how he was described by
John Emmerson, who worked with Dooman in the Embassy. His horn-
rimmed glasses and ever-present pipe gave him the look of a college professor. He did not have Grew's easy, gracious way with people. "He was a very
diffident man," Henri Smith-Hutton said of Dooman, "and difficult to get
to know." But Gene's intelligence and dedication did earn him the respect
of colleagues. Emmerson, for one, remembered Dooman's advice to junior
officers "that the clarity and accuracy of their drafting should be a source
of pride, since someday their handiwork would be displayed before posterity
in published State Department documents." It was a view shared by Grew.
"I try to get my staff," he told his daughter Lilla at one point, "to regard
every piece of work they turn their hand to as an opportunity for precision
and artistry, no matter how comparatively unimportant a particular task
may be."

Dooman had another quality that enhanced his relationship with Grew:
an interest in good food and fine wine, Grew saying that one dinner at
Gene's house in October 1941 was "to be remembered because his food and
wines were past all praise," adding that "Gene does things well." The two
men also shared an interest in developing harmonious relations between the
United States and Japan—an interest that, in Dooman's case, evolved from
a long history with the country.

He had been born in 1890 in Osaka, Japan, where his father was an
Episcopalian minister. His family moved to Tokyo when he was five, and it
was there that Gene attended a French missionary school, where many of
the Japanese students, as Dooman later remembered, "came from the most
important families." Those childhood connections—which Gene

maintained throughout his life—proved to be invaluable when Dooman and Grew tried to assess Japanese policy in the months before the Pearl Harbor attack. Many of those Japanese students had assumed influential positions in government and business, and Gene frequently turned to them for information and insight.

Dooman spent his high school years in the United States and then attended Trinity College in Connecticut. By then his parents were living in New York, and his mother urged her newly graduated son to take the examination to become a "student interpreter" in the Tokyo embassy. He scored well enough to receive appointment for one of the four vacancies, and by 1912, he was on his way back to Japan with a new position—and a new commitment. As he later explained to a State Department colleague, when he returned to Japan as a young language officer, "I made up my mind that my career in the service should aim toward contributing something toward averting war between the United States and Japan."

Although he was already fluent in Japanese, the two-year language program was, as Dooman later recalled, "extremely severe," encompassing, among other requirements, the ability to read Chinese classics in Japanese. After completing the program, he was appointed Vice Consul in the United States' consulate in Kobe and then spent ten years (between 1921 and 1931) at the embassy in Tokyo. That was followed by two years in London and four years at the State Department before his return to Tokyo in 1937.

The return was not happenstance. When Neville left, Hornbeck asked Grew if he had any preferences for a new Counselor. Grew requested Dooman. He had met the young foreign service officer on two prior occasions and had come away with an "entirely favorable" impression, in part because of Gene's "broad background of things Japanese" and his "poise and mature judgment." Dooman reciprocated the compliment, later saying of Grew that he was a "magnificent presence" and someone who was "very spiritualistic" and "very sensitive to what he thought was right and wrong."

Dooman's appointment was confirmed in January 1937. Grew wrote the new Counselor shortly afterwards, borrowing a comment that Charles Evans Hughes had made to the Ambassador many years earlier, telling Dooman, "You and I will be thick as thieves." And indeed they were.

The two men were in frequent communication on virtually every important matter throughout the next four years except when Dooman was on leave in the United States between August 1940 and February 1941. Their routine often included a conference in Grew's office at the end of the day, during which the two men would discuss the day's developments and pending issues. Dooman soon learned that the Ambassador was not one to make quick decisions if he could postpone them. He liked to ruminate on matters, thinking about what had happened, what was said, and what was appropriate. "Another little thing I've discovered by long experience," Joe wrote Elsie in September 1941 as he was wrestling with Japan's deteriorating relations with the United States, "is that when a problem crops up towards the end of the day, when I'm tired physically, mentally, and perhaps morally, the thing to do is not to touch it and to let myself worry about it until the next morning after a good sleep. It then generally looks entirely different and not nearly so important or at least the right solution is then often perfectly clear. There is, I think, a lot of wisdom in the advice 'Sleep on it.'" And so it was not uncommon for Dooman to receive a call from the Ambassador in the morning asking Gene to come to his office, where Grew would be pacing the floor and puffing on his pipe. When the Counselor entered, Grew would look up and say something like, "I've changed my mind."

One of the topics central to their deliberations in the early months of the relationship was American policy toward Japan in the wake of the Marco Polo Bridge Incident. They discussed it at length, and, in due course, a telegram from the Ambassador to Hull was drafted and circulated among the entire professional staff, which ultimately agreed with its content. "The present hostilities," Grew told the Secretary of State in that telegram of August 27, 1937, "are an inevitable corollary of the Manchurian conflict which left Japan with an eventual choice of two alternatives: either to establish complete control in North China or to be prepared for an eventual retreat from Manchuria. There could never have been any doubt whatever," he added, "as to the choice of alternatives." The United States, said Grew, had to reconcile itself to a prolonged conflict between the two Asian powers—although Grew correctly predicted that Japan had not given sufficient consideration to the "possible effects of almost endless guerilla warfare" even if Japan could defeat the Chinese army. He thought there would be little to gain in trying to assess the causes of the Marco Polo Bridge Incident and perhaps laying the blame on Japan. To criticize the Japanese, Grew explained, would "have no beneficial impact" and would deprive the United

States of a later opportunity to terminate the hostilities. "Japan will be more disposed to heed our counsel," the telegram said, "if she has confidence in our good will and impartiality than if her attitude toward us be one of suspicion and resentment." Grew therefore recommended that American policy should be focused on three objectives: to avoid involvement in a Sino-Japanese war, to protect American lives and property, and, "while reserving complete neutrality, to maintain our traditional friendship with both combatants."

The Secretary of State's response on September 2 left Grew surprised, bewildered, and very disappointed. Hull said that he could support the first two of Grew's recommended objectives—neutrality and protection of American property and lives—but that he could not support the third objective—namely, preservation of good relations with the combatant countries. The United States' first priority, said Hull, was the welfare of the United States. In pursuing that interest, the Secretary of State asserted, American policy "will be guided by laws and treaties, public opinion, and other controlling considerations." Hull's response did not reflect any newly-generated thoughts. He had entered the Secretary of State's office in March 1933 with "two points on the Far East firmly in mind"—one being an interest in maintaining China's independence "and in preventing Japan from gaining over-lordship of the entire Far East," and the second being a conviction that Japan had the diplomatic record "of a highway robber" who "had no intention whatever of abiding by treaties...."

As a lawyer and former circuit justice in his native Tennessee, it was hardly surprising that Hull would see reliance on laws and treaties as a bedrock of American policy toward Japan. It was a notion he held dear, an obsession that forever dominated his view of diplomatic relations in the Far East. Not surprisingly, it became a mantra that Hull would repeat almost endlessly in his discussions with Japanese representatives in the months before the Pearl Harbor attack, never seeming to realize—as Grew and Dooman did—that his cherished reliance on laws and treaties failed to account for the very different perspective of Japanese decision-makers.

"The unfortunate fact is," Dooman later explained, "...that the rule of law is not an integral part of the way of life of the ancient peoples of Asia, and although they have acquired laws and machinery for their enforcement, there has not prevailed among them that deeply-rooted respect for abstract

justice formulated by laws, which is an essential element of Western civilization." *New York Times* correspondent Otto Tolischus understood all this
after spending six months in Japan in 1941. "I saw the gulf that separates
Japan from the Western world," Tolischus said, "not only in distance, but
in mental, moral, political, legal and economic progress. I realized that this
was indeed a different world, to which none of the Western thought patterns
applied, because it lived in wholly different thought patterns of its own."
The Japanese, Tolischus added, "lived in a world not of cause and effect,
but of miracles and magic, people with myriads of gods and spirits who are
as real to them as physical existence."

From his long residence in Japan, Grew understood this perspective
as well, and he never tired in the months before the Pearl Harbor attack
of trying to explain to people in Washington that Western notions of laws
and treaties did not coincide with Japanese thinking. Still, in those days
well before the Pearl Harbor attack, Grew hoped that he could foster good
relations with Japan, orchestrate a peaceful settlement with China, and
help the United States avoid armed conflict with Japan. But those hopes
seemed to evaporate when Roosevelt gave his speech in Chicago on October 5, 1937.

The President was there to dedicate the opening of a bridge on Lake
Shore Drive. He was undoubtedly still smarting from the defeat of his legislative proposal to "pack" the United States Supreme Court with an additional
justice for every sitting justice was who more than seventy years and six
months old (up to a maximum of six additional justices). Roosevelt assumed
that his overwhelming re-election in 1936 (winning 523 of the 531 electoral
votes) had given him a mandate to deal with obstacles to his legislative
program. The Court—which had invalidated many of his New Deal measures—was certainly one of those obstacles.

Despite the defeat of the court-packing plan, Roosevelt believed that he
could take the initiative in other spheres. The expanding conflicts in Europe
and the Far East reflected a crisis that cried out for American leadership. Or
so the President thought. He knew that support for isolationism in the
country was strong. A 1937 Gallup poll, for example, showed that 70 percent of the public believed it was a mistake to become involved in World
War I. Roosevelt nonetheless believed that the public would accept his
leadership in curbing the conflicts in Europe and the Far East. And so he

decided to use his Chicago speech to condemn the "reign of terror" that had begun to engulf the world.

It was, said the President, "an epidemic of world lawlessness"that needed to be curbed. As was his custom, Roosevelt reduced the issue to one that people could understand from their own experience. "When an epidemic of physical disease starts to spread," the President intoned, "the community approves and joins in a quarantine of the patients in order to protect the health of the community against the spread of the disease." The President did not specify how to "quarantine" the aggressor nations, who were never named in the speech. No matter. The message was clear: the United States should join with other nations to isolate Germany, Italy, and Japan from the world community.

Grew was shocked and disheartened when he read the speech. It had echoes of Hull's earlier rejection of the Ambassador's proposal to preserve good relations with Japan despite the Marco Polo Bridge Incident. Duncan Laing, the Embassy administrator, walked out of Grew's office after the Ambassador had read the President's speech, telling other staff members, "The Old Man is sure upset." According to Laing, Grew said, "There goes everything I have tried to accomplish in my entire mission to Japan.'" Grew's disappointment found expression in his dairy. "This was the day that I felt my carefully built castle tumbling about my ears," he wrote, "and we all wandered about the chancery, depressed, gloomy, and with not a smile in sight." He added that he, Alice, and Elsie (who was visiting) went to see a movie and that he then "sunk myself in *Gone with the Wind*—which is precisely the way I felt."

Grew's gloom was premature. Although the "quarantine" proposal was a surprise to those in the State Department who had worked on the speech, Hull was initially "delighted" (as, no doubt, was Hornbeck—he had earlier recommended that Japan be condemned as "an outlaw" after the 1931 Mukden Incident). The euphoria in the State Department quickly evaporated amidst the adverse reaction from Congress, the media, and isolationist groups who wanted to reduce, not expand, American involvement in foreign conflicts. The adverse reaction also made Roosevelt realize that, as in the case of the court-packing plan, a landslide re-election did not eliminate the need to develop public support for his policies. "It's a terrible thing," he told Sam Rosenman, one of his speechwriters, "to look over your shoulder when you are trying to lead—and find no one there."

The impact on the President's thinking became evident in the months before the Pearl Harbor attack. Despite the escalation of the war in Europe and deteriorating relations with Japan, Roosevelt resisted efforts by some members of his cabinet to take more aggressive action that could embroil the United States in armed conflict with Germany and increase the risk of war with Japan. At one point in the spring of 1941, Hopkins told Treasury Secretary Henry Morgenthau Jr. that "the President is loath to get into the war and would rather follow public opinion than lead it." Roosevelt himself later told Morgenthau, "I am waiting to be pushed into this situation." It was a theme echoed in 1940 when Roosevelt had campaigned for a third term. He repeatedly told voters, "Your boys are not going to be sent into any foreign wars."

Not surprisingly, after October 1937, there were no references to any quarantine in the President's speeches or in directives from the State Department to its embassy in Tokyo. But Grew soon saw signs of efforts to isolate Japan and pressure the Asian empire to change its ways.

Japan was not blameless in the change in circumstance. The Japanese military continued to march through China. On Sunday, December 12, 1937, Japanese forces approached Nanking, then the capital of the Republic of China. Word spread that Chinese troops were evacuating civilians from the city by boat on the Yangtze River. The USS *Panay*, an American gunship, was peacefully patrolling the Yangtze River and could not have been mistaken for one of those Chinese boats. The United States Command had communicated the *Panay*'s location to the Japanese Command in Shanghai. Beyond that, the ship had the American flag painted on its awnings, there was a large American flag flying on the ship's mast, and it was a clear day. So the *Panay*'s crew was shocked when Japanese Navy planes bombed the ship (which soon sank) and then strafed the survivors with machine-gun fire as they tried to escape to the tall reeds at the river's edge.

For Joe Grew, Monday, December 13, 1937, was "a black day indeed." He had been planning to play golf, but those plans changed when he arrived at the Chancery and saw the telegrams which reported the Japanese shelling of retreating Chinese troops. And then Alice told Joe at 3 p.m. that Hirota Koki, the Foreign Minister, had called to say that he was on his way to the Chancery. Grew knew that a Foreign Minister's visit to an embassy was "an unprecedented step"and assumed it signified something ominous. His suspicions proved to be prescient. Hirota told the Ambassador about the sinking of the *Panay*.

The incident was, to Grew, "really incredible,"and he recognized at once that it could trigger a war with the United States because, as the Ambassador confided to his diary, "I 'remembered the *Maine*.'" But the Japanese government was quick to offer its apologies not only in Tokyo but in Washington as well (where the Japanese ambassador gave a statement of regret in English that could be included in film newsreels that were popular in those days). And so the matter passed without any immediate change in American policy. But the incident—coupled with the "Rape of Nanking," where thousands of Chinese were murdered, raped, and mutilated by Japanese troops—generated a swell of antipathy toward Japan among the American public. It was only a matter of time before that public disapproval was reflected in government policy.

The Roosevelt administration's ability to take punitive measures derived from Japan's considerable reliance on American trade. Most of Japan's oil and petroleum products, iron, and scrap metal—which were used for both military and consumer purposes—came from the United States. Japan also purchased many military products, including airplanes, from American suppliers. Beyond all that, the 1911 Treaty of Commerce and Navigation with the United States guaranteed Japan certain rights and privileges, including "most favored nation" status on trade.

Pressure to impose sanctions on Japan increased after Japan's Prime Minister—Konoye Fumimaro—announced in a radio address on November 3, 1938 that Japan would try to build "a new Far East" that would link "Japan, Manchukuo and China." Many American leaders viewed that "New Order" as an abandonment of the "Open Door Policy" in China that had been initiated by American Secretary of State John Hay in 1899 and that guaranteed all nations free trade with China. In December 1938, Hornbeck proposed that the United States institute "a comprehensive and thoroughgoing program of measures of material pressure" against Japan. He believed that such a program would discourage Japan's aggressive policies and thereby decrease the "danger of armed conflict" between the United States and Japan.

Grew disagreed that Hornbeck's proposal would lead to a change in Japan's policies. "I know Japan and the Japanese pretty well," he confided to his diary a couple of weeks before Hornbeck distributed his memorandum. "They are a hardy race, accustomed throughout their history to catastrophe and disaster; theirs is the 'do or die' spirit, more deeply ingrained than in almost any other people. They would pull in their belts another notch and continue." Grew was also concerned that economic sanctions were a double-edged sword. "I have consistently recommended against such measures," he wrote, "unless we are prepared to see them through to their logical conclusion, and that might mean war...."

Grew's insight was largely disregarded as the Roosevelt administration moved ever closer to a total embargo of trade with Japan. The State Department—reflecting outrage at the Japanese bombing of civilian populations in China—had already inaugurated what became known as a "moral embargo" against the export of certain items to Japan. In a letter to 148 American manufacturers on July 1, 1938, the State Department explained that the administration was "strongly opposed" to the sale of airplanes and airplane parts to Japan. The letter did not say the department would refuse to issue any necessary export licenses for that purpose, but it did make it clear that applications for such licenses would not be welcome. By early 1939, the "moral embargo" was extended to prohibit extensions of credit to Japan. And in July 1940, the administration—using power bestowed by the recently-enacted Export Control Act to codify the moral embargo— began to restrict or curtail the export of certain materials to Japan, which soon included aviation gasoline and high-grade scrap iron and steel.

By then, the 1911 Treaty of Commerce and Navigation had been terminated, and the United States was now at liberty to impose discriminatory tariffs on the import of silk and other Japanese products. Hornbeck had authored a memo in July 1938 proposing abrogation of the treaty, and in July 1939, Arthur Vandenberg, a powerful Republican Senator from Michigan, introduced a resolution that called for the termination of the treaty so that the United States would "be free to deal with Japan in the formulation of a new treaty and in the protection of American interests...." On July 26, 1939, Roosevelt announced that the 1911 treaty would be terminated as of January 26, 1940 in accordance with the treaty's six-month termination clause.

Grew was in the United States on leave when the President made that announcement, and he had become well aware of the growing animosity in the United States toward Japan (and would later reference that animosity in his "Straight from the Horse's Mouth" speech to the American-Japan Society in October 1939). Still, he continued to believe that one of the principal functions of the Embassy was to nurture "good relations between the United States and Japan." So he was very receptive when Japan's Foreign Minister, Nomura Kiichisaburo (who became Japan's ambassador to the United States in the months before the Pearl Harbor attack), approached Grew about negotiating a new commercial treaty and instituting a *modus vivendi* proposal to maintain the status quo during the negotiations.

In a telegram to Hull on December 1, 1939, Grew (now back in Tokyo) reiterated his earlier view that an American embargo of exports to and imports from Japan was unlikely to change Japan's China policy. The telegram repeated the comments from Joe's diary almost one year earlier, saying that "Japan is a nation of hardy warriors, still inculcated with the samurai do-or-die spirit which has by tradition and inheritance become ingrained in the race. The Japanese throughout their history have faced periodic cataclysms brought about by constant wars within and without the country. By long experience they are inured to hardships and they are inured to regimentation." For those reasons—and in light of Japan's disjointed political structure—Grew warned that it was foolhardy to believe that any embargo or other economic sanctions would undermine the Japanese military or create any public demand for a change in policy. "To await the hoped-for-discrediting in Japan of the Japanese army and the Japanese military system," he cautioned, "is to await the millennium."

Grew believed that there were two courses open to the United States: "complete intransigence" or a more pragmatic policy (which Grew thought "the wiser" approach) that would maintain the commercial status quo while a new trade agreement was negotiated. If that latter course were followed, said Grew, the United States could advise Japan that it could not secure the benefits of the new treaty unless and until Japan offered "concrete evidence"—including cessation of bombing and respect for American interests—that it was willing to adjust its policy. In pushing that approach, Grew made a veiled reference to Roosevelt's "quarantine" speech. "The argument is often advanced that Japan should and can be brought to terms through isolation," he said. But that approach carried risks because "[s]anctions commenced but not carried through bring in their wake a loss of prestige and influence to the nation declaring them. Sanctions carried through to the end may lead to war."

Grew's recommendation was not well received at the State Department. Hornbeck had already made clear his desire to "put the screws on" Japan. The Political Relations Adviser crossed out the word "intransigence" in Grew's telegram, and where Grew proposed to tell Japan about the benefits that would ensue if she should change her course, Hornbeck wrote in the margin, "We should not say this." Not surprisingly, Hornbeck's views prevailed. As Cordell Hull later explained in his *Memoirs*, "We obviously could not agree to negotiate a new treaty unless Japan completely changed her attitude and practice toward our rights and interests in China. To do so would condone what Japan had done, and would prevent our having the freedom of action toward Japan we needed in the event Tokyo continued its policy of discrimination and hostile actions against Occidentals in China." So the Secretary of State did not accept his ambassador's recommendation. Nor did he allow Grew to tell the Japanese exactly what the United States would require to initiate discussions for a new treaty.

Grew did not give up. He sent another telegram to Hull on December 18, 1939. "The simple fact is," said the telegram, "that we are here dealing not with a unified Japan but with a Japanese Government which is endeavoring courageously, even with only gradual success, to fight against a recalcitrant Japanese Army, a battle which happens to be our own battle." Grew added that a failure to respond favorably "may well bring about the fall of the present Cabinet." The choice, Grew concluded, was "either to direct American-Japanese relations into a progressively healthy channel or to accelerate their movement straight downhill." Hull was not moved. Negotiations for a new treaty were never commenced, and, as Grew anticipated, Hirohito felt compelled to replace the Prime Minister (along with the Foreign Minister).

The slide in American relations with Japan coincided with Germany's march across Europe in 1940. By June of that year, the Nazis had taken Norway and Denmark, swarmed across the low countries of Belgium, the Netherlands, and Luxembourg, and marched into the streets of Paris. German domination of all Europe—including Great Britain—appeared to be only a matter of time, and the Japanese took notice. "The German military machine and system and their brilliant successes," Grew confided to his diary on August 1, 1940, "have gone to the Japanese head like strong wine." Japan had already entered into an Anti-Comintern Pact with Germany in 1936 to defend against the communist regime in the Soviet Union. Pressure now mounted for Japan to enter into a broader military alliance with Germany and Italy. Such an alliance, it was said, would not only affiliate Japan with the dominant force in Europe; that alliance would also support Japanese interests in the Dutch and French colonies in Southeast Asia, especially Indochina, which had many of the natural resources that Japan lacked.

Grew tried to warn the State Department about a possible alliance with Germany. He also lobbied with his Japanese contacts against any such alliance. It was a losing battle (although Hornbeck, for one, did not really care, saying in a memo that Japan's entry into an alliance with Germany would not "substantially alter the effective course of world events"). Grew's lobbying effort was further undercut by Roosevelt's use of the Export Control Act to limit the export to Japan of aviation gasoline, lead, high quality scrap iron, and other critical materials. It was only one of several factors, but the impact was predictable. By the summer of 1940, many in the Japanese government believed that their country would fare better with the Nazis than with the Americans.

There were elements in the Japanese government who had concerns about an expanded military alliance with Italy and Germany. Japanese naval officers were troubled because Article III of the proposed agreement—called the Tripartite Pact—required each of the parties to come to the aid of the others if they were attacked by another country. The United States was actively supporting Great Britain in her struggles with Germany, and it was easy to envision circumstances in which the United States' alliance with Great Britain could lead to a conflict between the United States and Germany. Foreign Minister Matsuoka Yosuke, a principal proponent of the Tripartite Pact, had a different view. He argued that the alliance would decrease the chances of war with the United States because it "would force the United States to act more prudently in carrying out her plans against Japan." Hirohito was very skeptical. He remained fearful that execution of the pact might lead to a war with the United States that Japan could not win.

The Emperor expressed those fears to Konoye in a meeting with the Prime Minister on September 16, 1940. Despite his objections, Hirohito said he felt compelled to approve the Tripartite Pact because the agreement had broad support in the military and in the cabinet. "You must, therefore," he told the Prime Minister, "share with me the joys and sorrows that will follow." Konoye understood the Emperor's admonition. The Prime Minister had his own reservations about the Tripartite Pact. Years later, British ambassador Sir Robert Craigie reported "a well substantiated story" that, when the pact signatories gathered at the Prime Minister's residence to celebrate the execution of the agreement, Konoye "was seen to melt into tears and the party, from all accounts, was a distinct frost."

Whatever the concerns, Hirohito's remark to his Prime Minister proved to be a telling comment. The Tripartite Pact would become a major obstacle to Hull's willingness to enter into an agreement with Japan in the days before the Pearl Harbor attack.

Grew could not foresee those consequences, but he was greatly disappointed by Japan's execution of the Tripartite Pact on September 27, 1940. Not that it would have had any impact on his recommendations to Washington. He had already changed his mind by then about the utility of embargoes and other economic sanctions in trying to forge a more positive relationship between the United States and Japan.

Grew began to rethink his position after Konoye became Prime Minister for the second time in July 1940. On August 1, Konoye announced that his "New Order" policy of 1938—which encompassed Japan, Manchukuo and China—would now be expanded to include other countries in the "Greater East Asia Co-Prosperity Sphere" (an approach first articulated by Foreign Minister Arita Hachiro in June 1940). The new policy seemed to signal a willingness to use force to dominate all of East Asia. Grew's reconsideration was reinforced in early September 1940 when he read the report of A. T. Steele, the China correspondent for the *Chicago Daily News*, after a visit to Tokyo. In that report, Steele argued that economic sanctions could be applied against Japan with only a small risk of such sanctions leading to war. Grew continued to believe that the risk of war remained, but—in light of the cabinet change and its new policy—he concluded that a change in direction was warranted.

On September 12, after receiving input from the Embassy's professional staff, Grew sent Hull a telegram which he later referred to as his "Green Light" telegram. "[T]he time has come," said the telegram, "when continued patience and restraint on the part of the United States" would no longer suffice to preserve American-Japanese relations. "[A] show of force" through strong measures was needed. "My thought," Grew later told the congressional committee investigating the Pearl Harbor attack, "was that, by taking these measures, we would eventually bring…the sane-minded statesmen in Japan to the realization that, unless they stopped in their tracks, they were going to have war with the United States and Great Britain and other countries."

Grew later decided to send the President a personal letter setting forth his changed views. He had visited with Roosevelt at the White House during his leave of absence in the summer of 1939, and the President had told him, "When you have some thoughts on the situation, drop me a line." It now seemed appropriate to take Roosevelt up on that invitation.

He sent the "Dear Frank" letter on December 14, 1940, along with some new Japanese stamps that he thought would be of interest to the President. Grew's frustration was clearly evident. "After eight years of effort to build up something permanently constructive in American-Japanese relations," he lamented, "I find that diplomacy has been defeated by trends and forces utterly beyond its control, and that our work has been swept away as if by a typhoon, with little or nothing remaining to show for it." The Ambassador observed that the "pendulum in Japan is always swinging between extremist and moderate policies, but, as things stand today we believe that the pendulum is more likely to swing still further toward extremism than to reverse its direction." That seemed especially so because, as Grew told Roosevelt, "the Germans here are working overtime to push Japan into war with us."

Still, Grew saw no reason to retreat from the recommendations he had made in his Green Light telegram. "A progressively firm policy on our part" was needed, said the Ambassador. But he added that the United States had to be prepared to use armed force if Japan should prove unresponsive. "[I]f we take measures 'short of war' with no real intention to carry those measure to their conclusion if necessary," Grew opined, "such lack of intention will be all too obvious to the Japanese.…Only if they become certain that we mean to fight if called upon to do so will our preliminary measures stand some chance of proving effective and removing the necessity for war."

Those thoughts must have been uppermost in Grew's mind when he read the speech that Matsuoka was scheduled to give to the American-Japan

Society on December 19, 1940. It was a broad-ranging speech intended to quell any suspicion the United States might have about Japan's hostile intentions. Any such suspicions, said the Foreign Minister, were "absurd and untrue." Japan merely wanted to be "left alone" so that she could pursue her "constructive work unhindered." Of particular importance to the Japanese, he explained, was "to see the trouble in China and the war in Europe brought speedily to an end, without adding more participants, particularly such a powerful one as America." Matsuoka confirmed that Japan would abide by her obligations under the Tripartite Pact and would pursue her "truly vital" interests in China (as compared to the American interest in China, which he said was driven by "sentiment"). Matsuoka closed with "an earnest appeal" for the United States "to maintain calm judgment and quiet self-restraint."

As the President of the society—not to mention the United States' ambassador to Japan—Grew was entitled to comment on the Foreign Minister's speech. "This is no time for good-will speeches," Joe wrote in his diary before the event. "As I constantly say to those Japanese with whom I come into contact, the time has gone by when statements, assurances, promises, or pious expressions of hope can do any good; nothing can count now but facts, actions, and realities."

There was no rancor in Grew's comments when he delivered them to the American-Japan Society after Matsuoka had concluded his remarks. As in the case of the "Straight from the Horse's Mouth" speech, Grew spoke in a firm but friendly tone that avoided any personal offense. To be sure, he said, everyone would wish for calm judgment and self-restraint in pursuit of peaceful relations among nations. He did not try to address each of Matsuoka's points (although he did expressly reject the Foreign Minister's comment that American interest in China was based on sentiment). He did, however, emphasize that "what counts in international relationships today...is the concrete evidence of facts and actions, regardless of the persuasive garb in which such facts and actions may be dressed. Let us say of nations as of men: 'By their fruits ye shall know them.'"

Grew's remarks received widespread and very favorable comment in the United States. His "forthright reply to the honeyed words of the Japanese Foreign Minister," said the *Philadelphia Inquirer*, was all that Americans could expect from their "sturdy Ambassador." The *Washington Star* agreed, saying that Grew was an "ace" diplomat who knew "how to say the right thing at the right time." And the *Milwaukee Journal* added that Grew had made "an important contribution" by his blunt response to the Japanese Foreign Minister.

All of that—coupled with Grew's letter to the President—should have given comfort to Hull and Hornbeck. The Political Relations Adviser, in fact, supervised the draft of Roosevelt's reply to Grew's letter, and the reply made a point of saying, "I find myself in decided agreement with your conclusions." (Not knowing Hornbeck's involvement in drafting the reply, Grew sent the Political Relations Adviser a copy on February 25, 1941 for his "confidential information.") For all that seeming unity of opinion, the upper echelon of the State Department remained skeptical about the perspective of Grew and his staff. That was made all too clear when Dooman returned to the United States in August 1940 for six months' leave.

Grew thought it would be useful for his Counselor to meet with the President, and so he drafted a letter of introduction. "Dear Frank," the letter of August 8 read, Eugene Dooman "has been my right-hand man" and, "since our views coincide in practically every respect with regard to affairs in this part of the world, I believe it would be well worth your while if you could manage to see him if only for a few moments, for it would very much [be] as if I were talking to you myself." By January, Grew learned that the meeting had not yet occurred. So he sent a personal telegram to Roosevelt, repeating that Dooman "possessed my complete confidence," that the President could talk with the Embassy Counselor as though he were talking to Grew, and that he hoped Roosevelt would send for Dooman "before his departure" in February.

For his part, Dooman was looking forward to the opportunity to visit the President at the White House. But having served in the State Department and being well versed in bureaucratic procedures, Gene thought it best to ask Hull's permission to make the appointment with the President. He sent a memorandum requesting permission and also visited with the Secretary of State at his office in the State, War, and Navy Building. The feisty Hull was obviously not happy about the prospect of someone with Dooman's views speaking to the President. The Secretary of State initiated "a long harangue" about "the sanctity of treaties…and the condition precedent to a settlement—the withdrawal of Japanese forces from China." The Embassy

Counselor was no doubt respectful and patient, but it did him no good. Hull refused to allow Dooman to make the appointment with Roosevelt, and the President never sent for him.

It was a harbinger of things to come.

CHAPTER 6

The First Warning

Ricardo Rivera Schreiber, a tall man of medium build with balding hair combed straight back, deeply-set eyes, and a tight mouth, was skeptical. In the late fall of 1940, Felipe Akakawa, Schreiber's chief of staff, gave his boss some startling information conveyed by a Japanese interpreter in Peru's consulate in Yokohama.

As Peru's Minister to Japan since 1936, the forty-eight-year-old Schreiber was experienced enough to know that rumors abounded in Japan. It was an inevitable product of a society where open discussion was often discouraged and, in some cases, prohibited. Still, this rumor, if that's what it was, could not be easily disregarded. Akakawa told the Minister that the Yokohama interpreter was part of Japan's secret police and that he claimed to have a cousin in the Navy Ministry who had access to confidential information. The cousin said that the "Japanese squadron would, in a surprise move, sink the American squadron."

The circumstances surrounding the disclosure seemed to support its credibility. The Yokohama interpreter would visit the Peruvian embassy in Tokyo about once a week to report to Schreiber (because the interpreter had apparently been placed in charge of the consulate). In the evening, the interpreter and Akakawa would retreat to the servants' quarters and get drunk. It was during one of those encounters that the interpreter, feeling no pain, would brag about what he knew. So it did not appear to be a carefully calculated comment.

Schreiber's concern intensified over the ensuing weeks. On one occasion, Akakawa told the Minister excitedly that the Yokohama interpreter said that the Japanese attack on the American "squadron" would occur in the central Pacific. And on another occasion Akakawa reported that the attack would be "carried out by aircraft." The Yokohama interpreter added that Japanese aircraft carriers were at that time "steaming toward southern Japan with a view to beginning tests for the air attack which they were planning [to carry out] against the American squadron at Pearl Harbor."

Schreiber was not sure what he should do with the information. It could be nothing more than wild speculation. Or it could reflect an inadvertent crack in the veil of secrecy that surrounded Japan's military operations. There was no way for him to refute or verify the claims of the Yokohama interpreter. Or so he thought.

And then the Peruvian minister received a visit on Sunday, January 26 from Professor Yoshuda, a friend who taught courses on South America at the University of Tokyo. After an exchange of pleasantries, Yoshuda said with "great excitement" that "we were on the brink of a great misfortune which would bring everlasting ruin upon his country." The college professor proceeded to explain that Admiral Yamamoto Isoroku "had already outlined the plan to attack the American fleet in Pearl Harbor," that a "sham battle" was at that very moment being conducted in southern Japan, and that "the plan was ready to enter into action without the least doubt."

Some—but not all—of Yoshuda's information was accurate. Yamamoto had in fact conceived the plan for a surprise attack on Pearl Harbor. The Japanese admiral had authored two letters about his proposal in January 1941—one to the Navy Minister and another to Admiral Onishi Takijiro, a friend who espoused the use of aircraft carriers in warfare and would thus be receptive to a proposal to use aircraft carriers to attack Pearl Harbor. However, Yamamoto's plan had not been accepted by the Navy and would not be for many months. So there were no "sham battles" being conducted at the time. But there was one irony: around the time that Yoshuda was expressing his concern to Schreiber, Yamamoto was meeting with Onishi on a Japanese battleship anchored in southern Japan to discuss the Pearl Harbor project.

The details of that meeting were unknown to Schreiber. But Yoshuda's remarks did seem to confirm much of the information conveyed by the Yokohama interpreter. And more than that, there was nothing far-fetched about Japan making plans for an attack against the United States.

It was no secret that relations between Japan and the United States were deteriorating. In recent weeks, there had been repeated articles and editorials in the Japanese press decrying the precarious state of Japanese-American relations. In his diary entry for January 7, Grew cited one editorial which warned "the Japanese people that war between Japan and the United States will be necessary because of...Great Britain and America's entrance into the hostilities [in Europe]" and that these events "will shift the hostilities from Europe to the Pacific." The *New York Times* similarly reported shortly before Schreiber's meeting with Yoshuda that one of the Japanese government's principal anxieties "is the public's growing consciousness that relations with the United States have drifted into a dangerous position."

In light of the increasingly hostile environment, Schreiber decided that he had to convey his information about the possible Pearl Harbor attack to the American embassy. He was sure the American ambassador would be appreciative.

There was ample reason to believe that Grew would regard the information as credible. He certainly recognized the volatile state of Japanese-American relations. "With all our desire to keep America out of war and at peace with all nations, especially with Japan," Grew wrote in his diary on January 1, "it would be the height of folly to allow ourselves to be lulled into a feeling of false security. Japan, not we, is on the war path, and that path is not a whit the less dangerous to our own future welfare because it is camouflaged in such righteous-sounding terms as the 'New Order in Greater East Asia including the South Seas' and the 'Greater East Asia Co-Prosperity Sphere.'"

Grew was, of course, hopeful that armed conflict with Japan could be avoided. But the ever-optimistic envoy was not blind to undesirable outcomes. "In the meantime," he confided in that same diary entry, "let us keep our powder dry and be ready—for anything." He expressed similar trepidation to his friend Bill Castle in a letter on January 7. "As for our getting into war with Japan," he told the former Under Secretary of State, "that also rests on the lap of the gods....I do not think that we shall declare war on Japan and I think it is equally unlikely that Japan will declare war on us. A lot of future trouble is, however, on the cards and no one can predict anything whatever with certainty."

Part of Grew's concern reflected what was visible on the streets of Tokyo. A pronounced military presence seemed to be everywhere—even on school fields. "[I]t was a common sight in Japan and a startling one to recently arrived Americans," Grew later said, "[to] see little fellows scarcely big enough to walk togged out in military caps and playing military games. Anyone who passed a schoolyard would be even more startled to hear the blood-curdling yells coming from the throats of twelve-year-old boys as they charged across a field with real guns and bayonets, and in a manner so realistic as to be chilling."

Military training for Japan's youth was symptomatic of Japan's priorities. The country was on a war-time footing. On January 9, 1941, the Japanese press announced that Prime Minister Konoye's cabinet had decided to discuss the "national situation" informally with a newly-created body in advance of the Diet's opening session on January 21. As Hugh Byas reported in the *New York Times*, the purpose of the meeting was to "emphasize that Japan is virtually under a wartime government" and to explain that the government "requires from the nation greater exertions than it has yet made."

The government's announcement was hardly surprising. The conflict in China had been in progress for more than three years, and there were now about one million Japanese soldiers stationed there (mostly in Manchukuo and other North China provinces that were rich in the natural resources coveted by Japan). Beyond that, Japan had moved substantial military forces into northern Indochina, a French colony, after striking an agreement with the Vichy government, which controlled unoccupied France but was subject to pressure from the Nazis, who occupied the northern portion of France.

These and other military excursions had taken their toll on the Japanese economy and the Japanese populace. The military budget was enormous and required curbs on non-military expenditures. Rice was becoming more difficult to obtain, and by April 1941, rice could only be obtained in metropolitan areas through ration coupons; beef was almost impossible to find; use of metals for non-essential items was prohibited, and so toys were almost always made of wood; cotton, wool, and other natural materials were in scarce supply, and so clothing as well as shoes were usually made with "sufu," a wood pulp product that would dissolve in rain and from washing; and fertilizers to nurture over-planted farmland were difficult to secure, and so large trucks loaded with "honey buckets" of human excrement were, as Associated Press correspondent Max Hill remembered, a familiar sight on Tokyo's streets. "The odor," said Hill, "as you might well imagine, is none too pleasant."

The impact of all this was readily apparent to foreigners. "It seemed to me," said Henri Smith-Hutton upon his return to Tokyo in April 1939 after four years' absence, "that the people were more somber and subdued. Certainly their clothing seemed more shabby and made of poorer materials. There were shortages of all kinds of articles, especially metals and construction materials. Imported goods had almost disappeared from the stores, and prices were very high; and while vegetables and rice and fish were available, there was little meat, and people had to line up to buy bread."

The situation had deteriorated that much more by the time *New York Times* correspondent Otto Tolischus reached Tokyo in early February 1941. He was appalled by what he saw from a British embassy car in the ride from Yokohama to Tokyo. "Both sides of the road were lined with dirty, dilapidated, ramshackle wooden shops and shacks which had nothing in common with the pretty doll houses pictured in Japanese scenes at home," Tolischus remembered. "The people looked equally poverty-stricken. Most of them shuffled about in dirty kimonos or a bizarre array of Western dress, and most of them, though it was winter, walked about in bare feet shod in wooden clogs. Farmers, driving lumbering oxcarts, were completely in rags, sometimes covered with a raincoat made of straw." Tolischus had been expelled from Nazi Germany in March 1940 after almost seven years of residence there, and he could not help but make comparisons to wartime conditions in the Third Reich. "There were the same complaints about growing restrictions and declining standards of living," said Tolischus, "—about shortages of all sorts of things, especially imported goods, about queues before food shops and the scarcity of taxicabs, about the poor quality of ersatz materials and native whisky—that I had heard in Germany."

The decline in material comforts was accompanied by increased government surveillance and restrictions on speech. The government had taken steps to preserve secrecy and dampen dissent shortly after the China Incident commenced in the summer of 1937. The Military Secrets Preservation Law, as Robert Craigie later explained, "gave the police powers so wide that even the slightest indiscretion could be visited upon the victim with dire penalties." The law was complemented by new regulations from the Home Ministry designed to "smother anti-war or pessimistic expression" and to ensure that newspapers and other periodicals only included "correct data" that would "inspire an enduring, untiring spirit into the mind of the people."

These repressive measures were later strengthened by the National Defense Security Law, which was adopted by the Diet in March 1941 and went into effect in May 1941. The Home Ministry issued a warning to the people when the law went into effect "to be careful in their daily speech and avoid being utilized by spies." That warning was supplemented by a directive from the Justice Ministry that instructed people "to refrain from commenting in public or in newspapers or magazines on what their common sense tells them is unfavorable to the country if known by foreigners." (Knowledge of that law and those warnings did not help Tolischus or other correspondents for American publications. Almost all of them were arrested after the Pearl Harbor attack. In some cases, the correspondents were subjected to horrific torture, and in almost all cases, they were convicted for having sent information prior to the Pearl Harbor attack "to foreign agents harmful to Japan.")

The fear instilled in people was pervasive. By the end of 1940, Grew and his staff saw the impact. "[O]ur Japanese contacts, sources of information," he later explained to the congressional committee investigating the Pearl Harbor attack, "were falling away simply because they were being very carefully watched by the secret police and most of them did not dare come to the Embassy any more. They didn't dare meet me outside, and even when I went to the Tokyo Club, which was sort of a neutral meeting ground for Japanese and foreigners, I found that the Japanese I knew would quietly slip away into other rooms or corners." Marshall Green echoed that perception. "For the most part," said Green, "people were pretty damned supercautious about expressing their opinions and views, because there was the Kempeitai and other police and thought control organizations."

Those other "thought control organizations" were not all Japanese. The execution of the Tripartite Agreement in September 1940 resulted in a rapid influx of members of Germany's Gestapo, who were all too eager to assist their Japanese counterparts in suppressing any dissent. "These Gestapo agents," said Craigie, "undoubtedly found the officers of the Japanese Gendarmerie apt and enthusiastic pupils in all of the latest Nazi arts of political repression, police intimidation and mass terrorism." Grew himself soon reported to the State Department that there was "growing activity on the part of members of the Gestapo" and that "these gentry are reporting to the Japanese police the names of Japanese whom they believe to be harboring anti-Axis sentiments."

The effort to discipline the population was further fueled by a radical change in Japan's political structure. Political parties had been a staple of Japanese life for decades. But no more. The political parties—which provided at least some outlet for differing views on national policy—were dissolved by August 1940. On October 1, the government announced the formation of a new single party—the Imperial Rule Assistance Association—which would be the sole vehicle for dissemination of views on political issues. To ensure coordination with the government, the Prime Minister would be its president. Although it never achieved the same level of control that the Nazis exerted over the German populace, the creation of IRAA did result in fundamental changes. As Grew observed, the evolution of the new structure promoted "an economical way of life and a general frowning upon most forms of lightheartedness, bright colors, fun, sport, and general gaiety, so much loved by the Japanese, and, of course, 'dangerous thoughts.'"

The consolidation of political power in Japan only heightened American concerns with Japanese policies. All of that was made clear in Secretary of State Hull's statement before a congressional committee on January 15 with respect to the proposed Lend-Lease Act, legislation that would authorize the President to provide materials and other forms of support to any country—including China—whose needs were deemed vital to the defense of the United States. Hull used that statement to excoriate Japan's path of aggression, beginning with the invasion of Manchuria and continuing through the China Incident. "It has been clear throughout," said Hull, "that Japan has been actuated from the start by broad and ambitious plans for establishing herself in a dominant position in the entire region of the Western Pacific....It should be manifest to every person that such a program for the subjugation and ruthless exploitation by one country of nearly one-half of the population of the world is a matter of immense significance, importance and concern to every other nation wherever located."

Hull's statement triggered a flurry of angry editorials in the Japanese press. Mr. Hull's arguments, said one periodical, are "merely an exposition of American megalomania tainted with a fear complex amounting to phobia." The hostility of the editorials soon subsided, but on January 21, Prime Minister Konoye told the Diet that "a new order in East Asia" remained the backbone of Japan's foreign policy and that "Japan is firmly determined to achieve its program by destroying any parties, such as Chiang Kai-shek, who are resisting Japan and by cooperating with those who sympathize with Japan."

Grew monitored all these developments closely. There were some well-connected Japanese informants who advised him and his staff that they retained hope for improved relations with the United States. But those splashes of hope could not overcome a more realistic assessment of the Japanese government's perspective. "I have worked steadily during eight years to build up something permanently constructive in the relations between our two countries," Grew told one Japanese friend on January 13, but "those efforts are being defeated by trends and forces which seem to be beyond our control." And so, as he pecked out his thoughts on his Smith-Corona typewriter at the end of January, the American ambassador felt compelled to write that "[t]he outlook for the future of the relations between Japan and the United States has never been darker."

Schreiber was not privy to the comments in Grew's diary. But he did not need to read Grew's diary to decide how to handle the situation. The diplomatic community in Tokyo was a small, close-knit group. Schreiber was, Grew later said, "a close personal friend of mine" and someone he knew "very well." That sentiment was echoed when Grew testified before the congressional committee investigating the Pearl Harbor attack. "I trusted his word and I trusted his judgment," Grew said of Schreiber. And so conveyance of the information in Schreiber's possession should have been a simple matter. It was not. Quite the contrary. The sequence of events that unfolded at the end of January 1941 remains shrouded in mystery and inexplicable inconsistencies.

Schreiber recalled that he telephoned Grew immediately after Yoshuda left on Sunday, January 26, and explained that he had some important information to give the American ambassador. Schreiber probably did not describe the nature of the information when he talked with Grew on the telephone. "One has to live in Japan a while," Grew later confided to his diary, "to realize that we are constantly being spied upon and that telephone conversations are always and inevitably tapped." Like the American ambassador, Schreiber was very much aware of the ever-present surveillance by the Japanese government. He too would have undoubtedly assumed that their telephones were wiretapped. But Grew did not need to know the subject matter in that telephone call. He told his Peruvian colleague to have his car bring him to the American embassy.

Schreiber remembered that he left immediately and that he and Grew retreated to a small couch in the study of Grew's residence. The Peruvian minister wasted no time in recounting all that he had learned about the possible attack on Pearl Harbor. Ever the gracious diplomat, Grew listened intently, and Schreiber recalled that his American colleague "appeared to be quite moved" and "immensely grateful" for Schreiber's visit.

Grew probably did appreciate the gesture. But he may not have attributed any credibility to the rumored attack on Pearl Harbor. As he later explained to the congressional committee investigating the Pearl Harbor attack, the Japanese military seemed to leave no stone unturned in the effort to preserve secrecy over its activities. As one example, Grew pointed out that conductors on trains leaving Tokyo would routinely pull the shades down whenever the train passed a naval yard or other military installation. No risk could be taken that a foreigner or anyone else would see something that the military wanted to keep hidden. Given that obsession with secrecy, Grew thought it "very unlikely" that information concerning the military's planned attack on Pearl Harbor—or any other maneuver—"would have been allowed to leak out anywhere." And so it would have been "utterly impossible for any foreigner in Japan to acquire information of something that the Japanese military were going to do."

Grew recognized of course that the Japanese were capable of surprise attacks on their adversaries. The Japanese surprise attack on the Russian fleet in Port Arthur in 1904—which initiated the Russo-Japanese War—was well known. That attack had occurred after a stalemate in negotiations over the countries' respective interests in Manchuria and Korea. Grew knew that Japanese-American relations were on a downward slide—so much so that the State Department had issued a warning in October 1940 for all American women and children, as well as men "whose continued presence abroad is not highly essential," to return to the United States. But he could not yet reconcile himself to the notion that Japan and the United States were on the verge of armed conflict. "[W]ar between Japan and the United States seemed then so cataclysmic," remembered John Emmerson, "that, although rationally we saw it ahead, in our bones we could not feel that it would ever happen."

Schreiber recalled that he and Grew had discussed sending a cable to the State Department that would include the information conveyed by the Peruvian Minister. Schreiber said that Grew had responded that the two men should "jointly agree on a cable to be sent to the Department of State," but it is inconceivable that the American ambassador would have enlisted the assistance of another diplomat to draft any such cable. Not that it would have mattered. There is no evidence that Grew gave any consideration on that Sunday or even the following morning to sending a cable to the State Department about Schreiber's information. He did not even reference the Schreiber meeting in his diary—a remarkable omission, because the diary is replete with the smallest details of Grew's life in Tokyo. As one example, the diary entry for January 25—the day before the Schreiber meeting— recounts how a Japanese citizen "strong-armed" Joe out of a ticket line with "a heavy push," an encounter which led Grew to complain that "rough- necks" in Japan "seem to predominate." Given this attention to matters of trivial significance, it is difficult to understand why Grew did not include any reference to the Schreiber meeting in his diary—even if he did not attach any credibility to the information that Schreiber conveyed.

Subsequent events appeared to remove any need for Grew to correct the omission. Max Schmidt, the thirty-two-year-old Third Secretary in the Embassy, went to the Tokyo branch of the National City Bank of New York around noon on Monday, January 27. Schmidt (who changed his last name to Bishop after the Pearl Harbor attack) was a language officer who spoke fluent Japanese and was highly regarded by Dooman. He was, said the Embassy Counselor, "a young man of great ability" but "a very junior fel- low." Grew shared Dooman's favorable opinion of Schmidt and thought it would be useful for him to be on the Japan Desk at the State Department in Washington. So Schmidt was at the bank to exchange his Japanese yen for American traveler's checks in preparation for his return to the United States.

Schmidt's later recollections of what transpired at the bank vary in minor detail, but the essence remains consistent. In a 1979 interview, Schmidt said that he saw Schreiber in the bank lobby. The two men were acquainted with each other. They had seen each other at diplomatic functions and even participated in golf outings, which remained a favorite activity of Grew's and other Embassy staff members. In that 1979 interview, Schmidt said that Schreiber motioned him "over to one corner of the lobby." (In a 1988 letter Schmidt said that Schreiber tapped him on the shoulder and motioned him to a "side alcove.") According to Schmidt, Schreiber said that "the Japanese had a war plan involving a surprise all-out attack on Pearl Harbor if and when they decided to go to war." Schmidt said that Schreiber "did not name" his sources and that Schmidt "did not ask him who they were."

According to Schmidt, the conversation was brief. Still, Schmidt did not need more information to understand its significance. He raced back to the Chancery and immediately contacted other sources, including the United Press correspondent and other members of the Embassy staff, to try to verify the information conveyed by Schreiber. Although asked about those other sources in his 1979 and 1993 interviews, Schmidt did not describe any information received from other sources. The Third Secretary obviously did not regard confirmation as necessary. He drafted a telegram for Grew's signature and took it to the Ambassador that afternoon.

Grew discussed the draft telegram with Schmidt and other members of the Embassy staff but apparently said nothing to any of them about any meeting he had had with Schreiber the previous day. Schmidt never referenced a Grew meeting with Schreiber in his various statements about the telegram. Henri Smith-Hutton recalled Grew telling him only that he had "heard the rumor circulating in Tokyo that in the event of a break between the United States and Japan, the Japanese would make an all-out surprise attack on Pearl Harbor." Grew added, said Smith-Hutton, that "one of the main sources of the rumor was Dr. Rivera Schreiber, the Peruvian Minister to Japan." John Emmerson had a similar recollection of a conversation with Grew at the time. According to Emmerson, Grew told him that Schreiber had "whispered to an embassy officer that he had picked up a rumor that Japan had planned a surprise mass attack on Pearl Harbor in the case of trouble between Japan and the United States." When he published his recollection of that conversation in 1978, Emmerson was aware of statements by Schreiber saying that he had given the information to Grew directly and not to an "embassy officer." Emmerson, however, said nothing to reconcile the apparent discrepancy.

Grew ultimately made some edits to Schmidt's draft and sent the telegram to Hull on Monday, January 27 (one of Grew's lucky days). The telegram attributed its content solely to information conveyed by Schreiber to Schmidt, who was not identified in the communication. "My Peruvian colleague," the telegram said, "told a member of my staff that he had heard from many sources including a Japanese source that the Japanese military forces planned, in the event of trouble with the United States, to attempt a surprise mass attack on Pearl Harbor using all of their military facilities. He added that although the project seemed fantastic, the fact that he had heard it from many sources prompted him to pass on the information."

Grew did reference the telegram in his diary entry for January 27, but the entry was very vague and provided no additional detail. "There is a lot of talk around town," the entry read, "to the effect that the Japanese, in case of a break with the United States, are planning to go all out in a surprise mass attack on Pearl Harbor. I rather guess that the boys in Hawaii are not precisely asleep."

Grew did little to clarify the situation when he was questioned about the telegram at the post-war hearings to investigate the Pearl Harbor attack. When asked about the January 27 telegram by a board of the United States Army, Grew said that "the basis of that message was a statement made to a member of my staff by the Peruvian Minister." Grew added that "the Minister said that he considered it a fantastic rumor" but "felt that it was sufficiently important to justify his passing it on to me." In later testimony before the congressional committee, Grew said that the January 27 telegram "was based practically entirely on the report which had been brought *to me* by my Peruvian colleague."

Of course, it is possible that Grew's testimony before the congressional committee was not as precise as he intended and that he had in mind the report that was brought to him by Schmidt. Still, his response could have triggered questions from the congressional committee on the details of how Grew secured the information about the Pearl Harbor attack. But never once did the committee members or its counsel ask Grew to describe any conversations he had had with Schreiber about the rumored attack on Pearl

Harbor. And so the hearing records are silent on whether Grew did in fact meet with Schreiber on that last Sunday in January 1941.

Obvious questions thus remained unanswered. Why would a minister from a foreign country—regarded as a friend and held in high esteem by the American ambassador—convey important information about a planned attack on Pearl Harbor to a junior officer in the American Embassy with whom he had only a passing acquaintance? If the information was important—as Schreiber believed it to be—why would he have used a fortuitous encounter with that Embassy officer to convey the information? Schreiber did not acknowledge any meeting with Schmidt in his post-war statements, but even if he did discuss the Pearl Harbor attack with the Embassy's Third Secretary, why would the Peruvian Minister fail to mention that he had already communicated that same information to the American ambassador the previous day?

These and other questions loom large because Schreiber was upset when he later learned (after the war) that Grew had not sent a telegram to the State Department referencing his meeting with Schreiber but instead had sent a telegram referencing a meeting between Schreiber and a member of the Embassy staff. As Schreiber's wife later commented, her husband would not have communicated information he deemed important to "a subordinate functionary of the American Embassy" in light of her husband's "high rank of Minister Plenipotentiary, in addition to his personal friendship with Mr. Grew."

None of these questions appeared to trouble Hull or his staff. Grew's telegram was received by the State Department at 6:38 a.m. on that same Monday, January 27 (in light of the time difference with Tokyo). Hull reviewed it but did not see any need to ask Grew any questions about the information referenced in the telegram. Nor did the State Department staff. In fact, Grew never received any response from Hull or the State Department.

When he saw the telegram, Max Hamilton, the Chief of the Department's Far Eastern Division, decided to convene a meeting with his staff in his office in the State, War, and Navy Office Building. Frank Schuler, who had served in the American embassy and was now part of the Far Eastern Division staff, knew of Schreiber's high standing in the Tokyo diplomatic community and suggested that the warning "should be taken seriously." Still, the staff saw no need to press Grew for further information on the source of the rumor.

The staff's reaction to Grew's telegram was no doubt dictated, in part at least, by the staff's assessment of Japan's military capabilities. The prevailing view in government circles—both civilian and military—was that Japan would never attack the United States. That prevailing view reflected the vast difference in resources between the two countries. Another component of that prevailing view was racism. There was a deep-seated notion—perhaps epitomized by the Immigration Act of 1924 (which prohibited Japanese immigration to the United States)—that the Japanese were an inferior people, generally small in physical stature and incapable of matching Western intelligence and strategy in any armed conflict. "The Japanese are not going to risk a fight with a first-class nation," Pennsylvania Congressman Charles I. Faddis said around this time. "They are unprepared to do so and no one knows that better than they do." That sentiment was echoed by Commander Vincent Murphy, the assistant war plans officer for the Pacific Fleet. "I thought," Murphy later said, "it would be utterly stupid for the Japanese to attack the United States at Pearl Harbor."

Stanley Hornbeck shared that view. As early as January 1940, he wrote a memorandum to Hull dismissing Grew's fear that economic sanctions might lead Japan to go "insane," saying that there was no need to "baby" Japan in order to avoid any conflict with the United States. Grew's January 27 telegram had no impact on that perspective. The day after the telegram was received, Hornbeck circulated a memorandum to Hull and his State Department colleagues which urged them to "keep all the time in mind...that Japan is not prepared to fight (i.e., carry on) a war with the United States." And a few months later, the Political Relations Adviser advised the Secretary to discount any suggestion that the United States needed to negotiate an agreement with Japan to forestall any plan by Japanese authorities to attack the United States in the Pacific. The wording of Hornbeck's memorandum was convoluted, but the message was clear. "[T]hat those authorities will embark upon a war in the southwestern Pacific in the event of and because of lack of success in a 'negotiation' with the United States in the near future," Hornbeck told Hull, "I do not for one moment believe."

Hull's staff may have believed that the likelihood of an attack on Pearl Harbor was small, but they could not afford the risk of withholding Grew's telegram from the country's armed forces. The recriminations would be so catastrophic if the rumor reported in the telegram proved to be accurate. So Hamilton felt obliged to pass a paraphrase of Grew's telegram on to the Army and Navy. Ironically, Secretary of the Navy Frank Knox had sent a letter on January 24, 1941 to Secretary of War Henry L. Stimson saying, "If war eventuates with Japan, it is believed easily possible that hostilities would be initiated by a surprise attack upon the Fleet or the Naval Base at Pearl Harbor."

Despite that high-level sensitivity to a possible Japanese attack on Pearl Harbor, Grew's telegram stirred no interest on the part of either the Army or Navy. The Chief of the Naval Operations' staff decided that the information in the telegram should be forwarded to Admiral Husband E. Kimmel, the Commander-in-Chief of the Pacific Fleet stationed at Pearl Harbor. The task of preparing that message to Kimmel was assigned to Arthur H. McCollum, the forty-two-year-old Chief of the Far Eastern Section in the Office of Naval Intelligence. Like other members of the Navy staff, McCollum believed—without knowing—that the reports were nothing more than unconfirmed rumors with no basis in fact. He therefore prepared a message for the ONI Chief's signature which said that "[t]he Division of Naval Intelligence places no credence in these rumors" and that "no move against Pearl Harbor appears imminent or planned for in the foreseeable future."

Army intelligence officers had the same reaction. Brigadier General Sherman Miles, the fifty-four-year-old Assistant Chief of Staff, later testified at the congressional hearing investigating the Pearl Harbor attack that it "was inconceivable that any source in the know would have communicated that [information] to the Latin American Ambassador," that any attack on the United States by Japan would be "suicidal," and that, assuming the Japanese used "good sense," they were not going to risk losing ships they "could not replace" with a surprise attack whose success would depend on an assumption that the United States would be "unprepared to meet the attack." And so the Army too allowed Grew's telegram to die a natural death.

The telegram was not given any further consideration until after December 7, 1941.

CHAPTER 7

Matsuoka

I t was an experience never to be forgotten. He had enrolled in the University of Oregon Law School in Portland, Oregon, in 1898 at the age of eighteen. It was, in no small way, a reflection of his ambition, of his desire to succeed at whatever cost.

He had been born in March 1880 to a family in the Yamaguchi Prefecture in southwestern Japan. Providing for a family with seven children in a rural community was a challenge for his father, and one of the boy's earliest experiences was traveling with his mother along a narrow mountain path to visit relatives who might provide assistance. He was no more than four, but the memory of that trek never left him. "Young as I was," he later said, "I could still feel the embarrassment my mother felt." And so, he said, "I decided that I would make a name for myself to console her."

It was not an easy journey for the young boy. His father's merchant business soon collapsed, and in 1893 the family arranged with Methodist missionaries for the thirteen-year-old boy to be sent to Portland to live with William Dunbar, a widower, and his sister, Isabelle Dunbar Beveridge.

Their tranquil existence was disrupted in November 1894. William Dunbar—who owned or managed several companies—was convicted of smuggling in Chinese workers and drugs. Rather than face prison, he fled to Hong Kong. At some point after her brother's departure, Isabelle left the community.

However traumatic the experience for the Japanese youth, there was no forgetting Isabelle. She had doted on the boy, had urged him to pursue education at Oregon's public schools, and had arranged for his baptism as a Presbyterian Christian. He cherished her memory, and years later, after he had grown up and become a major force in Japanese politics, he returned to Portland to place a marker near Isabelle's grave. The inscription said that it was from the "loving hands of Yosuke Matsuoka" and expressed his "lasting gratitude for the sympathy and gentle kindness of a woman who, next to his mother, shaped his mind and character."

However much she influenced his mind and character, Isabelle had not called him Yosuke. He was in America, and he had to have an American name. So he became Frank Matsuoka.

In 1894, Frank's father died, and his older brother Kensuke decided to join him in Portland. But Kensuke had his own aspirations, and they did not include remaining in Oregon. He persuaded his younger brother to travel with him to Oakland where Kensuke had plans to open a restaurant. They were there for a few years, with Frank continuing to attend public schools, but Frank eventually returned to Portland when his brother's restaurant closed. One of his first decisions upon his return was to enroll in the University of Oregon's law school, believing that a law degree would feed the enduring hunger to restore his family fortunes. It was, in at least one respect, a bold move for a Japanese youth. Oregon, like other Western states infused with Asian workers, was awash in racial prejudice.

Frank was not insulated from that pervasive prejudice. One day he saw two other students coming toward him as he was walking down the street. As they passed Frank, one of the students grabbed his hat and threw it on the ground. When he bent down to pick it up, the student "gave him a kick in the backside and knocked him to the pavement." It was a telling moment, and the effect would linger long after Frank left Oregon.

Gene Dooman was one of those who heard the story from Matsuoka after he became Foreign Minister in July 1940, and the Embassy Counselor understood the impact. "There seemed to be within him," Dooman later said of Matsuoka, "some deep-rooted prejudice which was carefully concealed under a mannerism, which was extremely effusive and apparently friendly. But I think that there's no doubt that he had virtually a hatred of the United States and of Americans in general." Dooman's assessment may or may not have been correct. But there is no question that those years in America shaped Matsuoka's view on how Japan should treat the United States in any confrontation. "If you stand firm and start hitting back," he once told his eldest son, "the American will know he's talking to a man, and you two can then talk man to man."

Frank graduated from law school in 1900 and returned to Japan in 1902 when his mother became ill. Still, Matsuoka liked to believe, and certainly told others that he did believe, that those early years gave him an insight into the United States and its population that other Japanese leaders lacked. As Matsuoka told Grew at one point in the spring of 1941, he could talk to the American ambassador "as a man who regarded himself a quasi-American and...as if he were an American."

That apparent identification with America did not undermine Matsuoka's career in Japan. Although he was unable to secure admission to Tokyo Imperial University to obtain a Japanese law degree, he placed first among the 130 applicants who took Foreign Ministry entrance exams in 1904. Over the course of the next seventeen years, the aspiring diplomat held many assignments, including ones in Shanghai, Manchuria, Washington, and Paris (as a delegate to the Versailles Peace Conference). In 1921, he became a director and in 1927 vice president of the South Manchurian Railway Company, the semi-private organization which was the lifeline of Japanese military and business interests in northern China. Matsuoka resigned from the SMR vice-presidency in 1930, returned to Japan, and successfully campaigned to became a member of the House of Representatives in the Diet.

His participation in foreign policy and domestic policies—coupled with an unbridled self-confidence—made the fifty-two-year-old Matsuoka the ideal candidate to lead Japan's delegation to the League of Nations' sessions in Geneva, Switzerland, in the fall of 1932. This would not be a routine proceeding. A principal purpose of the sessions would be to consider a report by a five-member commission chaired by Lord Victor Bulwer-Lytton of Great Britain. The commission had been established under Article XV of the League's Covenant to evaluate the Japanese invasion of Manchuria. Its report—known as the Lytton Report—concluded that Japan had been the aggressor, that the Japanese puppet-state of Manchukuo should not be recognized, and that Manchuria should become a largely autonomous state consistent with Chinese sovereignty.

A man of medium height (for Japanese), with dark hair combed straight back, a round face punctuated by a dark toothbrush moustache, and round tortoise-shell glasses, Matsuoka welcomed the assignment. It would bring him into the limelight and cater to his ever-expanding ambition. But even he could not envision the impact the assignment would have on his career.

Through the late fall of 1932 and the early winter of 1933, Matsuoka spent hours meeting with delegates from other nations to persuade them that the Lytton Report failed, as Matsuoka later explained to the League Assembly, to appreciate Japan's desire "to preserve peace, to promote law and order, to benefit the people of Manchuria." By the time the Assembly met on the morning of Friday, February 24, in the auditorium of the Palais Wilson on Lake Geneva, Matsuoka knew, as did the other thirty or so members of his delegation, that their effort had been in vain. The budding politician had hoped for Japan's continuance in the League, but he received instructions from the Foreign Ministry on the evening of February 23 that if, as expected, the Assembly adopted the Lytton Report the next day, he was to walk out of the auditorium—but without using the word "withdrawal."

It was a very nervous man who walked up to the podium the following morning. He was a gifted speaker, but he was taking no chances. He had practiced his speech over and over again in the privacy of his room at the Hotel Metropole. He spoke in crisp English, gesticulating with his arm, and urged the delegates "not to accept this report for the sake of peace in the Far East and for the sake of peace throughout the world." Hugh Wilson, the American minister to Switzerland, was there, and he remembered that Matsuoka spoke with "a passionate conviction far removed from his usual businesslike manner." However passionate the speech, the delegates were not moved. All but one of the other forty-three countries in attendance subsequently voted to accept the report (with Siam abstaining).

As soon as the vote was completed, Matsuoka strode quickly to the podium again. The room was bathed in silence, the drama of the moment evident. Never before had the League used Article XV to censure a member. In his clipped but articulate English, Matsuoka said that, with "profound regret," he was forced to announce that the Japanese had "now reached the limit of their endeavors to cooperate with the League regarding the Chino-Japanese differences." He picked up his papers from the rostrum and resolutely walked down the center of the aisle, nodded to the two members of his delegation who had been seated with him in the auditorium, and led them out of the Assembly (with the other members of the Japanese delegation seated in the balcony following suit).

The strain on the Japanese spokesman was obvious as he stepped into the lobby. He was quickly surrounded by journalists and photographers who wanted to ask questions and take his picture. He pulled a cigar from his jacket pocket, clipped it, and tried to light it with a match, but the flame expired before the cigar could be lit. He soon left the lobby, puffing on the unlit cigar, stepped into the limousine with the flag of the Rising Sun on the radiator, and was swept off to the hotel.

For Matsuoka, the departure from the Assembly and Japan's later withdrawal from the League represented a failure of diplomacy. But not to the people back home. When the ship bringing him home docked in Yokohama, Matsuoka stepped off the gangplank in his bowler hat, puffing on a lit cigar (finally), to see thousands of people, many waving Japanese flags, all cheering the Japanese delegate who had dared to defy the Western powers. He was now a hero, a man who could, or so it seemed, provide the leadership Japan would need in a troubled world.

Matsuoka tried to use that new fame to promote an organization that would lead to the abandonment of political parties and the establishment of a fascist organization modeled after the one Benito Mussolini had built in Italy. He resigned from his seat in the Diet to devote his energies to the project, but the organization did not achieve the success Matsuoka had envisioned. He then returned to the South Manchuria Railway Company as president, but the passage of time did nothing to diminish his enthusiasm for his preferred political structure—a perspective which quickly surfaced when Matsuoka was selected by Prime Minister Konoye to be Japan's new Foreign Minister in July 1940.

It was a pivotal time for the country. Japan's political parties were being dissolved as a prelude to the establishment of the Imperial Rule Assistance Association—all in an effort to discourage dissent on political issues. The transition was undoubtedly on Matsuoka's mind when he discussed his views with *New York Herald Tribune* correspondent Wilfred Fleisher.

"The era of democracy," Matsuoka proclaimed to Fleisher, "is finished and the democratic system bankrupt." Totalitarianism, he said, "will achieve control." He added that it would take some years before Japan would achieve a totalitarian state but that it would be "unlike the European brand." There would be no concentration camps (and, in fact, Matsuoka would later facilitate refuge for European Jews in China), but the Japanese populace would have to share a common perspective on political matters.

Fleisher sensed from all this that the new Foreign Minister was "more intensely pro-Axis than any other Japanese with whom he [had] talked." The obvious question was how that attitude would affect Japan's relations with the United States. For his part, Fleischer was uncertain. The *New York Herald Tribune* correspondent told Grew he did not know whether the new Foreign Minister would "be disposed toward finding a reasonable basis for improving relations with the United States."

Some of that uncertainty would be removed in September 1940 when Matsuoka persuaded Hirohito to approve the Tripartite Pact with Germany and Italy. But that development—however discouraging to the American ambassador—did not dissuade Grew from doing what he could to forge a harmonious relationship with the new Foreign Minister. Whatever his political views, Matsuoka would be a critical component in the effort to minimize, if not eliminate, the risk of armed conflict with the United States.

Grew met with Matsuoka almost immediately after his appointment as Foreign Minister became official. As Grew explained to Hull in a telegram, the Foreign Minister said that "he had always been a frank talker and that in our contacts he might frequently say things which could be regarded as undiplomatic but he believed that much was to be gained by frank and direct speaking." Grew agreed with that approach, but he could not have anticipated the burden he would have to endure to accommodate Matsuoka's passion for candid conversation.

The Foreign Minister made it clear from the beginning that he wanted to have a close relationship with the American envoy. He was almost always available when Grew wanted to see him, was never shy in conveying what seemed to be his innermost thoughts about public policy, and told Grew to telephone him at his office or home "if at any point" he wanted "to check upon any doubtful point." On one occasion he even called Grew to thank him for a dinner at the Embassy—the first time any Foreign Minister had telephoned the American ambassador directly.

The problem—if problem it was—concerned Matsuoka's capacity for talking. "Yosuke Matsuoka," said the *New York Times* in the spring of 1941, "is one of the world's greatest talkers...." On one occasion in October 1940, Grew visited with Matsuoka to discuss the Tripartite Pact (which had been signed in the prior week). "As usual," Grew recorded in his diary, "Mr. Matsuoka did about ninety-five per cent of the talking because his continuous monologues can be broken only by forceful intrusion." On another occasion, Grew remarked that one emerges from a conversation with the Foreign Minister "feeling like a whirlpool, for the Minister's volubility is surpassed in my experience only by that of [the Turkish] Foreign Minister...." And when reporting to Hull on his conversations with Matsuoka in the spring of 1941, Grew acknowledged that the Foreign Minister sometimes made inconsistent statements. But those inconsistencies, he insisted, did not reflect adversely on Matsuoka's "intellectual and political honesty." "He talks so flowingly and freely, by the hour if time affords," said Grew, "that it is inconceivable that he should never make conflicting statements."

Matsuoka never acknowledged to Grew that his excessive talking—or the high energy which accompanied it—was an issue. His ego was so large, his self-confidence so robust, that it apparently never dawned on him that his comments—whether in private or public—were anything but insightful and eloquent. Alice saw evidence of that self-confidence when visiting with Matsuoka's wife at her home on the afternoon of January 22, 1941. The Foreign Minister walked in the house with an "air of satisfaction" after having given a lengthy and fiery speech at the opening of the Diet. In that speech, Matsuoka had urged the United States "to allay the impending crisis of civilization," saying, with words that would later have an ironic ring, that if the United States became involved in the European conflict, war with Japan would "take its furious course, unleashing formidable new weapons which have not hitherto been used...."

However much satisfaction he took from his pronouncements, Matsuoka's voluble manner created doubt among those inside and outside of Japan's government whether the Foreign Minister was of sound mind. He seemed to speak with a stream of consciousness that exceeded the boundaries of sane behavior (and would, for example, tell listeners how he often "indulges in thoughts in terms of one thousand or two or even three thousand years...."). After reviewing intercepted instructions which Matsuoka had sent to the Japanese ambassador in Washington in February 1941, Roosevelt forwarded the intercept to Under Secretary of State Sumner Welles with the comment, "These instructions seem to me to be the product of a mind which is deeply disturbed and unable to think quietly or logically." Several months later, Welles told Lord Halifax, the British ambassador to the United States, that a letter authored by Matsuoka was the product "of a man on the edge of a nervous breakdown...." Grew himself recorded in his diary around the same time that "by all criteria" the Foreign Minister "can only be considered as mentally ill-balanced...." These observations were not confined to American decision-makers. After one Liaison Conference—a meeting attended by the Prime Minister, selected members of his cabinet, and representatives of the military—the Navy Minister remarked to a colleague, "The Foreign Minister is insane, isn't he?"

Whatever the assessment of his mental faculties, Matsuoka remained an influential force within the Japanese government, in part because of his sustained popularity with the Japanese people. And in the winter of 1941, nowhere was that influence of greater concern to the United States—and its ally, Great Britain—than in the fate of Singapore.

Located at the tip of the Malaysian Peninsula, Singapore was a British colony and Great Britain's principal naval port in Southeast Asia. Protection of Singapore was a high priority for the British. Its security was central to England's ability to protect its interests in the Pacific.

Japan's placement of military resources in northern Indochina the previous September generated speculation in Washington and in London that Japan was preparing an attack on Singapore. On December 4, 1940, Grew had received a telegram from the State Department which described "the vital role of Singapore in the defense of the British Isles" and, perhaps more importantly, the inability of the British to protect Singapore. With all its resources devoted to the defense against the Nazis' Blitz on London and other British cities (not to mention rumors of a German invasion of the island), Grew concluded that the British government was "in no position today, and presumably will not be in the near future, to part with important naval units for the defense of Singapore."

Ever mindful of the situation, the British kept pressuring the United States to take firm action to dissuade the Japanese from moving against Singapore. On February 11, the British Foreign Office sent a telegram to its embassy in Washington (for communication to the State Department) that the British "felt certain that the Japanese are acting with the encouragement of Germany and that they are planning more vigorous aggressive measures in direct agreement with the German Government." On February 15, Winston Churchill sent a telegram to Roosevelt saying, "There are indications, from many drifting straws, that the Japanese mean to make war on us, or to do something which would compel us to make war on them, in the next few weeks or months.... Whatever you are able to do to instill in Japan anxiety as to a double war may succeed in averting this danger. Nevertheless, should we alone be attacked, it would be difficult to overstate the grave character of the consequences."

The President had been communicating with the British Prime Minister on a regular basis for almost two years, and he would have undoubtedly given close consideration to Churchill's warning. In fact, Germany had been pressing Japan, and Matsuoka in particular, to launch an attack on Singapore. Matsuoka understood the value of that strategy and advised German Ambassador Eugen Ott on February 10 that an attack on Singapore "had been planned" for later that spring.

Matsuoka's communication to Ott was more a reflection of his oversized ego than a carefully calculated military strategy. Under Japan's convoluted political structure, the Foreign Minister had no authority to initiate a war. Aside from rogue elements in the military who might operate independently (as may have been the case in the Mukden Incident), the initiation of armed conflict against another nation or its territories required the approval of the Army and Navy as well as the sanction of the Emperor. None of those prerequisites had been satisfied in the case of an attack on Singapore.

Still, rumors of a Japanese attack on the British colony were an open secret in Tokyo. Grew had already received reports of Japan's "firm intention to acquire jumping-off facilities for an eventual attack on Singapore." In the beginning of February, Grew recorded in his diary that Japan was "pouring further troops into Indochina...with a view to getting into a position for an eventual attack on Malaya, Burma, and Singapore." By the middle of February, *New York Times* correspondent Otto Tolischus, who had recently arrived in Japan, remembered that the picture was "alarming." Grew himself recorded in his diary that the situation was "tense." The American ambassador was particularly concerned that "the reckless do-or-die spirit of the military extremists may force the issue before Great Britain and the United States could or would intervene." And so, even without instructions from the State Department, the American ambassador knew that he had to do something.

The Embassy Counselor provided the vehicle for needed action. Gene Dooman returned to Tokyo from his six-month leave of absence on February 7, 1941. As late as January, Grew was concerned that Dooman would not be able to return that quickly. There were reports that he had experienced a recurrence of duodenal ulcers which might require an operation. ("Poor Dooman," Grew recorded in his diary.) But the operation was not necessary, and Dooman was able to return as planned. Even before Dooman's ship docked in Yokohama, Grew had cabled to ask if he would like a welcoming party (to which the Embassy Counselor responded, "You betcha"). An Embassy car was there on the ship's arrival and took Gene, Joe, Max Schmidt, and First Secretary Ned Crocker to a nearby course for a round of golf, which enabled the men to discuss unfolding developments. They then returned to the Chancery for dinner and an evening's discussion of the telegram Grew had drafted for dispatch to Hull.

The focus of the telegram was Singapore. Crocker had talked with his counterparts at the British embassy who were hoping the United States would send a portion of its Pacific Fleet to the vicinity in a show of force that might dissuade Japan from taking action. Dooman opposed that symbolic gesture, saying it would be regarded by the Japanese as a threat and might hasten rather than retard the risk of war. Everyone ultimately agreed with the latter assessment, and, according to Grew, the telegram was sent out that night "as originally drafted" without any recommendation with respect to the Pacific Fleet.

"Japan has edged her way cautiously to a position from which, with some added preparation, [it] could…eventually launch an attack on Singapore," said the February 7 telegram. "Such an assault," the telegram warned, "may well be planned to synchronize with the expected German all-out offensive against the British Isles." The telegram said the Embassy was not prepared to make a recommendation on how to handle the situation, but it did add "that the principal question before us is not whether we must call a halt to the Japanese southward advance, but when. Increased American naval concentration in the Far East would entail inevitable risks of war," the telegram observed, but might be less troublesome than the risk of allowing "the Japanese advance to proceed indefinitely unchecked."

Grew never received a response to the telegram, but he was disheartened when Sir Robert Craigie gave him copies of British telegrams on February 19 which detailed conversations Lord Halifax had had with Roosevelt and Hull on the same topic. "Of course," Grew recorded in his diary, "those conversations had not been reported by the Department to me, although they very closely concerned my job out here."

Despite the absence of any response from the State Department, the Embassy did not remain idle. About a week after the February 7 telegram was sent, Dooman exploited another opportunity to discourage a Japanese attack on Singapore. Grew had long been concerned that Japanese leaders discounted the possibility of any resistance by the United States because of an assumption that isolationist sentiment dictated American policy. "Whenever a speech by some prominent isolationist was made in America," Grew later told the congressional committee investigating the Pearl Harbor attack, "that speech was generally emblazoned in headlines in the Japanese press, and very few other speeches were ever allowed to be published." The result, said Grew, was that even the highest officials in the Japanese government were "amazingly ill-informed of American public opinion." The American ambassador saw Dooman's return as a way to dispel those misconceptions. The Embassy Counselor could advise the Foreign Ministry of what he had learned during his six-month leave to counter any notion that the United States would be indifferent to an attack on Singapore. And so Dooman scheduled a courtesy call on Ohashi Chuichi, the Vice Minister of Foreign Affairs.

As planned, Dooman opened the conversation (in his fluent Japanese) by saying that he wanted to pass on what he "had seen and heard while at home." He explained that, while Americans did not want to become involved in foreign wars, they were equally supportive of "helping England to the limit of our capacity." The consequence of that perspective, Dooman added, should not be lost on Japan. "It would be absurd to suppose," the Counselor intoned, "that the American people, while pouring munitions into Britain, would look with complacency upon the cutting of communications between Britain and British dominions and colonies overseas." And so, said Dooman, if Japan endangered those dominions or colonies, "she would have to expect to come into conflict with the United States."

Like his boss, Ohashi was a bountiful conversationalist. "He was," said Joe Ballantine, who knew the Vice Minister from his service in China, "the most talkative person that ever lived, and it was really like going to a circus to hear his comments." The Vice Minister did not disappoint in responding to Dooman. He said with great vigor that the United States and England were to blame for the current situation because they had tried to isolate Japan. Ohashi added that Japan "had no intention whatever of moving toward Singapore and the Dutch East Indies *unless* Japan was 'pressed' by other nations through the imposition of embargoes by the United States or by the sending of an American fleet to Singapore."

Dooman did not let those comments pass without again warning Ohashi of the consequences. "Do you mean to say," the Vice Minister replied with obvious astonishment, "that if Japan were to attack Singapore there would be war with the United States?" Dooman's answer was quick and to the point: "The logic of the situation," he said, "would inevitably raise that question."

Dooman then left, with Ohashi saying that "he would be glad to receive" the Embassy Counselor "at any time." But the impact of Dooman's words did not evaporate with his departure. A few minutes later, the Australian Minister—who had no knowledge of Dooman's visit—came to see the Vice Minister and found Ohashi to be "greatly agitated and distraught." Grew visited with Matsuoka a week or so later and advised the Foreign Minister that Dooman's comments were made with his "prior knowledge" and had his "full approval."

Grew's concern with the fate of Singapore was shared by Stanley Hornbeck. The State Department's Adviser on Political Relations remained fearful throughout the spring that the President—ever reluctant to engage in any hostile act that might lead to war—did not appreciate the importance of defending Singapore against a Japanese attack. On April 10, 1941, Hornbeck sent a letter to Grew asking that he send a letter directly to Roosevelt or to Hornbeck himself "volunteering a statement, which would be strictly your own," that stressed the need to "discourage a Japanese advance southward..."

Hornbeck became anxious when he did not receive any response to his request (largely because Grew did not receive Hornbeck's letter until the end of May). As an alternative, Hornbeck sent a memo to Under Secretary of State Welles on May 19, 1941, proposing that Welles forward to the President an excerpt of Joe's diary entry for March 30, 1941 (which Grew had previously sent to Hornbeck). In that entry, Grew had stated that it was "axiomatic that we cannot in our own interest and security afford to see Singapore fall" and that it was not "a question of whether we must act but when...." Welles agreed with the State Department adviser and sent a memo to Roosevelt on May 22. The memo quoted from Grew's diary entry of March 30 and placed particular emphasis on the Ambassador's warning that "we shall avoid war with Japan if Japan once becomes convinced that we mean business and that a Japanese attack on Singapore would inevitably result in war with the United States."

Roosevelt did not take any action in response to Welles' memo—in part because, long before then, he believed that the crisis over Singapore had abated. On February 20, shortly after Dooman had visited with Ohashi, Churchill had sent a telegram to Roosevelt saying that he had "better news about Japan." Matsuoka, Churchill had been told, was planning a trip to Berlin, Rome, and Moscow, and the purpose of the trip "may well be diplomatic sop to cover the absence of action against Great Britain."

Churchill's news proved to be largely accurate. The Foreign Minister not only wanted to assuage Germany's leaders about Japan's failure to take action against Great Britain. Matsuoka also hoped to persuade Adolf Hitler that Germany would benefit from a grand alliance that would include the Soviet Union as well as Japan. In conjunction with that latter purpose, Matsuoka wanted to execute a non-aggression agreement with the Soviet Union that would insulate Japan from an attack by its traditional nemesis. The execution of that agreement (as well as the creation of a grand alliance with Germany and Italy) seemed attainable because the Soviet Union was already an ally of Germany, having signed its own non-aggression pact with Germany in August 1939 shortly before the launch of Germany's attack on Poland.

Matsuoka departed from the Tokyo train station on March 12 for a journey that would take him through Siberia for an interim stop in Moscow, where he would meet with Soviet dictator Joseph Stalin and Vyacheslav Molotov, the Soviet Foreign Minister. From there, he would travel to Berlin to meet with Hitler and Joachim von Ribbentrop, the German Foreign Minister. That would be followed by a short visit with Benito Mussolini in Italy and then, on the return, another stop in Moscow for further meetings with Stalin and Molotov.

The Foreign Minister, with his hair now closely cropped, left Tokyo with high hopes. As he sipped vodka on the long train ride across the Soviet frontier, he told a staff member that he intended "to make puppets of Hitler and Stalin." Those intentions may not have not blossomed entirely as Matsuoka envisioned (in part because Ribbentrop intimated that a clash between Germany and the Soviet Union was on the horizon). Still, the Foreign Minister could not have been unhappy with his visit to Berlin. He was greeted by large crowds waving Japanese flags and the hospitality of smiling German officials. According to Grew, the Fuhrer was "reasonable and calm in all their talks" and showed "none of the excitable characteristics generally attributed to him"—although AP correspondent Max Hill later heard that "Matsuoka as good as said Hitler was a madman who screamed and pounded with his clenched fist on a table to emphasize his demands."

Whatever the truth about Hitler's conduct, the Russians proved to be more challenging. On his first stop in Moscow, Molotov deflected Matsuoka's proposal for a non-aggression agreement, which would have detailed provisions concerning the parties' relationship. Better, said Molotov, to consider a less complicated neutrality agreement. That kind of agreement would simply require each signatory to recognize the territory of the other country and agree to remain neutral in the event the other country was attacked. Matsuoka later met with Stalin, but he too resisted the non-aggression agreement that Matsuoka desired.

The Russians did not give Matsuoka an explanation for their position. Perhaps, like diplomats in Tokyo, the Russians simply grew weary of listening to the Japanese Foreign Minister. As Grew reported to Hull, the American ambassador had been told that Matsuoka "lectured" Stalin on Japanese ideology for fifty-eight minutes of their one-hour meeting. Stalin responded curtly that "he saw no reason why Russia and Japan could not be friends in spite of differences in ideology" and left the room. That was hardly a promising end to the conversation, and so Matsuoka could not have been optimistic about the possibility of securing a non-aggression agreement with the Russians.

Prospects for a non-aggression agreement did not seem any brighter when the Japanese Foreign Minister reached Moscow in early April on his return from Berlin. But the dynamic soon changed. At a meeting with Stalin on April 12, Matsuoka relented and indicated that he would accept the neutrality agreement Molotov had first suggested. Molotov's staff worked through the night with Matsuoka's aides on the agreement, and Stalin arranged a meeting in the Kremlin on April 13 for the signing of the Neutrality Pact (which consisted of four brief articles on two pages).

Stalin did not explain his motivations in seeking the neutrality agreement with Japan, but they were not difficult to fathom. The Soviet dictator undoubtedly suspected—and possibly even knew—that Germany would soon attack his country's western front, and Stalin surely wanted to avoid the prospect of simultaneously fighting Japan on the eastern front. Matsuoka did not trouble himself with Stalin's motivation. He signed the Neutrality Pact on behalf of Japan, and afterwards he and Stalin repeatedly toasted each other (with Stalin, who did not like wine, drinking some kind of "self-prepared red liquid").

Matsuoka may have preferred a non-aggression agreement, but the execution of the Soviet Neutrality Pact was no small achievement. "You Americans," one Japanese friend told Max Hill, "who have a continent to yourselves, with friendly nations on the north and the south, have no idea what it means to always have a bear clawing at your door." But the Japanese people understood. When his plane touched down at Tachikawa Airport outside Tokyo on April 22, Matsuoka was, according to *New York Times* correspondent Otto Tolischus, "[w]elcomed home like a victor entitled to the thanks of the nation." There was "a formal military reception and ceremony" at the airport, and the streets were lined with people shouting *Banzai!* as his motorcade brought him back to the city. "It was," said the *Japan Times and Advertiser*, "a triumphant close [to] one of the most notable chapters in Japanese diplomacy." The Foreign Minister held a five-minute conference with the press at his residence immediately afterwards. During his brief talk with reporters, the Foreign Minister sipped his favorite Scotch whiskey and was, as Hill later observed, "to put it charitably, on the tipsy side."

The impact of the achievement on Matsuoka's ego could not have been more dramatic. "He had come back from Berlin and Moscow," said Tolischus, "with a head far too large for his old hat." An enlarged ego was of no moment to Grew. The American ambassador was eager to speak with the Foreign Minister and assess the impact of all these developments on Japanese-American relations.

The meeting occurred on the afternoon of May 14 at the Foreign Ministry. Matsuoka was suffering from tuberculosis and coughing "badly" when Grew entered the office (although the Foreign Minister told the American ambassador it was bronchitis). Grew had some sympathy for the Foreign Minister's condition. He had recently written to his daughter Anita that he had not experienced any "serious colds" that winter and attributed his good health to a daily intake of a "Vegex" supplement, which included a Vitamin B complex. Grew told Matsuoka about the supplement and forwarded a bottle to him after he returned to the Embassy.

Grew's sympathy for Matsuoka's health did not seem to have any impact on the Foreign Minister's rambling remarks. They were, according to Grew, "bellicose both in tone and substance." Of particular concern to Matsuoka was the United States' persistence in sending convoys of ships to England with materials to assist in its defense against German attacks. Matsuoka told Grew that Hitler had "shown great 'patience and generosity' in not declaring war on the United States," but he was doubtful that such "patience and restraint could continue indefinitely." If the American convoys to England triggered a German attack on the United States, Matsuoka continued, he would regard it as an act of aggression by the United States that could require Japanese assistance to Germany under Article III of the Tripartite Pact. Accordingly, said Matsuoka, the "'manly, decent and reasonable'" course of action for the United States would be "to declare war openly on Germany...."

Grew responded heatedly that he resented any statement that his country "was guilty of unmanly, indecent and unreasonable conduct." Perhaps startled by the vehemence of the American ambassador's comment, Matsuoka immediately withdrew the statement. But as the conversation dragged on for another two hours, the Foreign Minister repeatedly stated that the United States was playing with fire and that "the whole future of the world and of civilization now lies in the hands of one single man, President Roosevelt."

Grew returned to the Chancery to write a report of the conversation for Hull, but before he could complete the draft, he received a hand-written note from Matsuoka apologizing for any "misapprehension" he might have caused Grew. In another long letter which Grew received a few days later, Matsuoka again tried to soften any ill feeling his comments may have generated. "I very often forget," the letter said, "that I am a Foreign Minister; to tell you the truth, I am seldom conscious of the fact that I am a Foreign Minister. Especially, I am apt to lose the sense of nationality when I converse with Your Excellency, pouring out my heart as man to man.... I honestly hate the so-called correct attitude taken by many diplomats which, as you know, hardly get us anywhere." Not surprisingly, Grew soon received an invitation from Matsuoka to come to his home on the afternoon of May 19.

The visit began with tea in the house (with Grew taking note of the inscribed photos on the mantelpiece of Hitler and Mussolini as well as Roosevelt, who had seen Matsuoka in Washington in March 1933 on Matsuoka's return trip from the League meeting in Geneva). The two men then strolled in the garden of the Foreign Minister's home, each smoking a pipe (with Matsuoka using tobacco Grew had given him as a gift). The Foreign Minister said that he was surprised to learn from the Japanese ambassador in Washington that Grew had reported to the State Department that he had "intimidated" the American ambassador in their last talk. Matsuoka again emphasized that he always thought it best "to lay aside as far as possible all formalities pertaining to our official positions and talk very frankly." Grew responded with a candor of his own, saying that he had reported to Washington that the Foreign Minister's tone and substance were "bellicose." "The Minister did not question the accuracy of my report," Grew later wrote, "but said smilingly that while his words might have been bellicose his heart and thoughts were peaceful." The conversation continued for another two hours or so, and, when they finally concluded, Matsuoka said that he "hoped for frequent future talks" and that the best format was "to gather informally around the tea table...."

In reporting the conversations to Hull, Grew said that Matsuoka "follows the carefully studied policy of painting the darkest picture of what will happen if the United States gets into war against Germany, probably in the mistaken belief that such tactics may serve to exert a restraining influence on American policy." Despite that perspective, and despite Matsuoka's unpredictable and often insulting comments, Grew added that his personal relations with the Foreign Minister "are of the best" and that he considered him "among my personal friends in Japan...."

That personal relationship did not blind the American ambassador to Matsuoka's precarious status with Japanese leaders. "It is not likely that Matsuoka will be replaced in the immediate future, because his stock with the public is too high," Grew recorded in his diary around this time, "but he is not liked and is regarded as a dangerous element in the Government, especially in risking war with the United States...." Nor did Grew's good relationship with Matsuoka provide any relief from the unrelenting repression that had now become a frightening staple of life in Japan.

Foreign correspondents remained a particular target of surveillance by the secret police. *New York Times* correspondent Otto Tolischus was told shortly after he arrived in Tokyo in early 1941 that his "wastepaper basket was being rifled by the police every day." The office boy of another foreign correspondent told his employer that he had received "a request by a policeman not to tear up matter thrown in the wastepaper basket, because it gave the policeman added trouble in putting it together again."

The surveillance was not confined to wastepaper baskets, and those who refused to comply with a request from the secret police could face dire consequences. A Mr. Matsuo, a Japanese interpreter employed by the American consulate in Taihoku (now Taipei), was sentenced to three years of imprisonment for espionage in the spring of 1941 because he refused a request from the military police "to divulge the combination of the office safe and other information which would enable the police to obtain access to the files of the Consulate." Grew was outraged by Mr. Matsuo's plight (writing in his diary, "I know of no case during my nine years in Japan that has made my blood boil more than the Matsuo case"). But the American ambassador's repeated pleas to Matsuoka for relief were all in vain.

Whatever his sympathies for Mr. Matsuo, Matsuoka was part of the problem. From the beginning of his tenure as Foreign Minister, he had taken actions and made pronouncements which reflected a bias against Westerners and sometimes even against whites. When he became Foreign Minister in July 1940, he vowed to remove those employees of the Foreign Ministry who had "gone Western." He also wanted to remove the Western presence from Pacific islands. One of his speeches in February 1941 said that Japan's

Co-Prosperity Sphere policy for "Greater East Asia" should include Japanese control of "Oceania," a geographic area that extended from Australia and included virtually all of the Western Pacific. A month or so later he made a public statement that "[w]hite men occupying Oceania are due to return it to the Asiatics." And shortly afterward, a Foreign Office spokesman advised the press that "Japan's true aim was to drive the white man out of Asia."

The bias against Westerners was reflected in the streets. As Grew complained to the Foreign Ministry, posters sometimes appeared with caricatures of Roosevelt, Churchill, and other foreign statesmen with the caption, "Strike the Enemies of the Imperial Nation." The bias against Westerners was also evident in the Japanese press, which routinely published articles and editorials saying that certain foreign powers, especially the United States and Great Britain, were trying to encircle Japan. Matsuoka, for his part, fully subscribed to that commentary. In discussing "encirclement" at a press conference with Japanese reporters in late February 1941, the Foreign Minister said he hoped that "the Anglo-Saxons" would refrain from taking "any measures tending to excite Japanese public opinion."

The dislike of Westerners bore unfortunate fruit shortly after Matsuoka made that statement. The commercial attaché from the French embassy was returning by taxi to the Yokohama docks to board the SS *President Coolidge* after having conducted business in Kobe. When a dispute arose with respect to the fare, the enraged taxi driver took an "iron tool" from his car and began to beat the attaché mercilessly. Five or six other tax drivers then joined the attack on the attaché, who by then was bleeding profusely and (as later determined) suffering from a broken leg. Apparently fearing for the attaché's life, the taxi driver took him to the police station after going through Custom Control, which did nothing to provide assistance to the injured attaché. The attaché was pulled from the taxi and thrown to the ground in front of the police station. After about fifteen minutes, he was taken to a local hospital and left waiting in the emergency room without care. The Consul from the French Consulate in Kobe eventually came to the local hospital and took the attaché to the International Hospital in Kobe for treatment.

As dean of the Diplomatic Corps in Tokyo, Grew wrote a letter of protest to Matsuoka which provided details of the incident. He pointed out that the experience of the French attaché was not unique. There were, said Grew, "other recent cases of bodily attacks or of insulting behavior on the part of

Japanese nationals against members of the Diplomatic Corps...." The Ambassador never received any satisfactory response to his complaint. But the incident with the French attaché confirmed that, however good his relations with the Foreign Minister, the American ambassador could not count on Matsuoka to facilitate an improvement in Japanese-American relations. Quite the contrary. The Foreign Minister proved to be a major impediment to any improvement.

CHAPTER 8

The Overture

Billy Hull was a lucky man. He was relatively small, weighing around one hundred forty pounds. And he was feisty. "Nervy as a tomcat," it was said, with a hot temper that would be inherited by his third son. Although living in Tennessee—which had seceded from the Union at the start of the Civil War—Billy was part of a group of Union bushwhackers who raided rebel farms on the northern border. After one of the raids, Billy got into an argument with Jim Stepp, another member of the group, over a rifle that Billy had snagged from a rebel farm. Stepp was not happy about the turn of events. He wanted the rifle for himself, and people in the back country of northern Tennessee were not always patient in settling disputes. So Stepp persuaded Riley Pikes, another member of the gang who was described as "slow-witted," to take care of the situation.

Pikes found Billy and a friend at the home of their neighbor, Cindy Lovelace. Pikes apparently made no effort to resolve the matter amicably. He just started firing his gun. The friend was killed instantly. The bullet fired at Billy entered his face between his nose and his right eye and exited the back of his head. As Billy lay prostrate on the ground, Pikes approached him with an obvious intent to fire again to make sure that Billy never got up. Cindy then intervened. She threw her apron over Billy's head and yelled at Pikes, "Lord a' mercy, don't shoot him again. He's dead now." Pikes relented and rode away.

In fact, Billy was not dead, and in time he recovered (although he did lose sight in his right eye and, as his son later remembered, "the wound never healed, keeping him in constant misery"). It did not take Billy long to learn that Stepp was the one who had instigated the attack, and Billy meant to get his revenge. He tracked Stepp down to a farm in Kentucky and found him sitting on a fence. When Stepp saw his former comrade, he tried to be friendly. "Why, hello, Billy," he said. But Billy was in no mood for talking. As Stepp started to run away, Billy pulled a pistol from a holster below his armpit and shot the fleeing bushwhacker. And then—no doubt remembering his own experience—Billy walked up to the fallen man and shot him again to make sure that he was dead.

Billy returned to Tennessee but never had to worry about prosecution under the law. Justice had been served. "He only did what any real person would," his son later said. "Everyone thought well of him for it."

The incident occurred before Cordell Hull was born on October 2, 1871. But his father's perspective and persistence were long remembered. The story was recounted in the opening pages of the *Memoirs* Cordell wrote in the 1940s, and Billy's son was capable of invoking the same mantra in dealing with issues that confronted him as Secretary of State: never forget, and never forgive. It was an approach that surfaced even when Cordell was discussing a settlement agreement with Japanese representatives in 1941.

Although he understood the value of reaching a mutually-satisfactory agreement with the Japanese, Hull could never get beyond his long-held notion that the Japanese were "one of the worst international desperados within the memory of man." To his mind, "it is the principal business of a desperado—whether a nation or an individual—to fight." And so he never really thought the Japanese were sincere in their ostensible effort to reach a settlement agreement with the United States. "I felt the Japs, as I say," he told the congressional committee investigating the Pearl Harbor attack, "were over here for the single purpose of inducing us to surrender our policies and principles and let her policy of war and conquest and so on continue intact."

Japan's Foreign Minister was the object of particular scorn. Hull had long regarded Matsuoka Yosuke as being "as crooked as a basket of fishhooks." In one of his meetings with the new Japanese ambassador in the spring of 1941, Hull said that "Matsuoka and others in his country have been talking loudly and acting aggressively" and that "such conduct and action were in the opposite direction of the entire spirit" of Japan's proposals. On another occasion, Hull told the Japanese ambassador that he would have "real difficulty to persuade even my associates of the absolute dependability of Matsuoka's acts and utterances." And at a later point, Hull told the Japanese ambassador that Matsuoka had been "more or less offensive in his references to this country" during a meeting with Ambassador Grew.

With this focus on Matsuoka, Hull should have been pleased—and more receptive to discussions of settlement—when Matsuoka was forced to resign from the Japanese cabinet in July 1941 because of his vigorous opposition to improved relations with the United States. But the Secretary of State could not let the Japanese representatives forget that Matsuoka had been a source of irritation and distrust during the early months of the discussions. And so, as those discussions continued through the summer and fall of 1941, Hull could not resist invoking Matsuoka's name—even though the man was no longer a part of Japan's decision-making apparatus. At the end of August 1941, Hull reminded the Japanese ambassador that "the war element" in Japan, "seemingly led by Matsuoka," had been "in favor of going forward with force on a program of unlimited expansion to establish the so-called 'new order.'" Less than a week later, Hull told the Japanese ambassador that "Mr. Matsuoka kept reasserting gratuitously Japan's alignment with the Axis" and that, "unless something was done to counteract the effect upon the American people, it might prove [to be] a source of serious embarrassment to the President...." And in October 1941, Hull again reminded the Japanese ambassador that, in earlier months, "Mr. Matsuoka was making public statements of a character inconsistent with the spirit" of their discussions.

Never once in these discussions—even when he and his staff repeatedly asked the Japanese representatives for evidence of Japan's good intentions—did the Secretary of State acknowledge what his ambassador in Tokyo had told him. The departure of Matsuoka, said Grew in a telegram to Hull on July 19, 1941, "removes from the Cabinet a Nazi-Fascist tinge which has proved fundamentally unacceptable to the Japanese nation." It was an obvious conclusion reported in the press as well. "[T]he elimination of Yosuke

Matsuoka," said the *New York Times* in an article on July 19, 1941, "is expected to eliminate the belligerent overtones that featured his diplomacy, especially after his return from Europe, thereby improving the diplomatic atmosphere between Japan and the United States and Britain, perchance opening up possibilities of understanding and even rapprochement."

The significance of Matsuoka's departure may have been clear to others but not to the Secretary of State. His world was one of unforgiving moral judgments, a place where precepts could not be clouded by the nuances of human relations. Nor was there any room for doubt. One can search in vain through Hull's *Memoirs* for any expression of regret for a mistake made in any decision or action on any matter relating to Japan. (He did, however, confess error as a member of his high school's debating society. "In my first effort to speak before this [debating] society," Hull recalled, "I was so excited that I remained completely speechless and sat down without having uttered a word.")

It was all a product, at least to some extent, of Hull's upbringing amidst the lingering haze and the smell of hickory trees in the foothills of the Cumberland Mountains in northern Tennessee. Billy Hull had relocated there after the Civil War and married a woman named Elizabeth Riley. She bore him five sons, and none of them took to learning the way Cordell did.

Elizabeth was a major influence on Cordell's education. She required all of her sons "to read the Bible as much as possible, and she herself read it constantly." Billy was a factor as well. He was nothing if not industrious. He had a moonshine business for a short time and then found considerable financial success in "timbering."

Cordell had been born in a small log cabin in Byrdstown, which his father rented and which may—or may not—have had glass windows. (Hull could not remember, but he did recall that none of his neighbors had glass windows—only holes in the walls with shutters to keep out the winter cold.) As his business prospered, Billy moved the family to a larger home that he had purchased in a nearby community. Like Elizabeth, Billy believed that education would be an important asset for his children's futures. So he hired a teacher to provide instruction in the winter and early spring months when the children were not needed on the farm. Cordell was a receptive pupil, and years later he remembered those nights when he "studied by the light of tallow candles made at home."

Billy continued to feed Cordell's hunger for learning. He sent his son to a high school and then to a ten-month course at the Cumberland Law School in Lebanon, Tennessee, in January 1891. By the time Cordell completed the course, he had already established a name for himself as a budding politician, having been selected as the chairman of the Democratic Executive Committee for Clay County in the summer of 1890 when he was not even twenty years old. That experience provided the foundation for his first victorious political campaign, and a month after his twenty-first birthday, the young lawyer was elected to the Tennessee State Legislature.

Hull's political career was temporarily interrupted by the Spanish-American War in 1898. Fueled by patriotic fervor, he organized a company of volunteers from Clay County that was sent to Cuba. He saw no combat, but he did learn some Spanish and also decided (for reasons he never explained) to give up poker before he returned home in May 1899.

In 1903, Hull was appointed by the Governor to fill the remaining term of a retiring judge, and the next year he was elected a circuit judge in his own name. That was followed by an election to the United States House of Representatives in 1906. The young Tennessean held that seat continuously until 1931 except for two years after the landslide election of Republican presidential candidate Warren G. Harding in 1920.

Hull quickly established a name for himself in Congress. He pushed for income tax legislation, and in 1913 (after the ratification of the sixteenth amendment to the Constitution), he became a principal draftsman of the law creating the first regulatory framework for federal income taxation. That focus on income tax legislation was supplemented by an interest in abolishing protective tariffs which raised the prices of imports from other countries. Hull called protective tariffs the "king of evils" because, in his view, they inhibited free trade and undermined consumer well-being. It was an interest that never subsided over his many years in Congress. He was constantly telling colleagues that protective tariffs fostered "economic wars," which in turn were "the germs of real wars."

The boy from Tennessee had made a name for himself. And so, when he lost his re-election bid in 1920, the Democratic National Committee elected him as its chairman. The position not only provided a platform for Hull to remain in national politics and facilitate his return to Congress in

1922; it also enabled him to strengthen his relationship with the Democratic Party's vice presidential nominee in 1920: Franklin D. Roosevelt.

As he struggled with polio and his own return to national politics, Roosevelt found in Hull a sympathetic listener. The two men saw each other frequently, usually when Roosevelt made a stop in Washington on his way to and from Warm Springs, Georgia, for treatment. In those discussions, they collaborated on the future of their party. Hull was the Chairman of the 1924 Democratic Convention in New York when Roosevelt made his "Happy Warrior" speech in support of the presidential candidacy of New York Governor Al Smith, and in 1928, Roosevelt told associates that he thought the fifty-seven-year-old congressman from Tennessee would be a good vice presidential candidate. "I am old fashioned enough to believe," said Roosevelt, "that the nominee for Vice President should be chosen with the thought that the Almighty might call on him to succeed to the presidency, and Hull would make a fine President."

Hull was elected to the United States Senate in 1930 and then worked diligently for Roosevelt's election as President in 1932. The President-elect (who had chosen House Speaker John Nance Garner III as his running mate) was no doubt appreciative. More than that, Roosevelt understood the value of including Hull in his cabinet as Secretary of State. The Tennessee Senator had not only established a reputation as an expert in international trade; he was also a political force from the South, which was no small matter for a President interested in good relations with a Congress dominated by senators and representatives from the same region.

Roosevelt had Louis B. Wehle, a political associate and nephew of Supreme Court Justice Louis D. Brandeis, make an inquiry with Hull about his interest in the position. Although Hull made no mention of the inquiry in his *Memoirs*, Wehle remembered that the Tennessee Senator's immediate reaction to the inquiry was one of resentment—not because of the proposed appointment but because of the lack of communication from Roosevelt. The President-elect, said Hull, had not shown any gratitude for the Senator's considerable labors on his behalf. But whatever disappointment Hull harbored was soon eclipsed by Roosevelt himself. He offered Hull the appointment as Secretary of State at a January 1933 meeting in the Mayflower Hotel in Washington, where the President-elect had stopped on another trip from New York to Warm Springs, Georgia.

The sixty-one-year-old Tennessee Senator had an appearance tailored to the position. Standing about six feet tall on a lean frame, his face had angular features, thin lips, deeply-set eyes punctuated by dark bushy eyebrows, and a receding hairline with short white hair. That aristocratic bearing was complemented by the black-trimmed pince-nez glasses with a black ribbon that he used for reading. But the majestic profile masked problems that could not be ignored.

The first issue concerned the social obligations of a Secretary of State. As *New York Times* columnist Arthur Krock reminded Hull, a Secretary of State needed a home suitable for large-scale entertainment. That was a matter of some concern for the Tennessee Senator. He was a fairly wealthy man by now, having received an inheritance in 1924 from his father of almost $300,000 (an enormous sum in those pre-Depression days). But he was then living in a modest hotel with his wife Frances. It was an arrangement that suited his wife because, as Hull told Krock, Frances "did not want to cope with a large house...."

Hull's deference to his wife was no surprise. Frances was the daughter of Isaac Witz, a banker from Staunton, Virginia whose roots could be traced back to an Austrian Jewish family (although Frances grew up attending an Episcopalian church, and Hull was not one to trumpet his wife's Jewish heritage). Her first husband had disappeared under mysterious circumstances during a business trip to East Asia. She and Cordell subsequently struck up a relationship in Washington, and they were married in November 1917. They had no children, but Cordell valued their relationship, saying in his *Memoirs* that Frances had given him "every help" in his public life "as well as deep contentment at home." The affection was reciprocal, and to accommodate her husband's new status, Frances agreed to relocate their home to a much larger apartment in the more elegant Carlton Hotel on 16th Street, which was only a few blocks from the White House.

The other problem was not so easily solved. Hull's health had never been robust. Upon meeting him in February 1933, outgoing Secretary of State Henry L. Stimson recorded in his diary that he "got a rather discouraging impression of his vitality and vigor." As a teenager in Tennessee, Cordell had to discontinue his study of the law with a local attorney because of health issues. In 1930, he felt compelled to check with his physician to determine whether his "uncertain state of health" would permit him to run for the Senate. The physician gave his approval, but that could not stem the tide of ailments. In early 1932, Hull's physician diagnosed a mild case of diabetes. And later that year the physician diagnosed the presence of tuberculosis in both of his lungs (a diagnosis that would not be disclosed to the public during Hull's tenure as Secretary of State). It was not enough to dissuade him from accepting Roosevelt's appointment, but Hull could not escape the consequences. Throughout his almost twelve years as Secretary of State, the Tennessee politician was subject to periodic bouts of severe coughing, high fever, and chills, which often required him to be bedridden for weeks at a time.

Hull may have been able to withhold information about these health issues from the public, but the President had to be aware of them to some extent, if only because of Hull's periodic absences from the office and his corresponding inability to attend meetings. Still, the relationship with Roosevelt appeared to start off on a good foot. As Hull prepared to sail to London in June 1933 for a conference on international monetary affairs, the new President penned him a note which said, "I want you to know once more of my affectionate regard for and confidence in you."

For his part, Hull's *Memoirs*—written after Roosevelt's death—conveyed only glowing memories of his relationship with the President. "Never an unfriendly word passed between the President and me during my twelve years in the State Department," Hull wrote. However positive, the remark was of only limited significance. It was a rare occasion for the ever-buoyant and charming President to criticize anyone directly. But Hull's post-war commendations for Roosevelt were not confined to the friendly nature of their conversations. The President, Hull added, afforded him a "full share in formulating and carrying out foreign policy" and, "with rare exceptions, [he] could scarcely have been more considerate toward me as Secretary of State throughout my twelve years in that office."

The truth was very different. Roosevelt often sidestepped his Secretary of State, and it was a matter of constant consternation to Hull. The President was prone to call upon others to handle foreign policy assignments in numerous situations. Part of it was undoubtedly Roosevelt's inclination to disregard lines of bureaucratic authority in selecting the right person for a particular task. Stimson, who later became Roosevelt's Secretary of War, referred to it as the "inherently disorderly nature" of the Roosevelt administration. But another part of it surely was Roosevelt's perception of Hull's temperament.

The Secretary of State was a very cautious decision-maker. It took him about a month to decide whether to accept the appointment as Secretary of State. Reaching conclusions on matters of public policy could take much longer. He scheduled long and often inconclusive meetings with his staff, and the impact on the pace of decision-making was apparent. At one point in 1937, Roosevelt mentioned to Adolf Berle, Jr.—a Columbia Law School professor who had been a member of Roosevelt's Brains Trust during the 1932 campaign—that the Secretary of State "was magnificent in principle but timid." At a later point, Roosevelt told Secretary of the Treasury Henry Morgenthau, Jr., that "Hull was slow" (although he "prepared his facts very carefully"). It was a trait noticed by other members of the administration as well. Breckinridge Long, a friend of Roosevelt's and an Assistant Secretary of State, said that Hull was "wary, slow to conclusion." Interior Secretary Harold Ickes shared that view. After Roosevelt suggested to Ickes in June 1941 that he give Hull three or four days to respond to a request, Ickes recorded in his diary, "If Hull moves that fast, it will be a new speed record for him."

The President may have accepted Hull's cautious approach to making decisions in some situations, but it did not stop Roosevelt from poking fun at Hull's manner of speech. The Secretary of State had a high, raspy voice with a pronounced lisp which resulted in his "r's" sounding like "w's." A favorite Washington rendition of a Hull statement on free trade was, "We must eliminate these twade baa-yuhs heah, theah, and ev-ywheah." The lisp would be that much more pronounced during one of Hull's tirades or when he became exercised over any particular matter. Those occasions—which were not infrequent—could result in a torrent of loud and colorful language that was unusual, if not unique, among the Roosevelt Cabinet members. "When the Secretary of State really gets wrought up," said syndicated columnist Drew Pearson in 1941, "he lets loose with the most vitriolic tongue-lashing of anyone in the Roosevelt Administration. All the feudal instincts of the Tennessee mountains come to the surface."

It was a display that Roosevelt witnessed more than once. "Hull was in a 'Chwist' mood today," he told his secretary Grace Tully after one meeting with the Secretary of State, "and the old boy was certainly good." And after Hull gave an excited discourse on Japan at a Cabinet meeting in

November 1941, the President said privately to Labor Secretary Frances Perkins (whom he had known since his days as Governor of New York), "If Cordell says, 'Oh Chwist' again, I'm going to scream with laughter. I can't stand profanity with a lisp."

Hull gave no hint in his *Memoirs* that he knew of the President's willingness to mock the Secretary of State's speech. But he certainly knew that Roosevelt was prepared to bypass him on matters of foreign policy. One matter concerned American policy upon the fall of France in June 1940. In dealing with the situation, the President had communicated directly with Bill Bullitt, the American ambassador to France. It was an approach that did not sit well with the Secretary of State. Hull told Henry A. Wallace, then Secretary of Agriculture (and soon to be Vice President), that Roosevelt had treated him "abominably" by dealing directly with Bullitt and that "he has been kicked around about all he can stand."

Another situation involved Under Secretary of State Sumner Welles. In January 1940, Roosevelt summoned Welles to the White House and told him that no stone should be left unturned in the effort to avoid American involvement in the European war. He therefore decided that someone should be sent as an American emissary to visit with the heads of state of England, France, Germany, and Italy, and that someone was the Under Secretary of State. Welles was certainly well qualified to undertake the mission, but the decision did not sit well with Welles's superior. Hull bitterly complained to Jim Farley, the United States Postmaster General and the chairman of the Democratic National Committee, "I was never even consulted on the Welles trip to Europe."

Another disturbing incident occurred during the war after the Pearl Harbor attack. Roosevelt asked Treasury Secretary Morgenthau—but not Hull—to accompany him to Quebec in September 1944 to discuss post-war planning with British Prime Minister Winston Churchill. Hull remarked to Arthur Krock shortly afterwards "that he could not understand why the President 'remained aloof from him and always had someone between them in matters of foreign policy.'" Frances was even more pointed in her criticism of Roosevelt when she discussed the Quebec conference with Krock a few weeks later. Her husband, said Frances, "could not understand how the President could conduct matters of such grave import, and foreign affairs in particular, with such irresponsibility and deviousness."

However much Roosevelt's approach to decision-making may have irked Hull, it was of no moment to Joe Grew as he tried to facilitate an agreement with Japan in 1941 to avoid an armed conflict. The American ambassador was far more concerned with the Secretary of State's mindset than his personal pique. And on that score, the American ambassador could not help but feel frustrated.

Grew had been dealing with Hull for almost eight years by the beginning of 1941. In accordance with tradition, he had submitted his resignation after Roosevelt's election to a third term in November 1940. On January 5, 1941, he received a telegram from Hull saying that Roosevelt was "eminently satisfied" with Grew's service and wished him to continue as ambassador. Grew referenced the telegram in his diary and, mindful of the United States's deteriorating relationship with Japan, added, "So another four years—maybe."

Grew knew that, as in the past, one of the challenges he would face in the coming months would be the Secretary of State's perspective. He was well acquainted with Hull's unwavering predilection for abstract principles. It was an approach that sometimes conflicted with Grew's effort to find pragmatic solutions to problems. Gene Dooman shared Grew's perspective. The Embassy Counselor later said that he had "the greatest respect" and "great affection" for Hull. But he believed that the Secretary of State failed to appreciate "the elements which motivated other nations" and also lacked the "flexibility" required for an effective Secretary of State.

There was perhaps no better example of Hull's inflexibility than the fate of the 937 Jewish refugees on the SS *St. Louis* in the spring of 1939 (the infamous "Voyage of the Damned"). When Cuba (the chosen destination) refused to admit the German refugees, frantic efforts were initiated to see if there was a way to admit the refugees to the United States or one of its territories. Henry Morgenthau, Jr. placed a call to the Secretary of State on the afternoon of June 5, 1939 to explore that possibility. It was a situation that cried out for an imaginative solution that would enable the United States to save the refugees without doing violence to American immigration laws.

That kind of flexible approach was ill-suited to the Secretary of State. He explained to the Treasury Secretary that it was "a matter primarily between...[t]he Cuban Government and these people" and that there was nothing he could do under the law to allow the ship to dock in the United

States or to accept the refugees. Hull added that he could not even grant the refugees tourist visas to disembark on the Virgin Islands because each refugee had to have "a definite home where they were coming from and in a situation to return to"—a comment of tragic irony because many of the refugees had been expelled from concentration camps on the promise that they would never return to Germany, and others were forced to leave homes that had been confiscated by the Nazis.

Grew had tried to warn Hull on many occasions that an inflexible policy would not succeed in overcoming the barriers that separated the United States and Japan. As early as December 1939, he had urged Hull to take "a realistic and constructive" approach rather than one based on "complete intransigence." The appeal from the Ambassador did not appear to have any impact. The Japanese representatives encountered that same rigid adherence to principles in their many meetings with the Secretary of State in 1941. To Hull, it was a matter of pride that could not be abandoned. In one of their last discussions in November 1941, the Japanese representatives struggled to find some way to elicit a favorable response from Hull that would facilitate their professed desire for an agreement. Hull was not moved, telling the Japanese representatives "that all we can do is to stand firm on our basic principles."

It was a response that could have been predicted from Hull's first days in office. One State Department colleague observed in those early days that, "when confronted with the obstacles and difficulties to his good intentions, [the Secretary of State] does not analyze them and figure out ways and means of licking them—but *preaches* merely against them." Still, the ever-optimistic Grew had reason to hope in early 1941 that there might be an opportunity to overcome the Secretary of State's steadfast reliance on honored principles.

The hope emerged from a most unlikely source. Bishop James E. Walsh was the forty-nine-year-old Superior General of the Catholic Foreign Mission Society of America at Maryknoll, New York, and Vicar General Father James M. Drought, age forty-four, was his second-in-command. The two men had spent about a month in Japan at the end of 1940 and the beginning of 1941. On the basis of conversations with unidentified sources in Japan (whom Stanley Hornbeck later referred to collectively as "John Doe" or the "John Doe associates"), the two priests believed that Japan would be receptive to a new agreement with the United States that would resolve all differences between the two countries. Upon their return to the United States, the two clergymen contacted Frank Walker, a fellow Catholic who was then serving as Postmaster General in Roosevelt's Cabinet. They were hopeful that Walker could gain them an audience with the President to discuss their proposal. The Postmaster General did not disappoint.

The two priests met with the President in the White House on the morning of January 23, 1941. In addition to Walker, Hull was also present. Fifteen minutes had been allocated for the meeting, but it lasted for almost one and a half hours.

As reflected in a memorandum they gave to the President at the meeting, the two priests explained to Roosevelt and his two Cabinet officers that American economic pressure and defense preparations "have been so politically successful that the Japanese would now welcome an opportunity" to alter their government's course and enter into an agreement with the United States to resolve outstanding issues. The memorandum identified three basic issues to be addressed in the agreement: Japan's alliance with Germany and Italy under the Tripartite Pact, the resolution of the China Incident, and the establishment of a new economic relationship that would encompass a "complete Open Door" policy. Speed, however, was essential. The Japanese officials with whom the priests had spoken said that "the Fascist element" would take control of the government if no agreement were reached before March or April. Another condition was secrecy. Japan's long history of political assassinations lurked in the background. Japanese authorities, the priests added, "dare not admit their readiness" to negotiate with the United States for fear that their lives would be in peril. The priests closed by proposing that Roosevelt select a representative, "with the full knowledge of Mr. Grew," to work out the agreement "with the utmost speed and secrecy."

A few days later, Roosevelt received another memorandum that Walsh had forwarded to Walker which referenced belligerent statements being made by Japanese leaders about the United States. Those statements were not to be taken at face value, said the memorandum. The "harsh talk" was "for home consumption" to prevent the Japanese leaders from being "supplanted by a group of Extremists." Roosevelt forwarded the memo to Hull with a note asking, "What shall I do next?"

On February 5, 1941, Hull forwarded to the President a memorandum under his signature drafted by Hornbeck and Max Hamilton, the Chief of the Far Eastern Division. As Hornbeck later told Grew, he had "great misgivings" about any new agreement with Japan, and that perspective was reflected in the memo Hull gave the President. The focus was the proposal submitted by the two Maryknoll clergymen. "I am skeptical," the memo said, "whether the plan offered is a practical one at this time. It seems to me," the memo continued, "that there is little or no likelihood that the Japanese Government and the Japanese people would in good faith accept any such arrangement at this stage." Hull separately told Roosevelt "there was not one chance of success in twenty or one in fifty or even one in a hundred." In fact, it is difficult to believe that Hull thought there was any chance of success.

Part of Hull's pessimism was dictated by his view of "Japan's past and present record." As the Secretary of State told *New York Times* columnist Arthur Krock a few days after the Pearl Harbor attack, "he had made up his mind in 1934 that Japan was determined to be the overlord of Asia, as Hitler of Europe, that their alliance was natural and inevitable, [and] that he never doubted" that Japan was destined to be in "common cause and action in war."

The absence of any realistic possibility of reaching an agreement also reflected Hull's view of what the agreement would have to include. Japan would have to renounce or otherwise separate itself from the Tripartite Pact that it had entered into with Germany and Italy; there would have to be a resolution of the China Incident satisfactory to China as well as the United States (with the almost certain removal of Japan's one million troops from her Asian neighbor); and there would have to be an unqualified commitment by Japan to honor the prior Open Door policy on free trade in China. Hull was prepared to work for an agreement which included those provisions, and Joe Ballantine—the head of the State Department's Japan Desk and the staff member who worked most closely with Hull in the discussions—later said that they "were sincerely and earnestly desirous of reaching agreement."

That was a tall order under any circumstance, but it was especially so for someone like Hull who had dark visions of Japan's history and character. As Hull later told Arthur Krock, he "was never an appeaser of Japan," and he had "little hope of a peaceful adjustment of the Pacific problems."

In other circumstances, it would have been relatively easy to determine whether Japan was or was not prepared to enter into an agreement that would be acceptable to the Secretary of State. Drafts could have been exchanged between the parties, the State Department could have included precise language in the drafts which reflected Hull's positions on the issues, and the Japanese response would have given Hull and his staff a clear idea on whether there was a basis to move forward. To facilitate matters, Hull could have involved Grew. The American ambassador had been in Tokyo for nine years, he knew virtually all of the country's principal decision-makers, and he had a good fix on Japanese psychology. He was therefore in a position to advise Hull on negotiating strategies and proposals. And he could have explained the American perspective to Japanese leaders as well, if not better, than any other American.

Hull did in fact inform Grew about developments at various points in the ensuing discussions, but it was a rare occasion when the Secretary of State asked his ambassador for advice—or even responded to recommendations that Grew felt free to convey. The Secretary of State's failure to fully integrate his ambassador into the decision-making process was not entirely surprising. From Hull's perspective, there was really little need to involve Joe Grew. Other, more paramount, considerations were at stake.

As a starting point, the United States and its allies were not prepared to defend themselves in the Pacific. "We had in the forefront of our minds," Hull recounted in his *Memoirs*, "the advice repeatedly given us by our highest military officers that they needed time to prepare the defense vital to ourselves as well as to the countries resisting aggression." The British and the Dutch—who had valuable interests in the Pacific—likewise advised Hull that "they were dangerously vulnerable in the Far East."

The vulnerability of the United States in the Pacific reflected, in part, the enormous resources that the United States was providing to Great Britain for its defense against Nazi attacks. As Hull told Krock almost immediately after the Pearl Harbor attack, the Navy "had urged him to gain as much time as possible, informing him that they could not be prepared for a long time for a war with Japan in view of our Atlantic commitments to Britain." That fear of a war in the Pacific also led Roosevelt to resist pressure from other Cabinet members who wanted the President to be more aggressive in his dealings with Japan. "It is terribly important for the control of the

Atlantic for us to help to keep peace in the Pacific," he told Interior Secretary Harold Ickes on July 1, 1941. "I simply have not got enough Navy to go round—and every little episode in the Pacific means fewer ships in the Atlantic." And so, as Hull later told the congressional committee investigating the Pearl Harbor Attack, he "constantly discussed with the President the question of gaining as much time as possible, and we had the subject very much in mind throughout the conversations with the Japanese."

Given the need for time to allow the United States and its allies to enlarge their defense arsenals, Hull did not want to push for an early determination whether the Japanese might be amenable to the kind of agreement he had in mind. An early determination could reveal what Hull expected: that there was no basis for agreement. That conclusion could in turn accelerate the point of armed conflict and force a defense of interests in the Pacific before the United States and its allies were ready. As Hull told the congressional committee investigating the Pearl Harbor attack, "I had been striving for months to avoid a showdown with Japan, and to explore every possible avenue for averting or delaying war between the United States and Japan."

One way to pursue that strategy was to avoid the submission of drafts that provided specific language delineating the American positions. "Our whole effort," said Joe Ballantine, "was to avoid making any original drafts of our own, but merely to reword their drafts." Part of the motivation for that approach was to clarify ambiguities in the language used by the Japanese. But the approach also had the added—and critical—benefit of dragging out the conversations.

Other tactics provided similar benefits. Hull or his staff would pepper the Japanese representatives with questions about their proposals and ask them to re-submit drafts with more precise language, sometimes before Hull and his advisors had even examined the particular proposal. At other times, Hull and his staff offered open-ended suggestions that left the Japanese leaders unsure of exactly what the Americans had in mind.

The absence of specific guidance from the State Department in those situations may have been frustrating to the Japanese representatives, but it served the State Department's overriding goal to delay any final resolution. That goal was also served by repeated requests from Hull and his staff for evidence of Japan's good intentions. At one point, Hull told the Japanese ambassador that he had "reluctantly come to the conclusion that this

Government must await some clearer indication than has yet been given that the Japanese Government as a whole desires to pursue courses of peace...." At another point, Ballantine told the Japanese representatives that the State Department "should have some clearer indication than the Japanese Government has yet given us of its peaceful intentions in order to counteract the effect of previous manifestations of Japanese policy." Even the President—reading a statement prepared by the State Department—told the Japanese ambassador in August 1941 (after Matsuoka had resigned) that Japan needed to "furnish a clearer statement than has yet been furnished as to its present attitude and plans."

Another part of the strategy for delay was to make it clear to the Japanese representatives that none of the discussions amounted to "negotiations." Only if the parties reached an *agreement* on preliminary matters would they proceed—and take the time—to engage in "negotiations." As Hull explained in one of his first discussions with the Japanese ambassador in April 1941, he was prepared to proceed "with certain preliminary discussions with a view to ascertaining whether there is a basis for negotiations," but that, "for the purpose of this preliminary discussion, there would really be no occasion for either side to present officially any completed documents." And so, as the discussions crawled along for months, any and every documented proposal that the State Department gave to the Japanese representatives was labeled "Unofficial, Exploratory and Without Commitment." Never did Hull agree that he and the Japanese representatives had entered into "negotiations."

The strategy did provide the delay that Roosevelt and Hull desired. But it was not without a cost. That point was pressed on Hull by Arthur Krock in the conversation they had shortly after the Pearl Harbor attack. "Well," said the *New York Times* columnist, "we were playing for time until we could be strong enough to smash the Japs, and they found it out and smashed us first. Isn't that so?" Hull responded in the affirmative.

Long before then, Hull had decided that he could not conduct any meaningful discussions with the John Doe Associates through the two Maryknoll clergymen. Instead, the Secretary of State wanted to deal directly with a Japanese official designated by the Japanese Government. As luck would have it, the new Japanese ambassador left Tokyo for the United States on January 23, 1941—the very day on which Walsh and Drought met with

Roosevelt and his Cabinet officers. It should have been an auspicious development—the new ambassador was someone well known to Grew and, beyond that, someone who had a genuine interest in better relations with the United States.

As time would tell, that was not enough.

CHAPTER 9

The New Ambassador

I t should have been a time of unspoiled gratification. Vice Admiral
Nomura Kichisaburo was in a reviewing stand in Shanghai with other
Japanese dignitaries to watch a parade of Japanese soldiers at the end of
April in 1932. It was not a routine occasion. Japan was about to sign a truce
to signal the end of months of hostilities which had resulted in the Japanese
repulsion of a formidable Chinese military force. As in many clashes
between Japan and China, the precipitating events were mired in conflicting
accounts. Some said the source of the hostilities was a spontaneous attack
by a mob of Chinese citizens on Japanese monks while others said that the
Japanese engineered the attack to create a pretext for an armed conflict.
Whatever the cause, matters quickly escalated into open combat between
Chinese and Japanese troops.

As Commander-in-Chief of Japan's Third Fleet in Shanghai, Nomura
had principal responsibility for protecting Japan's position. It was an assignment of considerable importance. Located in the Yangtze River Delta on the
east coast of China, Shanghai had long been a hub of international commerce, and the city's International Settlement included substantial represen-
tation from Japan, the United States, and other countries, including Great
Britain. Japan could not afford the commercial and military consequences

if it were expelled from Shanghai—and the other countries did not want to have their vested interests compromised by continued fighting.

Nomura's appointment as the Third Fleet commander in February 1932 had been welcomed by the United States, which had sent a cruiser, the USS *Houston*, and other ships to the waterways of Shanghai to protect American interests. In a telephone conversation shortly after Nomura's appointment, Secretary of State Henry Stimson advised Britain's Foreign Secretary that the United States Navy had a "very high opinion" of the new commander as a "liberal man" and that the State Department expected Nomura to exercise a "very restraining and conservative influence" on Japanese forces in Shanghai.

The commendations accorded the fifty-four-year-old Vice Admiral were not surprising. Nomura had spent three years as the naval attaché in the Japanese Embassy in Washington during Woodrow Wilson's administration. Upon Nomura's departure in June 1918, Navy Secretary Josephus Daniels commented that the Japanese attaché was an officer of "high professional ability" who had been of "great value" to the United States during the Great War (when Japan had been on the same side as the United States). Daniels' high regard for Nomura was shared by his Assistant Secretary, Franklin D. Roosevelt.

As the Embassy's naval attaché, Nomura was charged with evaluating American naval capabilities and assessing American attitudes toward Japan. The youthful Assistant Secretary was a valuable resource for the embassy officer. The two men would meet often—sometimes in Roosevelt's office, at other times at the exclusive Metropolitan Club (where Roosevelt was a member), and sometimes even at Roosevelt's residence in Washington. For his part, Nomura regarded Roosevelt as a "skillful" bureaucrat who was "entirely conversant with naval matters."

As in the case of his later appointment as Commander-in-Chief of the Third Fleet, Nomura's selection as the Embassy's naval attaché was not a matter of happenstance. It was the product of ambition and achievement a long time in the making. And it was all the more remarkable in light of Nomura's origins.

Nomura Kichisaburo had been born in Wakayama City in a rural area of southern Japan in December 1877. His father, Fukuda Zensaburo, was a member of the elite samurai class of warriors who had long been Japan's only recognized armed force. Their status declined when the government under Emperor Meiji decided to abolish the class system of the feudal era and create a modern army in 1873. Fukuda would forever be a member of that samurai class, but he soon lost the means to provide a comfortable life for his family.

Despite the change in his father's fortunes, Kichisaburo aspired to continue the family's military tradition and eventually secured an appointment at the Naval Academy at Etajima. Shortly afterwards, the teenager was adopted by the more affluent Nomura family, whose father was also a member of the samurai class and whose mother was the sister of Kichisaburo's birth mother. Adoptions of that kind were common in nineteenth century Japan, and however much he may have cared for his family, the event did not seem to affect Nomura's well-being.

After finishing second in his class at the Naval Academy, Nomura received assignments that took him to embassies and naval vessels in Austria, China, and Germany as well as the United States. Those assignments, coupled with his pleasant personality, made him a favorite in Japan's naval bureaucracy. In 1922, he was promoted to Rear Admiral and asked to be a tutor for twenty-one-year-old Crown Prince Hirohito, who had been appointed as regent for his ailing father.

Nomura had an imposing appearance that suited his new stature. He was about six feet tall—unusual for Japanese—with a medium build and a round face, closely cropped hair, a small but ready smile, and dark horn-rimmed glasses. With that large presence, Nomura was undoubtedly an easy figure to identify as he sat in the Shanghai reviewing stand on that spring day in 1932. Henri Smith-Hutton, a senior officer on the USS *Houston* (and later to become Grew's naval attaché), was standing about a hundred feet from the reviewing stand and had a vivid recollection of unfolding events. As the attention of Smith-Hutton and the dignitaries was directed to the marching soldiers, a bomb suddenly exploded and reduced the reviewing stand to "shambles." As Smith-Hutton later explained, a Korean nationalist—no doubt disturbed by Japan's policy toward Korea (which had been annexed by Japan in 1910)—had approached the reviewing stand unnoticed and "pushed a bomb close to the center of the group which was taking the review." There were many casualties, and Nomura was one of them. A splinter became lodged in his right eye, and the eye had to be removed. From that point forward, Nomura was forced to resort to an assortment of glass eyes as replacements.

The loss of his eye did not have any adverse impact on Nomura's subsequent naval career. But other factors required him to take an early retirement in 1937 at the age of sixty. He had promoted cordial relations with the United States and had been willing to accept the limitations on Japan's construction of new ships imposed by the 1922 Washington conference and the 1930 London conference. There were many elements in the Navy opposed to those positions, and however impressive his earlier contributions, Nomura could not any advance any further in the naval bureaucracy.

Nomura's perspective and prior experience in the United States became attractive qualities when former Army general Abe Nobuyuki became Prime Minister in August 1939 and needed a new Foreign Minister. Conversations were held, understandings were reached, and Nomura assumed the position in September 1939. His principal objective was to promote better relations with the United States generally and, more specifically, to engineer a new commercial treaty to replace the one that the Roosevelt administration had decided to terminate in July 1939. There were many meetings between Nomura and Grew to explore a new treaty, but the effort ended in failure. It was an unacceptable outcome for Japan's leaders. Nomura, as well as Abe and the rest of his cabinet, were forced to resign in January 1940 when the treaty's termination became effective.

Nomura might have lived the remainder of his life in retirement, but a new ambassador to the United States was needed in the summer of 1940. The new Foreign Minister asked Nomura to come out of retirement to take the position. The vacancy had occurred because of what one diplomat called the "Matsuoka Hurricane," when the newly-appointed Foreign Minister demanded the recall of ambassadors who did not appear to share his view of world affairs.

There were many considerations underlying Matsuoka's preference for the former Navy admiral as the new ambassador to the United States. Selection of Nomura—known for his friendly disposition toward the United States—could, or at least so Matsuoka thought, help deflect the Navy's resistance to the Tripartite Pact that Matsuoka wanted to sign with Germany and Italy. But there was more to it. Matsuoka had continually promoted the Tripartite Pact as a vehicle to discourage the United States from entering the European conflict, and the Foreign Minister needed a capable representative to convey that message to the Roosevelt administration. On that score, there seemed to be no one better qualified than the retired Navy Admiral. He was the one who had developed the friendship with Roosevelt during the Wilson administration. And so he could be the one to ensure the American president's receptivity to Japan's perspective. As Matsuoka told Nomura, "Besides your good self, there is no one who can talk with President Roosevelt over drinks."

Nomura was not persuaded—at least initially. Matsuoka had made a written inquiry to Nomura on August 24, 1940, and then met with him two days later. There were numerous factors to explain Nomura's resistance. Although he had served briefly as Japan's Foreign Minister, he was not an experienced diplomat. Beyond that, Nomura was concerned that the anticipated alliance with Germany would doom any effort to improve relations with the United States. "There is no way," he wrote to Matsuoka, "that we should think there is any chance of adjusting relations with the United States while Japan and Germany are working hand in hand." So Nomura declined the offer.

Matsuoka did not give up. He continued to press the retired admiral to accept the diplomatic post. Nomura's firm convictions were matched by an iron will (not to mention his perception of the Foreign Minister as a "sly fox"). He refused again, citing his concern that, even if he could prevail upon the United States to accept a new relationship with Japan, the bond could be undone by a different cabinet with a different Foreign Minister.

In the face of this unyielding resistance, Matsuoka brought pressure to bear upon Nomura from sources that would be more difficult to turn aside. Navy Vice Minister Toyoda Teijiro—a Nomura friend who would later replace Matsuoka as Foreign Minister—pleaded with his former colleague to accept the position so that Roosevelt would understand the Navy's opposition to war with the United States. And then another Navy admiral implored Nomura's acceptance with words that could not be ignored. "His Majesty," said Admiral Suzuki Kantaro, "desires a compromise in the Japanese-American negotiations" and asks that you accept the position "with its many anxieties" and that you "strive to meet the Imperial will."

Matsuoka telephoned Grew on November 7, 1940, to tell him that Nomura had accepted the ambassadorial post. The American ambassador was pleased with the appointment, recording in his diary that he regarded Nomura "as a man of high personal character" who had the Ambassador's "esteem and respect" and whom Grew believed "to be fundamentally friendly to the United States...." Grew met with the Foreign Minister for tea at Matsuoka's home a couple of days later. Matsuoka—never shy about patting himself on the back—explained that "his determination to persuade Admiral Nomura to accept the post and his final success in overcoming the Admiral's reluctance were eloquent testimony of his own attitude toward the United States."

Grew had to wonder about that attitude when he attended a farewell luncheon for Nomura in January 1941 that was hosted by Matsuoka. The Foreign Minister approached Grew as he was talking to Nomura, expressing his hope that the new ambassador would be able to help "improve American-Japanese relations." Matsuoka overheard the remark and could not resist interjecting. "They certainly couldn't be worse," he said, and then walked away.

Whatever he expected from Nomura, Grew recognized that the new ambassador had at least one shortcoming. After spending about thirty minutes talking with Nomura at another farewell party, the American ambassador concluded that Nomura "is clearly not at home in speaking English." Grew suspected that the failing would affect Nomura's effectiveness in the United States. "I can hardly picture him," said Grew, "in a group of hard-boiled American Senators or Congressmen or newspapermen or officials holding up his end in a discussion."

It was a prescient comment. When he began meeting with the new Japanese ambassador in February 1941, Secretary of State Cordell Hull noticed that Nomura was often a man of few words, prone to "bowing" and what Hull later characterized as a "mirthless chuckle." More importantly, Hull was not sure that the Japanese ambassador fully appreciated everything the Secretary of State was saying to him. "Nomura's command of English," Hull observed, "was so marginal that I frequently doubted whether he understood the points I was making."

It was a matter of no small importance to Hull. Through more than nine months of discussions with Nomura, the Secretary of State would frequently indulge in long-winded discourses on various topics, including Hitler's barbaric policies, the importance of free trade, and the difficulties of resolving the China Incident. (At one point Hull explained to Nomura that Japan's proposal to leave troops in northern China to defend against communists would be no more acceptable to the Chinese population than the placement of "northern troops…in the South after the Civil War" had been to people in the former Confederate States of America—a historical reference that undoubtedly eluded the Japanese ambassador's comprehension.)

Hull wanted—really needed—to make sure that Nomura could follow everything the Secretary of State was saying. After the first few meetings, Hull decided that he needed the assistance of Joe Ballantine, the only foreign service officer, other than his private secretary, whom Hull called by his first name. A tall man with a receding hairline and a pleasant personality, the fifty-two-year-old Ballantine was not only the head of the department's Japan Desk; he was also fluent in Japanese and could therefore clarify matters for Nomura. So Ballantine was asked to attend all of Hull's future meetings with the Japanese ambassador. The assignment, Ballantine later said, was "a very, very wearisome affair."

Most of Hull's meetings with Nomura and other Japanese representatives occurred in the evenings at Hull's apartment, sometimes during the normal work week but on weekends as well. If the meeting was at Hull's apartment, Ballantine would get there around 7:45 p.m. to review matters with Hull, and the meeting would commence around 8 or 8:30 p.m. When the meeting adjourned around 10 p.m. or so, Ballantine would go back to the State Department to write up his notes, which could take a couple of hours. Ballantine would return to the office the following morning at 8:30 to dictate a memorandum of the conversation. He would then remain in the office for the rest of the day to handle whatever responsibilities required his attention. As a result, Ballantine was working about sixteen hours a day almost every day of the week. By the time it all ended on December 7, 1941, said Ballantine, "I was a complete wreck."

The Japanese ambassador appeared to have no inkling of the stress imposed on Ballantine. He was obviously more concerned with understanding the Secretary of State's long-winded expositions and the President's careful comments. Although his fluency in speaking English may have been less than perfect, Nomura's diary indicates that he generally grasped the portent of remarks made to him by Hull and Roosevelt. His first meeting with the President occurred on February 14, 1941. Nomura no doubt hoped that this meeting would be more auspicious than the reception he had been given by the State Department. When the new ambassador reached Washington's Union Station on February 11—after traveling by ship across the Pacific and then by rail across the United States—the representatives from the German and Italian embassies on hand to greet him far outnumbered the solitary protocol officer from the State Department. Nomura met the next day with Hull in his office in the State, War, and Navy Building.

Construction of the five-story building had been completed in 1888, and, at the time, it was reputed to be the largest office building in the world. The front of the building faced Pennsylvania Avenue and was separated from the White House on the east side by a narrow street that later became a parking lot for staff members. The west side of the building bordered on 17th Street. Much of the building was designed by an Austrian, and the exterior appeared to reflect the baroque style of nineteenth-century Austrian and Prussian palaces. The interior reflected the same opulence. The twelve-foot-wide corridors were paved with alternate squares of black slate and white marble, the stairways were made of gray granite, and the balustrades incorporated polished bronze with mahogany hand rails.

Hull's expansive office was located on the second floor in the southwest corner of the south wing, with spacious windows facing the Washington Monument and, in the distance, the Potomac River. His large mahogany desk sat in front of the windows. On the left side of the desk were two phones, one of which was a direct line to the White House. On the right side of the desk was a speaker box that enabled the Secretary to communicate with his staff. The room was populated with bookcases, large engravings, paintings of former presidents, an assortment of chairs and couches, and a stone fireplace on the left side of the room. To the left of the fireplace was a door that connected to a small anteroom used by most visitors. Ambassadors, ministers, and other foreign dignitaries would typically enter from the more formal diplomatic room through an oversized door on the right side of the outer wall.

Nomura, wearing the formal diplomatic attire of striped trousers and a black cutaway coat, walked through that door to meet with Hull on February 12. The Secretary of State, believing that any substantive discussion should await the meeting at the White House two days later, spent only about four minutes with Nomura. The ambassador was ushered out of the office almost before he knew what had happened. The brevity of the visit disturbed Nomura. He later confessed to Bill Castle, the former Under Secretary of State and a Grew friend, that he was "unhappy that Hull had not been able to find any time to have a talk with him."

The Japanese ambassador's meeting with the President lasted much longer. Nomura and Hull, each wearing an overcoat and a hat, walked over to the White House from the State Department shortly before noon. Roosevelt greeted Nomura with his ever-present warmth and charm. The President recalled their friendship during the Wilson administration and said that, despite Nomura's new title, he "proposed to call him Admiral."

Roosevelt, guided by an earlier memo from the State Department, did most of the talking. Grew had already advised Hull that the situation in Southeast Asia in general and Singapore in particular was precarious. Japanese troops and war ships were congregating in strategic locations in or near Indochina. Patience could not be a virtue, Grew had explained, in these situations. "The general anxiety over the worsening relations with the United States, as indicated in my recent contacts with prominent Japanese," Grew had told Hull in a telegram a few weeks earlier, "has been more intense than at any time of my observations during the past eight years in Japan."

Roosevelt's remarks reflected that growing tension. He told Nomura that "the present relations between the two countries are not good" and that they were "deteriorating." Although the American people were "peace-loving," said Roosevelt, "it would be extremely easy" for some incident like the sinking of the *Panay* "to cause an overnight uprising...." The President added that he was glad that Nomura was now here to represent Japan because the two of them could talk in "the friendliest and frankest manner...." On that score, Roosevelt suggested that Nomura spend some time with Hull to "see if our relations could not be improved." In saying that, Roosevelt added that "there is plenty of room in the Pacific for everybody."

Nomura faced a challenge in responding to the President's remarks. The new ambassador had received written instructions from Matsuoka the day before he left Tokyo, but those instructions did little more than direct Nomura to impress upon the President the underlying rationale of Japan's positions and needs. In a meeting with Hirohito that same day, the Emperor admonished the new ambassador "to make peace with the United States at any cost." The problem was that neither Matsuoka's instructions nor

Hirohito's admonition gave Nomura any guidance on the particular agreements to be pursued (and he would not receive any such guidance from Matsuoka until April). So Nomura was not in a position to offer any specific proposal to Roosevelt. He said little more than that he would do his best "to promote and preserve peaceful and agreeable relations...."

Left without an anchor, Nomura appeared to drift in the days following his meeting with Roosevelt. He had sent a telegram to Tokyo requesting an advisor from the Army (no doubt believing that involvement of an Army representative in discussions with the United States would facilitate the acceptance of any agreement by his government). On February 27, Grew cabled Hull that he had received a visit from Colonel Iwakuro Hideo, who had been selected by the War Minister to travel to the United States to assist the new Japanese ambassador. Iwakuro told Grew that he "did not believe that American-Japanese problems could be permanently resolved at this time but that he hoped to contribute toward maintaining an equilibrium" until a solution could be found. Ironically, Grew sent Hull another telegram that same day reporting on a conversation with Matsuoka in which the Foreign Minister had said that "Japan rightly or wrongly had thrown in her lot with Germany and Italy, and regardless of the outcome she proposed to stand by her allies loyally to the end." It was a further indication of the ominous predicament facing the United States. "Since the conclusion of the Tripartite Pact," Grew added in another telegram to Hull a week later, "Japan's relations with the United States have progressively and dangerously deteriorated with little prospect of improvement."

Iwakuro was not the only Japanese citizen trying to help Nomura fashion a settlement agreement with the United States. On February 28, Postmaster General Frank Walker advised Roosevelt that a "Plenipotentiary Representative of the Japanese Government is here in Washington" and that he "is empowered to negotiate concrete terms for a settlement of all outstanding Far Eastern questions vis-à-vis the United States."

That purported "Plenipotentiary Representative" was a man named Wikawa Tadao, who happened to be a Catholic. He had worked in New York for Japan's financial commissioner and spoke good English, but most recently he had been the chief executive officer of the Central Bank of Cooperative Societies in Tokyo. He also had the distinction of being one of the John Doe Associates with whom Bishop Walsh and Father Drought had spoken in their quest to find peace in the Pacific. How Wikawa came to be regarded as a "Plenipotentiary Representative" is unclear (and, in response to Nomura's inquiry, Tokyo later sent a telegram to the Japanese ambassador advising him that Wikawa did not have "any connection whatsoever" with the Prime Minister or Foreign Minister).

Stanley Hornbeck was skeptical about Wikawa's bona fides even before Nomura received that cable, and Ballantine was sent to New York to meet with him in February as he prepared to travel to Washington. Wikawa told Ballantine that the Japanese did not trust the State Department and that he "wanted to talk only with the highest political appointees." But Ballantine otherwise felt that the purported Japanese representative was "not communicative." Upon his return to Washington, Ballantine reported to Hull that Wikawa was "a smoothie," and later, Ballantine concluded that he was "very untrustworthy."

The Secretary of State did not have to worry about meeting with Wikawa. Hull had told Roosevelt that he would only confer with Japan's official representative, and he had no intention of changing that position. Hull was therefore amenable to Walker's request for a meeting with Nomura. The Postmaster General suggested that the meeting be private to avoid any press coverage, which might create problems for Japan's leaders with the extremist elements in Tokyo. Wikawa, who had apparently spoken with Walker, soon passed word to Nomura that an appointment had been made for him to meet with Hull at the Secretary of State's apartment on the morning of Saturday, March 8, and that Nomura should use the back stairs at the Carlton Hotel to reach the apartment. The Japanese ambassador did as he was told. As Wikawa had promised, Nomura found the door to Hull's apartment unlocked. Nomura walked in and—perhaps to his surprise—saw the Secretary of State waiting for him.

Hull began the meeting by emphasizing to Nomura that he would not meet individually with the "good people" from his country who were trying to orchestrate a settlement agreement but would only deal with the ambassador. The Secretary of State then launched into a long discussion on the benefits of free trade and how that interest had been compromised by nations who had abandoned "this peaceful course of understanding and adjustment in accordance with basic rules and laws and policies...." Nomura responded that "all of the people in Japan, with very few exceptions, which included extremists, were very much averse to getting into war with the United States...."

Hull was skeptical, assuming, as he did, that "the military groups were in control" of Japan's government. Given that assumption, the Secretary of State wondered whether Japan "could possibly expect important nations like the United States to sit absolutely quiet while two or three nations before our very eyes organized naval and military forces and went out and conquered the balance of the earth...." Nomura responded that he did not believe Japan would make any further military movements "unless the policy of increasing embargoes" by the United States "should force his government, in the minds of those in control, to take further military steps." Hull was not moved, saying that any such military moves would be "a matter entirely in the hands" of Japan's government.

In the course of conversation, Hull referenced the "mutually profitable and genuine friendly relations" between Japan and the United States in earlier years. He then said that one of his "greatest ambitions" when he became Secretary of State in 1933 "was to work out a mutually satisfactory arrangement with respect to the" 1924 Immigration Act, which prohibited Japanese immigration to the United States and had long been a source of irritation to Japan. (The State Department's summary of the conversation said that Nomura "expressed his gratification at this," but it is hard to believe that the Japanese ambassador was satisfied with an aspiration that had not produced any results in eight years.) The meeting concluded with Hull pressing Nomura for "definite ideas" that might resolve the situation. But Nomura had none, and he left the apartment with Hull telling him that the President "would be only too glad" to see him whenever he wished.

Hull was as good as his word. Roosevelt met with Nomura and Hull a few days later. That meeting, as was the case with all of Nomura's meetings with Roosevelt, was imbued with a friendly spirit, but no progress was made. Much of the discussion focused on the Tripartite Pact and "the threatening nature of Matsuoka's acts and utterances," with Nomura saying at one point that the Foreign Minister "talks loudly for home consumption." But Nomura still had no specific proposals, and Hull closed the meeting by saying that Japan had "the responsibility" to propose something and needed, "above all," to "make it clear by words and acts" of its good faith desire to pursue peace. Hull did not explain what words and acts would satisfy that request.

On March 11—before Nomura's meeting with Roosevelt—Hull had forwarded to Grew a memorandum summarizing the conversation he had had with Nomura at his apartment on March 8. Hull did not provide any further elaboration or request any comment from his ambassador. Grew received a telegram from Hornbeck a few days later which said that Wikawa appeared to be the spokesman for the Japanese, that the State Department was handling the matter "in the strictest confidence," and that Grew should tell no one in the Embassy about the discussions other than Gene Dooman.

Neither telegram gave Grew any reason to believe that the growing tension in Tokyo would soon abate. A break was clearly needed, he thought, "to forget this horrid world"—not only for himself but for Alice as well (who, Grew confided to his diary, was "glued" to the radio much of the time, with her spirits rising or falling with the news). They had not been away from the Embassy for about eighteen months except for two weekend trips to Karuizawa the previous July. So Joe decided that they should take a five-day holiday at the Kawana Hotel golf resort on the Pacific Ocean, about a two-hour ride from Tokyo. They "thoroughly enjoyed" the holiday even though a substantial portion of the hotel's patrons were Germans, who were prone to give each other Nazi salutes as they passed each other on the walkways.

In the meantime, Grew decided that he could not take the leave he had requested in January 1941 to return to the United States for a few months beginning in June. "With great reluctance and disappointment," he confided to his diary, "I have given up all thought of taking [a] leave of absence this spring. This is no time for vacations while the world burns.... [S]omething of importance might happen when only the Ambassador could exert influence." The decision was especially frustrating to Grew because Harvard and Norwich University, a military college in Vermont, had each proposed to give him an honorary degree at their respective graduation ceremonies. But such displays of honor were hardly enough to change Grew's mind. "Duty first," he wrote a friend, "and the old New England conscience wins." (Grew sent a copy of his diary entry to Hornbeck, who in turn passed it on to Under Secretary of State Sumner Welles, with the Political Relations Adviser saying, in his convoluted syntax, that the entry provides "further evidence...of what Joe Grew is and how he thinks and how he performs—would that we had in adequate numbers in the service of this country such men.")

In retrospect, it might have been better for Grew to have taken that leave of absence to spend a couple of months in the United States. He could have spoken directly with the President about his opinions and recommendations. That personal interaction might have been more productive than sending Roosevelt an occasional letter which would invariably trigger a response drafted by the State Department rather than one penned by the President himself. Use of the leave might have made a difference.

CHAPTER 10

Commencement of the Conversations

It was another sign of the value Joe Grew placed on his wife's presence. In early May 1941, Alice had been taken by one of the Embassy cars to the Imperial Place to visit with the fifty-seven-year-old Dowager Empress, the mother of the Emperor. Alice had arranged the meeting on her own initiative—a reflection of the self-confidence that had evolved from the many years traveling the world with her husband.

The ostensible purpose of the visit was to congratulate the Dowager Empress on the engagement of her son, Hirohito's younger brother, and the engagement of her granddaughter. The two middle-aged women—contemporaries from different cultures—talked for thirty minutes on matters far and wide, including the jazz records that Alice had been sending to the fiancée of Hirohito's brother as well as Alice's interest in the deaf-and-dumb school. "Alice was amazed," Grew later said, "that the Empress knew so much about her, and being somewhat embarrassed by her thanks, she told several amusing anecdotes and had the Empress laughing heartily." As she prepared to leave, the Dowager Empress gave Alice orchids from the palace garden (the first time the Dowager Empress had given flowers to an ambassador's wife) and held Alice's hand for a long time in an obvious display of affection. In hearing about the visit, Grew could not help but reflect on the State Department's earlier advisory that American women and children leave Japan. "I am profoundly thankful," he recorded in his diary, "that our Government has never taken the step of insisting on the evacuation of the Embassy ladies, for it would be losing an important asset if Alice had to leave."

Half a globe away, Franklin D. Roosevelt was not in the same light-hearted mood as Alice during her visit with the Dowager Empress. On the sunny morning of Sunday, May 4, the President had been driven from Charlottesville, Virginia (where he had enjoyed some time off at the home of one of his aides) to Staunton, a rural Virginia community in the Shenandoah Valley between the Blue Ridge and Allegheny Mountains. The purpose of the visit was to dedicate the small white brick home where Woodrow Wilson was born as a national shrine. With the Secretary of State and other dignitaries seated to his right, Roosevelt, standing up and leaning on the black wooden rostrum, spoke to the several hundred people in attendance about the importance of democracy. "It is the kind of faith," he intoned, with his voice rising, "for which we have fought before—and for the existence of which we are ever ready to fight again."

The President did not feel the same vigor conveyed by his remarks. He was overcome by fatigue, and the correspondents who traveled with him could tell. "FDR looked as bad as a man can look and still be about," said the *Time* magazine reporter. The President had planned to attend a luncheon picnic in Staunton and a tea event at Newmarket, but those events were scratched from his schedule. To expedite the return to Washington, Roosevelt was placed on a train, with Steve Early, Roosevelt's press secretary, explaining the change in transportation mode as a way to avoid the heavy vehicular traffic on Virginia's roads.

When he reached the White House, Roosevelt discussed his symptoms with Ross McIntire. The President's personal physician immediately ordered blood tests, and the results no doubt disturbed him. The report showed that the President had only 4.5 grams per deciliter of hemoglobin, the iron-rich protein that gives blood its red color. A normal range for a man of Roosevelt's age would have been between 14 and 17 grams (and Roosevelt's last reading in March 1940 showed 13.5 grams per deciliter). In effect, the reading meant that the President had lost about two thirds of his blood supply in about fourteen months. It could have been—but was not—a simple case of bleeding from hemorrhoids, and even today, there is no clear explanation for the cause of Roosevelt's dramatic loss of blood. But subsequent blood tests—which showed a marked improvement in the hemoglobin count per deciliter—suggest that the President was given at least nine blood transfusions in the two months after his return from Staunton.

None of these details was disclosed to the public. The White House press office said only that the President was not feeling well and therefore had to postpone a speech planned for May 14. The Cabinet was not given much more information. Interior Secretary Harold Ickes reported that McIntire had told him that the President was suffering from "an intestinal disturbance which is not particularly important...." Regardless of the diagnosis, the President remained confined to his bed for most of the next few weeks and refused most visitors other than McIntire, his assistant Missy LeHand, and the ever-present Harry Hopkins.

Roosevelt was apparently not anxious to leave his bedroom even after he started feeling better. Robert Sherwood, the lean playwright who doubled as one of Roosevelt's speechwriters, remembered an encounter with Missy LeHand after a meeting with the President in his bedroom. Sherwood commented that Roosevelt appeared fine and never once coughed or sneezed. When Sherwood asked what the problem was, LeHand replied with a smile, "What he's suffering from most is a case of sheer exasperation."

There were consequences to Roosevelt's indulgence. He did not have any occasion during those first weeks in May 1941 to meet with Nomura. Nor could he engage in any long exchanges with Hull about the progress, such as it was, concerning the Secretary of State's dealings with the Japanese ambassador.

Hull's meetings with Nomura had taken a new turn by then. On April 9, one of Frank Walker's deputies in the Post Office left a detailed settlement proposal with the Secretary of State that had been largely drafted by Father Drought and Iwakuro Hideo, one of the so-called John Doe Associates. It was labeled as a proposal presented "through the medium of private American and Japanese individuals." Although it was favorable to Japan's interests, the mere notion of discussing settlement with the United States might have been enough to trigger a heated reaction from extremist elements in Japan. Even before Hull received the proposal, the Postmaster General had advised the Secretary of State that Prime Minister Konoye Fumimaro and other Japanese leaders were "endangering their lives" by pursuing settlement negotiations with the United States and that both Iwakuro and Wikawa

Tadao, another of the John Doe Associates, "expect assassination" for their participation in the process.

The proposal was replete with general expressions of intent on behalf of both Japan and the United States. It stated that the Tripartite Pact was designed only to prevent an extension of the European War and would not trigger any obligation on Japan's part except when one of the parties to the pact was "aggressively attacked" by another nation; that the United States' policy toward the European war would be dictated "exclusively" by considerations of "its own national welfare and security;" that the President of the United States would request Chiang Kai-shek to discuss settlement of the China Incident with Japan (and, if Chiang Kai-shek refused, the United States would discontinue aid to his government); that there would be a formal recognition of Manchukuo, the puppet state Japan had created in Manchuria; that Japan and the United States would agree to "a resumption of normal trade relations" as provided in the commercial treaty that the United States had terminated in January 1940; and that the parties' agreement would be finalized by Roosevelt and Konoye at a conference in Honolulu.

There were many meetings and memos in the State Department discussing the April 9 proposal. As a general proposition, Hull later commented, "our disappointment was keen." He and his staff regarded the document as "much less accommodating than we had been led to believe it would be, and most of its provisions were all that the ardent Japanese imperialists could want."

Stanley Hornbeck had a different perspective. Whatever the particulars of the document received on April 9, he did not think the United States should pursue an agreement with Japan. As the Political Relations Adviser later recounted in his unpublished autobiography, "The views, the reasoning and the purposes of Washington and of Tokyo differed so completely that there was no possibility of there being achieved a 'meeting of the minds.'" Even if an agreement could somehow be reached, Hornbeck was sure it would compromise American interests. "From the beginning," he explained in that autobiography, "I had been and was skeptical of the idea that a new agreement could be achieved, and I contended that the prevailing situation was such that, if achieved, the existence of a new agreement would in no way serve the interest and purposes of the United States but would, on the contrary, serve only the purposes of the Japanese, to which purposes the United States was opposed."

Given that perspective, Hornbeck wrote a memorandum for Hull's perusal—before the April 9 draft was received—saying that the State Department would be engulfed by "a super-colossal political bombshell" if it issued a public announcement that it had agreed to enter negotiations with Japan. The memorandum concluded with an aspiration. "I hope and trust," said Hornbeck, that "the highest officials of this Government" will decide not "to enter upon a negotiation with Japan...."

Those sentiments were echoed in telegrams Hornbeck sent to Grew. On April 5, the Political Relations Adviser told the American ambassador that the John Doe Associates "were endeavoring to draw this Government into an undercover negotiation" and that the State Department was "endeavoring to keep matters in suspense and to avoid the making of a commitment by this Government either affirmative or negative." In another telegram on April 10, Hornbeck said that the John Doe Associates were "pressing hard for a very comprehensive commitment by this Government" that would have substantial "potentialities for abuse...."

Hornbeck's perspective did not account for the directive that the President had given his Secretary of State in February: to undertake negotiations with Japan and to keep them active for as long as possible to allow the United States and its allies to bolster their defense capabilities. There was no mystery about Roosevelt's underlying concern. In a meeting with Secretary of War Henry Stimson toward the end of April, Roosevelt lamented the scarcity of available resources to manage conflicts in the Atlantic and Pacific Oceans, telling Stimson that "he did not have butter enough to spread over the bread he was supposed to cover." So Hull could not accept Hornbeck's advice to shun the negotiations. At the same time, Hull decided that he needed the Political Relations Adviser at his side throughout the eight-month process that ensued.

The two men agreed that Hornbeck would not attend any meetings with the Japanese representatives but would remain "in the background and off-stage" and participate as an "observer, analyst, and counselor." The role certainly suited the Secretary of State. As he later explained in his *Memoirs*, the State Department was able to keep abreast of the various proposals and explanations emanating from the Japanese representatives in large part because of Hornbeck's "precise draftsmanship and analysis of documents...."

For his part, Grew was not asked whether he shared Hornbeck's skepticism (although the Political Relations Adviser did tell the Ambassador that the Embassy "could be especially helpful" by being "alert in watching and reporting upon developments in Japanese internal politics...."). Grew did try to secure an appointment with Konoye in the beginning of April to discuss Nomura's mission in the United States. The idea had been suggested to Grew by a contact from a Japanese periodical who thought Konoye might agree to the appointment. The Prime Minister did not normally meet with ambassadors, but, reasoned the contact, he might do so now because of Matsuoka's absence from Tokyo (on his trip to Berlin, Rome, and Moscow). The idea of bypassing the Foreign Minister appealed to Grew, but Konoye, no doubt aware of Matsuoka's sensitivities, declined the request.

In the meantime, the tension was apparently having an impact on Grew's health. "Alice has no longer a monopoly on heart attacks," he mentioned in his diary entry for April 2, 1941. "[L]ast night for three or four hours," Joe confessed, "I learned something about that subject by firsthand information." He tried to discount the incident, later telling his daughter Lilla that "it was really nothing, just a temporary racing for a few hours...." At the time, he said that "it was not an agreeable experience while it lasts." But he apparently did not seek emergency medical care and said that he "felt all right the next day except for lassitude." All of which suggests that it may have been an incident of atrial fibrillation.

Grew did not report any of his health issues to Hull, and they were not on the Secretary of State's mind when he met with Nomura on the evening of April 14 at his new home in apartment 400G in the Wardman Park Hotel, a large red brick structure off Connecticut Avenue in Washington's Northwest quadrant. The Japanese ambassador said that he was familiar with the April 9 proposal and that "he had collaborated more or less" in its preparation. Like Hornbeck, Hull could not have entertained much hope that the April 9 draft would form the basis of an agreement between Japan and the United States. But the President's directive for time continued to loom large. And so Hull told Nomura that he was prepared to engage in "preliminary discussions" to ascertain whether the April 9 draft provided "a basis for negotiations" and that he would soon advise Nomura of the time and place for their next meeting. Nomura was agreeable but "emphasized the urgency of the situation." "[E]vents were moving rapidly," said the Japanese ambassador, and the prospect of "clashes" would increase "from week to week."

The two men met again at Hull's apartment on the evening of April 16. Hull explained that the April 9 draft "contained numerous proposals" with which the United States could agree but that "there were others that would require modification, expansion or entire elimination...." But another matter had to be addressed, said Hull, before they could discuss the specifics of the April 9 draft. The United States needed to know, the Secretary of State explained, that Japan was prepared "to abandon its present doctrine of military conquest by force" and, more specifically, that Japan was prepared to honor "the principles" which had formed the basis for the United States' "relations between nations." Hull then gave Nomura a document which set forth those principles:

> Respect for the territorial integrity and sovereignty of each and all nations.

> Support of the principle of non-interference in the internal affairs of other countries.

> Support of the principle of equality, including equality of commercial opportunity.

> Non-disturbance of the *status quo* in the Pacific, except as the *status quo* may be altered by peaceful means.

As Embassy officer John Emmerson later observed, "The word *China* did not appear in the principles, but China was the understood beneficiary of each of those four goals." Recognizing the principal beneficiary of the four principles may have been easy. But the principles provided no detail as to how they would be applied in specific situations—or, more importantly for Japan, precisely what the United States expected of Japan through its endorsement of the principles.

Nomura studied the document for a few minutes. The Japanese ambassador remarked that the preservation of the status quo—the fourth principle—"would interfere with the Manchurian situation." Hull brushed that comment aside, saying that "the *status quo* point would not affect" Man-chukuo, which would be addressed at a later stage of the discussions. Nomura then inquired about the prohibition of Japanese immigration to the United States. Hull responded, as he had before, that the immigration question was a matter of domestic policy, that one of Hull's ambitions since coming to the State Department had been to change that policy, and that "Japan would have to accept our good faith in this respect...."

Hull "was not sure" whether Nomura "fully understood each statement" the Secretary of State made with respect to the four principles, but he assumed that the Japanese ambassador did understand the more critical point Hull made when he handed the document to Nomura. The United States could not respond to a proposal that had been conveyed by unofficial agents of Japan. Hull needed a presentation from the Japanese government's chosen representative. Hull therefore suggested that Nomura give the April 9 draft to his government. "[I]f the Japanese Government should approve this document," said Hull, and if Nomura were instructed to formally present the draft to him, "it would afford a basis for the institution of negotiations" (although the Secretary later made it clear that they had "not reached the stage of negotiations"). Hull added that if Japan "is in real earnest about changing its course," he "could see no good reason why ways could not be found to reach a fairly mutually satisfactory settlement of all of the essential questions and problems presented." Shortly after that remark was made, Nomura left the apartment with the document containing the four principles and with Hull's promise to meet again if his government instructed the ambassador to proceed.

On April 24, Hull sent a telegram to Grew that summarized his discussions with Nomura on April 14 and 16, saying that he had told the Japanese ambassador that the Secretary of State would "consider any program which the Japanese Government might offer and which would be in harmony with the principles which I outlined to him...." Hull added, however, that he and his staff "were skeptical whether the Japanese Government would at this time be willing or be able to go forward with a program of the nature described." The Secretary of State did not request Grew's views or assistance in assessing Japan's interest in pursuing a settlement agreement.

Although he was undoubtedly pleased to receive the report from Hull about the conversations with Nomura, Grew continued to feel that the State

Department was leaving the Embassy in the dark on many matters. Embassy naval attaché Henri Smith-Hutton remembered Grew's "continuing complaint" at staff meetings about the lack of guidance from the State Department. Grew himself had told Hornbeck in a February 1941 telegram that at times he "felt just a little out on a limb here."

Grew's concern reached a new crescendo at the end of April when Sir Robert Craigie advised him that Lord Halifax, the British ambassador in Washington, had provided information to Hull on April 22 about a possible Japanese attack in "the South Seas" area, which included Singapore and the Dutch East Indies. As John Emmerson later recounted, Grew was "humiliated" when his British colleague told him about the conversation (as well as a related conversation that Under Secretary of State Sumner Welles had had with British and Dutch representatives on the same subject). As America's ambassador to Japan, Grew believed that the State Department should have sent to him the same information that the British government had sent to its ambassador in Japan.

Grew sent a telegram to let Hull and Welles know that he had received the information from Craigie but said nothing of his humiliation. That lament was reserved for his diary. It was insulting, said Grew, "to receive such information from a foreign colleague concerning the intimate affairs of my own Government.... The situation has irritated me for many years and there are officers in the Department who know it but, who while perhaps sympathizing, are evidently powerless to alter it."

Grew encountered a similar affront a few weeks later. Craigie again sent the American ambassador summaries of Lord Halifax's conversations with Hull and Welles with respect to the discussions the Secretary of State was having with Nomura (in which Hull said he was not taking the process "too seriously"). Grew forwarded the Craigie transmission to Hornbeck and dryly commented that the "difference in the methods of conveying this important information followed by the [State] Department and by the British is noteworthy."

Grew's irritation with the State Department did not affect his willingness to provide Hull and Welles with information that might be useful. On May 2, the American ambassador reported to Hull that Matsuoka was "in an intoxicated condition on the evening of his return from Moscow" on April 22 and that he had created a further strain with Prime Minister

Konoye by agreeing to provisions in the Neutrality Pact with the Soviet Union that had not been authorized by the Cabinet.

The schism between Konoye and Matsuoka was more dramatic than Grew reported to the Secretary of State. The Prime Minister had traveled to the airport to greet Matsuoka on his return and, more importantly, to tell him about the settlement proposal that Nomura had forwarded to Tokyo after his visit with Hull on April 16. The Prime Minister, knowing Matsuoka to be "an extraordinarily sensitive man," thought the best approach would be to explain the proposal when the two of them were alone in the car ride from the airport.

Konoye changed his plans when he saw the Foreign Minister after he disembarked from the plane. Matsuoka was not only feeling full of himself but also intent upon going to the Imperial Palace to make a report of his trip to Hirohito. Konoye asked Ohashi Chuichi, the Vice Foreign Minister, to travel with Matsuoka in the car ride back from the airport and explain the settlement proposal to him. In making that request, Konoye expected that Ohashi would tell the Foreign Minister what Konoye had assumed— that the proposal was one crafted by the United States. That mistaken impression was generated by the ambiguous telegram from Nomura. In forwarding the proposal to Tokyo on April 17, Nomura told Konoye that Hull had said "it would be all right to proceed with negotiations on the basis of" the proposal. Nomura had compounded the error by failing to forward the four principles that Hull had identified as the cornerstone of any agreement between the two countries (and he would not disclose those principles to Matsuoka until May 8, when he reported on further conversations with Hull).

The car ride from the airport was not a pleasant one for Matsuoka. He had discussed a possible settlement with the American ambassador to the Soviet Union while he was in Moscow, and he had assumed that the John Doe proposal was a product of that conversation. He bristled when the Vice Minister described what he thought was an American proposal. Although it had been largely drafted by unofficial agents of Japan and incorporated terms favorable to Japan's interest, it was not the agreement Matsuoka had discussed with the American ambassador. Nor did it reflect Matsuoka's views on how to resolve the China Incident or prevent the United States from entering the European war. And so the Foreign Minister declared that the proposal was "70% ill-will and 30% good-will." He said he would need two weeks to study it.

Matsuoka's negative reaction to the proposal exacerbated the "ill-feeling" among Army and Navy leaders, who were anxious to reach an accommodation with the United States. They resented the Foreign Minister's recalcitrant response. But Konoye, being familiar with Matsuoka's "complex nature," suggested that they give the Foreign Minister some time to reflect on the proposal. In due course, the Cabinet and the military acceded to Matsuoka's demand that "the whole affair be entrusted to his own diplomatic ability" and that the discussions with the United States be "left entirely to his discretion" without interference from Konoye, the Cabinet, or the military.

It was not an approach conducive to success. Hull did not conceal from Nomura his contempt for the Foreign Minister's leadership. It was "not comprehensible," he told the Japanese ambassador, that Matsuoka could represent Japan in settlement discussions when he was issuing "threatening expressions" against the United States and "sending enthusiastic congratulations to Hitler upon the brutal military attack on the poor little country of Greece and its defenseless people...."

The Foreign Minister did not make it any easier for Nomura. He demanded that the Japanese ambassador ask Hull about a non-aggression pact, which the Secretary of State quickly brushed aside when Nomura floated the idea in a meeting on May 7. Matsuoka also asked Nomura to present Hull with an "Oral Statement" (awkward terminology for a document which was nothing more than an explanatory exposition). The statement supported Germany and Italy's demand for Britain's "capitulation" and repeated Japan's intention to avoid any action "that might in the least degree adversely affect the position of Germany and Italy." Nomura was not comfortable in presenting the statement, but he did not have to worry. Hull already knew about Matsuoka's instruction because the United States was routinely intercepting Japanese diplomatic messages, which the Americans had dubbed as "MAGIC." Hull understood Nomura's discomfort and suggested that he not bother to submit the statement.

It was not until May 12 that Nomura was able to give Hull Japan's response to the April 9 draft (a delay occasioned by Matsuoka's desire to receive a reply from the German Foreign Ministry before submitting the response). "Very few rays of hope shone from the document," Hull recounted in his *Memoirs*. As far as he was concerned, the revised draft "offered little basis for an agreement unless we were prepared to sacrifice some of our most basic principles, which we were not."

For some reason, Hull and his staff were concerned about the rewording of some provisions in the new draft that appeared to reflect little or no difference from the earlier draft. The May 12 draft, like the April 9 draft, stated that the United States would discontinue assistance to Chiang Kai-Shek if he rejected an American suggestion to negotiate a settlement with Japan. The May 12 draft also stated that the United States would not be involved in any "aggressive measure as to assist any one nation against another." That language implied that the United States would have to suspend its aid to Great Britain but was not much different than the April 9 draft's statement that the United States would not be involved in any "aggressive alliance aimed to assist any one nation against another."

Another innocuous change was the deletion of the proposal for Konoye and Roosevelt to meet in Honolulu. Japan's May 12 draft said that, at least initially, an exchange of letters by the two governments would suffice. The change concerning economic activity in the Southwestern Pacific was more troubling. The April 9 draft stated that Japanese activities in that area would be conducted by peaceful means "without resorting to arms." The May 12 draft deleted the language "without resorting to arms," thus implying that Japan might use military means to expand its holdings in Indochina and other Southeast Asian countries.

Perhaps the most significant change to the April 9 draft concerned the Tripartite Pact. That document stated that Japan would have no obligation under that pact to participate in any hostilities against another nation unless that other nation "aggressively attacked" one of the parties to the pact. That language appeared to narrow the circumstances under which Japan might be drawn into armed conflict with the United States. The May 12 draft removed that explicit limitation and said only that Japan's obligation for military assistance under the pact "will be applied in accordance with the stipulation of Article III" of the agreement. The change implied that Japan might be obliged to join Germany and Italy in war against the United States even if the United States did not attack either Germany or Italy. The new language could mean, as Matusoka explained to Grew at one point, that

Japan would assist Germany in a war against the United States if the Nazis torpedoed American convoys shipping materials to Great Britain.

Hornbeck forwarded the new proposal to Grew along with summaries of Nomura's discussion with Hull on May 12 as well as on earlier dates. The Political Relations Adviser told Grew that, like the Secretary of State, he thought the new proposal "appears to offer a much less promising basis of an agreement or understanding than the earlier draft proposal." Hornbeck did not ask Grew for any comments or assistance in moving forward with the process.

The absence of any invitation from Hornbeck did not foreclose Grew's willingness to continue to provide helpful information. Quite the contrary. Throughout the spring of 1941, Grew sent a multitude of telegrams to Hull reporting on developments and dynamics that provided a window into the thinking of Japan's leaders. And while he often recounted the growing scarcity of meaningful contacts in a country that was becoming more repressive by the month, Grew still had access to many useful sources. The American ambassador's access to those sources was an open secret in Tokyo. At one point in the spring of 1941, Grew's diary referenced a confidential conversation he had had with an official of the Imperial Household who was "a little tight." The official told him that, in a lecture to the Imperial Household staff, a member of the secret police "said that the American Ambassador in Tokyo knows what is going on behind the scenes in Japanese politics even before the military or even the secret police know."

Grew relied on that inside information in his telegrams to Hull. A principal focus was the implementation of the Tripartite Pact. On the very day Nomura presented the May 12 proposal to the Secretary of State, Grew sent a telegram to Hull that discounted the likelihood that the Tripartite Pact would be used to involve Japan in a war with the United States—even if American ships were torpedoed by the Nazis. "Based on a careful estimate of official and public opinion in Japan," the telegram said, "it is my belief that predominant influences, including the Emperor, the Prime Minister, Baron Hiranuma, the majority of the Cabinet members and also the Japanese Navy, would be reluctant to incur war with the United States and would make every effort to find an interpretation of Article III which would release Japan from the mutual assistance obligation, provided that this could be done without sacrificing honor and without losing face vis-à-vis the United States."

In conveying that opinion, Grew was mindful that the Foreign Minister "is very much in the pocket of the Axis and amenable to pressure from Germany." He did not keep those thoughts to himself. In a telegram sent shortly after Nomura submitted the May 12 proposal, Grew advised Hull that he had no doubt that "the Axis Ambassadors have been stiffening the back of Mr. Matsuoka...." Still, Grew did not place any credence in Matsuoka's threats to use the Tripartite Pact as a vehicle to wage war against the United States. "I am certain," he told Hull on May 19, "that Mr. Matsuoka is well aware" that the Tripartite Pact "was a complete failure if not a disaster." Matsuoka had claimed—and had convinced Hirohito—that Japan's execution of the agreement in September 1940 would discourage the United States from continuing its support for Britain or from entering the European conflict. That claim was no longer tenable. The United States had not abandoned Great Britain or given any indication of revising its policies to account for the Tripartite Pact. As a result, said Grew, the Foreign Minister could not "placate" the United States now in Nomura's discussions with Hull without seeming to admit that the Tripartite Pact had failed to achieve its purpose.

That conclusion was reinforced by other intelligence Grew had received and passed on to Hull. A "trustworthy Japanese contact," Grew told the Secretary of State in the middle of May, had been asked by Marquis Kido Koichi, the Lord Keeper of the Privy Seal and the Emperor's principal adviser, to tell Grew that he should not be "unduly concerned over the statements and attitude of the Foreign Minister" because "there are persons in the Government who are exercising care to prevent the taking by Japan of hasty action." That same informant also told Grew that he had been asked by the Navy Minister to remind the American ambassador that "implementing any obligation which Japan might have under her alliance with Germany could not be taken by the Minister for Foreign Affairs alone."

Hull never gave any hint in his subsequent discussions with Nomura that Grew's cables had any impact on his views. Nor did Hull rush to give Nomura a complete response to the draft submitted by the Japanese ambassador on May 12. Instead, Hull gave Nomura some limited changes on May 16. They restricted Japan's obligations under the Tripartite Pact to situations where a party had been "aggressively attacked" by another nation, proposed a withdrawal of troops from China "in accordance with a schedule to be agreed upon," stated that any economic activity by Japan in Indochina would "be carried on by peaceful means," and affirmed that the future of Manchuria would "be dealt with by friendly negotiations."

Whatever the reason for limiting the changes, Hull was beginning to think that there might be some hope of extracting something useful from his discussions with Nomura. He would host meetings in his office on Tuesday mornings with Stimson and Navy Secretary Frank Knox to discuss policy matters affecting the Atlantic and Pacific fronts. In their meeting on Tuesday, May 13 (with Navy chief Harold Stark and Army chief George Marshall attending), Hull told the others that he "still thinks he has some chance"—which Stimson remembers Hull describing as one in ten—"to win something out of the negotiations with the Japs."

Hull's Political Relations Adviser clung to his contrary view. As discussions with Nomura proceeded from April into May, Hornbeck remained confident that any agreement with Japan would be a waste of time at best and counterproductive at worst.

The Political Relations Adviser was not one to keep his opinions to himself. He was a tireless writer when it came to matters involving Japan and China. (At an earlier point, Hull complained to another foreign service officer who had served in China that Hornbeck "just fusses at me all the time.") "Is there more reason for us to trust the militant militaristic element that is in control in Japan today (and which has been in control since 1931)," Hornbeck rhetorically asked in a memorandum on May 15, "than to trust the militant militaristic element that is in control of Germany today (and has been in control since 1933)?" The obvious answer left no room for doubt as to the appropriate course. "If we choose to conclude a treaty with Japan," he added, "that is one thing. But if we think that by the concluding of a treaty and by placing reliance upon pledges given by Japan in such treaty we shall have safeguarded our positions in the Pacific," he added, "... that will be quite another thing." Hornbeck preached the same sermon in another memorandum about a week later. "Japan has, in force today, with the United States," he said, "various treaties to whose provisions Japan pays no attention whatsoever. What reason have we to expect—and have we any reason to assume—that Japan will pay more or better attention to the provisions of a new treaty with us, if concluded now?"

In an apparent effort to assess Hornbeck's pessimism, Hull decided to reach out to his ambassador in Tokyo. On the evening of Saturday, May 24, Hull sent a telegram to Grew and Gene Dooman asking their "judgment" on the likelihood that the Japanese government "could carry out commitments...in good faith" with respect to a new agreement.

Hull's telegram was received in Tokyo at 4:45 p.m. on Sunday, May 25. Grew was excited to receive the inquiry. Nothing was more important to him than promoting peace with Japan. "Grew was," said Dooman, "passionately committed to the avoidance of war." And, given his continuing complaint about being ignored by the State Department, it was both refreshing and rewarding to finally receive the Secretary of State's request for his opinion on the ultimate question confronting Hull and his staff.

Hull's telegram indicated that additional materials were being forwarded to the Embassy for use in preparing its response. Pending receipt of those materials, Grew sent a telegram to Hull on Monday, May 26, to provide a "survey of the situation" in Japan that would serve as background. "In a country so politically backward as Japan," said Grew, "there is no set of principles which runs homogenously throughout the fabric of the nation, while medieval ideas which disappeared in the Occident centuries ago vie with political concepts—from Fascism to advance Liberalism—now current in the West." The absence of any attachment to principles, said the Ambassador, meant that Japan's foreign policies were "essentially susceptible to world developments and events." He could not make a definitive report on whether the extremists or the moderates carried more influence in shaping Japan's foreign policy at that juncture, but he thought the trend favored the moderates. In either case, said Grew, the situation was ripe for change because "under present conditions Japan is highly malleable."

The other materials referenced in Hull's telegram were received before Grew's survey was dispatched to Hull, and he gave them close consideration. He believed his next telegram would be "the most important telegram sent during [his] service in Japan." Grew began drafting it on the morning of Tuesday, May 27, "after a night of most careful and prayerful thought." He discussed it with Dooman, who "concurred completely" in the text. He then "mulled it over" during the course of the morning and finally sent it off, but "changed hardly a word from the first draft, which was dashed off on this little Corona as if the words had been planted in my mind overnight." The fact that the telegram was sent out on May 27—one of Grew's "lucky days" –gave him hope that the effort might bear fruit.

"There can be no doubt," the telegram said, that Japan "would carry out the provisions of the settlement in good faith to the best of its ability" if, as Grew assumed, the settlement was approved by the Emperor, the Cabinet, and probably the Privy Council as well. He recognized that there might be some elements in the Army and Navy who would oppose any settlement, but that concern was offset by a recognition that the government would not enter into any settlement "without the approval of the War and Navy Ministers, who in turn would not accord their approval without the support of the higher councils of the armed forces." On that score, said Grew, he had "good reason to believe that both the War and Navy Ministers in general terms favor a settlement along the general lines under discussion." Grew added that "the Japanese public would welcome such a settlement with a profound sense of relief."

Grew recognized that there was always a chance that Japan would not honor the commitments in a new agreement. But there was a saving grace. If Japan reneged on its new obligations, the United States would "be released" from any commitments it had under the agreement. "It therefore appears," the telegram observed, "that the United States has very much to gain from such a settlement and that, even if satisfactory implementation on the part of Japan should fail, which we doubt, no serious loss to American interests would necessarily be incurred." In view of all that, Grew proposed that the United States "proceed with the negotiations.... The alternative," he added, "might well be progressive deterioration of American-Japanese relations leading eventually to war."

Grew's telegram may have given Hull some hope that the United States could eventually extract some benefit from the discussions. But the telegram did not inspire the Secretary of State to expedite the process. On Saturday, May 31, the State Department delivered a draft proposal to the Japanese embassy. As had been the case with other documents submitted by the Department, this one was labeled "Unofficial, Exploratory, and Without Commitment." Hull later told Nomura and his associates that the President needed an agreement with "clear-cut and unequivocal terms...." That may have been so, but the May 31 redraft did not reflect an interest in achieving that goal. In accordance with the policy that Hull and his advisors had devised at the outset, the document did not provide an unambiguous recitation of American positions. It was instead little more than a regurgitation of the April 9 proposal, which was filled with vague pronouncements.

That point was exemplified by the Tripartite Pact. It remained a source of concern to Hull and his staff. Nomura knew this, and, as reflected in his conversations with Matsuoka before accepting the ambassadorial post, he also knew that it would be difficult to forge a new agreement with the United States as long as the pact remained in effect. But Nomura also knew that there was virtually no likelihood of Japan renouncing the agreement. It was a matter of honor. That perspective was evident in a conversation Nomura had with a friend from his Washington days, Navy Captain Ellis Zacharias. The new Japanese ambassador met with Zacharias in San Francisco in January 1941 as Nomura was preparing to travel to Washington to assume his new post. Nomura told his friend that the pact was signed amidst "a sharp division of opinion" and that Japan's leaders now realize it was "a mistake." But "nothing can be done toward cancelling it," said Nomura. "It must die a natural death."

Zacharias recounted the conversation in a letter to Harold Stark, the Chief of Naval Operations in Washington. The Navy chief no doubt shared it with Hull, who was told by Nomura in one of their early conversations that, as Grew had also told the Secretary of State, "the Japanese Government would make its own independent judgment" whether the pact required Japan's military assistance in any particular situation. Still, in later testimony before the congressional committee investigating the Pearl Harbor attack, the Secretary of State criticized the Japanese because they "had been consistently unwilling in the conversations to pledge their Government to renounce Japan's commitments in the alliance" and because "they wouldn't talk about getting out of this pact." (The irony was not lost on Japan: while he was promoting the sanctity of treaties, Hull was also hopeful that Japan would renounce the one it had with Germany and Italy.)

However strong Hull's views on the Tripartite Pact, the State Department's revised proposal of May 31 said nothing about Japan's renunciation of the pact. The proposal merely referenced Japan's claim that the pact's purpose was "defensive." In accordance with that perspective, the revised draft said that the agreement would "not apply" to acts of self-defense and that the United States' actions with respect to the European conflict had

been and would continue to be governed "solely and exclusively by considerations of protection and self-defense." In short, the State Department's
revised proposal of May 31 contemplated the perpetuation of the Tripartite
Pact as long as it did not penalize the United States for taking action that
the United States deemed to be defensive in nature.

Another key issue to be addressed was Japan's proposal to station troops
in North China after settlement as a defensive measure against communist
attacks—whether from Russia or the Chinese communists. Colonel Iwakuro,
who had accompanied Nomura to the meeting at Hull's apartment on May
20, explained that the stationing of troops in North China "had become a
cardinal objective in Japan's conflict with China and that it would be impossible for the Japanese to abandon it." Iwakuro did not provide any specifics
on the number of troops that would be stationed in North China. He said
only that it would be about one tenth to one fifth of the Japanese force cur-
rently garrisoned in North China. Nor did Iwakuro or Nomura offer a
timetable for the eventual withdrawal of those Japanese troops.

Hull suggested in a meeting with Nomura on May 21 that it might be
desirable to effectuate the withdrawal of all Japanese troops in "perhaps
twelve months," with the troops in North China being removed last. Another
alternative, said Hull, would be to have a commission of some sort deal with
the issue of "maintaining order in these areas." But Hull was quick to add
that "he did not wish to pass upon the merits of these suggestions" but was
only "raising them for consideration." In a conversation on May 30 with
Joe Ballantine and Max Hamilton, Iwakuro and Wikawa Tadao suggested
that the State Department draft language to address the issue, but the two
State Department officials—again reflecting the American reluctance to
draft specific proposals—deflected the request, saying that it would be better
if each side gave the matter "further consideration...."

The State Department's May 31 redraft added nothing to the mix. It
said only that the retention of Japanese troops in China was "subject to
further discussion." And on the other related question concerning Manchukuo, the redraft said that the status of the puppet state would be subject to
"[a]micable negotiation...."

Nomura came to Hull's apartment on the evening of June 2 to say that
he and his colleagues were in agreement with the May 31 redraft "with the
exception of some of the phraseology." In other circumstances, an adversary

in a contract negotiation might have welcomed that response. That should have been especially true here because Hull had received a telegram from Grew that very afternoon saying "that the potentialities for a successful outcome of the Washington conversations will decrease in direct ratio to the delay incurred in reaching an agreement...."

Speed may have been important to Japan (and the American ambassador as well), but it was not important to the Secretary of State. He knew, as Grew did not, that Roosevelt wanted to drag the discussions out as long as possible. So Hull was not interested in a quick fix or an early determination whether the Japanese and Americans could reach an agreement. Given the President's goal, the Secretary of State did not express any satisfaction when Nomura indicated at the June 2 meeting that Japan was prepared to accept the heart of the May 31 redraft. Instead, Hull "very slowly and deliberately" asked Nomura whether Japan "seriously and earnestly desired to enter into a settlement for peace" or whether, in light of Matsuoka's "loud statements," Japan was "only seeking a way to get out of China and otherwise to go forward with methods and practices entirely contrary to the principles which would have to underlie a settlement...."

Hull's response disregarded all those telegrams that Grew had sent to him in the preceding weeks (and, not surprisingly, apparently neither Hull nor Hornbeck sent Grew the summary of the conversation on June 2). The American ambassador had expressed his view that Japan would honor an agreement with the United States. Grew had also explained that the moderates seemed to have the edge in Japan's inner circles, that the War and Navy Ministers appeared interested in settlement, that the political situation in Japan was "highly malleable," that Matsuoka was becoming isolated from other Japanese leaders, and that, in any event, Matsuoka's belligerent statements should not be taken at face value because he could not initiate war by himself.

Nomura understood all that. In response to Hull's questions at the June 2 meeting, the Japanese ambassador said that Japan was indeed desirous of a settlement. That answer was not enough for the Secretary of State. Hull moved on to a different subject and inquired about Japan's interest in leaving "Japanese troops stationed in China indefinitely...." In keeping with the Department's planned approach, the Secretary of State did not offer any specific proposal to resolve that issue. He said only that he hoped that Japan was giving consideration to the concerns he had previously expressed.

Nomura may have sensed that Hull was in no rush to bring the matter to a conclusion. But he was too diplomatic to express that thought. He had a mission, and he left Hull's apartment with hope that he could still work out an agreement.

Time would tell that the hope was illusory.

CHAPTER 11

The Decision

J oe and Alice were avid readers, and in the spring of 1941, one book that captured their attention was the newly-published diary of William E. Dodd, the former University of Chicago history professor. Dodd had served as the American ambassador to Germany between 1933 and 1937, and his experiences would be recounted decades later in Erik Larson's bestselling book, *In the Garden of Beasts*. Dodd had died in 1940 at the age of seventy, but his diary was published the following year. The Grews were no doubt interested in comparing their tribulations in Japan with Dodd's time in Germany as Adolf Hitler consolidated power.

Grew did credit Dodd with "vision" because, despite Hitler's claims to the contrary, the one-time history professor saw that the Führer "aims at war" and that he was banking on the "pacifist" perspective of the English and French. But Grew's overall appraisal of Dodd's service was decidedly negative. Dodd "was obviously a bad misfit in the job," Grew confided to his diary. In part, that conclusion derived from Dodd's disdain for what he saw as a "clique" in the diplomatic service, "many of whom are Harvard graduates" and "connected to rich families." They were not "well informed," said Dodd, and they used the diplomatic service for "personal gratification" (all of which prompted Grew, "Mr. John Harvard," to write in his diary, "Dear me"). Dodd also denigrated the value of diplomatic functions, saying in his diary after one dinner that it "would have been far better to have dined at home and read a good book" (which prompted Grew to comment that Dodd's inability to obtain useful information from such functions "sizes up the author as well as any other"). But Grew's most pointed criticism concerned Dodd's failure to be more direct in his dealings with the German government. Despite his "bitter hatred of Nazis," Grew observed, Dodd refrained from "hard-hitting tactics, which is the only language the Germans understand...."

While the Grews were assessing the shortcomings of the former American ambassador to Germany, Japan's Foreign Minister was expressing to the Prime Minister his "displeasure and animosity" toward Japan's ambassador to the United States. From the beginning of his assignment, Nomura believed that he could modify or even ignore instructions he received from Matsuoka. When the Foreign Minister told his ambassador on May 12 to hand Hull a statement that said that any agreement with Japan would depend on the United States avoiding involvement in the European war and revising its relationship with China, Nomura bluntly responded that he had no intention of giving the provocative message to the Secretary of State. That did not sit well with the Foreign Minister. Matsuoka became equally enraged when he learned that Nomura had reportedly told Hull during one of their conversations in May that Matsuoka was the only cabinet member who opposed an adjustment in Japanese-American relations (which, according to Konoye's Memoirs, was true). And when Nomura explained in the beginning of June that he had received a counterproposal from the United States (the revised draft of May 31) and would forward it to the Foreign Minister after he had worked out revisions with the State Department, Matsuoka immediately fired back a telegram full of indignation. "[A]n important matter of this sort should be dispatched without delay," he said. The Japanese government could not formulate "policy toward the United States," the Foreign Minister snapped, if such information were withheld.

Nomura was infuriated by Matsuoka's comments. At one point, the retired admiral drafted a telegram to the Foreign Minister that explained his perspective as ambassador. He chided the Foreign Minister for using language in his instructions that "one would dare not use in talking even to a common soldier." But Nomura especially resented the insinuation that the Japanese ambassador was not doing his job. "I obey your instructions to the end," said the draft telegram, "but in carrying them out I am only using my discretion as to the order in which they should be put." He recalled the beginnings of their friendship of thirty years, saying, "This is absolutely not that heroic Matsuoka. In view of the circumstances which led me to come out of my retirement, the real Matsuoka should put more trust in me."

Nomura discussed the telegram with Iwakuro Hideo, who was now a military attaché in the embassy. Iwakuro apparently believed that the telegram would do more harm than good. So it was never sent. But Nomura's decision not to send the telegram had no bearing on his conduct in the continuing conversations with Cordell Hull and his staff.

Over the course of the first few weeks in June, Nomura and his colleagues met with Hull and his staff numerous times to review possible changes to the May 31 redraft. As before, most of the meetings were in Hull's apartment (and on at least two occasions, Hull remained bed-ridden for the entire conversation, which sometimes lasted as much as two hours).

A principal focus remained the Tripartite Pact. The State Department representatives wanted Japan to accept the American claim that all actions which the United States had taken or would take with respect to the European war were for self-defense and thus outside the scope of that pact. At a meeting on June 17, Far Eastern Division Chief Max Hamilton told Iwakuro and Wikawa Tadao that matters would move along more quickly if, as Hull had suggested, Japan would take "some unilateral act to indicate that it appreciates and understands the attitude of the United States toward the European war and realizes that that attitude is based on self-defense." Neither Hamilton nor Hull specified what "unilateral act" would satisfy the United Sates on that point.

There was also a concern in the State Department about Japan's proposal to delete the May 31 draft's reference to "the principle of non-discrimination in international relations" in "the Pacific area." The Japanese wanted to confine the language to Japan's "peaceful" activity in "the Southwestern Pacific." That limitation was unacceptable to Hull and his staff. Hull and his staff also remained uncomfortable with Japan's proposal to station troops in North China after settlement of the China Incident, but no progress had been made on that issue. In response to questions from the American representatives, Iwakuro said Japan could not give a time limit on how long the troops would remain there. He said only that "the troops would be withdrawn as soon as the cause for keeping them there should cease to exist." There was no discussion of—and therefore no agreement on—the Manchuria issue either because the American proposal of May 31 had repeated that the issue would be subject to "amicable negotiation" at a later point.

The meetings did little more than to highlight the absence of any agreement on these and other critical points. That was neither surprising nor unwelcome to Stanley Hornbeck. In a memorandum to Hull on June 10, the Political Relations Adviser expressed his long-held view that any agreement would be "something which neither the Japanese nation nor the people of the United States want and which, if consummated, will be distasteful to both." At the same time, Hornbeck—apparently educated about Roosevelt's interest in prolonged discussions—now saw value in continuing to talk with the Japanese about an agreement that should never come to fruition. "As I have said to you repeatedly," the memorandum continued, "I feel that certain useful purposes may be served by the carrying on and continuance of the conversations. But I would view with unqualified misgiving the eventuation of an agreement...." Hornbeck added that it was his duty, "in fairness to the Secretary of State," to tell him that, to best of his knowledge, "every officer of the Department who has been associated with or who has close knowledge of the progress of the conversations shares in the misgivings to which I have been and am giving expression...."

Hull certainly understood the underpinnings of his adviser's comments—especially because he was not pleased with the changes proposed by the Japanese representatives. In meetings with Nomura, the Secretary of State provided comments in person and in documents that expressed concern that the changes proposed by the Japanese representatives "carried the proposal away from the fundamental points" that the United States deemed essential "in establishing and preserving peaceful conditions in the Pacific area." But neither Hull nor his staff expressed any inclination to terminate the meetings or to expedite a determination whether an agreement was possible. Quite the contrary. Hull and his staff repeatedly explained to Nomura and his colleagues that reaching "a satisfactory understanding" would not be difficult if Japan would only "adopt courses which are in conformity with principles" espoused by the United States. Nowhere, however, did Hull or his staff provide any meaningful specificity with respect to the "courses" they desired.

The lack of specificity coincided with the American strategy to keep the balls in the air. At times, the strategy was even at odds with efforts to clarify the differences between the two countries. That resistance to clarification was evident at the meeting in Hull's apartment on Sunday morning, June 15 (when Hull was confined to bed). Nomura said that he "would like to come to an understanding with the Secretary as to what were the points in the Japanese proposal on which" there was agreement and "what were the points on which" the two sides "differed." Nomura said he needed that information to inform his government on the status of the conversations.

It was not an unreasonable request for a situation where two adversaries were interested in narrowing their differences. But that was not this situation. And so Hull brushed the request aside, saying that "such a procedure might give rise to misunderstanding on the part of the Japanese Government" and that Nomura should make a report to his government "on his own judgment as to the situation."

Despite that response, Hull and his staff decided there would be value in handing Nomura a further revised draft proposal. Hull handed the new draft, along with some explanatory documents, to Nomura at a meeting in Hull's apartment on June 21. There were a variety of changes, but the new draft was little different from the May 31 draft on key points. There was no explicit request for Japan's renunciation of the Tripartite Pact—only a reaffirmation of the earlier statement that all actions by the United States with respect to the European war had been and would be based "solely and exclusively" on self-defense. The proposal again stated that the United States would suggest that Chiang Kai-shek discuss settlement with Japan, but without any penalty to the Chinese if Chiang Kai-shek should decline. There was no provision concerning the stationing of troops in North China after settlement with China to defend against communist attacks—only a statement that the issue was "subject to further discussion." The draft again stated that all economic activity in the entire Pacific area would be subject to "the principle of non-discrimination." And the future of Manchuria was again left to "[a]micable negotiation."

Even as he handed the documents to Nomura on June 21, the Secretary of State expressed skepticism that the submission would be productive. The documents included an Oral Statement which acknowledged that "many Japanese leaders" might favor an adjustment in relations with the United

States. Unfortunately, the statement added, other "Japanese leaders in influential official positions are definitely committed to a course which calls for support of Nazi Germany and its policies of conquest...." The statement did not explicitly identify Matsuoka by name, but there was no doubt that the Foreign Minister was the object of that comment. In light of that unnamed leader's commitment to Germany, the statement rhetorically asked whether it was "illusory" to expect the parties to reach an agreement.

The Oral Statement did reference Japan's proposal to retain troops in North China to defend against communist attacks after a settlement between Japan and China. In accordance with Hull's strategy (and the language in the revised draft), it explained that the United States "does not desire to enter into the merits of such a proposal." At the same time, the statement questioned whether the proposal was in accord with the "liberal policies" that the United States wanted to incorporate in any agreement.

This observation, as well as others in the June 21 documents, made clear that little progress had been made. And if there was any doubt in Nomura's mind on that point, it was certainly removed by the last comment in the Oral Statement. "The Secretary of State has therefore reluctantly come to the conclusion," it said, "that this Government must await some clearer indication than has yet been given that the Japanese Government as a whole desires to pursue courses of peace...." It was not clear what "indication" would satisfy the United States. In his diary, Nomura said only that Hull "wanted the Japanese Government to show more sincerity one way or the other."

Throughout these several weeks in June, no communication was sent to or requested from the American ambassador in Tokyo with respect to the conversations that Hull and his staff were having with Japanese representatives. Grew himself commented in one telegram to Hull that he was "in the dark as to the progress and present status of the American-Japanese conversations in Washington." Grew's lament was warranted. He was not given any memoranda of the conversations. Nor was he given copies of any the proposals submitted by the United States or Japan. And nowhere did Hull or his staff request his views on any of the issues addressed in those proposals—although they remained mindful of Grew's earlier assessment. In analyzing the Japanese proposals for Hull just prior to the submission of the revised draft of June 21, Max Hamilton referenced the reports from Grew "that most of the Japanese Cabinet do not favor going to war with the United

States in the event that the United States becomes involved in the European war" and that "Matsuoka's attitude and policy are not supported by the most influential members of the Cabinet."

Ironically, as Hull was condemning Matsuoka's utterances on behalf of the Tripartite Pact and Germany during those June meetings, Grew was telling the Secretary of State that Matsuoka was becoming more and more isolated from the Japanese leadership. In a telegram to Hull on June 6, the American ambassador told Hull that he had received information from a reliable informant who told him that Prime Minister Konoye had told editorial writers for Japanese periodicals that "he was seriously disturbed by the efforts of Germany to persuade Japan to follow a course calculated to lead to war with the United States." In that same telegram, Grew also reported that a well-informed Japanese official had told him that "serious differences of opinion have developed between the Prime Minister and the Foreign Minister and that these differences will be publicly disclosed in the near future."

Other developments could have confirmed Matsuoka's diminishing stature to Hull. In May, the *Japan Times and Advertiser*—regarded by many as an organ of the Foreign Ministry—published an article that explained that people with "dangerous contagious thoughts" would be taken to prison and then to preventive detention facilities, where they would be kept "until there is unmistakable evidence that they have reformed and are no longer carriers of the infectious germs of subversive thoughts."

Government officials were not immune from that policy. On June 17, the Japanese press announced that the government had established within the Cabinet a new Bureau for Thought Control and that one of its primary objectives would be "the suppression of dangerous thoughts held by government officials...." Although the governmental apparatus was new, there was nothing novel about the effort to cleanse the governmental system of people with unacceptable opinions. As the creation of the new bureau was being announced, Grew learned that the government had already arrested 440 government officials in the past few months because their expression of "totalitarian views had rendered them amenable to the provisions of the Thought Control Law, which specifies penalties for persons who advocate the overthrow of the capitalist system."

The Foreign Minister was not beyond the reach of this new focus on government officials. Matsuoka had given a fiery speech on May 20 to a meeting of the Imperial Rule Assistance Association in which he had "ruthlessly" criticized the Japanese bureaucracy and "vigorously defended the totalitarian system of the Nazis...." Never one to be shy about promoting himself, the Foreign Minister had arranged for the production of 200,000 pamphlets with the text of his own speech. He no doubt hoped that distribution of the speech would enhance his popularity with the Japanese public. But the government had a different view. On June 19, Grew recorded in his diary that the Home Ministry had prohibited distribution of the pamphlets.

Whatever disappointment the Foreign Minister may have felt from the government's action was soon eclipsed by another incident: Germany's invasion of the Soviet Union on June 22. Grew had long expected the attack. His diary entry of April 25, 1941—written only days after Matsuoka's triumphant return from Moscow with the Neutrality Pact—recorded the Ambassador's view that such an attack was "almost inevitable." When he heard news of the invasion, Grew reiterated that view, saying that he "had long expected it" but "was surprised at the suddenness, believing that it would break somewhat later." Whatever the timing, it was, from Grew's perspective, a welcome development. "I think," he confided to his diary, "the German-Soviet war is the best thing that could have happened. Dog eat dog."

Like the American ambassador, Matsuoka should not have been surprised by the German attack on the Soviet Union. In his conversations with Ribbentrop the previous March, the German Foreign Minister had intimated that tensions were rising between Germany and the Soviet Union and that "a war might break out at any time...." In mid-April, the Japanese ambassador in Berlin had advised Konoye that Germany was on the verge of war with the Soviet Union, that the Soviet Union was unlikely to prevail, and that American and British aid to the Soviet Union "will have hardly any effect on the outcome...." Beyond all that, during the spring there were reports of Russian troops being moved to the Soviet Union's western border and movement of German troops to the east. The likely explanation for those movements was an expected clash between the two armies. And in June, the Japanese ambassador in Berlin dispatched other telegrams warning of an imminent attack by Germany against the Soviet Union.

Despite all these intimations, it appears that Matsuoka and other Japanese leaders discounted the prospect of an imminent German attack on the Soviet Union. They certainly had no formal notice from Germany about the attack. As *New York Times* correspondent Otto Tolischus observed on June 22, "[I]t was obvious that the Japanese were as much surprised by the timing of the event as the rest of the world." (Japan would later return the favor: Germany would not learn of the attack on Pearl Harbor until after it had commenced.)

In discussing the invasion with reporters, Matsuoka tried to appear calm. "Something must be wrong with the brains of those who are surprised," he told one Japanese periodical. In truth, the Foreign Minister was almost apoplectic at the turn of events. He was the one who had been hailed as a hero for securing the Neutrality Pact with the Soviet Union. It was a fitting complement to the Tripartite Pact, which Matsuoka had also advocated (in part because Germany had already signed its own non-aggression pact with the Soviet Union in 1939). The two agreements, at least on paper, safeguarded Japan from the prospect of war with its traditional adversary in Asia and with the dominant force in Europe. Japan would not have to worry about a direct attack from the Soviet Union. Nor would Japan have to worry about supporting Germany in any armed conflict it might have with the Soviet Union.

All those careful calculations evaporated with news of the invasion. Something needed to be done. But Matsuoka knew he had no power to act unilaterally. He could have contacted the Prime Minister to discuss alternatives, but that was not Matsuoka's style. He needed the sanction of a higher authority. And so, at 4 p.m. on that cloudy Sunday, he telephoned Marquis Kido, the Lord Keeper of the Privy Seal, and asked for an appointment with the Emperor. The meeting was scheduled for 5:30 p.m. that same day.

Kido was well aware of the differences of opinion between the Prime Minister and the Foreign Minister. Apparently expecting that Matsuoka would urge some action supportive of Germany, the Lord Keeper wanted to spare the Emperor from having to consider a policy that might not be supported by the Cabinet and, more importantly, one that might be inimical to Japan's interest. Kido suggested that Hirohito listen to the Foreign Minister and then ask if he had consulted the Prime Minister about any proposed action.

As Kido expected, Matsuoka was full of excitement when he saw Hirohito. There was, he told the Emperor, no time for delay. Japan's Neutrality Pact with the Soviet Union could not stand in the way of the appropriate policy. Japan, he said, "must cooperate with Germany and attack Russia."

Hirohito was, according to Konoye, "astonished" by Matsuoka's proposal. As Kido had suggested, the Emperor asked the Foreign Minister whether he had consulted with the Prime Minister. Matsuoka had not reached out to Konoye, and he now understood what he should have known from the beginning. Hirohito would not sanction any policy except through the recommendation of the Prime Minister and his cabinet. Matsuoka left the Imperial Palace with the knowledge that he had no choice but to contact Konoye.

The Foreign Minister had to know the implications of what lay ahead. The Prime Minister and the military had a different perspective than the Foreign Minister. They had no interest in undertaking the cost and risk of war with the Soviet Union unless it was necessary to protect Japan or unless German success on the Soviet Union's western front provided a propitious opportunity for Japan to initiate an attack on the Soviet Union's eastern front. But they did have an interest in relieving themselves of the tension and conflict created by the Foreign Minister.

The German invasion of Russia was the very incident they needed to orchestrate Matsuoka's removal from the Cabinet. His advocacy had placed Japan in the precarious position of being allies with two countries at war with each other. It was an untenable posture and, under the Japanese political system, someone would have to pay for the miscalculation. "Matsuoka will almost surely have to go," Grew confided to his diary at the end of the month.

No immediate decision was made on the Foreign Minister's status— although his stature and public standing were clearly diminished by the German invasion of Russia. The more pressing problem for the Japanese Government was to craft a response to the German initiative. In doing that, the Japanese government did not want to grapple with open discussion among the people. "The police issued a special warning against groundless rumors," Tolischus recorded on June 25, "and threatened severe punishment to all, including 'big men in all walks of life, who, because of their special knowledge, are believed to be the source of the rumors.'"

That warning may have applied to Matsuoka, but it did not preclude remarks from the Prime Minister. He gave an interview to the foreign press on Sunday, June 29, to emphasize that "Japan is very anxious to maintain friendly relations with the United States" and that he saw "no reason why our two countries cannot remain friendly." Speaking in English and appearing "unhurried and very courteous," Konoye added that the "chief purpose" of the Tripartite Pact was "defensive in nature" and should not pose an obstacle to maintaining those friendly relations with the United States.

Konoye's comments were derided as meaningless by Joe Ballantine, who told Hull that the Prime Minister's remarks about a "friendly" relationship with the United States were no "different from those which have been repeatedly announced by spokesmen of the Japanese Government for the last several years." Ballantine did not share his skepticism with Grew, who was in a position to provide a countervailing view. "Only a few days ago," he recorded in diary on July 2, "Prince Konoye asked a close Japanese friend of mine whether I fully realized his strong desire for friendship with the United States." That information was buttressed by a report from another "reliable contact" who told Grew that Konoye had spoken to him "very confidently of the prospect of adjusting relations between our two countries."

In the meantime, Konoye as well as other members of the Cabinet and representatives of the Army and Navy met almost continuously in Liaison Conferences to review the country's options. Support for Germany was in short supply. The German ambassador had been, according to Grew, "seeing Matsuoka or other high Japanese officials constantly." But Grew knew the meetings would not overcome the bitterness many Japanese already felt or were beginning to feel toward the Germans. The Reichstag representatives had been persistently pushing Matsuoka and other Japanese officials to pursue aggressive military action against the United States. At one point in the middle of June, the American ambassador sent a telegram to Hull that conveyed information from a member of the Diet who had sent a written message because he was afraid to be seen going to the American embassy. According to the informant, the Germans had urged the Foreign Minister to initiate an attack in the South Seas because "the United States is in no condition to engage in hostilities in both the Atlantic and Pacific...."

Many in the Japanese government recognized the German pressures for what they were—an incitement to action more likely to serve the Führer's interest than Japan's. "Today," Tolischus reported in the New York Times, "Japan knows that she is not a partner but merely an object in

Hitler's policies. And she also knows, as one Japanese newspaper has said, that Hitler throws off treaties like worn-out sandals, and all those who sought to profit by cooperating with Hitler paid a terrific price for it." Grew explained the prevailing attitude toward the Germans more succinctly in his diary. "[M]any high Japanese," said the Ambassador, "are fed up with them."

Not surprisingly, most of the participants in the Liaison Conferences at the end of June were more focused on a policy that would serve Japan's interest rather than Germany's. The military wanted to proceed with the establishment of a presence in southern Indochina, which was still under the purported rule of the Vichy government. Moving southward, they argued, would give Japan access to needed natural resources, provide a means to restrain American and British aid to Chiang Kai-shek, and, not coincidentally, give Japan a springboard for military advancement to other points in Southeast Asia if, as many junior officers in the Army hoped (despite Konoye's expressed desire to the contrary), Japan should find itself in armed conflict with the United States.

For his part, Matsuoka acknowledged that he bore some responsibility for Japan's dilemma. "As a matter of fact," the Foreign Minister told the other conferees at the first Liaison Conference on Wednesday, June 25, "I concluded a Neutrality Pact because I thought that Germany and Soviet Russia would not go to war. If I had known that they would go to war... I would not have concluded the Neutrality Pact." But that mistake could not stand in the way of the need to support Germany. "When Germany wipes out the Soviet Union," he argued, "we can't simply share in the spoils of victory unless we've done something. We must either shed our blood or embark on diplomacy. And it's better to shed blood."

A surprising perspective from a Foreign Minister. But it was not enough to carry the day with the Cabinet or even the military. That became clear when they all gathered on July 2 for an Imperial Conference in front of the Emperor in the Meiji Palace on the Imperial compound.

Unlike the more informal Liaison Conferences, Imperial Conferences were a vehicle to have the Emperor sanction policy choices made by the Cabinet and the armed forces. They were not an everyday occurrence. There had only been three Imperial Conferences since the inauguration of the China Incident in 1937. The setting was commensurate with the importance of the event. Tall ceilings punctuated with large glass chandeliers. Purple-colored silk hangings with floral patterns affixed to the walls. Two long rectangular tables—covered in multi-colored silk sheets—only a short distance from each other. There the participants sat, ramrod straight, looking at each other. The Emperor, dressed in his army uniform, sat on a chair in front of a gold screen facing the two rectangular tables.

The conference had been requested by Konoye the day before to bring closure to the discussions the Cabinet members and military representatives had been having in the previous ten days. Their decision now needed the Imperial Seal of approval. The proceedings began at 10 a.m. The Prime Minister rose from his seat, bowed in the direction of the Emperor, and read from a document entitled "Outline of National Policies in View of the Changing Situation." The document referenced the need to implement the Greater East Asia Co-Prosperity Sphere policy "no matter what changes may occur in the world situation." The document said that the government would "continue its efforts to effect a settlement of the China Incident." That goal, the document added, would "involve steps to advance south."

To that end, the document said that Japan would execute plans set forth in another policy statement which detailed "various measures relating to French Indochina and Thailand." In carrying out those measures in the "southern regions," the document said that Japan "will not be deterred by the possibility of being involved in a war with Great Britain and the United States."

No reference was made to any attack on Pearl Harbor. Commander Genda Minoru—who had been given responsibility for the air assault—had initiated test flights by torpedo bombers in the southern islands, but Admiral Yamamoto's plan had not been formally approved by the Navy. His scheme was not even known to the War and Navy Ministers, let alone the civilian members of the Cabinet. (Ironically, Tolischus had told Grew about an indirect interaction with Yamamoto on an earlier train ride from the beach town of Hayama to Tokyo. The *New York Times* correspondent had asked two members of the Diet, who were also on the train, about a report that the Japanese Navy would intercept any American ships moving across the Pacific toward the Red Sea. The Diet members immediately consulted Yamamoto, who was also traveling on the train. He not only denied the report but also said "that it was Japan's intention to avoid complications in the Pacific and that his own influence was and would continue to be exerted wholly in that direction.")

The new policy statement being considered at the Imperial Conference did address the German-Soviet conflict but deferred any response. In deciding how to proceed, the document said that Japan would be guided by the Tripartite Pact but that Japan would "decide independently as to the time and method of resorting to force." The document promised involvement in that conflict only if the war should develop to Japan's advantage. It closed with a statement that the government's immediate attention would turn "to placing the nation on a war footing" and to making sure that "the defense of the homeland will be strengthened."

The document did not explicitly explain how the move into southern Indochina or Thailand would help resolve the China Incident. Presumably, a military advance into those countries would enable Japan to close the Burma Road, a highway in Burma—then a British colony located southwest of China—that was used to provide supplies to Chiang Kai-Shek's regime. Whatever the details on that situation, the participants understood that other benefits would ensue as well—the ability to secure more natural resources, the opportunity to secure an advantage in any military campaign in the Southwest Pacific, and, not incidentally, the ability to discourage German intrusions into Southeast Asia if, as some conference participants believed, Germany was on the verge of victory against the Soviet Union and thus in a position to move into Asia.

The participants should have known that the planned move into southern Indochina was a decision fraught with risks. The United States had not been pleased when Japan had moved its military into northern Indochina in September 1940. Japan had ultimately secured an agreement with the Vichy government to effectuate that move, but it had been preceded by combat initiated by Japanese armed forces. That tactic fostered a widely-held belief (at least in the United States) that any new agreement with the Vichy government would be a prelude to Japan's use of armed force. Beyond that, the Roosevelt administration recognized that a substantial Japanese military presence in the French colony would facilitate Japan's ability to launch attacks on the Philippines, Singapore, and other points in Southeast Asia. In explaining the United States' displeasure to the press, Hull had pointed out that the United States advocated "abstinence by all nations from the use of force in the internal affairs of other nations." Another administration official was more direct. "The danger," said Federal Security Administrator Paul McNutt, "lies in powerful men-of-war steaming into Manila Harbor, into Guam, and the Hawaiian Islands...."

The Roosevelt administration did not counter the Japanese move into northern Indochina with armed force, but it did institute an embargo on Japan's importation of scrap steel and scrap iron. It was not an insignificant action. Japan needed scrap iron and scrap steel to make machinery of all kinds, including military hardware. (In fact, Japan had purchased about 90% of her scrap iron and scrap steel from the United States in 1939.) The reaction by the United States to a move into southern Indochina could be expected to be that much more adverse even it were accomplished through peaceful means. For his part, Hull would undoubtedly view the move into southern Indochina as a rejection of his repeated requests to Nomura for some indication that the Japanese government had abandoned its policies of military conquest.

Nomura, for one, understood the implications—at least if military force were used. Matsuoka sent a cable to the retired admiral on the day the conference ended to inform him of the decision to move into the southern regions. "[I]f you are resolved to use armed force against the Southern Regions at this time," the Ambassador responded on July 3, "there seems to be no room at all for adjusting Japanese-American relations."

Although he shared that concern, Hirohito believed he was obligated to sanction a consensus reached by the government and the military. At the same time, he wanted the Imperial Conference participants to consider the risks of the proposed decision to move into southern Indochina. But he would not be the one to raise concerns at the conference. Bearing in mind the guidance which Prince Saionji had given him years earlier, the Emperor believed that his questions should be voiced by Hara Yoshimichi, the seventy-four-year-old President of the Privy Council.

A small man with a thin moustache and horn-rimmed glasses, Hara did not hesitate to confront the Cabinet members and military representatives with Hirohito's apprehensions at the July 2 conference. His questions were, as Army Chief Sugiyma Hajime later said, "relevant and pointed." A principal theme of Hara's questions was the impact on Japan's relations with the United States. "I want to avoid war with the United States," he bluntly stated. Given that goal, he asked whether it might not be better to join Germany in an attack on the Soviet Union. "I do not think that the United States would take any action," he said, "if we were to attack the Soviet Union." Conversely, he asked whether moving into southern Indochina carried that risk of war with the United States.

The Foreign Minister was quick to respond. "I cannot exclude that possibility," he said. Unlike Matsuoka, Sugiyama was willing to give Hara the answer he wanted. The Army chief did acknowledge that the "occupation of Indochina will certainly provoke Great Britain and the United States." But they could not worry about adverse American and British reactions. The movement into southern Indochina was "absolutely necessary" to protect Japan against an uncertain future. That posture seemed especially justified, said Sugiyama, because he did "not believe that the United States will go to war if Japan moves into French Indochina"—assuming, as he did, that the occupation would be accomplished "peacefully."

It was a perspective born of the Japanese leaders' view that the United States was in the grip of isolationist sentiment that shunned involvement in foreign conflicts. "I am convinced," said Tolischus a couple of months earlier, "that Japan's leaders were being deceived regarding American strength and morale by labor strikes and isolationist and pacifist activity in America, which were being exploited in the Japanese press." It was a view shared by Grew. In late April, he had cabled Hull and Under Secretary of State Sumner Welles that "the extremists in Japan who favor carrying out the southward advance have been encouraged by reports from the United States in their stubborn belief that we would not go to war with Japan short of a direct attack on the Philippines...[U]nder these circumstances," Grew suggested, "it might be helpful if either the President or the Secretary should call in Admiral Nomura and should talk to him in a way which would disabuse the extremists of the foregoing beliefs."

The suggestion might have been beneficial to the United States (and Japan) as Konoye's cabinet and the Japanese military decided on their country's new policy at the July 2 Imperial Conference, but neither Roosevelt nor Hull had any such conversation with Nomura. And so there was no discussion at that conference about whether the United States might respond with embargoes or other sanctions.

The absence of any such discussion did not trouble Hara. He had the assurance he wanted that there would be no war with the United States. A vote was taken, and the new policy statement was unanimously adopted. The document was signed by Konoye and the military chiefs and then brought to the Privy Seal's office for the affixation of the Imperial Seal. The decision to establish a military presence in southern Indochina was now the official policy of Japan. About two hours after the conference ended, the Foreign Minister issued a public announcement which stated that "[a] decision regarding the Government's fundamental policy was reached at the Imperial Conference today" and that "a super emergency period is developing in the Far East which will directly affect Japan." No mention was made concerning the particulars of the decision.

Hara may have been satisfied with the decision, but Konoye's concerns endured. The Prime Minister decided to send a letter to Matsuoka on July 4 because, in his view, "the Foreign Minister's ambiguous attitude could no longer be disregarded." Among other matters, the letter referenced the Navy's judgment that simultaneously fighting a war against the Soviet Union and the United States would pose "almost insurmountable difficulties." In light of that judgment, said Konoye, the "invasion" of southern Indochina "should, if possible, be abandoned" until the Soviet issue was resolved. That suggestion assumed that the move into southern Indochina could spark an armed conflict with the United States. A corollary to that suggestion was Konoye's admonition to Matsuoka that it was "necessary" to bring Nomura's discussions with Hull to "a successful conclusion...."

Konoye's letter did not surface in public, but word soon slipped out about the move into southern Indochina (which would ultimately be accomplished by another agreement with the Vichy government). British Ambassador Sir Robert Craigie registered a protest with the Foreign Ministry Office on July 5 to say that England would consider it "a serious problem" if there was truth to the report that the Japanese military would soon move into southern Indochina.

Grew sent a telegram to Hull the next day after hearing the news from various sources, including Otto Tolischus. The Imperial Conference, said the telegram, had decided to "sit on the fence" with respect to the German-Soviet conflict but, in the meantime, to acquire military bases in southern Indochina "gradually and step by step in order to avoid an open conflict with the United States." The Ambassador explained that this move was dictated in part by a desire on the part of Japanese leaders to consolidate

Japan's position in Southeast Asia "before Germany is in a position to inter-fere with Japanese ambitions...." Grew also reported that Matsuoka had told Craigie that "the mutual confidence between the allies of the Tripartite Pact remains unimpaired...." But he added that no credence could be given to that statement. It "is so palpably contrary to the truth," said Grew, "that we must take the Minister's statement with reserve."

In the midst of all these developments through the late spring and early summer of 1941, Grew still found time to write letters to his daughters, each of whom remained with their respective families in a different American legation outside Japan. The dispatch and receipt of such letters could take weeks. And so it was not until the middle of June that the doting father was in a position to write Elsie a long letter to thank her for the good wishes she had sent on May 27, Grew's sixty-first birthday.

"I don't know," said Joe, "whether life actually begins at sixty-one, but one certainly gets a lot more out of it.... Another advantage of sixty-one over twenty-one," he continued, "is the fact that by that time one has either devel-oped a happy home or ended like the Sergeant whom the Colonel lambasted for getting a divorce after all those years of matrimony." (According to Grew, the Sergeant told the Colonel, "You've got it all wrong. I'm not a deserter. I'm a refugee.") For Grew, the importance of a successful marriage could not be overestimated. "[O]ne finally arrives at that most agreeable situation in life," he told Elsie, "where complete understanding, contentment and happi-ness in the home has developed a philosophy where one doesn't give much of a damn what happens outside the home, relatively speaking of course."

It was a perspective that would be tested in the months that lay ahead. As Japan and the United States slid closer to war, tensions increased. And Grew would become that much more frustrated as he tried to do some-thing useful.

CHAPTER 12

The Response

I t was not just another train ride. On a sweltering day in September 1940, the President assembled a large entourage of Cabinet members and other administration officials to travel with him by train from Washington to Jasper, Alabama, to attend the funeral of William Bankhead, the former Speaker of the House of Representatives and the father of acclaimed actress Tallulah Bankhead. The sixty-six-year-old Bankhead had collapsed a few days earlier as he was about to give a radio address in Baltimore, the victim of a ruptured abdominal aneurysm. The President's train left Washington's Union Station around 5 p.m. on Monday, September 16. Another train included a large congressional delegation, Bankhead's family, and the casket. They would all congregate the next day in the First Methodist Church in Jasper, where Bankhead had maintained his home.

The Secretary of State would have been included in the President's party, but Cordell Hull was ill. Instead, Sumner Welles, the Under Secretary of State, was asked to represent the State Department. It would prove to be a fateful ride for the forty-seven-year-old executive.

He was, by appearance, background, and temperament, a man of aristocratic bearings. Standing about six foot-three inches, Welles displayed lean features, a receding hairline, a thin white mustache, and striking blue eyes. His tailored suits were purchased from British clothiers, and the image of self-assurance was reinforced by his erect carriage and the walking stick he often used when strolling down the street. That self-assurance was reflected in meetings and other interactions with colleagues and staff members. He could be brisk, almost abrupt, and was rarely suffused with doubt. Welles' self-confidence was not always well received by others. Interior Secretary Harold Ickes referred to him as "one of the most conceited men I have known."

Welles could trace his lineage back to 1636 when Thomas Welles first arrived in Boston. Over the course of the next two centuries, the family amassed considerable wealth. By the time he grew up in a fashionable New York City townhouse in the late 1890s and early 1900s, young Sumner's family was, as Welles' son later recounted, surrounded by "butlers, maids, coachmen and grooms...." The young boy's reliance on ever-present servants did not fade as he grew older. As the country suffered through the Depression in the 1930s, he would use a chauffeur to drive him to the State Department in a Rolls Royce.

Welles did not try to shield others from his lavish life style. When he was a rising star at the State Department at the end of Woodrow Wilson's administration, Welles tried to meet with Secretary of State Bainbridge Colby late one afternoon. It was apparently a pressing matter, and the young staff member waited until about 10 p.m. before returning home. Colby learned of Welles' desire to see him and called his house later that evening, only to be told by the butler, "Mr. Secretary, Mr. Welles told me—particularly if you called—to say that he had retired." (The incident had no bearing on Colby's high opinion of Welles. "He is brilliant, tireless," the Secretary of State later told a friend. "When there is work to be done—the clock does not exist.") In later years, social events at one of Welles' homes—whether the mansion of one hundred rooms on Massachusetts Avenue in Washington (which later housed the upper crust Cosmos Club) or the estate in Oxon Hill, Maryland (a 250-acre manor located near Washington on the Potomac River)—featured all the accommodations and blandishments one would expect for a man with Welles' wealth.

However comfortable his environment, Welles was not one to while away the hours in leisure. His considerable ambition was fueled by his years at Groton and Harvard. It was there that he pursued relationships with students and others who would facilitate his entry into government. And it was there too that he suffered one of the most traumatic events of his young life. His mother, who had doted on him as a boy, died in his freshman year at Harvard. She was never to be forgotten, and for years afterward, Sumner would wear a black tie as a sign of mourning.

Shortly after graduating from Harvard, Welles entered the diplomatic service, an appointment engineered in part through family connections with Washington politicians. He spent two years as a Third Secretary in the embassy in Tokyo (where he saw that "behind the veneer" of a country trying to assimilate the attributes of Western civilization "lay a primeval military instinct"). He was later assigned to a post in Argentina before returning to the State Department. There, he ultimately captured the attention of Charles Evan Hughes, President Warren Harding's new Secretary of State.

It was the beginning of a close working relationship that catapulted Welles into the highest echelon of the State Department hierarchy in the early 1920s. He was unmistakably intelligent and endowed with leadership qualities. Welles was the "outstanding man in the State Department," Hughes told one dinner companion. "Presidential timber." More than that, Welles was invested with an ability to express himself in crisp language. (That would later be a point of comparison in Roosevelt's administration when Welles would attend Cabinet meetings at the White House if Hull was unavailable. "If Welles were representing the State Department, as frequently he was," remembered Attorney General Robert H. Jackson, "he usually gave a quick and very intelligent resume of the week's developments and trends. He was a much more informative person, and a much more informed person to all appearances, although it was never possible to tell how much Hull might know because he was so reserved.")

By the age of twenty-nine, Welles was the head of the State Department's Latin American Division. He resigned in March 1922 only to return months later at Hughes' request to settle simmering disputes in Central America (a role well-suited to Welles' talents, in part because he was fluent in Spanish). In all, it was work that received the highest accolades from the State Department and even the President. In his memoirs, Hughes praised Welles' "special aptitude for negotiations" with Latin American countries. Under Secretary of State Joseph Grew referenced his "fine work" in trying to orchestrate an agreement with rebels in Honduras. And in a meeting in the Oval Office,

President Calvin Coolidge thanked him for his "accomplishments" in resolving problems in the Dominican Republic.

The bloom soon fell off the rose. While working at the State Department, Welles became infatuated with Mathilde Townsend Gerry, a tall woman with large eyes and delicate facial features who was eight years older than Sumner. The problem was that she was married to Peter Goelet Gerry, a Democratic senator from Rhode Island. The other problem was that Welles was also married (to Esther Slater, a woman from Boston and, like Mathilde, the heiress of a considerable family fortune). In due course, Welles divorced Esther and married Mathilde, who had divorced Senator Gerry.

The June 1925 marriage of the two divorcées was mentioned in the *New York Times*, and one of those who learned about it was Calvin Coolidge. It did not sit well with the puritanical president. In the middle of July, Joe Grew, still Under Secretary of State, forwarded to the White House a list of people who should be invited to an event to honor fifteen nominees to a tribunal in the Dominican Republic which Welles had helped to create. Coolidge approved all the proposed invitees except one. "All O.K. except Sumner Welles," the President scrawled in a note at the top the list. "If he is in government service, let him be dismissed at once."

The presidential directive could not be disregarded, and Welles' tenure at the State Department came to an abrupt end. After leaving the government, he spent considerable time writing a two-volume, thousand-page history of the Dominican Republic (*Naboth's Vineyard*). Much of his other time was spent traveling with Mathilde and enjoying his homes. And throughout it all, there was excessive drinking, sometimes at speakeasies that evaded the restrictions of Prohibition. It was an indulgence that would prove to be his undoing.

In the meantime, Welles had another outlet to regain entry into government service: Franklin D. Roosevelt. His connection to the Roosevelt family dated back to his boyhood. His mother and Eleanor Roosevelt's mother were close friends (so much so that twelve-year-old Sumner was a page at Eleanor and Franklin's wedding in March 1905, carrying the train of her wedding dress as President Theodore Roosevelt walked his niece down the aisle). Franklin Roosevelt, then Assistant Secretary of the Navy in Wilson's administration, was among those who wrote letters of recommendation for Welles when he was trying to enter the diplomatic service in 1915. Roosevelt told

Secretary of State William Jennings Bryan that he had known Welles "since he was a small boy" and that he "should give a very good account of himself in the service."

The two men had maintained sporadic contact over the years. Welles had, in fact, reached out to Roosevelt after he suffered the polio attack in 1921. By 1923, the men were communicating more frequently, with Welles eventually providing the erstwhile presidential candidate with thoughts about American foreign policy. By the time Roosevelt reached the White House in March 1933, Welles had prepared the outlines of what would become the new President's Good Neighbor Policy for Latin America.

Not surprisingly, Roosevelt found a place for Welles in his new administration, first as the Ambassador to Cuba (where rebel forces threatened to overthrow the government) and then as Assistant Secretary of State with responsibility for Latin American policies. The two men forged a close working relationship, and Roosevelt decided to ask Welles to become Under Secretary of State in 1937 to fill the vacancy created when Bill Phillips left the position to become the ambassador to Italy.

The President's proposal to promote Welles did not sit well with the Secretary of State. Hull favored the appointment of his friend Walton R. Moore, a seventy-seven-year-old former congressman from Virginia and the Assistant Secretary of State in charge of congressional relations. Ever the hopeful mediator, Roosevelt settled on a compromise that he presumably hoped would leave no ruffled feathers. Welles would get the appointment as Under Secretary, and Moore would fill the long-dormant position as Counselor to the State Department. The compromise did not satisfy Hull or Moore. "Mr. Welles has won his fight with the President and with the Secretary," Moore wrote to William C. Bullitt, then the United States ambassador to France and one of Welles' most bitter antagonists. "It is desired that I shall win the consolation prize."

Welles strived to be solicitous of Hull, but the circumstances made good relations difficult. Hull recognized that Roosevelt was prone to reach out to people regardless of their status in the administration hierarchy, and that would be especially so here, where the Under Secretary had a long-standing personal relationship with the President. As Under Secretary, Welles had direct responsibility for the operational details of the State Department, and that too became a sore point with the Secretary. "I don't see the President very often," Hull complained to Jim Farley at one point. "Most of the details are handled through Welles."

The Secretary tried to accept the situation, but it was not easy. As he later explained in his *Memoirs*, Hull wanted to give Welles "reasonable latitude" in meeting directly with the President (as if Hull could control Roosevelt's schedule), but the Under Secretary "abused this privilege by going to the President at times without my knowledge, and even attempting to secure a decision, again without my knowledge." Given this perspective, the Secretary could be suspicious of Welles if there was any public criticism of Hull or any decision he made. "Hull," said *Foreign Affairs* editor Hamilton Armstrong, "is one of the most sensitive and suspicious people who ever held office."

That suspicion surfaced in December 1940 when syndicated columnist Drew Pearson—a Welles friend—wrote a column stating that Hull had tried to arrange a $100 million loan to Spanish dictator Francisco Franco but that Welles had gone directly to the President to block it. Hull was infuriated because the story was not true. The Secretary assumed (wrongly) that Welles had been the source for Pearson's column, and he did not conceal his anger from the Under Secretary. Welles later told Pearson "that he had never been castigated by anyone in his life as he had been by Hull." The particulars of other situations may have differed over time, but Hull's view of his deputy did not. "[E]very department has its thun-a-bitch," he told a friend in his lisp, "but I've got the all-American."

With all this simmering distrust, Welles should not have been surprised when Hull exploited the reported incident on that September 1940 train ride to have Welles removed from office. After Bankhead's funeral, the President's entourage returned to the train station in the late afternoon for the ride back to Washington. Many began to imbibe liquor, and as the train rumbled through Tennessee in the early morning hours of September 18, Welles was still drinking with Henry Wallace, the Democrats' Vice Presidential nominee, and Federal Works administrator John Carmody.

When the train approached Roanoke, Virginia around 5:30 a.m., John Stone, a black porter, was summoned to bring coffee to Welles' compartment. Upon arrival, an inebriated Welles reportedly offered Stone twenty dollars to perform oral sex while Welles remained clothed. Stone refused and returned to the dining car. It was alleged that Welles made "indirect" approaches to other porters who were also asked to come to his compartment with coffee. The disturbed porters reported the encounters to the dining car manager, and he, in turn, alerted Dale Whitehead, the head of the President's Secret Service detail. Whitehead tried to observe a porter delivering coffee to Welles' compartment, but the Under Secretary apparently saw Whitehead and kept his compartment door closed until the train reached Washington later that morning.

Rumors of the incident circulated among the press as well as members of Congress and the administration. Welles himself had heard that Bill Bullitt had passed the rumor on to Burton Wheeler, the Democratic senator from Montana and a sometime antagonist of the President's. The Under Secretary discussed the situation with his friend Bob Jackson, the Attorney General. Welles acknowledged that "he had been drinking rather heavily and was no doubt considerably under the weather. . . ." He remembered taking a sleeping pill and also requesting coffee because, he said, he was experiencing heart pain (a chronic condition), and coffee was the one thing that could help him deal with the pain. But he said he could not recall making any proposition to any of the train's porters.

By early January 1941, the rumors had reached the White House, and Roosevelt asked the Federal Bureau of Investigation to investigate the matter. FBI Director J. Edgar Hoover presented the bureau's findings in a visit with Roosevelt in the Oval Office around 4:30 p.m. on January 29. Hoover told the President about the allegations that "Welles had propositioned a number of the train crew to have immoral relations with them." However, the bureau had not interviewed Welles to hear his side of the story. Nor had the bureau interviewed John Stone, the porter who allegedly received the most direct proposition, because he had died two weeks before the bureau began its investigation.

The President listened impassively to Hoover's report. He did not comment or seek the FBI Director's advice. But that did not free him of the pressure to do something. On the morning of April 23, 1941, he met with Bill Bullitt, who said that Judge Moore (who had unsuccessfully vied with Welles to become Under Secretary of State) had summoned Bullitt while "on his deathbed" and given him documents concerning the alleged incidents on the train. Bullitt presented Roosevelt with one of the documents. The President turned it aside, saying, "I know about this already. I have had a full report on it. There is truth to the allegations." Bullitt pressed Roosevelt to dismiss Welles, saying that Hull also knew about the allegations and "considered Welles worse than a murderer." Roosevelt was unwilling to commit to any action (perhaps because, as his son Elliot later said, the President "believed Welles' version—that it was the porter, bribed on Bullitt's behalf, who had made the overture").

The pressure for the President to do something did not abate. Bill Bullitt's hatred of the Under Secretary was unremitting, and he was relentless in his effort to have Welles dismissed from office. And in that effort, he had a willing accomplice: Cordell Hull. The Secretary had discussed the matter with Judge Moore shortly before he had died, had reviewed at least a portion of the FBI files, and had repeatedly asked the President to remove Welles as Under Secretary of State. On August 11, 1943, Roosevelt summoned the Under Secretary to the White House and told him that Hull "had been trying for a year and a half to make it clear that he wished [Welles] to be replaced." Despite his affection and high regard for Welles, Roosevelt knew that the rumors of the 1940 incident were too rampant and too damaging to be ignored.

Welles told Mathilde that he would have resigned within twenty-four hours if Hull had only asked for the resignation himself. He could not let the matter pass without discussing it with Hull. That was his way. So he made a final visit to the Secretary's office a day or two later. He pointedly asked Hull why he had not spoken to him directly to request his resignation. "I didn't speak to you," Hull angrily responded, "because you're an intimate friend of the President, much closer to him than I." But Hull did not mince words about the need for Welles to leave. "Your continuation in office," he said, "would be, for the President and the State Department, the greatest national scandal since the existence of the United States." With that, Welles stood up, shook Hull's hand, and left the office without saying anything further. A few days later, he submitted his resignation to Roosevelt. (Hull did not accept any responsibility for Welles' resignation, saying in his *Memoirs* that the President had made the decision to request Welles' resignation "on his own" to improve "the efficiency" of the State Department.)

Long before then, the Secretary of State needed Welles to assume direct responsibility for conducting the discussions with Nomura and the other Japanese representatives. The tubercular condition that had forced Hull to remain in bed during some of his meetings with Nomura in June 1941 continued to deteriorate. Fever and frequent bouts of coughing made it increasingly difficult for the Secretary to attend to work. Hull's doctor therefore recommended that he go to the Greenbrier resort in White Sulphur Springs, West Virginia, for an extended rest. Hull departed for the Greenbrier on June 24. Before leaving, he told the Japanese ambassador that "he was leaving for the country for a few days to recuperate ...." Sumner Welles, who had largely been isolated from matters involving Japan, would be there to fill the void as Acting Secretary of State.

One of Welles' first actions concerned rumors that Japan might attack the Soviet Union. Roosevelt and his administration worried that such an attack would widen the European war and force the United States to re-evaluate its position. On July 5, the Acting Secretary sent Grew a message from Roosevelt to the Japanese Prime Minister to inquire whether it was "the intention of the Japanese Government to enter upon hostilities against the Soviet Union." Any such action, the message said, "would render illusory the cherished hope of the American Government" for "peace in the Pacific area ...."

Upon receiving the communication, Grew sent a letter to Konoye at his private residence to tell him that he had a message from the President and that he "would be glad to meet him at any suggested place in order to avoid publicity." The Prime Minister's secretary responded that Konoye "feared publicity" if Grew came to his residence. The secretary suggested that they meet on a golf course. But that suggestion proved to be unworkable because it was Sunday and the golf courses would be crowded. Konoye ultimately told the American ambassador that the Foreign Minister would respond to Roosevelt's message when he returned from a brief holiday.

True to that promise, Matsuoka delivered a statement to Grew on July 8 which stated that rumors "are abundantly bred not only in Japan but in all countries," that Japan had always desired to prevent "the European War from spreading to the regions of Greater East Asia," and that Japan "had not so far considered the possibility of joining the hostilities against the Soviet Union." Matsuoka did not mention the relevant clause in the policy statement that had just been adopted at the Imperial Conference. It said that Japan would resort to armed force against the Soviet Union if the situation developed "to the advantage" of Japan.

For reasons never explained, Welles did not ask Grew to make a similar inquiry about Japan's intention to secure military bases in southern Indochina. That omission was particularly noteworthy because the United States knew—from the MAGIC intercepts—of that planned action almost as soon as the decision was reached at the Imperial Conference on July 2. In his *Memoirs*, Hull recounted that the United States had intercepted Matsuoka's telegram to Nomura on that same day, which alerted the Japanese ambassador to the "southward advance" and the execution of Japan's policy "with reference to French Indo-China and Thailand...." That intercept dovetailed with information that Grew had sent to the State Department shortly after the Imperial Conference. And it coincided too with a direct inquiry that Far Eastern Division Chief Max Hamilton had made with Nomura in a meeting on the evening of Saturday, July 5 at the Japanese embassy in Washington.

At that meeting, Hamilton referenced reports in the *New York Times* about Japan's move into southern Indochina and asked the Japanese ambassador for "a prompt denial or frank confirmation of those reports." Nomura did not admit or deny the reports (saying in his diary that he told Hamilton that he too had "read the paper" but had "received no information" from his government). The Japanese ambassador nonetheless felt compelled to justify any southward movement by his country. He said that Japan had to prepare itself for "possible eventualities," that there had been reports of the United States making plans for "the encirclement" of Japan, and that Japan had to prepare against "the possibility of an executive order being issued" by Roosevelt that would foreclose the shipment of petroleum products to Japan. He added that Americans "were apt to treat war lightly and some blindly believed that they could beat Japan in a few months."

Hamilton reported the substance of his conversation with Nomura to Hull, who was still at the Greenbrier. The Secretary of State was not satisfied, and he subsequently directed Hamilton to make another inquiry with the Japanese ambassador. The Far Eastern Division Chief, along with Joe Ballantine, met with Nomura again on July 15 at the Japanese embassy. Hamilton referenced "recurrent rumors and press reports" that Japan was "planning to acquire naval and air bases in French Indochina." Nomura again replied that he "only knew what had been reported in the press" but that he would not be surprised by any such move into southern Indochina for reasons he had articulated earlier.

Hamilton's inquiries no doubt placed Nomura in an uncomfortable position. He knew about the planned move into southern Indochina, but he had not been authorized by his government to convey that information to the United States. His responses to Hamilton reflected that equivocal posture. In the July 15 meeting, Nomura said that he would refer Hamilton's question to his government for a response.

However stoic his responses to the State Department representatives, Nomura was churning inside. On July 10—after his first meeting with Hamilton—the ambassador sent a telegram to Matsuoka with a request that he be allowed to return to Japan. There was a possibility of a "rupture" in diplomatic relations with the United States, said Nomura, and it would be "meaningless" for him to remain in Washington. Matsuoka rejected his request, but Nomura reminded the Foreign Minister that he was "an amateur" who had given Matsuoka "so much trouble" and that, "from a long-range view of things," it would be best if he could be replaced soon by a "skilled person." Matsuoka was not persuaded, and Nomura did not receive permission to leave.

Nomura may have struggled in giving a response to Hamilton's pointed inquiries, but it was a discomfort he had to bear alone. Grew was never asked to make a similar inquiry about Indochina with Japan's Prime Minister or its Foreign Minister. Nor was Grew asked to advise the Japanese government of the consequences that would ensue if, as the United States expected, Japan did expand its military presence in southern Indochina. Welles' failure to make such requests of the American ambassador was all the more perplexing because Roosevelt had already decided that Japan's expansion into southern Indochina would trigger a forceful reaction from the United States.

On July 10—days before Hamilton made his second inquiry to Nomura—Welles was asked by British ambassador Lord Halifax what the United States would do "in the event that Japan occupied Indochina entirely." Welles responded that the President had authorized him to say that "in the event that Japan now took any overt step through force or through the exercise of pressure to conquer or to acquire alien territories in the Far

East, the Government of the United States would immediately impose various embargoes, both economic and financial...."

That anticipated reaction was confirmed in a Cabinet meeting on July 18. Welles told the group that he anticipated that Japan would move into southern Indochina within the next few days. Treasury Secretary Henry Morgenthau, Jr., asked the President what he planned "to do on the economic front against Japan if she makes this move?" Roosevelt responded that he was not prepared to stop all shipments of oil to Japan because it might cause Japan to launch an assault against the Dutch East Indies (another source of oil for Japan) and that "would mean war in the Pacific." Welles then interjected that the United States would "freeze Japanese assets" in the United States if Japan made the move into southern Indochina.

It was not on its face the total and unqualified embargo that some Cabinet members wanted. But the freezing of Japan's assets could (and ultimately did) represent a far more stringent sanction than any that had previously been applied. Welles did not explain exactly how the freeze would work, but, at a minimum, it would give the United States the flexibility to decide whether to allow Japan to withdraw funds from American banks to pay for oil or other exports. As Roosevelt later told the Cabinet, he wanted "to slip the noose around Japan's neck and give it a jerk now and then."

The proposed imposition of the freeze order against Japan flew in the face of Grew's earlier comments in his "Green Light" telegram of September 12, 1940, and his letter to Roosevelt in December 1940. The Ambassador had explained in those communications that economic sanctions were unlikely to alter Japan's policy unless it was made clear to Japan that the United States was prepared to go to war. The contemplated imposition of the freeze order also disregarded Nomura's earlier comment to Hull that economic sanctions could result in military action if Japan felt cornered. (The State Department, as well as Roosevelt, may have been influenced by Stanley Hornbeck's contrary view. Joseph E. Davies, a former ambassador to Belgium and then an assistant to Hull, sent the Secretary of State a memo on March 17, 1941, to report a conversation he had had with Kurusu Saburo, the former Japanese ambassador to Belgium and someone Davies knew well. Kurusu, said Davies, had explained to him in a recent visit that "the application of economic sanctions" against Japan could create a sense of "sheer desperation" and "cause them to fight...even if it meant defeat." After reading the memo, Hornbeck wrote in the margin, "This is nonsense.")

Grew was not asked about the efficacy of the freeze order against Japan if the country moved into southern Indochina. But he was told about it shortly before the Cabinet discussion on July 18. A few days later, Sir Robert Craigie gave him copies of telegrams expressing the British belief that "the British and American Governments should warn Japan in advance that certain economic sanctions will be imposed if these bases are taken." Grew told Welles (as he had previously told both Welles and Hull in April) that there was much to be gained "by letting the Japanese Government know of our intentions, privately and without publicity, preferably through Admiral Nomura...." The advice reflected Grew's long-held belief that sanctions would do little to alter action already taken. "A clear unambiguous statement of such intentions might conceivably exert a deterrent effect," Grew added, "but, once an occupation were effected, Japanese prestige would render subsequent withdrawal out of the question."

Welles did not accept his ambassador's renewed suggestion. The Acting Secretary met with the Japanese ambassador in his office at the State Department (which adjoined Hull's office) in the afternoon of July 23. Nomura told Welles what the Acting Secretary already knew—that "the Japanese Government would send military forces to occupy certain portions of southern Indochina." Nomura tried to justify the policy by reference to Japan's need for natural resources as well as the country's need to defend itself against "a policy of encirclement" being pursued by the United States and other "foreign powers." Nomura was, as Welles later reported, "exceedingly conciliatory," repeatedly telling Welles that the United States should not "reach hasty conclusions."

Welles knew it was too late for that. He said that there was no basis to believe that the United States and other foreign powers were engaged in a policy of "encirclement." He added that the agreement that Nomura had been discussing with Hull would provide Japan with ample economic benefits and render a "policy of force and conquest" unnecessary. But the Acting Secretary said nothing about a possible freeze on Japanese assets in the United States if Japan moved into southern Indochina. Welles said only that he had been authorized by Hull to say that, if Japan did move into southern

Indochina, they could no longer pursue "the conversations in which he and the Ambassador had been engaged."

Welles sent Grew a copy of the memorandum of the Acting Secretary's conversation with Nomura. That information would prove useful to the Ambassador. But even before then, Grew had been in touch with Welles on other matters concerning the formulation and implementation of American policy toward Japan.

CHAPTER 13

Deadlock

J oe Grew was frustrated. Tension was rising in Tokyo, and the State
Department was still failing to provide him information relating to
American policy for Japan. In late June, Grew registered his complaint
with Stanley Hornbeck. In a letter to Grew on June 26, Hornbeck explained
that information was sometimes withheld because of a fear among some
State Department officials that "the codes can be and are likely to be broken." At the same time, the Political Relations Adviser told Grew that "it
might be helpful" if he were to write Sumner Welles or the President directly
to explain that information reached him "belatedly or not at all."

The motivation to accept Hornbeck's suggestion surfaced in early July
when Robert Craigie gave Grew a copy of a "most secret" communication
which the British ambassador had received from his Foreign Office. The
communication detailed a conversation between Welles and Lord Halifax
on July 3 as well as a separate conversation that the Director of United States
Naval Intelligence had had with the British Naval attaché. Each of the conversations concerned unfolding developments with respect to Japan.

As he confided to his diary, Grew had written many telegrams complaining about the State Department's failure to keep him informed but
had "usually torn them up, chiefly because I am always reluctant to complain about procedure in the Department when I well know the

tremendous strain under which everyone is working there." But enough was enough. Beyond that, the Ambassador knew that the Acting Secretary would be sympathetic. Grew had long been one of those who respected Welles' talents. In the summer of 1925, Joe reported to Welles that, as Under Secretary of State, he was working with the new Secretary of State—Frank B. Kellogg—to bring Welles back to the State Department as Assistant Secretary for Latin America (an effort which never came to fruition). Welles reciprocated the admiration, saying in his 1944 post-resignation memoir that Grew's reports from Tokyo "from the outset of his mission to the last days—seen in the light of the present—reflected with amazing accuracy the true trend of events."

Grew sent the telegram to Welles on July 10. The telegram referenced the "most secret" cable received by Craigie and bluntly stated, "I feel very strongly that the information revealed in those conversations should properly have been brought promptly to my attention." The reason for Grew's complaint should have been obvious, but the Ambassador was leaving nothing to chance. "Please remember," he told Welles, "that in Japan we are generally groping in the dark, and that now, more than ever, it is exceedingly difficult to ascertain what is going on behind the scenes, especially since few of our former Japanese contacts dare come to the Embassy or meet us elsewhere." He could not do his job, Grew told Welles, if he were "deprived of intelligence or clues available in Washington pertinent to issues which I am asked to deal with or to estimate here."

Welles responded the next day, saying, "I appreciate and sympathize with the point of view you express." As Hornbeck had previously explained, Welles pointed out that many people in the State Department were "convinced that it is not safe to entrust" confidential information "to the cable or to the radio...." At the same time, he said they realized "the importance of your having promptly significant information having relationship to the very difficult mission with which you are charged and which you are discharging with such credit." Welles promised to make "a special effort" to remedy the problem, and for a time thereafter Grew noticed that he was receiving "a great deal more important, confidential and helpful information"—including the memorandum of Welles' conversation with Nomura on July 23 (but never would Grew learn of the MAGIC intercepts until he returned to the United States in 1942).

Improved communications with the State Department coincided with other developments in Japan. Even before Grew received Welles' response to his complaint of July 10, he was telling the Under Secretary about new decrees issued under the 1938 National Mobilization Law. They reflected the mandate of the July 2 Imperial Conference to put "the nation on a war footing." Beginning on July 12, the Japanese populace was inundated with policy pronouncements and sweeping measures that gave concrete meaning to Matsuoka's post-conference announcement that the nation faced a "super emergency."

For months, Grew had witnessed the ever-increasing grip of the government on the Japanese populace. He had been told by his dentist to have bridge work done sometime in February because the government would be confiscating everyone's gold at the end of the month and there would thus be no gold available for dental work (a governmental action which led the Ambassador to make a plea to the Foreign Office to allow one embassy employee to keep a gold watch that he had been given for twenty-five years of service). In March, a popular golf course was taken over by the Army to be used as an aviation training ground ("sayonara golf match at Asaka," Grew recorded in his diary). And in May, the revised Peace Law went into effect and authorized "procurators," or prosecutors, to "seize, detain, question and search suspects as they please."

Now the grasp of the government reached new heights. Men between the ages of thirty-five and forty-two were called up for military service with only a day or two of notice (with Grew remarking that the Embassy lost one of its cooks). Tennis tournaments and other athletic contests in Tokyo had to be cancelled because trains used by students to reach events were needed for the transport of troops. And the daily lives of the Japanese people—already seemingly stretched to the limit—were made that much more difficult. The Chamber of Commerce and Industry told people that Japan is "engaged in a large-scale war and the nation is therefore called upon to lower its standard of living in order to enable the state to effect its enormous consumption." Working hours were increased from ten hours to twelve a day, six days a week, and people were advised to consume more rice and sardines and less meat. Imported goods remained virtually unobtainable. Even coffee was replaced by another brew about which, according to *New York Times* correspondent Otto Tolischus, "it was better not to ask too many questions."

Other restrictions were imposed to reduce the risk of espionage. Foreigners were not allowed to travel to certain areas near military installations (whether on land or water). And conversations over the telephone had to be conducted in Japanese—a restriction that drew loud protests from Grew and other members of the diplomatic community, who pointed out that their countries did not impose similar restrictions on Japanese diplomats.

In reporting all these developments to Welles, Grew said that there was a "high nervous tension" among the Japanese people as well as the diplomatic community. But all was not as it appeared to be. The ostensibly united front presented by the government in making all these announcements and taking all these actions concealed heated disputes. And few were as critical as those involving Japan's relationship with the United States.

At the end of June, an informant told Grew that he expected "'startling developments' within the next week or 10 days," with the implication that they would be "favorable to the American position." Grew had to suspect that the "favorable" developments concerned the Foreign Minister. "Mr. Matsuoka," Joe confided to his diary on July 6, "has repeatedly been challenged to refute the evidence of Germany's deliberate deception of Japan in attacking Soviet Russia in the face of the advice which Hitler is alleged to have given Matsuoka in Berlin that Japan should improve Soviet-Japanese relations by concluding a pact with the Soviet Union."

Whatever difficulty he had in responding to questions of Nazi duplicity, Matsuoka undermined his status in the Cabinet with a strident response to the Oral Statement that Hull had handed Nomura on June 21. Although the statement did not mention him by name, the Foreign Minister assumed—correctly—that he was the target of the Oral Statement's reference to "Japanese leaders in official positions" who called for "support of Nazi Germany." Matsuoka regarded the comment as an "outrageous statement" which implicitly called upon the Japanese Government to remove him from his post. The United States, he told a Liaison Conference on July 10, had no right "to demand that Japan, a great world power, change her Cabinet." Matsuoka understood that there was a need to respond to the draft proposal which Hull had given Nomura on June 21. But the Foreign Minister wanted to send Nomura instructions to reject the Oral Statement before submitting any revised draft to the United States.

The other cabinet members, as well as the military representatives, shared Matsuoka's view about the Oral Statement. But they did not share Matsuoka's view that the statement should be withdrawn before the submission of Japan's response to the proposal of June 21. Like Konoye, they feared that the United States might regard such a procedure as a reflection of Japan's "intention to discontinue the negotiations" that Nomura was having with the American Secretary of State.

Nor did the other leaders share Matsuoka's view that the negotiations should be discontinued because there was "no hope for success." Japan was about to move military resources into southern Indochina, the prospect of war with the Soviet Union could not be dismissed, and the last thing they wanted was war with the United States. "As the Foreign Minister proposes," said Home Minister Hiranuma Kiichiro, "it is permissible to reject the 'Oral Statement;' but with regard to the negotiations, even though the possibilities of success might be slight, I would like to see them carried on...." No one disputed Hiranuma's comment, and the group concluded that a revised draft should be presented to Hull simultaneously with a rejection of the Oral Statement.

Matsuoka heard his colleagues' comments and appeared to accept them. He did draft a revised proposal that could be given to Hull. But after the conferences concluded, he disregarded the consensus and instructed Nomura to reject the Oral Statement before submitting the revised draft to Hull (and also asked his staff to forward to Germany the revised proposal which had not yet been submitted to the United States). Konoye was not pleased. "[I]n spite of my efforts," Konoye later said, "Foreign Minister Matsuoka's attitude became increasingly uncooperative. It became clear that his attitude was one of opposition to the Japanese-American negotiations." Because of that, the Prime Minister convened a secret meeting with Hiranuma, a former Prime Minister and perhaps the most influential member of the Cabinet, along with the Ministers of War and Navy. Their reaction was unanimous. "[A]t this point," said War Minister Tojo Hideki, "we have no choice but to take decisive action, either by replacing the foreign minister or by having the entire cabinet resign—one way or the other."

Konoye discussed the matter with Kido. The Lord Keeper of the Privy Seal wanted to secure Matsuoka's resignation without forcing a change in the entire Cabinet, but the Prime Minister disagreed. He was concerned that the solitary resignation of the Foreign Minister would be used by Matsuoka and his supporters as propaganda to say that the Cabinet had succumbed to pressure from the United States. Kido discussed the matter with Hirohito, who agreed with Konoye.

The Prime Minister secured the resignations of all the cabinet members (including Matsuoka, who was ill and at home in bed) and presented them to Hirohito at his beachside resort in Hayama at 8:50 p.m. on July 16. After receiving the advice of a council of Senior Statesmen consisting of former Prime Ministers, Hirohito summoned Konoye to the Imperial Palace (where the Emperor had relocated) and asked him to form a new cabinet. The task was completed by July 18. There was no change among the principal cabinet members except for the Foreign Minister. That post was given to Toyoda Teijiro, who had been the Minister of Commerce and Industry since April 1941.

The irony of the cabinet change was that Nomura had followed Matsuoka's instructions and requested the withdrawal of the Oral Statement without submitting Japan's response to the American proposal of June 21. In his July 15 meeting with Hamilton, Nomura said that the Japanese government regarded the Oral Statement as an improper "interference in the internal affairs" of Japan by requesting "a reconstruction of the Japanese Cabinet." After discussing the matter with Hull (who was still at the Greenbrier), Hamilton withdrew the Oral Statement a couple of days later. The Far Eastern Division Chief gave Nomura a formal statement that said that Japan had misunderstood the Oral Statement and that the United States was only "hoping to find in the attitude, utterances, and acts of the Japanese Government as a whole" an interest in pursuing peace in the Pacific. During that July 15 discussion with Hamilton, Nomura said nothing about Japan's response to the American proposal of June 21.

Nomura continued to withhold Japan's revised proposal even after Hamilton withdrew the June 21 Oral Statement. The Japanese ambassador apparently believed that he should await further instructions from the new cabinet before proceeding. It was not an unreasonable decision. Nomura was well acquainted with the new Foreign Minister and had reason to assume that Toyoda's approach to Japanese-American relations would be different from Matsuoka's.

Their appearances were as different as their politics. Standing about the same height as Matsuoka, Toyoda had a round face, a receding hairline, and a scraggy mustache. His background also distinguished him from Matsuoka. Prior to joining Konoye's cabinet in 1941, Toyoda had spent his entire career in the Navy (including service as the naval attaché in Japan's embassy in London). For a short time, he was the Vice Minister of the Navy in 1940, and he had retired as an admiral before becoming the Minister of Commerce and Industry.

Although Toyoda had supported Japan's execution of the Tripartite Pact, Grew and his staff were pleased by his appointment as Foreign Minister. "He was a soft-spoken officer who spoke English well," remembered Henri Smith-Hutton. "He was well known in Tokyo for his moderation. So when he became Foreign Minister, we were all very pleased." Grew recorded similar views in his diary, saying that Toyoda "is a very good man" who "is believed to be friendly to both Great Britain and the United States" and "appears to be honest, frank and communicative...."

Toyoda met briefly with each of the chiefs of the foreign missions on Friday, July 25. In his meeting with the American ambassador, the new Foreign Minister said that his appointment "had come as a great surprise" and that he would need Grew's assistance because he "was an amateur at diplomacy...." Grew responded that improvement in relations between Japan and the United States was his paramount concern but that "we must remember friendship is not a one-way street." Toyoda said he understood and thought that it would be good if the two men could have a longer conversation. Grew agreed of course, and the two men met at the Foreign Ministry at 9:30 p.m. that same day.

Toyoda gave Grew a document that attempted to justify Japan's move into southern Indochina with the same reasoning that Nomura had expressed to Welles—the need for natural resources and the need to defend against the "encirclement" by the United States and other foreign powers. Toyoda added that Japan's action reflected peaceful intentions and that Japan had no plans to use the move into southern Indochina as "a base of armed advanced against adjoining areas...."

Grew did not mince words in responding. He said that the charge of "encirclement" was an "utter fallacy" because the United States' intentions were peaceful and did not in any way threaten Japan. He also emphasized that he could not take the new Foreign Minister's assurances of peaceful intentions at face value. The American ambassador recounted that he had experienced "many bitter disappointments during the past several years" in dealing with other Foreign Ministers and that the United States was "now obliged to rely on facts and actions rather than upon words." Toyoda did not try to rebut Grew's arguments, but in closing, he urged the American ambassador to use his "best efforts" to persuade the Roosevelt administration of Japan's peaceful intentions and to avoid actions "which would provoke the Japanese people...."

Trying to convince Roosevelt of Japan's peaceful intentions was a steep climb. Shortly before Grew had his meeting with Toyoda, the President had conferred with Nomura (on Thursday, July 24, in Washington, still fourteen hours behind Tokyo time). The Japanese ambassador, recognizing the crisis that was about to emerge, had requested the meeting in the hope that Roosevelt could do something to stem the tide. The two men convened in the Oval Study around 5 p.m. on that Thursday, with Welles and Navy chief Harold Stark also in attendance (in part because Stark had been in periodic contact with Nomura and had scheduled the meeting at Nomura's request).

Roosevelt told the Japanese ambassador that "this move by Japan in Indochina created an exceedingly serious problem for the United States." But the President had a proposal that he hoped could resolve the problem. Roosevelt explained that the idea had come to him shortly before Nomura had arrived and that the President had not had time to discuss it with Welles. If Japan agreed to refrain from moving her armed forces into southern Indochina—or, if that movement had taken place, if Japan "would withdraw such forces"—Roosevelt said he "would do everything within his power" to secure agreement among the United States, Great Britain, and the Netherlands to guarantee Indochina's status as a "neutralized country." In that event, said Roosevelt, "Japan would be afforded the fullest and freest opportunity of assuring herself of the source of food supplies and other raw materials in Indochina which she was seeking to secure."

It was a proposal that might have generated some interest at an earlier stage. But, as Grew predicted, the die had already been cast. Japanese forces were already on their way to southern Indochina in accordance with Japan's agreement with the Vichy government. Nomura told Roosevelt that effecting a withdrawal "would be very difficult at this time on account of the face-saving element involved...." Nomura said he would "immediately" report the President's proposal to his government but, as Welles wrote in his summary of the conversation, the Japanese ambassador did not seem "optimistic about the result."

As promised, Nomura did send a brief summary of Roosevelt's proposal to Toyoda immediately after the meeting. He also expressed his view that, if Japan rejected the proposal, "somehow or other economic pressures are very close to being realized."

Shortly after the transmission of that telegram, the White House issued a statement announcing the freeze of Japanese assets in the United States. Grew was disheartened when he read the announcement. "The vicious circle of reprisals and counter-reprisals is on," he later confided to his diary. "Unless radical surprises occur in the world, it is difficult to see how the momentum of this down-grade movement in our relations can be arrested, nor how far it will go. The obvious conclusion is eventual war." But that was not to say that he would throw in the towel. "Meanwhile," he added, "I am taking no defeatist attitude here and am doing what little can be done to avoid catastrophe."

That was Grew's attitude when Toyoda summoned him for another meeting on Saturday, July 26—not only to discuss the freeze, but also to address Welles' earlier statement to Nomura that any move into southern Indochina would result in the discontinuance of the conversations with Hull. The Foreign Minister appeared "distressed," said Grew, and he told the Ambassador that he "had hardly slept at all in recent nights." Toyoda was "profoundly concerned at the rupture of the Washington conversations." He also wanted to know from the American ambassador whether the United States was planning to take any "further retaliatory measures."

Grew could not do much more than repeat what Welles had told him and what was contained in the White House statement. But the American ambassador said he was "reluctant to end" the conversation "in an atmosphere of defeatism." So he urged Toyoda to use his "best efforts" to prevent a further deterioration in Japanese-American relations, which would "inevitably occur if Japan made any more aggressive moves in the Pacific area." (It was a comment that drew criticism from the State Department's Political Relations Adviser. After reading a summary of Grew's conversation with Toyoda, Hornbeck commented that Grew's unwillingness to close the conversation with Toyoda on a "defeatist" note "may well have indicated to the Minister that once again the United States was prepared to start over again on the basis of accepting Japan's acts of aggression in the hope that the latest will be the last.")

On Sunday, July 27, Grew received the summary of Nomura's conversation with the President, which included Roosevelt's proposal to neutralize Indochina and assure Japan of the resources she desired. One of Grew's first reactions upon reading the telegram was relief. On Friday, he had cabled Welles to ask whether, in light of unfolding developments, he should stay in Tokyo or take advantage of a weekend in Karuizawa. Welles replied that he had "no reason" to ask Grew to remain in Tokyo and told him to use his own judgment. Ever the conscientious diplomat, Grew had decided to remain in Tokyo, and now, as he read Welles' telegram, he thanked his "stars" that he had made that choice.

Grew's other reaction to Welles' Sunday telegram was excitement. Here was a proposal that might be responsive to Japan's stated concerns. Here was an initiative by the United States that might break the stalemate in diplomatic relations. Here too was something that confirmed the wisdom of his decision not to take that leave of absence to return to the United States. Roosevelt's proposal represented "precisely the sort of juncture" that he had in mind when he had forsaken that leave of absence.

Toyoda had not mentioned the proposal in their discussions on Saturday, perhaps because he had not yet received word of the proposal from Nomura. But surely, Grew thought, the Foreign Minister knew of the proposal by now. It cried out for immediate discussion. So the Ambassador decided not to bother with a telegram to the State Department to request authorization to discuss the proposal with Japan's Foreign Minister. He knew that could delay any meeting by at least a day, if not longer. That could be a problem because time was of the essence. He knew too that he understood the situation in Tokyo better than anyone in Washington. And he was sure that Roosevelt "would wish nothing to be left undone to ensure that maximum consideration should be given to his proposal. . . ." So he telephoned the Foreign Minister and asked for a meeting. Toyoda told him to come to the Foreign Minister's official residence at 11:30 that morning.

As soon as he saw the Foreign Minister, Grew confided to his diary, he made "the strongest appeal of which [he] was capable" to advocate Japan's acceptance of Roosevelt's proposal. To Grew's "astonishment," Toyoda told him that he had not seen the proposal. That may have been a lie, because

Nomura had in fact sent a summary of the proposal on the day of his meeting with the President (and, if it had been read by Toyoda, it could have inspired questions for the Japanese ambassador about the details). Or perhaps the Foreign Minister simply overlooked Nomura's telegram. Whatever. It really made no difference. After listening to Grew's description of the proposal, the Foreign Minister told the American ambassador—as Grew might have anticipated—that "he was afraid the President's suggestion had come too late." Although public opinion had little, if any, impact on the government's decision to move into southern Indochina, Toyoda (perhaps understanding the importance which Americans placed on public opinion) explained that "Japanese public opinion" had been "greatly exercised against the United States" and that no conciliatory action could be taken until that public opinion "had had an opportunity to cool...."

Even though he may have expected that reaction from the Foreign Minister, Grew was pleased with the initiative he had taken. He recounted that satisfaction in a letter to his daughter Anita the next day. "On the 26th," he told Anita, "everything here looked very black indeed, and I could see no prospect whatever of any opportunity to do something useful...." But the situation dramatically changed with his receipt of Roosevelt's proposal on Sunday. It was July 27—another one of Grew's "lucky" days. Roosevelt's proposal, said the proud father, presented "a wonderful opportunity," and he "immediately asked for an appointment with the Foreign Minister." He explained to his daughter that he did not have any authorization from the State Department to discuss the proposal with the Foreign Minister, but he did not have "the slightest doubt" about the wisdom of his decision to schedule the meeting. And, he added, "I don't give a damn whether the State Department approves or not."

Grew need not have worried. After reading his ambassador's report of the meeting, Welles responded that he had made the right decision in scheduling the meeting with Toyoda.

In the meantime, the Japanese were not feeling as lucky as the American ambassador. From all appearances, they were shocked by Roosevelt's decision to freeze the country's assets in the United States. Grew recorded in his diary that he was "entirely convinced" that Japanese officials (including Toyoda) believed "that the United States would not resort to measures of retaliation" and were surprised by the announcement of the freeze. Not surprisingly, said Grew, the Japanese astonishment was accompanied by resentment toward the United States. *New York Times* correspondent Otto Tolischus agreed. "It was obvious," Tolischus reported, that the statements by Roosevelt and Welles announcing the freeze were received "with consternation and bitterness" in Japan.

Those in the United States who might have expected some favorable response from Japan were disappointed. The Japanese may have been "stung to the quick," said Tolischus, "but not stung enough to yield." The validity of Tolischus' observation was confirmed in press reports. "There is no greater misconception," said one Japanese newspaper, "than to think that Japan would become more conciliatory should the United States strengthen economic pressure." Another periodical proclaimed, "Japan will not succumb to economic blockade. Economic blockade may be a step for exhausting others without fighting, but to think that Japan can be ruined by economic pressure is an insult to the Japanese spirit."

There were other voices that cast a different light on the Japanese reaction. While the man in the street may have been stunned by the freeze, neither Toyoda nor other Japanese leaders should have been surprised. At a Liaison Conference on July 24—a couple of days before the freeze was announced—Toyoda told the group that Japan's "occupation of Indochina" would cause the United States to take punitive measures, including "freezing Japanese funds...." Toyoda's warning was echoed by Ushiba Tomohiko, the Prime Minister's private secretary, at a private dinner a few days after the announcement of the freeze. A couple of members of Grew's staff were at the dinner, and the conversation turned to the American freeze. In response to one staff member's questions, Ushiba said that the American reaction to Japan's move into southern Indochina was "as strong as Japan had expected" and that "the Japanese were relieved" that the United States had "not taken stronger measures." It all indicated to the Japanese that the United States was reluctant, "if not entirely unwilling," to precipitate a war in the Pacific.

However much the freeze may have been expected in some quarters, Admiral Nagano Osami, the Chief of the Navy General Staff, was not happy. Quite the contrary. He was incensed and felt the need to visit with Hirohito shortly after the freeze order went into effect. On the one hand, Nagano told the Emperor that Japan should "avert" a war with the United States "as much as possible." On the other hand, said Nagano, the freeze would deprive the country of oil needed for military operations and might require an immediate strike against the United States. Nagano told Hirohito that Japan had enough oil to last for perhaps two years if there was no war, but far less than two years if there was war. If Japan did nothing now, the Navy chief explained, the country would be powerless to protect itself down the road.

Hirohito was horrified by Nagano's suggestion to initiate war against the United States, in part because the Navy chief could provide no assurance of victory. And so the Emperor told Kido afterwards that war with the United States was "out of the question."

Hirohito's desire to avoid a war that Japan might not win was certainly understandable. But Nagano's concerns about the availability of oil proved to be well-founded. The freeze order did not expressly curtail or even limit the oil that Japan could acquire. As the *New York Times* reported the day after the freeze order was announced, Japan could apply for a license under the freeze order to obtain oil and other products, and the Roosevelt administration would then decide whether and under what conditions the license would be granted. On its face, then, the freeze order contemplated that there might still be some oil sales to Japan. But that possibility did not account for Dean Acheson, the tall, immaculately-dressed Assistant Secretary of State.

As de facto chairman of the Foreign Funds Control Committee (FFCC)—an inter-department group that included representatives from the Justice Department, the State Department, and the Treasury Department—Acheson was responsible for drafting regulations to implement the freeze. He was also among those in the Roosevelt administration who had advocated the imposition of harsh economic sanctions against Japan, and he meant to exploit the opportunity he had been given. He gave Welles a memo for the President's review that would prohibit the export to Japan of petroleum products that could be used for military purposes.

Roosevelt approved Welles' memo on Thursday, July 31, and on the morning of Friday, August 1, Acheson telephoned Interior Secretary Ickes (who similarly opposed any "policy of appeasement") in "great triumph." Roosevelt, the Assistant Secretary explained, had just signed "certain orders" which imposed a flat ban on Japan's importation of high-octane gasoline and crude oil, which could be used by Japan for airplanes and other military purposes.

Acheson soon had other reasons to gloat. Although the memo approved by Roosevelt on July 31 did not foreclose the sale of all exports to Japan (including other petroleum products), those sales never materialized. The freeze regulations contemplated a two-step process for Japan to purchase oil or any other American product: Japan would first have to secure an export license from the State Department for the product, and then Japan would have to secure a license—to be approved by the FFCC—to pay for the product with funds in American banks. The memo expressly stated that the FFCC would "hold without action" on license applications for *all* petroleum products until the administration had established a coherent policy. That temporary suspension of action on other petroleum products soon became a total embargo on all exports to Japan. Acheson was placed in charge of reviewing license applications, and never would he allow the FFCC to approve any of them.

Hull was in White Sulphur Springs and did not know of Acheson's actions to forestall Japan's importation of all gasoline and other products (and would not learn of them for about a month). Not that it would have mattered. Hull's mindset on Japan was now immovable.

By the first week in August, the Secretary of State had returned to Washington, and Nomura arranged to meet with Hull in his apartment at 6 p.m. on August 6. The Japanese ambassador gave Hull his government's response to Roosevelt's proposal to neutralize Indochina. Nomura himself had little hope that Japan's counterproposal would be well received, and for good reason. It was not anything the United States could be expected to accept. There was nothing in the counterproposal that contemplated a neutralized Indochina. Instead, the counterproposal said that Japan would not station troops anywhere in the "Southwestern Pacific except French Indochina" and that those Japanese troops stationed in Indochina now would be removed upon settlement of the China Incident. The counterproposal included other provisions that would lead to resumption of trade between the two countries, an American initiative to promote discussions between Japan and Chiang Kai-shek, and the United States' suspension of "military measures in the Southwestern Pacific areas." None of that was likely to hold any interest for the Secretary of State. He placed the counterproposal in his pocket and said that he would respond in due course.

Even before he met with the Japanese ambassador, Hull had decided that further conversations with the Japanese ambassador would be a futile exercise—except to serve the American interest in delaying any armed conflict in the Pacific. "From now on," Hull later explained in his *Memoirs*, "our major objective with regard to Japan was to give ourselves more time to prepare our defenses." The Secretary of State confirmed that perspective when he met with Henry Stimson a couple of days after his meeting with Nomura. "He has made up his mind," the War Secretary said of Hull, "that we have reached the end of any possible appeasement with Japan and that there is nothing further that can be done with that country except by a firm policy and, he expected, force itself."

Later that same day, Hull handed Nomura a document that explained the United States' rejection of Japan's counterproposal. He said the Japanese ambassador "might care to glance at the document." Nomura read the document and said that "he understood its import." Nothing in it was a surprise to Nomura. Hull then remarked that Japan's move into southern Indochina "made it clear that those elements in the Japanese Government which favored peaceful courses had lost control" and that there was no longer any reason to pursue the "understanding" that he and Nomura had previously been discussing. Hull closed the meeting with a reference to the points he had made in earlier conversations with Nomura. "[I]t remained with the Japanese Government," the Secretary of State said, "to decide whether it could find means of shaping its policies accordingly and then endeavor to evolve some satisfactory plan."

Hull did not specify what that plan should be, but Nomura understood that the Secretary of State had reached the end of the road. "[T]here is no mistaking that the United States government has made up its mind," he telegrammed Toyoda on August 6, "to take in stride any contingency whatever." And after he met with Hull on August 8, the Japanese ambassador telegraphed Tokyo that "[t]here is no longer any room for talks unless there are changes in our policy" and that "it will be difficult to overcome the deadlock...."

Hull would have undoubtedly agreed with Nomura's assessment. As far as he was concerned, nothing could be offered to reverse the State Department's position. It was now only a matter of time before the deadlock would result in war in the Pacific. But the Secretary of State underestimated his ambassador in Tokyo.

Joe Grew was not one to give up—no matter what the circumstances. As he later explained to the congressional committee investigating the Pearl Harbor attack, Grew likened his position to that "of a candidate for political office who knows that he is going to be defeated but he does not admit it until it is all over." The same persistence applied to him. "For any diplomatic officer in the foreign service or for any foreign service officer to go abroad and throw up his hands and say, 'War is inevitable,' might as well go home, because he would be a discredit to the service...."

Joe Grew did not intend to be a discredit to the foreign service.

Joe and Alice Grew with Edith, their first child, circa 1907. Edith died in 1924 after contracting scarlet fever on a school trip in Europe. *Courtesy of Robert English.*

Joseph C. Grew in 1924 shortly after he had been appointed Under Secretary of State. *Library of Congress.*

Left to right: Grew, now ambassador to Japan, with granddaughter Edith, daughter Elsie, daughter Lilla (Edith's mother), grandson Jay Pierrepont (Peter) Moffat, Jr. (Lilla's son), and Alice circa 1934. *Courtesy of Robert English.*

Left to right: Baseball player Lefty O'Doul, Joe Grew, Babe Ruth, and professional golfer Charles Akibashi, November 6, 1934, during Ruth's tour of Japan. *Courtesy of Robert English.*

seph Grew at a plomatic reception in kyo circa 1935. The hite-haired gentleman n Grew's right is scount Saito Makoto, e Lord Keeper of the ivy Seal. Saito was sassinated on February 5, 1936, after attending dinner at the American nbassy the previous ght. Grew went to see ito's body the next y, later saying it was a arrowing experience." *ourtesy of Robert English.*

Joe and Alice Grew in San Francisco in November 1936 as they were about to return to Tokyo after a few months' leave in the United States. *Getty Images.*

Secretary of State Cordell Hull sitting at his desk in the State, War, and Navy Building in Washington, D.C. One of the two telephones on Hull's left is a direct line to the White House. *Wikimedia Commons Images.*

Eugene H. Dooman with his wife and son in front of their Alexandria, Virginia, home in April 1937 shortly before Dooman returned to Tokyo to become the embassy's counselor. *Courtesy Russell Dooman.*

Stanley K. Hornbeck, the political relations adviser to Secretary of State Cordell Hull. *Library of Congress.*

Grew playing golf in Japan with Marshall Green, his private secretary, circa 1940. *Courtesy of Edward Green.*

Emperor Hirohito circa 1928. *Getty Images.*

Secretary of State Cordell Hull and Under Secretary of State Sumner Welles walking from the State, War, and Navy Building to the White House on May 10, 1940, for a meeting with President Roosevelt. *Getty Images.*

mbassador Grew and Prime Minister Konoye Fumimaro at the Tokyo train
:ation circa 1941. *Courtesy of Robert English.*

Foreign Minister
Matsuoka Yosuke
meeting with Adolf
Hitler in Berlin in the
spring of 1941. *Getty
Images.*

Foreign Minister Matsuoka Yosuke meeting with Joseph Stalin in Moscow in the spring of 1941. *Getty Images.*

Joseph Grew meeting with Toyoda Teijiro shortly after he was appointed foreign minister in July 1941. *Getty Images.*

Tojo Hideki, the war minister in Prime Minister Konoye's cabinet and the one who succeeded Konoye as prime minister in October 1941. Tojo was prime minister when Japan attacked Pearl Harbor. *Getty Images.*

Togo Shigenori, who became foreign minister in October 1941. *Getty Images.*

Secretary of State Cordell Hull walking to the White House from the State, War, and Navy Building on November 17, 1941, with Japanese Ambassador Nomura Kichisaburo (on Hull's right) and Kurusu Saburo, Japan's special envoy, for a meeting with President Roosevelt. *Getty Images.*

President Roosevelt signing the Declaration of War against Japan on December 8, 1941, in the White House Oval Office with members of Congress standing behind him. The black band on Roosevelt's left arm is a memorial to his mother, who had died the previous September. *Getty Images.*

CHAPTER 14

The Meeting Proposal

Hiranuma Kiichiro was prepared. He knew he was a target for assassination by the ultra-nationalist organizations, and he was not above taking necessary precautions. He had increased the bodyguards around his Tokyo home and had even taken to wearing a bulletproof vest. But he knew there was no way to eliminate all risks.

It was, in a way, an ironic turn of events for the seventy-three-year-old statesman. His political career had been one of the more illustrious ones in the modern history of Japan. He had served as the head of the Supreme Court, Minister of Justice, President of the Privy Council, and even for a short time as Prime Minister. His accomplishments had resulted in him being knighted as a Baron before he was forty. By August 1941, his countenance suited his stature. A lean, almost ascetic-looking man (who did not drink but was a heavy smoker of English cigarettes), he had thick gray hair parted on the left side, horn-rimmed glasses, and a smile that boasted large teeth.

Through most of those years of prior service, he had been a favorite of radical right-wing organizations. He had even helped found one himself. He had promoted their interest in securing Japan's rightful place in the world—even if it meant, as in the case of the Manchurian Incident and the China Incident, the use of armed force. It did not matter to him that these organizations regarded assassination—or the threat of assassination—as an appropriate tool to dispose of those in government who frustrated their aspirations. Indeed, it was reported that the soldiers who orchestrated the revolt in February 1936—and assassinated many Japanese leaders in the process—hoped that Hiranuma would become the new Prime Minister.

One of the more notorious ultra-nationalist organizations was the Black Dragon Society, which had been founded in 1901. The name sounded ominous, but its origins were benign. It was called the Amur River Society at the start because the group's initial goal was to keep Russia on the northern side of the Amur River, which separates eastern Russia from northeastern China. The Chinese characters for Amur mean "black dragon," and so that became the group's name in the Japanese language.

The leaders of the Black Dragon Society, as well as some of the other radical organizations, commanded considerable respect among the public. When he first arrived in Tokyo in 1932, Grew learned that Toyama Mitsuru, the head of the Black Dragon Society, was "looked upon by a large section of the public, including the military, as a sort of super-patriot...." AP correspondent Max Hill remembered the time he saw the eighty-six-year-old Toyama enter a Sumo wrestling match in 1941. A thin man with a long white beard and a "weathered, tired face," Toyama moved toward his seat. As he did so, said Hill, the hundreds of Japanese in attendance "rose and bowed to him with a reverence which could be compared only to their attitude toward the emperor."

Neither Toyama nor the other leaders of the nationalist societies generated the same respect in the diplomatic community. The societies' reliance on assassinations, as well as blackmail and fraud, did not sit well with the more genteel men who populated the foreign legations. "We looked on these patriotic societies," said Henri Smith-Hutton, "as gangs of thugs."

Still, they were a force to be reckoned with in Japan. Prime Minister Konoye—whose father was a patron of the Black Dragon Society in its early days—recognized that influence. It was reported that Toyama—who issued a statement in April 1941 that the "red-hair barbarians" should be expelled from East Asia—had told Konoye in early 1941 that Japan could discuss a possible settlement with the United States as long as the country simultaneously prepared for war. Toyama's blessing no doubt gave Konoye comfort that, at least for the time being, the initiation of talks with the United States would not result in reprisals by the Black Dragon Society (or, hopefully, by similar organizations). And on August 4—after the issuance of the American freeze order—Konoye summoned Toyama and leaders of other patriotic societies to a luncheon where he described the government's contemplated response to Roosevelt's proposal for a neutralized Indochina.

These overtures to the Black Dragon Society and the other ultra-nationalist groups may have been useful, but there were no guarantees in this business. Grew learned of that uncertain danger shortly after the Imperial Conference of July 2, where it was decided to secure military bases in southern Indochina. Hiranuma, the Home Minister in Konoye's cabinet, had by now forsaken his earlier extreme right-wing leanings and was more interested in relaxing Japan's ties with Germany and finding an accommodation with the United States. This more moderate perspective brought him into conflict with Matsuoka and the extremists.

On July 3, *New York Times* correspondent Otto Tolischus advised Grew that Hiranuma had threatened to exercise his powers as Home Minister to secure the arrest of Nakano Seigo, the head of one of the more belligerent patriotic societies and someone who had clashed with Hiranuma on policy matters in recent years. According to Tolischus, Hiranuma was told by Nakano in a telephone call that, if the police tried to arrest him, they would be "overcome" by forces loyal to Nakano and that "Hiranuma himself would be assassinated shortly thereafter." Hiranuma was apparently persuaded to postpone any arrest of Nakano, but matters changed after Konoye formed a new cabinet in the middle of July (where Hiranuma remained as a minister without portfolio but, because of his stature, was regarded as the Vice Premier). Japan was now facing a possible showdown with the United States, and impediments to an adjustment in relations had to be removed. As Grew learned from the British embassy, "One of the first moves of the new Government was to arrest Nakano for a few days."

Hiranuma should have been more suspicious when thirty-three-year-old Natchiko Mishiyama came to his door on August 14 with a letter of introduction and a request for a sample of the Baron's handwriting. Almost immediately after he stepped into the house, the young man pulled a pistol from beneath some colored papers he was carrying and shot the cabinet minister three times in the neck and jaw, with one shot, according to Hill, "ripping out his tongue." Harmed and bloody but not disabled, Hiranuma chased the assailant as he fled the house, where he was captured by the minister's bodyguards.

The attempt on Hiranuma's life could not have been far from Konoye's mind as he confronted the challenge of dealing with the United States. By then, the Prime Minister had already embarked on a new path to break the deadlock in the discussions his ambassador was having with the American Secretary of State. It was a path, he knew, that increased the risks of his own assassination.

The new path focused on the way to communicate with the United States. Matsuoka was not the only one who had been frustrated by Nomura's seeming ineptitude. Konoye too sensed that the retired admiral was not well suited to the delicate and very demanding task that lay before him. The Prime Minister was especially troubled by Nomura's failure to explain to Hull the significance of Matsuoka's removal from the cabinet.

But, in a way, those were minor details. The larger obstacle to success was Hull's intransigence. The Prime Minister knew that something different, something dramatic, was needed to overcome that intransigence and reverse the inescapable spiral toward war. As Grew later told the congressional committee investigating the Pearl Harbor attack, the Prime Minister "saw the handwriting on the wall." And so Konoye finally decided that only he could provide the needed antidote. He would travel to American territory to meet with the American president.

The initial draft understanding prepared by the John Doe Associates in April had proposed a conference in Honolulu that would be attended by American and Japanese delegates and be opened by Roosevelt and Konoye. The proposal had been removed in Japan's reply of May 12, but Konoye now seized upon that possible conference with one major revision—it would not be a meeting of delegates but a personal meeting between Roosevelt and the Prime Minister (albeit supported by whatever staff they each chose to bring to the meeting). Success was more likely, Konoye thought, if the two leaders could discuss in person the issues that now divided their countries.

More was at stake for Konoye than an adjustment in American-Japanese relations. He felt a compelling need to atone for past mistakes. He had been prime minister when the China Incident erupted in July 1937. Now, after four years of fighting and the incurrence of hundreds of thousands of casualties, the matter was no closer to being settled. "I have made big mistakes on

Japan's relations with China," Konoye confided to a friend. "I am so ashamed and cannot face up to my ancestors. I do not want to repeat such a mistake. And I want to avoid war with the United States at all costs."

Konoye broached the possibility of the Roosevelt meeting with the Navy Minister and the War Minister on the evening of August 4. Nomura had not yet submitted Japan's response to Roosevelt's proposal for a neutralized Indochina, but the Prime Minister had little hope that the response would turn the tide. Something more was required, and Konoye knew that the Navy and War Minister's approval was critical to any change in strategy. Oikawa Koshiro, the Navy Minister, gave the Prime Minister his approval to the Roosevelt meeting later that evening. Tojo Hideki, the War Minister, was not as quick. He consulted other members of the Army staff, and they were less than enthusiastic. "We can't say that Konoye can't go to the United States," Tojo told the Army General Staff. "We figure it's 80 percent certain that his trip will end up a failure, but even if he does fail we'll have pinned the prime minister down about not resigning."

The following day, Tojo sent Konoye a written message. He explained that the Army did not regard the meeting to be "a suitable move." The War Minister said that the Army was nonetheless willing to support the proposed meeting on one condition: the Prime Minister would have to "firmly support" the July 2 resolution to go to war with the United States "if the President fails to comprehend the true intentions of the Empire." The message also included the admonition that Konoye "shall not resign on the grounds that [the meeting] was a failure...."

On the morning of August 6, Konoye presented his proposal to Hirohito. The Emperor—who favored a diplomatic resolution—summoned the Prime Minister back to the Imperial Palace on August 7 and told him to proceed. Hirohito was especially concerned about the oil embargo instituted in conjunction with the American freeze. "In view of this," he told Konoye, "the meeting with the President should take place as soon as possible."

Konoye immediately sent instructions to Nomura to raise the proposal with Hull. Toyoda followed up with a separate telegram to the Japanese ambassador. "In his heart-to-heart talks with the president," said the Foreign Minister, "the prime minister will not limit himself to the August 5 proposal [which dealt with Indochina and other issues] but will try to come up with a breakthrough in the situation from the larger perspective of preserving world peace."

There was no precedent for a Japanese leader to travel to a foreign country to negotiate a treaty. It was, in that sense, a bold move. But it was one, Konoye knew, that would not sit well with the ultra-nationalist organizations. They would invariably regard it as a sign of weakness, an implicit confession that the pressure exerted by the United States was too much to bear. It was not a confession those organizations and other extremists were likely to welcome.

Other advisers recognized the danger the meeting posed to the Prime Minister. "If you push it through," said one friend, "you will be killed." That was not enough to dissuade Konoye. "I do not care much about my life," he responded. He knew that that it was something that had to be pursued. More than that, he knew that he was the only Japanese leader who could pull it off. It was all a reflection of his family's history, his upbringing, and his personality.

The forty-nine-year-old Prime Minister looked and acted like the aristocrat he was. Konoye Fumimaro stood almost six feet tall, with dark hair combed straight back, a bronze complexion, a recessed chin, and a Charlie Chaplin-like moustache. A man with a medium build, he had, said Robert Craigie, "the easy gait of the athlete," but his eyes, the British ambassador added, were "his best feature, denoting intelligence and political acumen."

Konoye was a member of the Fujiwara family, which had reportedly "descended from a god who sat in on the Heavenly Conference summoned by the Sun Goddess before she sent messengers down to create the Japanese Islands." The family's prominence was second in nobility only to the Emperor's family and entitled Konoye to the honorific title of "Prince."

The trappings of his life reflected that status of nobility. He was a fastidious man who had the resources to lead an indulgent lifestyle. He enjoyed the comfort of many homes. He had a seemingly successful marriage that produced five children, but he also enjoyed the company of Geishas who could serve him food or double as his mistresses. He could shave himself but had a barber attend to his hair every week. And he could remain in bed for hours during the day, reading, watching movies, eating meals, and sometimes conducting conferences with subordinates (not unlike Roosevelt, who was prone to spend mornings in bed reading and consulting with people).

Konoye was the only child of his father's first marriage because his mother died eight days after his birth. His father then married his mother's younger sister. He was only twelve when his father died, propelling him to the head of the family but also leaving him with a mountain of debt. Advisers who had once flocked around his father disappeared, and the young Fumimaro had to grapple with the family's problems with only minimal assistance. The experience drove him to seek refuge in the writings of Jean-Jacques Rousseau, Karl Marx, and other revolutionary thinkers. "I was a gloomy young man with [a] biased disposition," Konoye later admitted, "and I sought consolation in radical Western literature."

As a member of Japan's nobility, Konoye was appointed to the Diet's House of Peers when he was a twenty-one-year-old university student. For many years, he remained in the background. But he had qualities that induced other men to seek his counsel. He was smart. He was patient. And he was good listener (although, if he was bored by a meeting, he tended to increase his consumption of cigarettes). By 1931, he was elected Vice President of the House of Peers, and in 1933, he became its president. By 1936, he was viewed in many circles as an ideal candidate to become Japan's Prime Minister. It was not merely his status in the House of Peers or his noble lineage. He possessed a personality that enabled him to draw support from divergent and often conflicting segments of Japanese society—a trait which explained in part the Army's insistence that Konoye not resign if his proposed meeting with Roosevelt ended in failure. He was not one to pound the table and insist on adherence to his views. He was a leader who sought consensus.

It was a combination that finally resulted in his selection as Prime Minister in June 1937. But he grew frustrated with the stalemate in China and the emergence of other pressing problems. He resigned in January 1939 and left many supporters perplexed. ("I really have no idea why Konoye quit," said one cabinet minister at the time.) None of that diminished Konoye's standing among the public or the competing factions of society. In July 1940—as international crises mushroomed—he acceded to Hirohito's request that he return as Prime Minister.

Ironically, the same qualities that made him attractive to so many people produced criticism from many of those same people. His willingness to listen, his interest in reaching accommodations, and his patience—all these traits were viewed as signs of weakness. "Few are completely satisfied with him," Otto Tolischus reported in the *New York Times* in August 1941, "and some accuse him of weakness, vacillation, and even of lack of courage...." Grew was among those who shared that view. The Prime Minister, the American ambassador confided to his diary shortly after Konoye became prime minister for the second time in July 1940, is "a man of weak physique, poor health and weak will."

Grew's reference to Konoye's poor health was not based on inside information. The Prime Minister's health was a matter of public discussion. As a boy, he suffered from tuberculosis and other ailments. His frailty was a constant concern, and it led him to deflect requests that he become prime minister immediately after the 1936 revolt. However genuine that concern, it seemed that the Prime Minister was always retreating to his bedroom during a crisis to cater to some unspecified illness. "He uses his frail health," said *Time* magazine in a 1940 profile, "as a sort of storm cellar, into which he retires whenever he sees a political twister coming." The routine did not escape the attention of the Japanese press. As the government wrestled with Matsuoka's desire to attack Singapore in February 1941, Konoye's absence drew a comment from one newspaper, which said that "there seems to be room for criticism of his continued absence and his occasional illnesses at the most critical times."

However much he may have treasured the sanctity of his bedroom in times of crisis, Konoye knew that he could not remain in isolation if he was truly interested in pursuing the meeting with Roosevelt. He needed the support of Japan's leaders. It became a constant topic of his conversations with others, especially the Foreign Minister. But all that discussion could not salvage a proposal that seemed doomed almost from the start.

As instructed, Nomura immediately raised the prospect of Konoye's meeting with Roosevelt when the Japanese ambassador met with Hull on Friday, August 8. The Secretary of State did not respond to the inquiry. Instead, he veered off into a monologue concerning the "patience" shown by the United States so that the Japanese Government "as a whole and [Japanese] public opinion could be brought into line to support policies" that he had been discussing with Nomura. When Hull finally finished, Nomura asked whether the Secretary of State's commentary "could be taken as a reply to the suggestion he had made for a meeting of the responsible heads of the two Governments." Hull again sidestepped the question. In his report of the conversation to Tokyo, Nomura suggested that Toyoda might want to consider "conveying your intentions through Grew...."

Nomura's advice to contact Grew was well-taken. The Secretary of State had no intention of providing any encouragement for a meeting between the Japanese prime minister and the American president. That became clear when Hull spoke with Stimson the day after his meeting with Nomura.

The Secretary of War was a rugged outdoorsman who had made his fortune as a Wall Street attorney and generally spent weekends at High-hold, his 100-acre estate in Huntington Township on the north shore of Long Island. The weekend of August 9 was no exception. After he returned from a morning horseback ride on that Saturday, the seventy-three-year-old Stimson received a message from Brigadier General Sherman Miles, the assistant chief of Army intelligence in Washington, that he was sending a plane to Long Island with a MAGIC intercept that had just been received. As Stimson soon learned, the intercept included the instructions to Nomura about the proposed Konoye-Roosevelt meeting. To the War Secretary, this was not an overture for peace but "another example of Japanese duplicity." As far as he was concerned, "the invitation to the President is merely a blind to try to keep us from taking definite action." So Stimson promptly called his cabinet colleague to make sure he was aware of the proposal's sinister implications.

Hull no doubt assured Stimson that he was of the same view. As the Secretary of State later told the congressional committee investigating the Pearl Harbor attack, "We knew that the Japanese leaders were unreliable and treacherous." In his view, "the military element in Japan" would never allow the Japanese government "to stop Japan's course of expansion by force and to revert to peaceful courses." And so he was "thoroughly satisfied" that Roosevelt's meeting with Konoye "could only result either in another Munich or in nothing at all, unless Japan was ready to give some clear evidence of a purpose to move in a peaceful direction." It was not apparent what evidence would have satisfied Hull, but it really made no difference. "I was opposed to the first Munich," he told the congressional committee, "and still more opposed to a second Munich."

Part of Hull's reasoning reflected his assessment of the Japanese Prime Minister. The Secretary of State reminded the congressional committee that

Konoye had been prime minister when the China Incident had erupted; he had been prime minister when Japanese bombers sank the *Panay*; he had been prime minister when Chinese forces had committed the outrageous "rape of Nanking;" and he had been prime minister when Japan had signed the Tripartite Pact with Germany and Italy. It was not the kind of record, said Hull, that inspired confidence that any meeting with Roosevelt would produce "concrete and clear-cut commitments toward peace."

Konoye might have guessed the American Secretary of State's perspective. But that could not be a deterrent. The Prime Minister was a man with a mission, and he decided to accept Nomura's advice. Grew would have to be involved if there was to be any chance of success.

CHAPTER 15

The Dinner

The President advised his Secretary of State that he wanted to see the Japanese ambassador as soon as he returned from his conference with Winston Churchill near the Argentia Naval Base off the coast of Newfoundland. The two leaders had converged there on separate warships in the beginning of August to discuss matters of mutual interest. One of the topics was Japan. Churchill proposed to Roosevelt that their two countries both issue warnings to Japan that any further military aggression by the Empire of the Rising Sun would trigger forceful reprisals from Great Britain and the United States. It was hoped that the warnings would deter further military moves by Japan in East Asia and thus serve both leaders' desire to avoid war in the Pacific.

Sumner Welles had accompanied the President to the Atlantic conference and had drafted the warning to be issued by the United States. It was a strident statement, telling Japan that, if she "undertakes any further steps in pursuance of the policy of military domination," the United States would "be forced to take immediately any and all steps of whatsoever character it deems necessary in its own security, notwithstanding the possibility that such further steps on its part may result in conflict between the two countries."

After reviewing the draft on Friday, August 15, Hull and his advisers agreed that the statement "needed toning down." They were concerned that Japan would regard the message as a threat and thus trigger the very opposite reaction than the one desired. They revised the draft to state that, if Japan took any further military actions in East Asia, "the United States will be compelled to take immediately any and all steps which it may deem necessary toward safeguarding the legitimate rights and interests of the United States...." Nothing was said about a possible conflict.

Joe Ballantine brought the revised statement to Hull's apartment on the morning of Sunday, August 17 before the meeting that had been scheduled for Nomura at the White House at 4:30 that afternoon. Ballantine also brought along another lengthy statement that referenced Nomura's proposal for the meeting between Konoye and the President (which Nomura had raised with Hull again in a meeting they had had on Saturday). The second statement did not respond to the meeting proposal. Instead, the second statement said that the United States was prepared to resume the conversations that the Japanese ambassador was having with the Secretary of State if Japan provided "a clearer statement than has yet been furnished as to its present attitude and plans...."

The second statement was, as Ballantine later acknowledged, an "olive branch" to counterbalance the warning in the first statement. In discussing their aversion to any conflict in the Pacific, Roosevelt had reportedly told Churchill that he would "baby the Japanese along." Ballantine, for one, resented the implication of that alleged statement—namely, that the United States was not genuinely interested in an agreement with Japan. But the proposed resumption of conversations with Hull served that purpose.

As always, Roosevelt greeted the Japanese ambassador with an air of cordiality when Nomura came into the Oval Study at 4:37 p.m. After an exchange of pleasantries, Roosevelt asked Nomura "if he had anything in mind to say in connection with the situation." The Japanese ambassador withdrew a document from his pocket that referenced Japan's desire for "peaceful relations" and that explained that "Prince Konoye feels so seriously and so earnestly about preserving such relations that he would be disposed to meet the President midway, geographically speaking...and talk the matter out in a peaceful spirit." Roosevelt then said—incorrectly— that "he had dictated what he was about to say" and read to Nomura the warning that Ballantine had given Hull earlier that morning. That was soon followed by the President's reading of the second statement. For his part, Nomura was impressed that Roosevelt had wanted to see him on a Sunday as soon as he had returned from the Churchill meeting. He was also pleased by the President's friendly demeanor. But the Japanese ambassador could not give any assurances to Tokyo that the meeting with Konoye would materialize.

Hull would send Grew a summary of Nomura's conversation with Roosevelt the following Monday evening. By the time he received that summary, the American ambassador was already aware of the importance that the Japanese Government placed on the proposed meeting between Konoye and Roosevelt.

At 3 p.m. on Monday, August 18 (1 a.m. in Washington), Gene Dooman met with Terasaki Taro, Chief of the American Bureau of the Foreign Office. Terasaki explained that he had requested the meeting to ask that the Embassy Counselor advise the American ambassador that his scheduled meeting with the Foreign Minister at 4 p.m. that same day "would be of the greatest importance." Terasaki said he hoped Grew's meeting with Toyoda would "eventually yield a satisfactory adjustment of American-Japanese relations." It was not a casual comment. It was an admonition that that the two countries were running out of alternatives. "If a Cabinet under the leadership of Prince Konoye should prove unable to adjust relations with the United States," said Terasaki, "it would be inconceivable for any other Japanese statesman to succeed where he had failed." There was a caveat to all this. In no event, the Foreign Ministry section chief added, should the United States be under any illusion that economic sanctions would make Japan more pliable. Japan, he insisted, "will under no circumstances give in to any form of pressure."

Grew's meeting with Toyoda lasted two and one-half hours—"the longest conversation" he had ever had with "a Foreign Minister anywhere." Toyoda had much to explain, and the setting was less than desirable. There was no air conditioning in the Foreign Office and thus no escape from the sub-tropical heat of the Tokyo summer. As the Foreign Minister proceeded with his extensive comments, heat and sweat overwhelmed both men. After about an hour or so, Toyoda ordered cold drinks and cold wet towels to swab off the sweat, but that was not enough. Toyoda finally stood up and, with a small smile and look of hope at his guest, made a move to take off his suit jacket—a highly unusual gesture in the formal world of diplomacy. But the American ambassador was a practical man. He nodded approvingly, and both men removed their jackets and rolled up their shirt sleeves.

It was the kind of gesture that appealed to Grew. "He is a very sympathetic and very human type," Joe said of Toyoda in his diary, "and I think I like him more than any other Foreign Minister I have ever dealt with." Toyoda's informality also made it easier for Grew to take the copious notes that would form the basis of long telegrams to Hull. The Foreign Minister reviewed the most recent proposals and responses of the two countries and then tried to underscore the opportunity—and risk—that lay before the United States and Japan. These two countries, he said, "hold the key for maintaining world peace." It would "leave the greatest black spot on human history," he continued, if they should fail to rectify the breakdown of their relationship. The only way to "eliminate this critical situation," he opined, would be for the countries' two leaders to "directly meet each other and express their true intentions toward each other...." To that end, he said, Konoye was prepared "to proceed to Honolulu and have talks personally with President Roosevelt...." Toyoda emphasized that Konoye's willingness to go abroad had "no precedent in Japanese history" but that Konoye had "made up his mind with an extremely strong determination to meet the President" despite "the objections in certain parts of the country."

Mindful of the obligation to be a spokesman for his country's official position, Grew repeated many of the points that Hull had made in his recent conversations with Nomura, including the mantra that, in reviewing Japan's proposals, the United States would "only be guided by facts and actions and not by words." Grew said that he would have to withhold comment on Konoye's proposed meeting with Roosevelt until his government had had a chance to review the proposal. But he wanted the Foreign Minister to know that the overture had found a sympathetic listener. "[I]n the interests of peace," said the American ambassador, he would give the proposal his "own personal support."

Grew worked into the late hours of the night and early the next day to perfect the telegrams that needed to be sent to Hull. The telegrams included minute details of the conversation, and, true to Grew's word to Toyoda, they included pleas for a favorable response as well.

In his telegram of August 18, the Ambassador urged "with all the force at his command, for the sake of avoiding the obviously growing possibility of an utterly futile war between Japan and the United States, that the Japanese proposal not be turned aside without very prayerful consideration." A more detailed analysis of the proposal was included in the telegram of August 19. Konoye's proposal, said Grew, "shows a remarkable degree of courage because, if the proposal should become prematurely known, or, if taking place, the meeting should fail to achieve its purpose, it would in all probability lead to further attempted assassinations" and "the downfall of the [Japanese] Government." Given the unprecedented nature of the proposal, said Grew, "the Prime Minister deserves whatever support we can properly accord him in his courageous determination to override the extremists and to sacrifice if necessary not only his political life and that of the Government, but his own life as well." But time was of the essence. The "rapid acceleration" of American economic sanctions, the Ambassador explained, would soon weaken "the moderate elements in the country" and "reinforce the extremists."

These were the first of many heartfelt entreaties from the American ambassador, almost none of which would be answered by Hull. There was no mystery to the State Department's silence. Back in Washington, the Ambassador's telegrams would be dissected by Stanley Hornbeck and members of the Far Eastern Division who had a very different perspective.

As Joe Ballantine later explained, "Hornbeck did not under any circumstance want to have the President meet with the Japanese." Roosevelt prided himself on his ability to advance American interests through meetings with foreign leaders (and would have many such meetings during the war). Hornbeck was nonetheless afraid, said Ballantine, that the President would be "trapped" into making vague commitments that the Japanese would later "interpret to their liking." Hornbeck expressed those views in his unpublished autobiography, saying that he regarded Konoye's proposal "from the outset with suspicion and disfavor." Any agreement made at any such meeting, said Hornbeck, would "be very general in [its] terms" and "be susceptible of widely different interpretations...."

Hornbeck did not hide his opinions from the Secretary of State. Quite the contrary. Almost every telegram from Grew was countered by a memorandum from the Political Relations Adviser. On August 21, Hornbeck sent a seven-page memo to Hull commenting on Grew's telegrams of August 18 and 19. The Political Relations Adviser was not impressed with the Ambassador's prediction that a failure to accept Konoye's proposal would result in a new cabinet that would pursue "an all-out do-or-die effort to extend Japan's hegemony over all of 'Greater East Asia'.... (How many times have we heard this during recent years?)" But Hornbeck obviously did not want to appear arbitrary. So he concluded his memo with two recommendations. First, any meeting between Konoye and Roosevelt "should be made contingent upon" the two governments having reached a "'meeting of the minds'" on an agreement. And second, the meeting should transpire "only if the Japanese authorities gave evidence, by a suspension of offensive military operations, of a desire to have and to maintain peace...."

In telegrams sent later in August, Grew underscored the importance of an expeditious response to Konoye's proposal. "Daily life," Grew told Hull in one telegram, "is increasingly constrained by a [mass] of restrictions, and queues for bread, sugar, vegetables, and other daily necessities are a common sight on every street." The use of cars was another casualty of American sanctions. Tolischus recorded at the beginning of August that "oil restrictions had almost eliminated taxis from the streets," but that some "were now being equipped with charcoal gas engines which could not make even the slightest incline...." (Nomura himself told Hull that "taxicabs in Japan had ceased operating" because gasoline was not available.) Grew warned Hull that these deprivations were not likely to make the Japanese more receptive to American demands. "In Japan," he told the Secretary of State on August 27—as Kurusu had told Davies months earlier—"a psychology of despair leads characteristically to a do-or-die reaction."

Hornbeck's reaction to this warning of a suicidal war was no different from his reaction to Davies' earlier message. "The Japanese Government," he told Hull at one point, "has no intention of making war on the United States." This assessment was based in part on an assumption that the country had exhausted its military resources through the China Incident. "We are not in great danger vis-à-vis Japan, and Japan is not capable of doing us any great injury," Hornbeck advised Hull at another point. "Japan, involved and weakened as she is by the 'Chinese Incident,' does not possess military capacity sufficient to warrant an attack by her upon the United States."

Given his perspective on Japan's weakened state, the Political Relations Adviser remained convinced that the oil embargo and other economic sanctions would ultimately bring Japan to her knees without the need for a meeting between Konoye and Roosevelt. The passage of time had no impact on Hornbeck's view. When John Emmerson returned to the State Department in October, he asked the former Embassy staff member, "What do you people in the Embassy think about war with Japan?" Emmerson responded that Japan could be driven "to war in desperation." Hornbeck was incredulous. "Name me one county," the Political Relations Adviser responded with derision, "which has ever gone to war in desperation."

Hornbeck's rejection of the Embassy's on-the-ground assessment was not based on firsthand knowledge. Tolischus, for one, had a different view of Japan's military capabilities from his perch in Tokyo. "Far from exhausting herself in the China war, as the world believed," the *New York Times* Tokyo correspondent wrote on July 15, "Japan had been using the China conflict as a screen behind which she built up a mighty war machine...." By contrast, Hornbeck's perspective was based largely on conjecture secured firmly in a framework of long-established convictions. And so the Political Relations Adviser had no patience for Grew's "great solicitude for the Japanese point of view...." Especially because the American ambassador had recognized in his "Green Light" telegram of September 12, 1940 (as well as in other earlier communications) that economic sanctions could be useful in changing Japan's policies.

The Political Relations Adviser did not withhold his perspective from the American ambassador. On August 7, Hornbeck had forwarded to Grew a seven-page compilation of selected statements from the Ambassador's Green Light telegram and other earlier communications. The compilation highlighted comments that the time had come for the United States to forgo a passive acceptance of Japan's military moves and to impose economic sanctions to make Japan more compliant.

Grew was offended when he received Hornbeck's package after the meeting with Toyoda. "I don't quite know just what was in Stanley Hornbeck's mind in sending me these excerpts," he confided to his diary, "unless it was in the belief...that I am now advocating so-called 'appeasement'...." Grew pointed out that he had proposed the use of economic sanctions to promote "a complete regeneration of thought" in Japan, and he believed that the United States' actions in the prior eight months had produced that precise result. Japan had now decided to make a meaningful effort for a diplomatic accommodation with the United States. To the Ambassador, it was an opportunity worth pursuing. "What the eventual outcome will be, I do not know," he concluded, "nobody knows; but defeatism is not within my philosophy."

In the meantime, Nomura was doing what he could to extract a favorable response from Hull and Roosevelt to Konoye's meeting proposal, but it was not easy. The Japanese ambassador had several meetings with Hull after his conference with Roosevelt on August 17, but the Secretary of State did not give Nomura any encouragement. At Nomura's request, another meeting was scheduled with Roosevelt in the Oval Office at 10:45 on the morning of Thursday, August 28.

Nomura opened the meeting by expressing his appreciation for the President's time and then handed Roosevelt a message from Konoye. "The present deterioration of the Japanese-American relations," the message said, "is largely due, I feel, to a lack of understanding....I consider it, therefore, of urgent necessity that the two heads of the Governments should meet first to discuss from a broad standpoint all important problems between Japan and America...."

Roosevelt's reaction could not have been more satisfactory to the Japanese ambassador. As Nomura later reported to Tokyo, Roosevelt "highly commended it as very splendid." The President's only qualification was the choice of Honolulu as the location for the meeting. A meeting in Hawaii would require him to spend three weeks away from Washington. He offered Juneau, Alaska, as an alternative because, in his view, it would involve less time.

Nomura then gave Roosevelt a separate document that responded to the request Roosevelt made at their meeting on August 17 for a clear statement of Japan's intentions. The document said that Japan's move into Indochina had been taken "to accelerate the settlement of the China Incident," that Japan would welcome "an exchange of views" to reach a "lasting and extensive peace in the Pacific area," and that Japan would withdraw her troops from Indochina "as soon as the China Incident is settled or a just peace is established in East Asia."

Toyoda, ever mindful of the risks of an adverse reaction from ultra-nationalist organizations and other extremists (not to mention the Germans), had instructed Nomura to avoid any public disclosure of Konoye's proposed meeting with Roosevelt. Grew had similarly advised Hull that it was important to hold the proposed meeting "in strictest secrecy." Despite those admonitions, Nomura and Hull "mutually agreed" that they should make an announcement to the press after the Roosevelt meeting on August 28 that the Japanese Prime Minister had sent a personal message to the President "without any reference to the contents of the message." It proved to be a miscalculation. Speculation and rumors erupted in Japan and the United States on what the message said. Neither the White House nor Hull would provide any detail. For his part, White House Press Secretary Steve Early denied reports that the Japanese Prime Minister had "proposed that he and President Roosevelt hold a personal conversation aboard a Japanese warship in the Pacific Ocean." Early said that "the only Presidential sea voyage in the near future was a weekend cruise 'from Annapolis, down the Chesapeake Bay and up the Potomac River to Washington.'"

The optimism with which Nomura made his public announcement evaporated when he met with Hull at the Secretary of State's apartment the evening after the announcement was made to the press. Roosevelt, ever confident of his ability to handle personal meetings, embraced the notion of a meeting with the Japanese Prime Minister. But the views of Hornbeck—supported by Ballantine and Far Eastern Division Chief Max Hamilton—prevailed. There would be no meeting unless and until the parties had reached an agreement. It was a condition that Roosevelt accepted on Hull's recommendation. "Mr. Hull," Ballantine later said, "was the one that dissuaded him from going."

Nomura opened the discussion on that Thursday evening by expressing "his appreciation" for the Secretary of State's assistance in scheduling the meeting with Roosevelt that morning. The Japanese ambassador added that he felt "much encouraged" by the President's response and proposed a meeting sometime between September 21 and 25. Hull threw cold water on that euphoria and made clear that a September meeting date was unrealistic. The Secretary of State then talked about "the desirability of there being reached in advance of the proposed meeting an agreement in principle on the principal questions...." He said that "serious consequences" would ensue if the meeting "failed to result in an agreement." For that reason, he continued, it would be better to use the meeting as a "ratification of essential points already agreed to in principle."

Hull did not hide his skepticism on the likelihood of the parties reaching any kind of agreement. He said "it would be unfortunate to proceed now" when "one half of the Japanese Government was disposed to go along a course of peace" while "the other half" was "pulling in the opposite direction."

Hull's approach placed the United States at cross purposes with the Japanese Government. Konoye wanted to use the meeting to bridge the gap between the two countries. Hull wanted to have the meeting after that gap had already been bridged.

Nomura was plainly disappointed, but he was a reserved man. He did not argue with the Secretary of State. He closed the meeting by saying that Konoye "was a man of great courage and was prepared to assume great risks...." But the despair he felt was evident in his report to Tokyo. "[H]e is very careful and cautious in handling this question," the Ambassador said of Hull, "and he seems to have been giving it careful consideration from every angle." That was not a good omen for Konoye. "So it is my observation," Nomura concluded, "that the meeting of the leaders will not materialize unless both parties reach an agreement on the main points."

Nomura continued to meet with Hull almost daily over the next few days, but little progress was made. For his part, Grew was sending Hull telegrams almost every day to report on conversations with Japanese officials and to make recommendations to facilitate a meeting between Roosevelt and Konoye. "In liberal circles," the Ambassador told the Secretary of State in a telegram on August 30, "Prince Konoye is characterized as weak, but it is doubtful if those circles have [a] true conception of the fundamental difficulties and dangers which confront him from extremists and pro-Axis elements." Grew said "it was certain" that Konoye and other Japanese leaders "already realize the fundamental error that was made in concluding the Tripartite Alliance." Still, he added, it would be helpful if the United States could generate publicity in Japan to counter the unceasing propaganda from the Nazis and their supporters. He therefore proposed that Roosevelt make some dramatic gesture that would be given publicity in Japan and that would emphasize the benefits of an adjustment in Japanese-American relations. One possible opportunity, he suggested, would be the Labor Day speech that Roosevelt would soon deliver. Much good would be accomplished, said Grew, if that speech could emphasize, however briefly, "the potential beneficial future rather than the unhappy past...."

Hornbeck was not impressed. "There is no way," he wrote in red pencil on his copy of the telegram, "that we can get it through to the Japanese people except as their officials are willing to let it through...." So Grew never received any response to his proposal. Instead, when Hull met with Nomura on September 1, the Secretary of State merely mentioned that "there was no assurance that the Japanese Government could obtain public support" for any settlement and that it might be useful if the Japanese Government could "exercise its influence with the Japanese press...to point out the benefits that would flow to Japan from a peaceful program such as the Secretary and the Japanese Ambassador had in mind."

Nomura did allude to Hull's suggestion in his report to Tokyo, but his subsequent discussions with Hull did not generate any movement toward the meeting that Konoye sought with Roosevelt. Any hope for immediate progress was dispelled when the Japanese ambassador met with the President and the Secretary of State in the Oval Study around 5:15 p.m. on Wednesday, September 3.

Roosevelt had requested the meeting to respond to Konoye's message to him with respect to the meeting. But the first order of business was to set forth the American position. To that end, the President almost immediately began reading a lengthy Oral Statement which referenced the four principles that Hull had given Nomura in their meeting on April 16 and that remained fundamental to the American position. The Oral Statement concluded with a hope that "the Government of Japan will surely recognize that the Government of the United States could not enter into any agreement which would not be in harmony" with those principles. Roosevelt then read his reply to Konoye. He "noted with satisfaction the sentiments" expressed in the Prime Minister's message and said he was "prepared to proceed as rapidly as possible toward the consummation of arrangements for a meeting...." At the same time, said Roosevelt's reply, he had to take "cognizance" of elements in Japan who could raise "obstacles to successful collaboration." For that reason, the reply continued, it would be "highly desirable" to immediately commence "preliminary discussion of the fundamental and essential questions on which we seek agreement."

The ambiguous language of the statements left Nomura uncertain. As soon as Roosevelt had finished reading them, the Ambassador asked whether the President "was still favorable to a conference...." Roosevelt replied that he was, but that it "was very important to settle a number of these questions beforehand...." He, as well as Hull, also emphasized the need for the Japanese Government "to clarify its position on the question of abandoning a policy of force and conquest...." Konoye's request for a meeting, and his message to the President, would obviously not suffice. And if the United States and Japan should ultimately reach agreement, said Roosevelt, his administration would then have to review the matter with the British, the Dutch, and of course, the Chinese.

Grew had no prior notice of Roosevelt's meeting with Nomura—and Hull had not asked for his advice in framing the Oral Statement or the reply that Roosevelt gave to Nomura at that meeting. The American ambassador nonetheless understood the steep hurdles that Hull was creating in demanding an agreement before the two leaders could meet. So he tried to soften the American position after meeting with Toyoda on the afternoon of September 4.

The Foreign Minister had requested the meeting so that he could give the American ambassador a new settlement proposal (even though Nomura had not yet given the United States the counterproposal to the American proposal of June 21). Toyoda opened the meeting by saying that Konoye would "leave no stone unturned" to arrange the meeting with Roosevelt "at an early date" and "to ensure the success of that meeting...." But the Foreign Minister wanted Grew to appreciate the risk involved. If the meeting should "fail to achieve its basic aim," said Toyoda, "he was afraid that further efforts would be useless."

Toyoda then gave Grew the new Japanese proposal. It was not a revision of the American draft that Hull had given to Nomura on June 21. It was instead a much more concise document that took account of recent developments. The new draft said that Japan would "not make any military advancement" from Indochina into other East Asia countries, that the attitude of Japan and the United States toward the European war would be determined by "concepts of protection and self-defense," that

Japan would "independently" decide whether any activity by the United States triggered Japan's obligations under the Tripartite Agreement, and that Japan was "ready to withdraw its armed forces from China as soon as possible in accordance with the agreements between Japan and China." Nothing was said about retaining troops in North China to protect against communist activities.

For his part, Grew told Hull that the new proposal reflected "a difference in tone and substance" that, to the American ambassador, reflected "the earnest wish of the Japanese Government to achieve a basic settlement with the United States." But Grew remained concerned about timing. As he had repeatedly told Hull, Konoye could not afford the delay of a long, deliberative process. In conveying Toyoda's proposal of September 4 to Hull, Grew tried to make sure the Secretary of State understood that time limitation. "[I]t would not be possible," Grew told Hull, "... to work out a detailed agreement" within the timeframe available to Konoye to have the meeting with Roosevelt. But he had a proposal to ease Hull's concern about entering into an agreement that could later be misinterpreted by the Japanese. The United States could withhold relaxation of existing sanctions only when satisfied that Japan had implemented its commitments. That way, said Grew, the United States "would always retain in its hands the leverage" to ensure Japan's compliance with the agreement.

It was another proposal that received no response from the State Department. The American ambassador was therefore left to wonder whether Hull appreciated the need for expedition.

Grew was not the only one concerned that time was growing short. It was becoming more and more clear to many in Japan's military and its cabinet that the United States might never be pinned down to an agreement and that application of American economic sanctions would soon deplete Japan of resources needed to fight a prolonged war with the United States. "In various respects," Navy Chief Nagano said at a Liaison Conference on September 3, "the Empire is losing materials" and "we are getting weaker" while "the enemy is getting stronger." If "we get into a long war without a decisive battle," Nagano continued, "we will be in difficulty, especially since our supply of resources will become depleted." There was general agreement on these points among the other conferees, and a new policy statement was proposed.

The new policy statement said that Japan would "complete its preparation for war" but would "concurrently take all possible diplomatic measures" to resolve Japan's differences with the United States and Great Britain. If "there was no prospect" of Japan's demands being satisfied through diplomacy by October 10, the Japanese government would "immediately decide to commence hostilities against the United States, Britain, and the Netherlands." The policy statement included Japan's "minimum demands," some of which would never be accepted by the United States and Great Britain (such as the demand that the United States and Great Britain close the Burma Road that had been used to provide supplies to China and that those two countries otherwise "cease to assist the Chiang Kai-shek regime"). The "maximum concessions" identified in the policy statement consisted primarily of those already included in the draft proposal that Toyoda had given to Grew on September 4.

After the new policy statement was approved by the cabinet on September 5, Konoye requested a meeting with Hirohito to explain the government's recommendation and to request an Imperial Conference so that the new policy statement could receive the Emperor's approval. Kido questioned the Prime Minister on the wisdom of establishing an October deadline for a diplomatic resolution, but Konoye held firm. The consensus among the military and the government was a fragile one, and trying to revise the deadline could undermine that consensus.

Hirohito was nonetheless troubled by the new policy statement. He told the Prime Minister that the new policy statement seemed "to give precedence to war over diplomatic activities." He was not willing to shield those concerns from the military. He told Konoye that he would question the chiefs of the Army and Navy General Staffs on their priorities at the Imperial Conference, which had been scheduled for the following day. Konoye responded that there was no difference in the importance between diplomacy and war and that "the Government intended to pursue diplomatic negotiations as long as possible and to commence preparations for war only when there seemed [to be] no prospect for [a] successful negotiation." Konoye also suggested that it would be better for the Emperor to question the Army and Navy chiefs now—before the Imperial Conference—rather than at the conference. And so Hirohito summoned Navy Chief Nagano and Army Chief Sugiyama to the Imperial Palace.

Hirohito told the military chiefs that he wanted to give priority to a diplomatic resolution. He then asked Sugiyama "the probable length of hostilities in case of a Japanese-American war." The Army Chief thought it would take about "three months." The Emperor was not buying. "When the China Incident broke out," Hirohito responded, "you were our army minister. I remember you telling me then that the conflict would be over in about a month. But after four long years, it hasn't ended!" Sugiyama struggled to find an answer, saying that the "hinterland" of China was "extensive." At this, Konoye remembered, the Emperor responded in a raised voice, saying that if the Chinese hinterland was extensive, "the Pacific was boundless." After some further discussion, the Emperor asked the two military chiefs whether they would give "precedence to diplomacy." They both answered in the affirmative.

About twenty minutes before the Imperial Conference convened at 10 a.m. the next day—Saturday, September 6—Hirohito told Kido that he wanted to question the participants to emphasize the priority that should be given to diplomacy. The Lord Keeper of the Privy Seal said that he had already talked with Privy Council President Hara about the need to ask questions. Still, Kido understood the Emperor's desire to break his silence on the matter. He suggested that the forty-year-old Emperor say something at the end of the conference to urge everyone to "cooperate to bring about success in the diplomatic negotiation."

Konoye opened the conference with a statement that straddled the need to pursue diplomacy with the need to prepare for war if diplomacy failed. The Empire must, he said, "try to prevent the disaster of war by resorting to all possible diplomatic measures. If the diplomatic measure should fail to bring about favorable results within a certain period, I believe we cannot help but take the ultimate step in order to defend ourselves." That general theme was echoed in statements by Nagano, Sugiyma, Toyoda, and other participants. When the preliminary statements were concluded, Hara took the floor and conveyed the Emperor's perspective. "The draft seems to suggest," he said, "that the war comes first, and diplomacy second, but I interpret it to mean that we will spare no efforts in diplomacy and we will go to war only when we can find no other way." Nagano was quick to confirm the Privy Council President's interpretation.

As the proceedings drew to a close, Hara focused on Konoye's proposed meeting with Roosevelt. "When Prime Minister Konoye goes to the United States," said the Privy Council President, "it is essential for him to feel that his main objective is to adjust relations somehow or other through diplomacy, bearing in mind that we shall be preparing for war while doing everything possible in terms of diplomacy. If this proposal receives the Imperial Assent," he said to the chiefs of the Army and Navy General Staffs, "I ask your cooperation...."

Neither Nagano nor Sugiyama gave any immediate reply. The participants were then stunned to hear the Emperor interject in his high-pitched voice. Hirohito had not spoken at an Imperial Conference since 1936. "The question Hara has just asked makes sense," Hirohito said. "Why doesn't the high command answer?" Before Nagano and Sugiyama could say anything, Hirohito pulled a piece of paper from the breast pocket of his khaki army uniform and read the words on that piece of paper. They consisted of a poem written by Hirohito's grandfather, the venerable Emperor Meiji:

All the seas in every quarter are as brothers to one another.
Why, then, do the winds and waves of strife rage so turbulently
throughout the world?

"I always read this composition with humility," Hirohito added, "endeavoring to be instructed in the late emperor's peace-loving spirit."

Nagano and Sugiyama were not about to take issue with the Emperor. They quickly agreed that a diplomatic solution would receive priority.

That priority certainly squared with Konoye's perspective. But time was running out. He was now confronted with a deadline of October 10 to conclude the negotiations with the United States, and his ambassador in Washington had made it clear that neither the Secretary of State nor the President was in any rush to reach an agreement and facilitate his visit with Roosevelt. Continued reliance on Nomura to secure an expeditious response from the United States was foolhardy. Another avenue would have to be used.

Protocol generally precluded the Prime Minister from meeting alone with the American ambassador, but this critical situation justified an exception. Konoye had Ushiba telephone Dooman on the afternoon of September 5 to request that he and Grew attend a secret meeting with the Prime

Minister that evening at the home of a friend. But then Konoye decided that the meeting should be postponed to the following evening after the Imperial Conference concluded. Ushiba told Dooman that he would transport the Counselor and the Ambassador to the meeting in his car.

Around 5 p.m. on the evening of September 6, 1941, a large black automobile—devoid of license plates to conceal its ownership—passed through the gates of the American Embassy and pulled up to the Ambassador's residence. Grew and Dooman emerged through the front doors, got in the car with Ushiba, and were driven to the home of Baron Ito Bunchiko, one of Konoye's confidants. Aside from Ushiba, the Prime Minister, and Konoye's Geisha mistress (whom Grew mistakenly thought was "probably the daughter of the house"), no one else was in attendance.

After dinner (which Grew described as "especially delicious"), the Prime Minister explained the purpose of the meeting: to sidestep normal diplomatic channels to expedite the meeting with Roosevelt and hopefully reach a settlement with the United States. Although he spoke English, Konoye's comments were made in Japanese and then translated by Ushiba.

One of the Prime Minister's first comments later became a point of controversy with the State Department. Konoye later recalled that he began the conversation by saying that Hull's four principles "were splendid as principles, but when it came down to actual application a variety of problems arose." One of the purposes of his proposed meeting with Roosevelt, said Konoye, was "to solve those very problems." Dooman's recollection squared with the Prime Minister's. "Konoye said that he accepted the four points which Secretary of State Hull had laid down as a basis for building relations between our two countries," the Embassy Counselor later remembered. "But, in the same breath, he said, 'But, however, they will have to be applied in the light of conditions as they actually existed.'"

Unfortunately, the telegram that Dooman later prepared and that Grew sent to Hull did not clearly set forth that qualification. The telegram recounted Konoye as saying that he and the Japanese government "conclusively and wholeheartedly agree with the four principles enunciated by the Secretary of State as a basis for the rehabilitation of relations between the United States and Japan." The telegram did add that the points embraced in the proposal given by Toyoda to Grew on September 4 "may need clarification and more precise formulation...." That language may have been intended to capture Konoye's qualification, but Hull and his advisers did not read it that way. Later, when they learned of the Prime Minister's qualification, Hull and his advisers chalked it up to another sign of Japanese duplicity.

Konoye could not have anticipated that later disparagement when he met with Grew and Dooman. The Prime Minister did, however, acknowledge his own responsibility for "the present regrettable state of relations" between the United States and Japan. But that admission was not enough to discourage a change in direction. While not wanting to appear immodest, Konoye insisted that "only he" could turn the situation around. If he should fail, he cautioned the two Americans, "no succeeding Prime Minister, at least during his own lifetime, could achieve the results desired."

The Prime Minister said he was very much aware of the skepticism expressed by Roosevelt and Hull whether any agreement with the United States would have the support of the military. Yes, he said, there were "certain elements within the armed forces who do not approve his policies." But Japan's naval and military leaders had "subscribed to his proposals," and the Ministers of War and the Navy had also "given their full agreement to his proposals...." In fact, said the Prime Minister, he had already arranged for high-ranking Army and Navy officers to accompany him to his meeting with Roosevelt.

Konoye did not give Grew or Dooman "any inkling" of the substance of his proposals. According to Dooman, he said only that he would make a proposition that "'President Roosevelt could not afford' (I think those were his exact words) 'to reject.'" But time was of the essence. Konoye made no reference to the Imperial Conference that had been held that morning or to the deadline of October 10 that had been incorporated into the policy statement and approved by the Emperor. Instead, Konoye explained that American economic sanctions were taking their toll on the Japanese populace and that something needed to be done before the growing anger made any agreement impossible. The importance of expeditious action was especially important because, in his view, "it might take half a year to a year to work out all the details...."

The Prime Minister added what was probably self-evident to Grew and Dooman—namely, that it would be "impossible for the two governments to negotiate through ordinary diplomatic channels." In his view, the two countries could reach agreement only through a meeting with the heads of state. That was especially true, said Konoye, because the Foreign Office "abounded with Axis sympathizers...." For that reason, he had not even told Toyoda about his meeting with Grew and Dooman. Nor had he advised Toyoda or the other civilian members of his cabinet about the proposals he was prepared to offer Roosevelt. And he did not want to rely on Nomura as a vehicle for communicating with the President. If Roosevelt wanted to convey any message to him "personally and confidentially," said the Prime Minister, he would be glad to arrange "secret meetings" with Grew.

Although he did not describe the proposal he was prepared to make to the President, Konoye emphasized the benefit of the leaders' meeting in dealing with the China Incident. As soon as an agreement was reached with the United States, the news would be dispatched to Tokyo and instructions would be issued "to the commander-in-chief in China to suspend hostilities."

All of this was conveyed to Grew by Ushiba, who translated the Prime Minister's comments into English as they were being spoken. Immediately after making that last remark to Grew, Konoye turned to Dooman. "Now," he told the Embassy Counselor in Japanese, "I am going to tell you something that I don't want you to repeat to Mr. Grew or in any way disclose. This is purely for your information so that you can advise the Ambassador with more intelligence as to what my thinking is." Dooman thought for a moment and then said he would agree to that restriction if "the information related to some matter internal to Japan." The Prime Minister said that it did. "The fact is," said Konoye, "that as soon as I reach agreement with the President, I will report immediately to the Emperor, and it will be the Emperor who will command the army to suspend hostilities." Reaching an agreement, however, was critical. "You have lived a long time in this country," Konoye told the Embassy Counselor, "and you well understand that the Emperor cannot be involved before a definite agreement has been reached. But the fact is that he is ready to take a decisive step."

Konoye concluded the meeting by saying that he was "determined" to adjust relations with the United States "regardless of cost or personal risk."

The meeting with Konoye lasted about three hours. As they left the Ito residence, Grew and Dooman knew that there was only a short window of time to save the situation. They were nonetheless hopeful that the Prime

Minister had given them some leverage to facilitate the conference with Roosevelt and, with the conference, an amicable adjustment of relations between their two countries.

Still, they understood the challenges involved. In trying to save the situation, their principal adversary might not be the Japanese government but their own State Department.

CHAPTER 16

Frustration

I t was not the life they had expected. Alice and Joe had experienced many ups and downs in different legations around the world (including service in Berlin during the Great War), but nothing could compare with the tension and terror of Tokyo in September 1941. Their personal safety remained a principal concern, especially because Grew had learned that some groups had targeted him for elimination. The fear was heightened after Grew learned of the attempted assassination of Konoye. As the Ambassador recounted in his diary, "[F]our men with daggers and short swords jumped on the running board of [Konoye's] car as he was leaving his private residence and tried to get at him. The doors were fortunately locked, however, and the assassins were quickly overpowered by the plain-clothes men at the residence."

The guard at the entrance to the Embassy was strengthened, but the Grews knew that might not be enough to deter assassins from scaling the walls that surrounded the Embassy. Joe began to carry a handgun beneath his suit jacket. "I don't like heroics," he confided to his diary, "but [I] have no intention of letting a group of those roughnecks carve me up without a reasonable attempt at repartee." He was not alone in taking precautions against assassination. During a conversation with Terasaki, the American Bureau chief took the Ambassador's hand and placed it over his heart. "I thought," Grew later said, "he meant to convey the idea that his heart was in the right place, but it felt like a very hard heart, and I soon grasped the idea that the hardness wasn't his heart at all but a very business-like gun."

The routines of daily life had also become more difficult. The government announced that an additional 150 consumer items—including can-openers, cocktail shakers, and finger bowls—had been added to the list of banned iron products. The reciprocal freeze that Japan had placed on American funds in July continued to make it impossible for anyone in the Embassy to withdraw money from the bank or to cash checks (a situation that led Grew to seek assistance from the State Department, saying that for six weeks, everyone in the Embassy had been living on borrowed funds). The Embassy had stockpiled gasoline for its cars, but the supplies had to be used sparingly. Still, exceptions could be made. Alice authorized an Embassy car to take the Grews' good friend Yoshida Shigeru, the former ambassador to Great Britain, to the hospital two or three times a week to visit his wife, who was dying of throat cancer—a welcome gesture, because Yoshida had no car of his own "owing to the gasoline restrictions."

There were moments of cheer in these dark days. One occurred when Mizzie, the Grews' long-time servant, came to Joe and Alice one evening while holding one of the two canaries in the Embassy residence. The bird's eyes were closed, and it appeared to be on the verge of death. But, as Grew recounted in his diary, Alice "suggested the proper medicine." So the Ambassador put a few drops of Bourbon whiskey in the bird's mouth, and Mizzie took the canary back to its cage. "The next morning," said Joe, "I dropped in to view the corpse, but there was the little fellow a-tilt on his perch, preening his feathers and singing as if his heart would burst with the joy of living."

These incidental diversions at the Embassy residence had no impact on the pace of activity in the Chancery. It remained frenetic. There was a steady stream of meetings. Grew himself had twelve meetings with Toyoda in the space of one seven-day stretch. The burden on the staff was considerable. They had to help the Ambassador prepare for his meetings, attend to meetings of their own, review and summarize the daily press, and generate the plethora of telegrams that had to be sent to the State Department. Routine social events were now a thing of the past, in part because the Embassy was largely a bachelor establishment. Almost all the women and children had been evacuated except for Alice, Mizzie, Jane Smith-Hutton (wife of naval attaché Henri Smith-Hutton), the Smith-Hutton's five-year-old daughter Cynthia, Marion Arnold, Grew's long-time secretary, and some file clerks and secretaries.

Despite all that, it was an exhilarating time. In late August, Grew had suggested to John Emmerson that he defer his scheduled return to the United States. "I can't imagine your wanting to leave the embassy now," he told the Third Secretary, "when you have this opportunity of a lifetime to see history made."

That opportunity of a lifetime disappeared in the five weeks after Grew's dinner with Konoye. The logistics of discussing an agreement—which Hull perpetually portrayed as a condition for any meeting between Konoye and Roosevelt—were initially compromised by Nomura. On September 4, he gave Hull a counterproposal which he characterized as a "redraft" of the State Department draft of June 21. The Japanese ambassador failed to disclose that the new counterproposal was not a document authorized by the Japanese government but rather one that Nomura had prepared on his own initiative (probably with the assistance of the John Doe Associates). It was not until September 10 that the State Department learned of the document's true origin.

Prior to learning of that faux pas by Nomura, Hull had sent a telegram to Grew that discussed Nomura's draft as well as the proposal Toyoda gave to Grew on September 4 (and which Nomura had given Hull on September 6). A primary consideration was the settlement terms Japan would propose to China. Hull explained to Grew, as he had previously told Nomura, that there could be no agreement between the United States and Japan unless the United States was "satisfied that these terms were in harmony with the principles" to which the United States was committed. Hull remarked that the parties had "reached an impasse" in the earlier discussions on two principal points: Japan's proposal to station troops in North China after a settlement had been achieved, and Japan's failure to make "explicit commitments" with respect to "non-discrimination" in its post-settlement commercial relationship with China. Hull proposed that the American ambassador question the Japanese about those issues and others relating to the Japanese proposals.

Grew met with Toyoda on September 10 to discuss the questions raised by Hull. To facilitate that discussion, he gave the Foreign Minister a document that referenced the "deadlock" on the two issues relating to the settlement with China. On a more general level, the document expressed the State Department's view that the Japanese proposals appeared "more limited" than the terms "on which tentative agreement had previously been reached." As one example, the document stated that the American draft of June 21 had promoted non-discrimination in economic relations in the "Pacific area" while Toyoda's proposal referenced non-discrimination only in the "southwest Pacific." Hull similarly told Nomura in a separate conversation on September 10 that the State Department believed that Toyoda's proposal of September 4 "had narrowed down the spirit and scope of the proposed understanding."

Toyoda met with Grew on September 13 to discuss Hull's concerns and to dispel any notion that Japan had tried to limit the scope of any prior understanding. The Foreign Minister explained that the Japanese government had drafted proposals that would hopefully "obviate [a] long drawn out discussion of details...." In no event, said Toyoda, had Japan intended "to reduce or curtail in any way whatever" any "preliminary agreement" that the parties had previously reached. In response to Hull's questions about the parties' agreement in general and the terms of a China settlement in particular, the Foreign Minister gave Grew a copy of instructions that had been sent to Nomura that same day. The instructions explained that Japan wanted to station troops in North China after settlement of the China Incident "for a certain period" agreed to by China and Japan to prevent "communistic and other subversive activities." Those instructions also confirmed Japan's commitment to "the principle of non-discrimination with regard to commerce in China...." And the instructions made clear that the proposal had referenced the Southwestern Pacific—not the entire Pacific area—because that was where Japan was active and thus the area of most concern to the United States. In the course of his discussion with the American ambassador, Toyoda again emphasized "the urgency" of arranging the meeting between Konoye and Roosevelt "with the least possible delay."

The request for urgency fell on deaf ears at the State Department. In fact, Hornbeck was on vacation when the State Department received the telegram that described Grew's conversation with Toyoda. Nomura had reported to Tokyo that Hornbeck was planning to go on vacation for two weeks beginning on September 20 and that Hornbeck had told an

Associated Press correspondent "that no progress...was to be expected during his absence." That report caused considerable consternation among the Japanese, and Grew conveyed that consternation to Hull on September 20. The Secretary of State was quick to respond that Hornbeck had actually gone on vacation on September 13 and had returned on September 21.

Whatever the dates, the Political Relations Adviser did not share Toyoda's concern about the need for expedition in responding to Konoye's request for a meeting with Roosevelt. Nor was there any change in Hornbeck's disdain for the adverse consequences that would allegedly ensue if the meeting were not held. On September 6—the day of Grew's dinner meeting with Konoye—Hornbeck made a note of "certain themes" that dominated the Ambassador's dispatches and that the Political Relations Adviser obviously deemed unworthy of consideration: "time is of the essence; may be [the] last chance; assassination possible; national hara-kiri; etc."

Hornbeck's continued opposition to a meeting between Konoye and Roosevelt was not a secret within the department. "The holding by the President of the United States now of a rendezvous with the Premier of Japan," he had written Hull on September 5 in his convoluted syntax, "would be, so far as the United States is concerned, a gesture born of lack of confidence in the present position (actual military capacity) of the United States." The specter of Munich loomed large in the background. Any meeting between Konoye and Roosevelt, Hornbeck added, "would more nearly resemble meetings which were held between Mr. Chamberlain and Mr. Hitler."

Hornbeck's perspective mirrored prevailing public opinion in the United States. The isolationist fervor that had frustrated Roosevelt's effort to become more involved in Britain's struggle for survival did not apply to a possible conflict with Japan. In mid-July—before the American public learned about Japan's move into southern Indochina—a Gallup poll showed that 51% of those surveyed agreed that the United States should "take steps to keep Japan from becoming more powerful even if this means risking a war." By early September, the number had jumped to 70%. Much of America's opposition to any accommodation with Japan was driven by a deep affection for China (perhaps instilled in some small part by *The Good Earth*, Pearl Buck's 1931 best-selling novel about a Chinese family). Whatever the source, that opposition was reflected in editorials in the American press.

"We are confident," said the *New York Herald Tribune* on September 16, 1941, "that, so far as the State Department is concerned, [Japan] will win no more appeasement from the United States government than it would win from the man in the street." Nothing, the editorial said, "would move us to let the Chinese down." That sentiment was shared by many senior officials in Roosevelt's administration, some of whom were constantly pressing the President for more aggressive action in dealing with Japan. Interior Secretary Harold Ickes was among those senior officials. He confided to his diary on September 5 that he would resign with "a very carefully prepared statement" if the administration should return "to our policy of appeasement of Japan."

Nomura was mindful of the growing sentiment against Japan, and he did his best to convey the American public's mood in telegrams to Tokyo. For its part, Konoye's cabinet was eager to minimize the risk of failure. On September 22, Toyoda handed Grew a document that set forth the settlement terms that Japan would propose for China. The terms included the fusion of Chiang Kai-Shek's regime with the puppet regime Japan had established in Nanking, the recognition of Manchukuo (the puppet regime Japan had established in Manchuria), and the withdrawal of all Japanese troops from China except for those needed in certain areas to prevent "communistic and subversive activities...." In giving Grew the settlement terms, Toyoda repeated that the Japanese proposal of September 4 "had widened rather than reduced the subject matter of the negotiations...." He then added, in obvious frustration, that Japan was "still awaiting" some response from the United States.

Grew understood that frustration. He and Dooman had discussed the slow progress incessantly. Their views had been articulated in a continuous stream of telegrams to the State Department. Explanations of possible benefits from Konoye's meeting with Roosevelt. Ways to preserve leverage over Japan. Warnings of dire consequences if the meeting were not held. None of those communications had generated a meaningful reaction from the State Department. And so, on the very afternoon when Toyoda gave him the proposed terms of a settlement in China, Grew sent a "Dear Frank" letter to the President.

Konoye, Joe told Roosevelt, "is courageously working for an improvement in Japan's relations with the United States." True, the Prime Minister "bears the heavy responsibility for having allowed our relations to come to such a pass." But, said Grew, "he no doubt sees the handwriting on the wall and realizes that Japan has nothing to hope for from the Tripartite Pact...." And so there was now an opportunity for reconciliation. But that opportunity would not survive indefinitely. "It seems to me," Grew wrote, "highly unlikely that this chance will come again or that any Japanese statesman other than Prince Konoye could succeed in controlling the military extremists...." And then came a plea for favorable action. "I therefore must earnestly hope," Joe concluded, "that we can come to terms, even if we must take on trust, at least to some degree, the continued good faith and ability of the present Government fully to implement those terms."

The letter did not produce the result Grew might have expected and certainly wanted. There was no change in the State Department's strategy. Joe did not even receive a response from the President until October 30—long after the prospect for a meeting with the Japanese Prime Minister had disappeared.

Like Grew, Konoye was distressed by the American failure to respond to his proposal to meet with Roosevelt, especially because the patience of the Japanese military was wearing thin. To implement the policy statement of the September 6 Imperial Conference, the Army and Navy decided that preparations for war would commence if the negotiations with the United States did not produce an agreement by October 15. That decision was accepted at a Liaison Conference on September 25.

The decision was consistent with the policy statement adopted at the September 6 Imperial Conference. The statement had referenced the need for military action if there was "no prospect" of Japan's demands being met in "the first ten days of October." Still, Konoye was surprised and disappointed by the military's adoption of a hard deadline. He had "no confidence" in a war with the United States. And he still had faith that he could work out an agreement with Roosevelt. Given that perspective, he told Kido that, "if the military insists on the October 15 deadline," he might have no choice "but to think of resigning."

Kido was not pleased. He had cautioned Konoye before the Imperial Conference of September 6 that it was not wise to establish an October deadline for the successful conclusion of negotiations. And now the Prime Minister, this Prime Minister, the one on whom so much hope had been placed, was threatening to walk away. "You cannot leave the decision hanging and just disappear," he told Konoye. Alternatives could be considered. Perhaps, Kido suggested, Konoye could "propose a reconsideration" of the decision made at the September 6 Imperial Conference. The notion of reconsidering a decision approved by the Emperor was not a course to be taken lightly and would likely draw opposition from the military. Konoye responded to Kido's suggestion by leaving Tokyo on September 27 for the security of his home in nearby Kamakura.

The Prime Minister's absence did not affect the continued efforts of his cabinet and Nomura to elicit a favorable response from the State Department. On the very day on which Konoye left for his home in the suburbs, Toyoda met with Grew to convey "the anxiety of Prince Konoye and the entire Cabinet lest the proposed meeting between the heads of our two Governments might be indefinitely delayed...." Toyoda also gave the American ambassador a detailed statement that reviewed the prior deliberations and that now proposed a meeting between Konoye and Roosevelt between October 10 and 15. The statement also explained that all the logistics for Konoye's trip to Juneau had been completed—the military officers who were to accompany the Prime Minister had been identified, and the warship itself had "been put into momentary readiness to sail."

Nomura gave a copy of Toyoda's statement to Hull on September 29. In the meantime, the Japanese ambassador had suggested that Tokyo submit a counterproposal to the State Department draft of June 21. That new counterproposal was given to Grew on September 25, and on September 27, a member of the Japanese Embassy in Washington gave a copy to Ballantine. The counterproposal reiterated many of Japan's prior positions, including a statement that it would "independently" decide whether any action by the United States in the European war triggered any obligation under the Tripartite Pact. The embassy also gave Ballantine an Oral Statement that Terasaki had delivered to Dooman on September 23 and that explained the need for Japan to station troops in North China after a settlement of the China Incident.

By the last weekend in September, Grew had not received any response from the President to his letter. No matter. He would not give up. He spent all day on Sunday, September 28, preparing a detailed review of the situation for the Secretary of State. After reviewing the draft with Dooman, the telegram was dispatched at noon on Monday, September 29. It was, Grew remarked, "one of the longest" telegrams he had ever sent.

"Japan is now trying to get out of an extremely dangerous position caused by miscalculation," the telegram explained. As a result, said Grew, "the political soil in Japan [is] hospitable to the sowing of new seeds which, if carefully planted and nourished, may lead…to a complete readjustment of Japan's relations with the United States." There were two approaches to planting those seeds, Grew continued. One was "progressive economic strangulation…." The other was negotiation—"not so-called appeasement," but what Grew called "constructive conciliation." It appeared to the Ambassador that the Roosevelt administration had wisely chosen this latter approach because the United States would always retain the option to employ "progressive economic sanctions…." A meeting between Konoye and Roosevelt, said Grew, provided "substantial hope" that the American approach could succeed.

Grew did not want that prospect of success to be extinguished by the State Department's insistence on securing a comprehensive agreement before the meeting. "The question arises," he told Hull, "whether we are not now presented with the opportunity to halt that [Japanese] program [of expansion] without war or the immediate risk of war, and whether, if the present opportunity fails us, we shall not be confronted with the greatly increased risk of war." In trying to elicit a productive response from the Japanese, the Ambassador continued, "it is essential to understand Japanese psychology, which is fundamentally different from the psychology of any Western nation. We cannot measure reactions to any given set of circumstances and predict Japanese actions by any Western measuring rod. For a country so lately emerged from feudalism," Grew continued, "this fact is hardly surprising."

For that reason, he added, it was futile to require the clear-cut commitments so cherished by Hull as a prerequisite to any meeting between Konoye and Roosevelt. "If we expect and wait for the Japanese Government to agree in the preliminary conversations to clear-cut commitments…in point of principle and concrete detail, the conversations will almost certainly drag on indefinitely and unproductively to a point where the Cabinet and those supporting elements who desire *rapprochement* to the United States will reach the conclusion that the American Government is merely playing for time and that the outlook for an agreement is hopeless." In that event, said Grew, "war would be difficult to avoid" because the Konoye Cabinet would fall and be replaced by "a military dictatorship."

However much he may have hoped for a positive reaction, Grew's telegram was given short shrift in Washington. Even before the telegram had been received, Roosevelt had accepted Hull's recommendation that there be a further delay in the discussions with Japan. The Secretary of State had given the President a handwritten note—probably sometime before Roosevelt left on Friday, September 26, for a weekend trip to his estate in Hyde Park. Hull said that the Japanese had "*narrowed* their position" on basic issues. The Secretary of State therefore suggested that he ask the Japanese to "go back to their original liberal attitude so that we can start discussions *again* on agreement in principle before the meeting...." The response, said Hull, could also emphasize Roosevelt's "desire for a meeting." The President sent Hull a typewritten response on Sunday, September 28, that said, "I wholly agree with your penciled note...."

Hull's note to Roosevelt was premised, in part at least, on a memo Ballantine had given the Secretary on September 23. The Japan Desk officer—speaking on behalf of all the Foreign Service officers involved in the conversations—first reviewed the proposals that had recently been received from the Japanese (which, he said, had "served to narrow" the "application of principles" necessary to any agreement). He then evaluated the options available for any response by the State Department. One obvious option was to "present a counterproposal to the Japanese Government." That option was not favored—even if Japan agreed to the counterproposal. "One disadvantage of such a course," said Ballantine, "would be that we could never be sure that the Japanese, in subscribing to a draft which we had prepared, have, in fact, reached a meeting of minds with us." (It was a perspective shared by Hull as well as others in the Roosevelt administration. At a meeting with the Secretary of State on October 6, Stimson said that "no promises of the Japs based on words would be worth anything." The War Secretary recorded in his diary that Hull "agreed.") The other disadvantage to an American counterproposal, said Ballantine's memo, is that it might "reveal so clearly the wide discrepancy in our viewpoints" and then be utilized by "reactionary elements in Japan to torpedo any proposed agreement."

Given those disadvantages, Ballantine said the group preferred to give the Japanese a reply that offered no counterproposals but made the American position "unmistakably clear," was "friendly in tone," and left "the door open for a continuation or resumption of the conversations...." Use of that option, said Ballantine, would shift the burden to Japan if the conversations were terminated. Hull explained the strategy to Grew several weeks later, telling the Ambassador that the State Department did not want "to exert pressure on the Japanese Government by presenting in detail the specifications of commitments which we have desired Japan to give." Better, said Hull, to let the Japanese fend for themselves in figuring out precisely what the United States wanted. That logic may have made sense to Hull and his advisers, but it was not a logic the Japanese could understand.

By Thursday, October 2, the Secretary of State was prepared to move forward on the strategy he had proposed to Roosevelt. It was a special day for Cordell Hull—his seventieth birthday. When he entered the reception room just outside his office for a noon press conference, the Secretary of State saw a cake on the long table. The correspondents had placed twenty-one candles on the cake to symbolize the twenty-one American republics and the Roosevelt administration's Good Neighbor Policy. Hull was moved by the gesture and offered a few remarks. "Today we are living through a dark period," he said. It was therefore important "to hold fast to the faith...in the destiny of free men and the supreme worth of Christian morality...." Hull then blew out the candles (taking seven breaths to do so).

It was a fitting cap to a morning in which Hull had taken another step, or so he believed, to protect America from Japanese aggression. He had asked the Japanese ambassador to come to his apartment at 9 o'clock that morning to give him an Oral Statement that would respond to the proposal that Toyoda had given Grew on September 4. Max Schmidt—the former Third Secretary in the Tokyo Embassy who was now part of the Far Eastern Division staff—had been asked to prepare the initial draft. His instructions were clear. There would be no counterproposals. Instead, he was told to "just keep it on the basis of principles."

The Oral Statement acknowledged Roosevelt's gratification in receiving Konoye's message of August 28 and his expression of "Japan's desire and intent to pursue courses of peace...." The Oral Statement said that the

United States wanted to proceed in arranging the meeting between Roosevelt and Konoye "as rapidly as possible...." But there had to be an agreement before any meeting could be held, and Toyoda's proposal showed that there was a "divergence in the concepts of the two Governments." Japan's proposal, coupled with its subsequent explanatory comments, appeared "to narrow and restrict" the application of the four principles that needed to be the basis of any agreement.

As an example of that divergence, the Oral Statement pointed out that Japan's proposal would apply only to the "Southwest Pacific area" instead of "the Pacific area as a whole." Reference was also made to Japan's proposal to station troops "for an indeterminate period" in portions of China after settlement of the China Incident. The Oral Statement did not acknowledge, let alone evaluate, Japan's explanations for that proposal; it merely said that the retention of troops in North China was "open to certain objections" because it seemed to be "out of keeping with the progressive and enlightened courses and principles" advocated by Hull. The Oral Statement added that it would be helpful if Japan could provide "a clear-cut manifestation of Japan's intention" with respect to the withdrawal of troops from China as well as Indochina.

The Oral Statement did not offer any analysis of Japan's assertion that it would "independently" decide whether the Tripartite Pact imposed any obligation on Japan if the United States became involved in the European war. Hull later said in his *Memoirs* that Japan's response was unacceptable because it enabled Japan alone "to judge what constituted self-defense...." But the Oral Statement did not express that objection. It merely said that "it would be helpful if the Japanese Government could give further study to the question of possible clarification of its position."

In view of Japan's various qualifications and exceptions to Hull's principles, the Oral Statement asked whether Japan believed that a meeting between Konoye and Roosevelt "would be likely to contribute to the advancement of the high purposes which" the two countries "had in mind." Not that it seemed to matter what Japan thought. As Hull and Roosevelt had previously agreed, the Oral Statement closed by expressing Roosevelt's "earnest hope" that further discussion of "fundamental questions" could facilitate the convocation of that meeting.

Hull gave Nomura the Oral Statement when the Ambassador reached the Secretary's apartment on that Thursday morning in October. In a meeting with Stark three days earlier, Nomura had told the American Navy chief he "was overwhelmed with shame for [his] failure to bring about satisfactory results since [his] arrival here." That sense of guilt was now compounded by despair. Nomura told Hull that "his Government would be disappointed" by the Oral Statement because of Japan's "very earnest desire to hold the meeting." Hull responded that "he had no desire whatever…to cause any delay." But the position of the United States remained unchanged. There had to be "a meeting of the minds on essential points before holding the proposed meeting." After a short time, the Japanese ambassador left, repeating his conviction that "the Konoye Cabinet was extremely desirous of reaching an agreement with the United States." In his report to Tokyo, Nomura said that the negotiations "have finally reached a 'deadlock.'"

As Dooman later said, the October 2 Oral Statement "was the turning point in the negotiations…." The disappointment in Tokyo, as Nomura predicted, was considerable. Japan had submitted three proposals to the United States in September—the one Toyoda gave to Grew on September 4, the peace terms for China given to Grew on September 22, and the draft of September 25. Substantial effort had been expended in preparing those proposals in the hope that they might elicit a favorable response from the United States—or at least some meaningful progress toward an agreement that could facilitate a meeting between Konoye and Roosevelt. And now the United States had responded with an Oral Statement that was largely confined to broad pronouncements and further questions for the Japanese government. "[T]he Japanese alone," Konoye later said in his Memoirs, perhaps with some hyperbole, "were stating their opinions on all sorts of problems. The Americans merely criticized or attacked these and did not at all try to show what was in their minds."

Not surprisingly, the October 2 Oral Statement generated numerous meetings in Tokyo. Ushiba met Dooman for breakfast on October 7 at the Counselor's home and expressed his government's concern with the Oral Statement. "It was true," said the Prime Minister's secretary, "that the American Government had given a full presentation of its principles, but it had not precisely specified what it wanted the Japanese Government to undertake." Many in the Japanese government, he said, believed that Japan "had fallen into a trap." The United States had extracted "an exposition" of Japan's "policies and objectives," and, having decided that they were unacceptable, the United States had decided not "to make an agreement with Japan...." The only option left for Japan, said Ushiba, was "to ask the American Government" to explain "the undertakings" that the United States wanted Japan to give.

Later that same day, Grew travelled to the Foreign Office to meet with Toyoda. The Foreign Minister initially objected to the Oral Statement's comment (borrowed from Grew's earlier report of his dinner with Konoye on September 6) that the Prime Minister "fully subscribed" to the four principles which Hull had given Nomura back in April. That was not an accurate description of Konoye's position, said Toyoda. The Prime Minister had accepted those points "in principle" only. Modification would be required when they were applied "to actual conditions."

On a more general level, the Foreign Minister wanted to know if Grew could give him, "unofficially and privately," his own opinion "on the position of the United States Government as outlined" in the October 2 Oral Statement. In truth, Grew was not pleased with the Oral Statement. It not only reflected an "uncompromising" and "almost completely inflexible" attitude; it also disregarded virtually everything Grew had said in his telegram of September 29 (as well as his earlier communications): the explanation of Japanese politics, the comments on Japanese psychology, and the recommendations for appropriate action. It was not something the Ambassador could ignore. "I have the feeling," Grew would confide to his diary about a week later, "whether justified or not, that my opinions are not particularly welcome nowadays."

However deep Grew's disappointment, it could not be disclosed to the Japanese Foreign Minister (or to the State Department, for that matter). The Ambassador was a loyal representative of his country. So he told Toyoda that the October 2 Oral Statement was nothing more than an effort by the United States "to assure itself that Japan would genuinely and fully observe those principles" that were essential "for a lasting peace in the Pacific area. . ."

The conversations with Dooman and Grew left the Japanese unsatisfied. Further information was needed. Terasaki thus held separate conversations with Grew and Dooman on October 8 and 9. In each case, the American Bureau chief questioned the American representatives on the request in the October 2 Oral Statement that Japan provide "a clear-cut manifestation of Japan's intention" with respect to the withdrawal of troops from China and

Indochina. Did the United States expect, Terasaki inquired, that Japan would withdraw troops before there was an agreement?

Neither Grew nor Dooman could give Terasaki an answer to that question or the others posed by the American Bureau chief. Grew said that he thought the October 2 Oral Statement was "friendly in tone and helpful in substance" but that he had "no authority" to interpret the document. It would be better, he said, for Nomura to pose questions to Hull on its meaning.

CHAPTER 17

Resignation

Nomura knew he had a steep hill to climb. He had received the instructions from the Foreign Minister on October 4—before Toyoda had met with Grew to discuss the October 2 Oral Statement. The instructions directed the Japanese ambassador to ask Hull to "set forth in precise terms the obligations which the United States Government wished the Japanese Government to undertake" with respect to the three principal issues: application of the Tripartite Pact if the United States became involved in the European war; the retention of troops in North China after settlement of the China Incident; and "equal opportunity in China." Nomura had sensed as long ago as September 4 that the Secretary of State's position had "considerably stiffened" and that he seemed unwilling to compromise on any issue. That was shortly after Hull had said there could be no meeting between Konoye and Roosevelt unless the parties first reached agreement. Little had changed in the American posture since that time. Hull remained a tough negotiator. Nomura made an appointment to meet with the Secretary of State at his apartment at 9 a.m. on Thursday, October 9. He would try to extract answers to the Foreign Minister's questions, but the Japanese ambassador could not have been very optimistic about the outcome.

Nomura's pessimism was well-founded. The previous Monday—an unusually hot day in Washington, with the temperature exceeding 90 degrees—Stimson had come to the State Department to discuss the Far East situation with the Secretary of State. The Secretary of War told Hull that he "needed three months to secure our position and to be protected from an explosion of the Japanese Army during that time." Stimson then read to Hull a memo that he had prepared on October 2 for his staff. "[W]hile I approve of stringing out negotiations during that period," said the memo, "they should not be allowed to ripen into a personal conference between the President and [the Prime Minister]. I greatly fear," the memo added, "that such a conference if actually held would produce concessions which would be highly dangerous to our vitally important relations with China." Hull listened as his cabinet colleague elaborated on his views. By the end, said Stimson, the Secretary of State "agreed to all of this." So there was little chance that Hull would try to facilitate an agreement by giving Nomura the information desired by Toyoda.

Hull reiterated his view at the October 9 meeting that the Japanese proposal of September 4 seemed "to narrow down" the principles that had to be the foundation of any agreement (and again cited the Japanese proposal's reference to "the southwest Pacific area" instead of the entire Pacific). The conversation then shifted to Japan's proposal to retain troops in North China after settlement of the China Incident. Hull did not think the Chinese would find the proposal acceptable. Remembering the history of his native Tennessee, Hull remarked that there was "bitter resentment" when Union troops were stationed in the South "after the civil war." Nomura may not have grasped the relevance of that attempted analogy, but he surely understood that Hull was not going to give him the information he wanted. Nomura remarked that Japan was at a "crossroads" and "in a very difficult position." Although 99 percent of the Japanese did not want "trouble with the United States," they were, said the Ambassador, "a very disciplined people and would fight if commanded to do so."

Hull did say in the meeting that it might be useful for Nomura to meet separately with Ballantine and Hamilton "to see whether any points in our respective documents could be further clarified and shades of meaning brought out." Nomura accepted that offer, and later that afternoon, he and some of his colleagues met with Ballantine, Hamilton, and Schmidt at the Japanese Embassy.

The Japanese representatives initiated the two-hour meeting by saying that they wanted to review the Japanese draft of September 25 "point by point" to understand the United States' objections. A reasonable approach perhaps, but not one that the State Department staff members were prepared to accept. They repeatedly rebuffed the Japanese representatives' requests for specific information on the United States' positions. "We pointed out," said Schmidt's summary of the conversation, "that... another way of approaching this problem, which might serve to avoid becoming lost in a maze of details and minutiae and to get back to fundamental principles, might be [for the Japanese] to take the October 2 document and to study it in the light of other statements" that the United States had made in documents and that Hull had made in conversations with Nomura. The Japanese ambassador finally turned to his colleagues and said that he would have to send a report to Tokyo "stating that the American Government had no concrete counterproposal to make" and that Japan "could either redraft its proposals or could prepare a new document...."

Toyoda was obviously frustrated when he received Nomura's reports of the conversations with Hull and his staff. And the Foreign Minister did what he invariably did in these situations where the State Department was uncommunicative: he asked the American ambassador to come see him.

Toyoda explained to Grew that Nomura had been unable to obtain information on the specific undertakings that the United States wanted Japan to take. A week "of very valuable time" had been lost in the process, he said. Time was growing short. So he asked Grew to secure answers to the same questions that Toyoda had posed to Nomura. In making that request, Toyoda explained—as Grew already knew—that Konoye would "make commitments of a far-reaching character" in his meeting with Roosevelt but that the full scope of those commitments "could not be set forth prior to the meeting."

Grew was prepared to do what he could (although he did tell the Foreign Minister that reports of Japan's plan to send 50,000 additional troops to Indochina "would create a very delicate situation" and would, in Grew's opinion, "seriously and adversely affect" Nomura's conversations with Hull). Grew forwarded to Hull that same day a summary of his conversation with Toyoda. And when no response was forthcoming, the Ambassador sent another telegram to Hull on October 14.

While he was awaiting Hull's response, Grew received the State Department's summary of a long conversation on October 13 between Wakasugi Kaname, the Minister-Counselor in the Japanese embassy, and Welles (apparently because Hull was not available). Wakasugi said that he had just returned from a two-week trip to Japan and that he wanted to convey "his impressions" from conversations he had had with Konoye, Kido, Toyoda, and other Japanese authorities.

The situation, said the Minister-Counselor, was not good. The people with whom he talked, Wakasugi explained, were "unanimous" in the "desire for peace between Japan and the United States...." But that common desire, he added, was undermined by growing frustration because "it seemed impossible for the Japanese Government to find out what in reality were the desires of the United States and what in reality was the agreement which the United States desired to achieve."

If Wakasugi was expecting further clarification on the American position, he was soon disappointed. Welles repeatedly said that the United States' position had "been very clearly set forth in an oral statement given the Japanese Ambassador on October 2" and that there was nothing he could add to the comments already made by Hull and in other State Department documents. Welles—who already believed that war with Japan was imminent—was not moved by Wakasugi's comments about a possible change in government. (If there should be a change in the Japanese cabinet, said the Minister-Counselor, "because of assassination or because it could see no hope of reaching any satisfactory adjustment with the United States, there was no telling what the result might [be].") Nor was Welles moved when Wakasugi told him that "he believed that within twenty-four or forty-eight hours, his Government must reach a final decision on the basic questions involved."

Wakasugi knew what he was talking about. Two days later—shortly after Grew saw Hull's non-committal response to his earlier telegrams—Konoye resigned as Prime Minister.

The resignation was the culmination of an intense debate among the Japanese cabinet and the military leaders that commenced upon receipt of Hull's Oral Statement of October 2. Tojo expressed frustration at the Liaison Conference on October 4 that was no doubt shared by the other participants. "The American reply ought to be 'yes' or 'no' or something in between," the War Minister remarked. "But the reply that has come is neither 'yes' nor 'no.'" Naval chief Nagano was also tired of waiting. "There is no longer time for discussion," he said. "We want quick action." Despite their displeasure, the Liaison Conference participants did not reach any decision on how to respond to the Oral Statement of October 2.

Over the next twelve days, there was an almost endless series of meetings to assess the situation and explore Japan's options. For his part, Konoye wanted to continue the pursuit of a diplomatic solution, but Tojo thought the prospect of a diplomatic solution was hopeless. "The United States does not concede an inch," he remarked at one point. In a conversation with Tojo on October 5, Konoye focused on the question of stationing of troops in China. In the Prime Minister's view, that was the key issue. He believed that the other two principal issues—the Tripartite Pact and equality of opportunity in China—could be resolved. "What if in principle," he asked Tojo on October 5, "we aim at withdrawing troops, while stationing some troops in the name of protecting resources?" The War Minister had no interest in that approach. "That's just a ploy," he responded.

Tojo remained adamant throughout the conversations in his opposition to any concession on the stationing of troops in China. The principal question for Tojo was the Navy's confidence in a war with the United States. The Navy would bear the brunt of the responsibility for conducting any war—especially at the outset. "If the Navy has no confidence about a war," Tojo said in a meeting on October 7, "we must reconsider our position."

The Navy did in fact have reservations about its ability to be victorious in a war with the United States. In late September, Yamamoto—whose proposal for a surprise attack on Pearl Harbor had not yet been approved by the Navy General Staff—said that "a war with so little chance of success should not be fought." But having those reservations was one thing. Expressing them at a meeting of civilian and military leaders was quite another. Perhaps it was a matter of saving face. Or perhaps it was a reflection of how decisions should be made. It made no difference.

Shortly before a conference of the Navy, War, and Foreign Ministers on October 12 (Konoye's fiftieth birthday) at Tekigaiso, his stylish mansion in the suburb of Ogikubo, Konoye received a message from the Chief of the Naval Affairs Bureau. "The Navy does not want the Japanese-American negotiations stopped and wishes to avoid war if at all possible," the note read. "But we cannot see our way to expressing that openly at the meeting." Tojo learned of the note and pressed Oikawa on the Navy's position at the meeting. The Navy Minister would not yield. "We have indeed come to the crossroads where we must determine either upon peace or war," said Oikawa. "I should like to leave this decision entirely up to the Premier."

Hirohito and Kido did not remain aloof from the discussions. Konoye met with each of them often during the debates. For his part, the Lord Keeper of the Privy Seal continued to see the decision of the Imperial Conference of September 6 as the stumbling block. Establishment of an October deadline for completion of negotiations seemed "too extravagant" to Kido—especially because a war with the United States "would offer little chance of our victory...." In light of those concerns, he had advised Konoye on October 9 that the best course was "to reconsider" the Imperial Conference decision. Tojo was not receptive to any reconsideration when that option was posed to him. To change a course of action approved by the Emperor, he said, would require a change in the leadership of those responsible for recommending the decision to the Throne.

At 9 a.m. on October 14, Konoye asked the War Minister to come to his official residence before the cabinet meeting that was scheduled for 10 a.m. "I have a very great responsibility for the China Incident," he told Tojo, "and today when this Incident has lasted four years and still sees no settlement, I find it difficult to agree, no matter what is said, to enter upon a great war the future of which I cannot at all foresee." Tojo was not persuaded. "If at this time we yield to the United States," he responded, "she will take steps that are more and more high-handed, and will probably find no place to stop." It was all a matter of taking a necessary risk. "We as persons sometimes need to jump from the platform of Temple Kiyomizu [a Buddhist temple in Kyoto]," Tojo told the Prime Minister. Konoye could not agree. "If we consider the two thousand and six hundred years of...our nation and the fate of our hundred million Japanese nationals," he replied, "we as government officials...should not do such a thing."

The War Minister expressed his opposition to concessions with great vigor at the cabinet meeting later that morning. As Konoye himself later said, Tojo's excited remarks "were so sudden that the other Cabinet Ministers were somewhat taken aback and there was no one who would open his mouth to answer."

The War Minister was now a man obsessed. And his patience with the Prime Minister had been exhausted. He passed word to Konoye that he would no longer meet with him because "he was not sure he could stifle his feelings." He added that, in light of the Navy's refusal to openly express its reservations about war, "there is no other way but that at this time we all resign...and reconsider our plans once more."

Konoye had already decided that it was hopeless to continue. He tendered the resignations of the entire cabinet to Hirohito at 5 p.m. on October 16. "To plunge into a great war," he said in his letter of resignation to the Emperor, "the issue of which is most uncertain, at a time when the China Incident is still unsettled, would be something which I could not possibly agree to, especially since I have painfully felt my grave responsibility for the present state of affairs...." Hirohito was disappointed with this turn of events (later expressing his disappointment in Konoye's "lack of firm conviction and courage"). But the Emperor—rightly or wrongly—felt powerless to prevent the resignation.

The Brazilian ambassador called Grew about 8:15 p.m. that evening to tell him about the Cabinet's resignation which had just been announced on the radio. The American ambassador had not heard the news because he was with about a dozen other men in the study at his residence for a farewell party to an American banker who was returning to the United States. Although he was "surprised" by the timing, Grew had known the resignation was only a matter of time given "the failure of progress in the American-Japanese conversations...." A telegram with the news was sent to Hull by 9 p.m.

Dooman was getting dressed the following morning when he received a telephone call from Ushiba. Konoye's private secretary asked if he could come to the Embassy Counselor's house. Dooman, of course, agreed. He was having breakfast when Ushiba arrived.

Dooman knew Ushiba to be a man who "was normally well composed." But not today. He was "nervous and excited," said the Embassy Counselor, telling Dooman that "he had been up all night helping Prince Konoye make arrangements" for the appointment of the next Prime Minister. They had accomplished "a miracle," said Ushiba. Konoye would be succeeded by someone who would continue the conversations in Washington. But the principal purpose of the visit, Ushia explained, was to give Dooman a personal letter that Konoye had written to Grew.

"It is with regret and disappointment," the letter said, "that my colleagues and I have had to resign owing to the internal political situation....I feel certain, however, that the cabinet which is to succeed mine will exert its utmost in continuing to a successful conclusion the conversations which we have been carrying on up till today." The letter concluded by expressing Konoye's "heartfelt gratitude" for Grew's "friendly cooperation" and his hope that Grew would "give the same privilege to whomever succeeds me." Konoye had no reason to be concerned. "I need hardly assure you," Grew said in a letter sent to Konoye later that same day, "that your successor may count fully on my own earnest cooperation" in trying "to achieve a successful outcome." But no longer would that cooperation include an effort to arrange a meeting between the Japanese Prime Minister and the American President.

Later, after the war, there would be considerable conjecture whether any meeting between Konoye and Roosevelt would have been productive. Herbert Feis, who had been the State Department Economic Advisor for International Affairs in 1941, wrote a book that said that Konoye was "a prisoner, willing or unwilling, of the terms precisely prescribed" in the policy statements approved at conferences at which he had presided, including the Imperial Conference on September 6. Any terms Konoye could have offered Roosevelt at a meeting, said Feis, would have been based on those policy statements and would have been unsatisfactory to the United States. There were many who shared that view.

Dooman had a different perspective. Feis had asked the former Embassy Counselor to review his book before it was published in 1950, and Gene told his former colleague that he thought the manuscript "absorbingly interesting." But he disagreed with Feis' conclusion that virtually nothing could have been done to halt the road to war. "You say not once but many times," Dooman wrote Feis, "that we in Tokyo could give Hull no substantial reason to support our belief that even a shadowy gesture of conciliation would bear fruit. I think you will admit," he pressed the former State Department economist, "that our Tokyo record on the question whether or not Japan would capitulate to American economic and other pressure is, to put it moderately, rather better than Washington's....[W]ould it not be rational and reasonable," he continued, "to think that Grew and I had good grounds for believing that something from Washington in the nature of a crumb of good will could have been effectively used by those Japanese who, if you cannot believe were our friends, were at least desperately anxious to avert war?"

Dooman's faith in his assessment was reinforced after a meeting with Ushiba in 1953. The former secretary told Dooman that Konoye never disclosed to him the precise terms he would have proposed to Roosevelt but that "those documents [on which Feis relied] were not to be taken too seriously." To Dooman, Ushiba's comment indicated that Konoye had in mind "a completely different set of proposals" for the United States other than those reflected in the September 6 policy statement and the other documents that had become public.

That perspective remained intact when Waldo Heinrichs, Grew's biographer, visited the former Embassy Counselor many years later at his home in Connecticut. Heinrichs had given Dooman a copy of the pre-publication manuscript to review. Dooman, then in his seventies, was not pleased. The book cast doubt on whether a meeting between Konoye and Roosevelt would have been productive. "[H]e was somebody who didn't like what I was saying," Heinrichs later recalled. He was "very fierce" and "very angry."

For his part, Grew knew there could be no assurance that any meeting between Konoye and Roosevelt would be successful. But he was in favor of taking the risk—especially because, in his view, the United States would retain ample resources and options to deal with Japan if the meeting proved to be a failure. Nor did he share the State Department's concern about the military extremists. "We in Tokyo were closer to the scene than was the Administration in Washington," Grew wrote in his post-war memoir, "and we believed, on the basis of the highest possible evidence...that the Japanese Government at the time *was* in a position to control the armed forces of the country." There was also the matter of pride, which played no small part in the Japanese mind. As a former prime minister told Grew in early October (and as he reported to Hull at the time), "it would be unthinkable for Prince Konoye to return to Japan from a [meeting with Roosevelt] which had ended in failure...." And beyond all that, Grew thought that the Prime Minister might have benefitted from Kido's suggestion that the decision of the September 6 Imperial Conference be reconsidered. There were some who later agreed with the American ambassador.

But none of that post-war speculation was of use as Grew—and the Roosevelt administration—prepared to deal with a new Prime Minister.

CHAPTER 18

The Second Warning

The letter from Anita reminded Joe that he had not written his daughter in many weeks—an unfortunate consequence of the enormous demands on his time. But he would soon rectify that. "[Y]ou are always in our loving thoughts," he wrote Anita at the end of October. "Our life in Japan," he continued, "seems to consist [of] just one long crisis, year in and year out, and we are passing through very difficult times...." Despite the persistent stress, Joe tried to be upbeat with his daughters. And so he assured Anita that he still believed "that we shall pull through somehow" because "war would be so utterly stupid." But in his heart, he knew that the prospect of war was very real.

One of the crises Grew had to address as he was writing to Anita was an assessment of the new Prime Minister: Tojo Hidecki. Tojo's selection on October 17 had capped a whirlwind of meetings that had commenced days before Konoye had tendered his resignation to the Emperor. After telling Konoye that the Cabinet should resign in the face of an irreconcilable conflict, Tojo had delivered a message to Kido on the morning of October 15 saying that the new prime minister needed to be someone who could "harmonize the Army and the Navy with the Imperial will." One candidate who satisfied that criterion, according to Tojo, was Prince Higashikuni Naruhiko. The fifty-three-year-old Army General also happened to be a member of the

Imperial family, having married Emperor Meiji's ninth daughter. When he met with Kido in the afternoon of October 15, Konoye likewise recommended the Prince as the next prime minister. "The prince is bent on opposing war," Konoye had told one cabinet member, "and has urged me again and again to make a success of the negotiations with the United States."

Kido was opposed to the recommendation. The Army and the Navy were not yet united in their views and, beyond that, "serious problems" remained unresolved. It would not do, the Keeper of the Lord Privy Seal explained, to place a member of the Imperial family in the precarious position of leading a government that might not be able to achieve its mission. The Emperor's standing among the people—not to mention the ability to retain his position—could be put at risk. Better to have someone else. But Kido agreed with Tojo and Konoye that the someone else would have to be a person who could command the respect of the military and honor Hirohito's desire for a diplomatic resolution of the conflict with the United States.

Konoye told Kido that the best alternative candidate to fulfill those expectations was Tojo. Kido ultimately agreed, as did the Senior Statesmen (the former Prime Ministers) who were consulted about the selection.

Unlike Konoye, the fifty-six-year-old former War Minister was not a large man. He stood about five feet, four inches with a medium build. He was almost bald, and, as Max Hill observed, "had a scraggy, untrimmed mustache touched with gray." Robert Craigie noticed other prominent features. There was, said the British ambassador, a "certain pallor under the swarthy skin." And then there were the "dark eyes, looking through oblong spectacles," which were "clear and penetrating." But his demeanor overshadowed all those physical characteristics. There was "an incisive speech and quick brain," said Craigie, all augmented by an "erect carriage" that seemed to denote "energy and determination."

His nickname was the "Razor." There were various explanations for the nickname. One said it was because of his "sharp intellect." Another said it reflected "a sharp and cutting mind" that had little patience for indolence or stupidity. (If a student yawned while he was teaching at the War College, Tojo would suspend the lecture and scold the student.) And still others said it was because of "his insistence that office work be dispatched with lightning speed...." Whatever the source of the nickname, all the explanations bespoke a man with a keen intellect who treasured discipline and hard work.

It was all no doubt a product of his upbringing and experience. He had grown up in a samurai family in Tokyo. From childhood, he had learned that skill and courage were more important than size. There was a well-told story of how he had returned home crying after he had been struck down by a classmate at school when he was a young boy. There was no sympathy from his mother. Only an admonition. Yes, he was small, said his mother. But he could do something to offset that disadvantage. And so he became an expert in jujitsu.

His ascension in the Army was rapid. Graduation from the military college at twenty-one. Completion of studies at the Imperial Military Staff College at twenty-nine. Appointment in 1935 as Commander of the Kwantung Army's military police ("the Japanese Gestapo," according to Tolischus). Promotion to Lieutenant General and appointment as Chief of Staff for the Kwantung Army by 1937. Selection as the Vice Minister of War in 1938. And appointment as War Minister when Konoye became Prime Minister in July 1940.

Tojo's personality and experience were complemented by his loyalty to Hirohito. "[T]he Emperor is a sacred being," he had told subordinates. "Even the prime minister is unimportant in front of the Emperor." That perspective was of no small importance to Kido and Hirohito. They needed a prime minister who would respect the Emperor's wishes. Hirohito wanted the new Prime Minister to focus on a diplomatic resolution of the growing crisis with the United States—even if it required disregarding the October deadline established by the September 6 Imperial Conference. Konoye, for one, believed that Tojo would satisfy those needs. "From the way Tojo has talked over the past two or three days," Konoye told Kido in a telephone call on the morning of October 17, "he was not necessarily to be regarded as an advocate of immediate war between Japan and the United States."

Tojo was not sure why he was summoned to the Imperial Palace in the late afternoon of October 17. He suspected that he would be reprimanded for his role in forcing the resignation of the Konoye cabinet. So he was surprised by Hirohito's words.

"We direct you to form a cabinet and to abide by the provisions of the Constitution," the Emperor commanded. "We believe that an exceedingly grave situation confronts the nation. Bear in mind," Hirohito continued, "that cooperation between the army and the navy should be closer than ever before...."

Almost as soon as the stunned Tojo left the Imperial presence, Oikawa was ushered in to see Hirohito. The former Navy Minister received the same directive for cooperation between the Army and Navy that Hirohito had given Tojo.

Tojo was waiting with Kido in the anteroom when Oikawa emerged from his meeting with the Emperor. Protocol precluded Hirohito from imposing any conditions on the directive to form a new cabinet And so it was left to the Lord Keeper of the Privy Seal to make the Emperor's wishes known. "Deep consideration, a careful attitude, and freedom from the decision of the council on the 6th of September were things wished for in the establishment of the fundamental policy of this country," said Kido. It became known as "the emperor's message to wipe the slate clean." It was a message that Tojo would try to honor in the final weeks before the Pearl Harbor attack—although he still remained subject to the demands for consensus in the Japanese political system.

The new Prime Minister was unlike many—if not most—who preceded him. Other military men had previously become prime minister but, in most cases, only after retiring from the service. By contrast, Tojo was promoted to a full general and remained in active service (thus preserving his influence with the Army). He retained his position as War Minister and also assumed the portfolio of Home Minister—a consolidation of positions that also distinguished him from most of his predecessors.

But there was another side to the new Prime Minister that was unusual. He wanted the Japanese people to get to know him. And more than that, he wanted to mingle with the populace and help inspire the personal sacrifices that would remain a staple of their lives. (Shortly after Tojo's appointment as prime minister, the new Vice Minister for Finance gave a radio broadcast in which he appealed to his countrymen for "an increase in savings and a reduction in living standard as the most effective means to maintain a solid economic front....") Periodicals published human interest articles about the new Prime Minister and his family of seven children. He himself would take to riding his horse in the streets of Tokyo on many mornings. Sometimes he would visit schools, dismount from his horse, and talk with children. On one occasion, he visited the central fish market. He dismounted from his horse and walked among the stalls, many of which displayed baskets that were half-empty. There was a shortage of fish, he was told, because there was no gasoline for the boats. Complaints of that kind could not be tolerated if Japan were to survive. "Get up earlier," Tojo responded. "Work harder."

However useful these interactions with the public, the new Prime Minister's first and foremost responsibility was the selection of his cabinet. Securing the inclusion of a new Foreign Minister was not easy.

Togo Shigenori, a fifty-eight-year-old diplomat, received the call at his home around 7:30 p.m. on October 17. The new Prime Minister asked him to come immediately to the War Minister's Official Residence. When Togo arrived, Tojo explained that he wanted Togo to join the cabinet as Foreign Minister.

Tojo's interest in Togo was undoubtedly a reflection of the new Prime Minister's desire to honor Hirohito's message to "wipe the slate clean." Togo's diplomatic experience was varied and extensive, but, most importantly, he appeared to be someone who would support an improvement in Japan's relations with the United States.

Togo had served in many missions abroad—including China, Switzerland, and the United States—beginning in 1912. After serving as the chief of the European-American Bureau in Tokyo, he was appointed ambassador to Germany in 1937. That assignment lasted only about ten months. Togo opposed Japan's interest in developing closer ties with the Axis at the expense of Japan's relationship with the United States and Great Britain. That opposition made him a *persona non-grata* in Berlin. He was transferred to Moscow as Japan's ambassador to the Soviet Union (taking with him the German woman he had married). There, Togo flourished. Grew later confided to his diary that he had heard that Togo "was held in high regard by the Soviet Government as the most acceptable representative from Japan who had been sent to Moscow in recent years."

Togo was a victim of the Matsuoka "Hurricane" in the summer of 1940 when the then-new Foreign Minister decided to purge the ambassadorial ranks of those who opposed closer ties with the Axis. Upon his return to Tokyo, Togo refused Matsuoka's requests that he resign from the diplomatic service because a resignation would, in Togo's view, "be tantamount to approval by me of his policies...." So Togo sat by idly, watching Matsuoka nurture a closer relationship with Germany and preaching "the necessity of doing everything possible for success in the negotiations [with the United States]...." Dissenting views like Togo's were not welcomed by the Foreign

Office under Matsuoka, and members of the Kempeitai would routinely visit with the former ambassador two or three times a month to "inquire" about his opinions.

Togo initially declined Tojo's offer to become Foreign Minister. He questioned the new Prime Minister closely in that evening meeting on the reason for the fall of Konoye's cabinet, saying that he had heard it had stemmed "from the uncompromising attitude of the Army toward the stationing of Japanese troops in China." Tojo acknowledged that was so and that the Army would continue "to maintain a resolute stand in the negotiations." Togo said he could not become Foreign Minister under those circumstances because the negotiations with the United States "would certainly break down" if the Army remained "obdurate" and unwilling to make "genuine concessions." Tojo did not want to lose Togo's service. He relented, assuring Togo that he was prepared to review "the problem of troop stationing, as well as the other issues...." Thus assured, Togo accepted the position.

His appointment as Foreign Minister was well received at the State Department. Hamilton reported to Hull that Togo had a reputation as "an experienced, patient, and capable negotiator" and that his appointment might signal "continued efforts toward a negotiated settlement with the United States...." Grew did not get an opportunity to meet with the new Foreign Minister until October 30. But he was not simply biding his time. The Ambassador was busy sending long telegrams to Hull with reports of recent developments in Tokyo and his preliminary assessment of the Tojo cabinet.

Although he had earlier predicted that the fall of the Konoye cabinet would lead to a military dictatorship, Grew advised Hull on October 20 that "it would be premature to characterize the new Cabinet as a military dictatorship committed to the pursuit of...war with the United States." On October 25, Grew sent another telegram to Hull recounting the views of an "informant" who had been in contact with "the highest circles" and who believed that, "for the first time in ten years, the situation at present and the existing political set-up in Japan offer a possibility of a re-orientation of Japanese policy and action." And on October 26, Grew sent yet another telegram based on information from a "wholly reliable source" who recounted Hirohito's "unprecedented step" to command that the Army and the Navy obey his wishes for a diplomatic resolution of the conflict with the United States. The Emperor's active pursuit of a *"rapprochement* with the United States," said the Ambassador, might presage "a more positive effort on the part of the new Prime Minister and Foreign Minister to bring the preliminary conversations" to a successful conclusion. In the Japanese leaders' views, said Grew, the principal obstacle to that successful conclusion was the stationing of troops in China after settlement of the China Incident. But even there, said Grew, his informant believed that complete withdrawal "will be accomplished if Japan is not pushed into a corner by the expectation on the part of the United States that such withdrawal shall be executed all at once."

Grew's telegrams received a mixed reaction in Washington. Hornbeck was, as expected, skeptical about any possible *rapprochement*. The Political Relations Advisor focused on the statement in Grew's telegram of October 25 that there was now a "possibility of a re-orientation of Japanese policy and action." "This had been said several times previously," Hornbeck wrote with his red pencil. And in a separate note, Hornbeck mocked the reference in Grew's October 26 telegram to a "wholly reliable informant" who talked about resolving the issue with respect to the stationing of Japanese troops in China. "It used to be 'reliable informant,'" Hornbeck wrote. "It has become the 'wholly reliable informant.'"

For his part, the Secretary of State appeared to be more impressed by Grew's comments concerning the involvement of Hirohito. "Hull thinks he has the Emperor on his side," Stimson confided to his diary on October 28. If so, Hull told the Secretary of War, the United States might be in "a wonderful position."

Hull's optimism—which proved ephemeral—did not signal any change in American policy. The need to delay any conflagration in the Pacific remained intact. "The entire purpose of the State Department, under the orders of the President," Welles later told the congressional committee investigating the Pearl Harbor attack, "was to find every means possible to prevent a break in the negotiations...." That purpose undoubtedly remained uppermost in Roosevelt's mind as he reviewed intercepts of Japanese diplomatic messages that reflected the heated debates between Konoye and Tojo concerning Japan's policy toward the United States. Whatever the ultimate policy, the President knew it would take time for the Japanese leaders to reach agreement and then implement the decision. The day before the cabinet resignations were announced, Roosevelt cabled Churchill with good news. They had gained "two months' respite in the Far East."

In all this, there was apparently no concern at the White House or in the State Department about Grew's earlier prediction that the fall of Konoye and his cabinet would lead to a military dictatorship and a more belligerent approach toward the United States. Still, some discussion was required. After learning of Konoye's resignation, Roosevelt cancelled the Cabinet meeting scheduled for the afternoon of October 16 and replaced it with a meeting of his "War Cabinet," which included Hull, Stimson, Stark, Marshall, and Knox (along with Harry Hopkins). Nothing was decided in the two-hour meeting—although the focus, Stimson later recorded, was on "the delicate question" of making sure "that Japan was put into the wrong and made the first bad move...."

Nomura obviously knew nothing of what was said in the White House meeting on that Thursday, but he was despondent. Upon learning of Togo's appointment, the Japanese ambassador sent a telegram to the new Foreign Minister. "It is a matter for regret that I have been of no service though I have tried my utmost in compliance with the previous cabinet's policies," he told Togo, "and I feel myself greatly responsible for it. Indeed, I am burning with shame...." For that reason, he said, he wanted "to return to Japan at the first opportunity...."

There was no response from the Foreign Minister, and so Nomura sent a separate telegram on October 20 to Admiral Shimada and Shigetaro, the new Navy Minister. The Japanese ambassador expressed his disappointment in failing to secure an agreement on the China issue but explained that Hull was not at all "conciliatory." He told Shimada that he had earlier proposed a standstill agreement, or *modus vivendi*, to the Secretary of State that would enable the countries to restore some kind of trade relationship while they explored solutions to the China problem. The initial reaction was not encouraging. Hull, Nomura said, had "rigidly maintained the indivisibility of the Chinese question" with the other issues. The Japanese ambassador still saw some benefit in that *modus vivendi* proposal and had discussed it with Lord Halifax on October 16 in the hope that the British ambassador might put in a favorable word with the American Secretary of State. But all that was secondary to Nomura's principal purpose in writing to the new

Navy Minister: he wanted to come home, and he hoped Shimada would support that request if Togo asked for his opinion. When he received no response from either the Navy Minister or the Foreign Minister, Nomura cabled Togo again on October 21, reiterating his request to come home because he could no longer be useful. "I am now," he said, "so to speak, a skeleton of a dead horse."

Nomura's repeated requests for permission to return to Japan remained unanswered, and it was left to Wasakugi to visit with Welles on October 24 to express the new cabinet's interest in continuing the conversations "without delay." The Counselor-Minister also told the Under Secretary of State that he had been instructed to inquire whether the United States would be making any counterproposals. Welles predictably replied that the American position "had been set forth with complete clarity" in the proposal of June 21 and the Oral Statement of October 2 and that no counterproposals from the United States were needed. But Welles added that the United States "would be glad to sit down" with the Japanese representatives if they had any "changes in phraseology" that they wanted the United States to consider. Wakasugi had no further suggestions to make, and he left the meeting with a promise to return after he had received further instructions from his government.

There matters stood when Grew received an invitation from Togo to meet him at the Foreign Minister's residence at 3 p.m. on October 30. "On entering the Minister's room," Grew later remarked, "I encountered the usual solid army of press cameras and movies and we posed for several minutes, and then they were shooed out...." Togo was a fit-looking man of average height for Japanese, with a shock of dark hair parted on the left side, a broad nose, a small moustache, and large round glasses with black frames. The Foreign Minister was accompanied by Kase Toshikazu, the Foreign Minister's Secretary and a new Section Chief in the American Bureau. Kase had been educated at Harvard and Amherst and was there to interpret the Foreign Minister's remarks.

"What a difference between Admiral Toyoda and Togo," Joe confided to his diary. "[T]he former cheery and very friendly and always with a little exchange of pleasantries before getting down to business. The latter grim, unsmiling, and ultra-reserved. He speaks English well enough," said Grew, "but talks so low that few can understand him and I not at all, so I'm glad that he is using an interpreter." (Dooman, who had known Togo for many years, said he "was a person completely devoid of any personal charm" and was "the closest thing that I have ever known to a piece of ice.") Kase sat beside Grew on the sofa in that first meeting, and so the American ambassador was confident that his deafness would not impede the discussion with the new Foreign Minister.

Togo had already studied Nomura's reports on the conversations with Hull and his staff. The prospects for success seemed daunting. "The United States," he later remarked, "had shown no sign of making concessions, merely reiterating after the latter part of June her position...." The situation had deteriorated that much more after the late July announcement of the freeze on Japanese assets in the United States. It seemed to Togo that the United States had become "extremely uncompromising and seemed only to be trying to prolong the discussions rather than to reach an agreement." The Foreign Minister conveyed those perceptions to Craigie, who had asked for an emergency meeting with Togo on October 29. "[T]he attitude of the United States," the Foreign Minister told the British ambassador, "is entirely too theoretical, and if this continues there will be slight chance of a settlement."

Togo conveyed those same concerns to Grew in the meeting on October 30. Japanese-American relations, he said, had "progressively worsened" since his return to the Foreign Office in the late 1930s. If the trend was not reversed, said the Foreign Minister, the situation posed "the gravest dangers." The Foreign Minister remarked that progress could only be made if the United States was willing to "face certain realities and facts." That was particularly true with respect to the Japanese proposal to station troops in North China after settlement of the China Incident. Togo remarked that other nations "maintained troops in certain areas of China," pointing to "the Soviet soldiers stationed in Outer Mongolia." The Foreign Minister concluded by saying that he hoped to have further conversations with the American ambassador in due course. Grew responded that Hull wanted the conversations to be continued in Washington, but that he would be prepared, as before, to have "parallel talks" in Tokyo.

The Foreign Minister's remarks did not give Grew any reason to be optimistic that Tojo could succeed where Konoye had not. That sense of impending doom was undoubtedly reinforced by Roosevelt's response to

Grew's letter of September 22. Joe had written the letter in the hope that a personal appeal to the President would overcome the State Department's resistance to Konoye's request for a meeting. Roosevelt's response of October 30—which would have been received in Tokyo after Grew's meeting with Togo—sidestepped the arguments Grew had marshalled in support of that meeting. The response had been drafted by the State Department and reflected the perspective and convoluted syntax that were Hornbeck's trademarks. The meeting had not materialized, the letter made clear, because of Japan's failings. "It seems a pity," said the President's response, "that during the time [Konoye] was Premier there could not have been rallied in Japan a wider and stronger support for a moderate and peaceful policy." The implicit message was clear: the Roosevelt administration would not be any more flexible with Tojo than it had been with Konoye.

Washington's continued disregard of Grew's opinions and recommendations could not justify a change in course for the Ambassador. He was still America's representative to Japan. And he still had a responsibility to convey his thoughts, however unwelcome they might be in Washington. That was especially so now. The optimism expressed by informants before his meeting with Togo appeared unfounded. "If Tojo should succeed," Joe confided to his diary at the end of October, "it would indeed be little short of miraculous." True, Hirohito's increased involvement might prolong the conversations in Washington. But Grew could not "avoid the conviction that, with the passing of Konoye, the outlook is far less favorable than it was before." He had to warn Washington about the possible—and perhaps imminent—consequences.

Dooman had already prepared a draft of a telegram. Grew used that as a base and spent most of Sunday, November 2, expanding and refining it. That evening, he reviewed the draft with Dooman and Chip Bohlen, a thirty-seven-year-old Foreign Service officer who had arrived at the Embassy in January after service in the United States embassy in Moscow. They could not leave Washington in any doubt as to the risks that lay ahead. "I don't want our country to get into war with Japan," Grew recorded in his diary, "through any possible misconception of what the Japanese, especially the Japanese army, are capable of doing, contrary to all logic and sanity."

The telegram was sent to Hull at 3 p.m. on the following Monday, November 3. It restated Grew's view that economic pressures would never bring Japan to her knees. True, he said, "the greater part of Japan's commerce has been lost, Japanese industrial production has been drastically curtailed, and Japan's national resources have been depleted." But Japan, he warned, would not bend if American economic pressures were retained or even strengthened. It would, said Grew, be an "uncertain and dangerous hypothesis" to believe, as some in the United States did, that war could be averted "by progressively imposing drastic economic measures...."

Grew remained mindful of claims that any agreement with Japan would constitute the kind of "appeasement" that had fallen short with Hitler. As he had told Hull in his telegram of September 29, a more appropriate label for his approach was "constructive conciliation." Still, he knew with whom he was dealing in the State Department. So it was a point worth repeating. The telegram said that the Ambassador was not advocating "any 'appeasement'" that would reflect a retreat "from the fundamental principles" that Hull had "laid down" as the foundation for "American relations with Japan...." But, the telegram said, Grew did not want the United States to become "involved in war with Japan because of any possible misconception of Japan's capacity to rush headlong into a suicidal struggle with the United States." He knew that many in the United States thought any such action by Japan would be foolhardy, but there too he observed—as he had before — that assumptions about the Japanese mindset could be fallacious. "While national sanity dictates against such action," the telegram said, "Japanese sanity cannot be measured by American standards of logic."

In all of this, said Grew, it was important to remember, as the Roosevelt administration well knew, that Japan was mobilizing and expanding her military resources. "[I]t would be short-sighted," the telegram explained, "for American policy to be based upon the belief that Japanese preparations are no more than saber rattling, merely intended to give moral support to the high pressure diplomacy of Japan." In making that statement—as well as others in the telegram—Grew had in mind Japan's surprise attack on the Russian fleet in February 1904. The Russians were caught off guard, and their fleet was decimated. Grew had to wonder whether "the same technique" might be used against the United States. And so, Grew concluded, "an armed conflict with the United States may come with dangerous and dramatic suddenness."

Grew considered including three other paragraphs in the telegram that focused on the withdrawal of Japanese troops "from foreign soil." Grew did not think Japan would withdraw her troops from China or Indochina "unless and until" Japan had a "hard-and-fast agreement on paper with the United States, if then." However firm his views on the subject, the Ambassador decided to omit those paragraphs from the telegram he sent to Hull. Grew apparently felt uncomfortable giving the Secretary advice on how to conduct the discussions with the Japanese representatives. At the same time, he believed that those additional paragraphs were worthy of consideration by someone involved in the process in Washington—and, more than that, someone he could trust to use those paragraphs to try to steer the discussions in the right direction. And so Grew sent the three omitted paragraphs in a separate telegram to that person: Sumner Welles.

In the first omitted paragraph, Grew expressed doubts that the conversations in Washington could ever produce an agreement "which would be mutually acceptable." Part of the problem, he wrote, was that agreements were "almost always open to varying interpretations, however carefully they may be drafted." Much better, he said, to rely on "facts and actions rather than any written commitments...." To that end, he rhetorically asked, whether it would "not be the better part of wisdom to say with entire frankness to Japan" that the United States would agree to provide particular benefits (such as resumption of trade relations) only when Japan had offered "concrete evidence" of having taken a particular step to demonstrate her peaceful intent (such as withdrawing troops from southern Indochina)?

Although that strategy might work in adjusting Japanese-American relations, Grew believed that China involved different circumstances that required a different approach. To him, there seemed to be only one possible solution—if a solution was indeed desired. China and Japan had to initiate "preliminary and exploratory conversations" between themselves concerning a possible settlement. As Hull had made clear to Nomura, there were many in the Roosevelt administration—as well as in China—who opposed such direct talks, at least until the United States had approved the terms of any settlement. (Stimson, for one, had warned Hull back in April about "the desire of the Japanese to negotiate alone with the Chinese on the all-important matter of the termination of the present Chinese Incident.") And even then, some American and British advisers had expressed concern about the consequences for the United States and Great Britain if one million Japanese troops were re-deployed outside China. But Grew's recommendation was based on a logic devoid of those considerations.

In all this, said the last omitted paragraph, the fruit was there for the taking. "I believe we can accept as fact," Grew opined, "that the Emperor is now taking an active and positive stand to bring about a *rapprochement*...." Progress could therefore be achieved, the third paragraph concluded, if the United States could show "a somewhat greater degree of flexibility...."

Even without those omitted paragraphs, Grew was satisfied with the telegram he sent to Hull. It soothed his conscience. He had left no stone unturned in the effort to warn his country about a possible surprise attack by the Japanese. "If war should occur," he wrote in his diary at the end of November, "I hope that history will not overlook that telegram...."

CHAPTER 19

Kurusu

oe Boxley may have been surprised on that day in May 1929 when the
sheriff's posse arrested him and took him to the jail in Tennessee's
Gibson County. He was a black sharecropper who worked on land
owned by John James, a prominent citizen in nearby Crockett County
(named for Davy Crockett, the former Tennessee congressman who had
died at the Alamo).

The arrest was not indiscriminate. Someone had raped James' wife.
When they found the stricken woman, it was said that she murmured the
word "Joe." Suspicion immediately surrounded Boxley, and in that part of
Tennessee, people did not always wait for a trial to determine if a black man
was—or was not—guilty of an assault on a white woman.

"Lynching" was a term that probably derived from the practices of
Charles Lynch, an American revolutionary in Virginia who took it upon
himself to punish people who supported the British. In time, the term came
to mean execution by a mob. Usually, but not always, it involved a hanging.
Lynchings were particularly rampant in the South after the Civil War. In
Tennessee alone, it was reported that more than 200 blacks had been
lynched. Joe Boxley was one of them.

A mob descended on the Gibson County jail to get the incarcerated
sharecropper. "They have been trying to break in with a railroad iron," one

of the peace officers reported. Fearful that the mob would succeed, the sheriff sneaked Boxley out of the jail and took him to the jail in Alamo, the principal town of Crockett County. A mob of more than one hundred men broke into the home of the county sheriff and took the keys to the jail. They dragged Boxley from the jail and hung him from a nearby tree.

Cordell Hull—who then had a home in Carthage, about 200 miles northeast of the hanging site—may or may not have known about Boxley's lynching (although it was reported in newspapers). But the fifty-seven-year-old congressman certainly knew that lynchings were a part of his state's history. It was something he could recall with ease—even when he was discussing war and peace with Japanese representatives many years later.

As the Secretary of State later said in his *Memoirs*, from "the outset," he thought the chances of reaching an agreement with the Japanese "were no bigger than a gnat." In his view, it was only a matter of time before the Japanese military took some action that would precipitate armed conflict with the United States. For that reason, he had a keen interest in reports from Grew concerning military matters in Japan, and he gave a close reading of the Ambassador's telegram of November 3.

Hornbeck, for one, was not impressed. "The reasoning of this telegram," he told the Secretary of State, "as in many which have preceded it, runs to the general effect that, although Japan misbehaves, we must not apply strong pressures to Japan—because that would probably cause Japan to…bring on war…." Hull had a different perspective. By early October, he believed that the initiation of a Japanese attack "was rapidly approaching." Grew's telegram of November 3 reinforced that suspicion (although the Secretary of State never imagined that the sudden and dramatic conflict anticipated by Grew would involve a surprise attack on Pearl Harbor). Still, Hull wanted to do what he could to reduce, or at least delay, the chances of that armed conflict. And so he contacted his ambassador on November 5 about the editorial in the *Japan Times and Advertiser*.

On November 5 (November 4 in Washington), the newspaper published an editorial that proposed that the United States adopt a program of "restitution" for Japan. That program included termination of aid to Chiang Kai-Shek, recognition of Manchukuo, cessation of a military "encirclement" of Japan, lifting of the freeze on Japanese assets in the United States, and restoration of normal trade relations. In a telegram to Grew, Hull explained that the American press had "widely circulated" the editorial because the newspaper was believed "to be the official English language mouthpiece of the Japanese Foreign Office...." Dissemination of the editorial, the Secretary of State believed, undermined his effort to continue the discussions with the Japanese representatives. "The uncompromising and truculent tone of articles of the sort appearing on November 5," he told Grew, "lends color to the suspicions of many Americans in regard to Japanese official policies and objectives and considerably strengthens the position of critics of Japan." Hull therefore instructed Grew to use his discretion in conveying the Secretary's displeasure to Japanese authorities.

Grew was more than willing to undertake that task. He had already confided to his diary that the editorial was indeed "nasty" and that it could have far-reaching consequences. "If anything could render utterly hopeless the prospect of our coming to an understanding with Japan," he wrote, "this editorial, from a newspaper known to be the organ of the Japanese Foreign Office, would appear to do it...." It was especially discouraging to Grew because he still wanted to believe that war could be avoided. "I have about given up hope of the Washington conversations making any progress," he added, "but if the door can be kept open and a complete breakdown avoided, it may be that we can tide things over until the inevitable crack in Germany...."

Grew raised the matter with Togo at a reception at the Soviet embassy the day after he received Hull's telegram. The Foreign Minister "appeared to know nothing about the editorial" and said that he "was sure" it "had not been inspired by the Foreign Office." After speaking with the American ambassador, Togo approached the editor of the *Japan Times*, who was also at the reception. The editor then talked with Grew and explained that "he alone was responsible for the editorial...." In a further conversation, Togo told Grew that, "while the Foreign Office had not exerted control over the *Times and Advertiser* up to the present, it was jolly well going to exert such control from now on." The next day, Grew reported to Hull that "the flow of invective" in the morning's newspapers "appears suddenly to have ceased...."

However much satisfaction they may have taken from a change in the newspapers' tone, Togo and Grew both knew that it was not enough to bridge the gap between their two countries. Something more was obviously needed. And they both undoubtedly hoped that the something more might be Kurusu Saburo. Even as Grew and Togo were discussing the editorial in the *Japan Times*, Japan's new Special Envoy to the United States was in route to Washington.

It was a decision a long time in the making. On August 4—shortly after the announcement of the freeze on Japan's assets in the United States—Nomura told Toyoda that "there is a limit to [his] humble ability" and that the Foreign Minister should send "a veteran diplomat" to assist him. He floated one name as a possible candidate: Kurusu Saburo.

There was nothing surprising about Nomura's choice. The fifty-five-year-old Kurusu very much looked the part of the seasoned diplomat he was. Of average height and build for a Japanese, he had silver hair combed straight back, a small moustache, and a face—punctuated by horn-rimmed glasses—that bespoke a pleasant demeanor. He had served in a variety of foreign missions beginning in 1914, including appointments as Japan's ambassador to Italy and then Belgium (where he had befriended the American ambassador, Joseph Davies, who was now an assistant to Hull). More than that, he was fluent in English. It was a product of his extensive travels in the United States, having served for six years in the Japanese consulate in Chicago, where he met his American wife.

There was, however, one aspect of his experience that might have made him an inappropriate selection to negotiate an agreement with the United States: as Japan's ambassador to Germany, he had been the one to sign the Tripartite Pact in September 1940. But even there, Kurusu's record was not what it seemed. "Immediately after the signing of the treaty," he later wrote, "I sent in my resignation by wire." Kurusu had "not been in favor of this alliance" and resented that it had been negotiated "secretly over [his] head."

Toyoda had tried to enlist Kurusu's assistance in the discussions with the United States shortly after the formation of Konoye's third cabinet in July 1941. Kurusu had declined the offer. He suffered from high blood pressure and a weak heart, and he feared for his health. But more than that, the Foreign Minister was a former admiral, and the retired diplomat opposed "the participation of military men in foreign diplomacy...."

Despite that rejection, Kurusu's name surfaced again as the new Foreign Minister (who was not an active or former military officer) returned from a trip outside Tokyo on November 3. "While on the train," Togo later recalled, "I could not prevent my thoughts from recurring to the Japanese-American negotiations and the quest for ways and means of warding off a catastrophe. It was at this time that the idea of sending Ambassador Kurusu to the United States occurred to me."

The timing of Togo's idea was not coincidental. Japanese leaders had just concluded ten days of almost continuous Liaison Conferences to formulate a policy. It had not been easy. The United States, they knew, would not be making any counterproposals. Japan would have to take the initiative to change course.

The first Liaison Conference on October 23—like many that were to follow in that ten-day period—was contentious. Nagano expressed impatience at the outset. "The Navy is consuming 400 tons of oil an hour," the Navy Chief of Staff told the conferees. "The situation is urgent. We want it decided one way or the other quickly." Tojo counseled restraint. He had been asked by the Emperor to "wipe the slate clean," and he meant to honor the Imperial command. "I would like to have us decide whether the Government can assume responsibility for the September 6 decision at it stands," he responded, "or whether we must reconsider it from a new point of view." He then asked the Army and Navy chiefs whether they had objections. They were not about to challenge Hirohito. And so the debate ensued.

The last conference on November 1 was the longest and most inflammatory. It lasted seventeen hours "amid great tension and angry exchanges between the participants." The focus was two alternative proposals that Togo had submitted for consideration—one designated as Plan A and the other as Plan B.

Plan A was designed to resolve all outstanding issues, and none was more controversial than Togo's approach to the removal of Japanese troops from China. Togo proposed that most troops be withdrawn within two years after China and Japan had reached settlement and that troops in North China (as well as in certain other designated areas) be withdrawn within five years. Togo pointed out that "it was not reasonable to station troops in territories of other countries indefinitely." However rational the Foreign Minister's logic, it "drew heavy fire from the military services." They argued vigorously that retention of troops in North China and related areas was "necessary" to protect the extensive Japanese enterprises in those areas.

The conferees ultimately adopted a Plan A that specified no timetable for the withdrawal of troops in North China but added a note to address the situation if the United States pressed for a timetable. In that event, said the note, Japan would say twenty-five years. Plan A repeated that Japan would "act independently" in deciding its obligations under the Tripartite Pact, explained that all troops would be withdrawn from Indochina upon settlement of the China Incident, and (in response to Hull's repeated complaints about Japan's prior position on trade) stated that Japan would "recognize the principle of nondiscrimination in the entire Pacific region, including China, if this principle is applied throughout the world."

Togo realized that Plan A faced a high hurdle in being accepted by Hull as a basis for negotiation. Plan B was the fallback position. As the Foreign Minister later explained, it was a standstill agreement, or *modus vivendi*, "to be used as a last resort in arriving at agreement on a few items essential for averting the outbreak of war." The *modus vivendi* would allow the parties to restore a limited relationship in certain areas while they pursued solutions to more fundamental problems. But even that alternative proposal would face tough sledding in the United States. The plan required that Japan and the United States pledge not to make any armed advance anywhere in Southeast Asia or the South Pacific "except French Indochina," that the two countries restore trade relations as they were prior to the American freeze on Japanese assets, that the United States supply Japan with all the petroleum it needs, and that the United States refrain from taking any action that "may hinder" the efforts of Japan and China to reach a settlement (which presumably would require the United States to terminate its assistance to Chiang Kai-Shek). Plan B also included a note that, if pressed by the United States, Japan would agree to move all its troops in southern Indochina to northern Indochina.

Neither the final Plan A or Plan B was entirely satisfactory to Togo. Part of the Foreign Minister's distress was tied to the deadline imposed by the conferees. Nagano had approved Yamamoto's plan to attack Pearl Harbor and had settled on a target date of December 8 (December 7 Hawaii time). None of that was discussed at the Liaison Conferences because the military kept a tight lid on operational matters. But the conferees agreed that boundless patience was not a virtue. "To adopt a policy of patience and perseverance," said Tojo "...was tantamount to self-annihilation of our nation." So a decision had been made to initiate plans for war by December 1, with the understanding that the negotiations with the United States had to be completed five days prior to that deadline, or November 25. Still, the Foreign Minister was encouraged by Tojo's promise to support the Foreign Minister in securing "further concessions" by Japan if the United States responded favorably to either Plan A or Plan B.

Although the Prime Minister's promise gave Togo some hope, Hirohito was disheartened when Tojo (accompanied by the chiefs of the Army and Navy General Staffs) made his report on the Liaison Conference decisions to the Emperor at noon on November 2. Tojo later said that the Emperor's face was filled with despair. There was now a deadline for breaking the deadlock with the United States and initiating war, and it was hard to be optimistic. War "may be unavoidable," Hirohito told the Prime Minister, "but I want you to try your very best to find a way out through diplomatic negotiations."

Kurusu knew nothing of Tojo's presentation to the Emperor—but he would soon become the instrument of Hirohito's directive to the Prime Minister. Kurusu's telephone was not working on November 3, and he was awakened around midnight by a policeman who said that the Foreign Minister wanted to see him immediately. As soon as Kurusu arrived, Togo explained the need for the diplomat's services. He would be sent to America to assist Nomura (whose English was not the best) and to make sure the Japanese ambassador followed instructions. Despite lingering concerns with his health, Kurusu could not refuse an assignment of such importance. Togo told Kurusu that he planned to send both Plan A and Plan B to Nomura, who would be instructed to present Plan A to Hull before Kurusu reached the United States. But the Foreign Minister assented to Kurusu's request that he be the one to present Plan B to Hull if, as expected, the United States rejected Plan A.

Kurusu understood the challenge of the assignment but was buoyed by his meeting with Tojo the following evening. The Prime Minister assured the Special Envoy that he would "doggedly support and carry out" any compromise reached by his diplomatic representatives "even in defiance of the strong opposition of various circles within our country...." Although he thought the chances of success were no more than 30%, Tojo left his new envoy with a plea. "Please do your best," he told Kurusu, "to reach an agreement."

One immediate logistical problem loomed large. Togo wanted Kurusu to reach the United States by November 13. That would require him to take the Pan Am Clipper that departed from Hong Kong on the morning of November 5. There was no way Kurusu could reach Hong Kong by that time, and, if he missed that plane, Kurusu would have to wait two weeks for the next departure. Kase explained the problem to Grew on November 4. Could the American ambassador use his influence to delay the plane's departure for two days? Dooman called Max Hamilton in Washington, where it was around midnight. The Far Eastern Division Chief worked through the night to secure the delay, and the American ambassador soon called Togo with the good news.

Kurusu came to visit Grew at the Embassy residence around 9 p.m. that same evening. The two men were well acquainted with each other. Grew considered him to be "one of Japan's outstanding diplomats with a well-nigh perfect grasp of the English language...." There was also a family connection: Kurusu's daughter Jaye was a good friend of Elsie's. The new Special Envoy told the American ambassador that he had been studying the documents, that he "was going merely to bring a fresh point of view to the conversations," and that he would "leave no stone unturned to reach an agreement." Grew asked if Kurusu would be bringing "a new plan of settlement." Kurusu was not at liberty to tell the American ambassador about Plans A and B, and so he responded negatively. He saw a look of disappointment on Grew's face. Without a new proposal, said the Ambassador, it would be "useless" for Kurusu to go to the United States.

Alice appeared as Kurusu was about to leave. She knew—as did her husband—that they could be on the verge of a complete collapse. She could not hold back the tears as she said good bye to their friend. "I was deeply moved with an indescribable emotion," Kurusu later said. But whatever inspiration he drew from Alice would not be enough. The American Secretary of State remained intractable.

Togo forwarded Plans A and B to Nomura on November 4 (before they were approved by the Emperor at an Imperial Conference on November 5). The Foreign Minister explained to his ambassador that the proposals represented Japan's "final effort" and that the Japanese ambassador was to "strictly" abide by his instructions with "no room for discretion." Despite that admonition, Nomura gave Hull only a portion of Plan A when he and

Wakasugi met with the Secretary of State at his apartment on the morning of November 7. Hull did not give any immediate response to those portions, but he did ask Nomura—perhaps in response to the omitted paragraphs that Grew had sent to Welles—whether Japan would respond favorably "if the Chinese were now to say that they desired a real friendship with Japan...." Nomura and Wakasugi were "very much impressed" with that suggestion, but Hull gave no details on how it might be implemented. Instead, he "expressed hope" that some "concrete statement" could be developed with respect to Japan's relations with the Axis.

Nomura responded that his government had already explained its position on the Tripartite Pact, but that was not enough for the Secretary of State. He wondered whether any statement by the present cabinet would "cover the situation should some new government come into power in Japan." It was a question the Japanese representatives could not answer. They soon left, but not before the Japanese ambassador expressed his hope that Hull appreciated the "urgency of the matter." The situation in Japan, he said, was "critical."

That expression of hope had no impact on Hull. He had seen intercepts of Togo's cable to Nomura establishing the November 25 deadline for the conclusion of the discussions. That deadline—coupled with Grew's telegram of November 3—convinced him that Japan was bent on war. That impression was reinforced by Togo's reference to Plans A and B as Japan's "final effort." American translators interpreted that term to mean that the Japanese proposals constituted an ultimatum—another sign that Japan had reached the end of the road. And so, when he met with Roosevelt and other members of the cabinet for their weekly meeting at that White House on the afternoon of November 7, Hull felt compelled to issue a warning. "We should be on the lookout," he told the President and his cabinet colleagues, "for a military attack by Japan anywhere at any time."

Roosevelt remained hopeful that there would no attack any time soon. He had received a memo from Marshall and Stark a couple of days earlier in which the Army and Navy chiefs had said that "[w]ar between the United States and Japan should be avoided" so that the United States could build up "its defensive forces in the Far East...." And in no event, said the military chiefs, should any "ultimatum be delivered to Japan."

The President was no doubt mindful of that memo when he explained to his cabinet on November 7 that he had rebuffed Churchill's earlier request to become involved in hostilities in the Pacific because "he wanted to delay such action as long as possible." Still, the President knew that the United States could be thrust into a conflict because of some action taken by Japan. So he initiated a discussion with his cabinet on whether the American people would support the administration if the United States got "into [a] shooting [match] with Japan if she attempts to go into Singapore and the Dutch East Indies." The Cabinet was unanimous in saying that the public would support the administration—although there were some comments about the need to further educate the public on "the freedom of the seas."

Grew was not given any information about Hull's warning or the other comments made at the November 7 Cabinet meeting. But if he needed any further reminders about the precarious state of the situation, they were provided in the meeting Grew had with Togo on the morning of November 10. The Foreign Minister was frustrated with the American response to Japan's proposals. "[T]he American government," Togo told the Ambassador, "had taken no step toward meeting the Japanese position and had yielded nothing...." In fact, he continued, the United States "had perhaps taken a more advanced position." All of which, he said, was forcing the Japanese government to wonder about "the sincerity of the American Government in continuing with the conversations." The question of stationing troops in North China illustrated the point.

Togo did not understand the United States' continuing objection. After all, he said, Soviet troops were stationed in Outer Mongolia, which "was universally recognized to be a part of China." Beyond that, said Togo, the American freeze on Japanese assets in the United States "had stopped supplies of many important raw materials to Japan." That kind of economic pressure, he continued, could jeopardize Japan's existence "to a greater degree than the direct use of force" and might force Japan "to resort to measures of self-defense."

Grew did what he could to counter Togo's complaints, saying that the United States did "understand the realities of the situation" and that the whole purpose of the conversations in Washington was to facilitate Japan's ability "to obtain such necessary supplies...." But the American ambassador was handicapped by an inability to offer any meaningful response.

And—while Grew sent Hull a summary of his discussion with Togo—there was no change in strategy when Nomura came to the White House for a meeting with Roosevelt hours after Grew's meeting with Togo. As the President told a British Undersecretary the day before, "[h]is present Japanese policy is one of stalling and holding off."

Nomura's meeting with Roosevelt and Hull on that tenth day of November did nothing to improve the situation. The Japanese ambassador read a long statement detailing the particulars of Plan A. The President responded by reading a shorter statement that said, in part, that the United States was doing its "best to expedite the conversations." Nomura could draw no encouragement from Roosevelt's comments. He left the meeting with a comment that it was "not [his] wish to be the last ambassador [to the United States]."

Togo's frustration reached new heights when he received Nomura's report of the meeting with Roosevelt. Kase was sent to see the American ambassador on November 12 to convey the Foreign Minister's concern. Togo was "shocked," the secretary told Grew, because "the United States Government does not fully grasp the urgency of successfully concluding the current conversations in the shortest possible time." The extraordinary length of time devoted to the conversations, Kase continued, was giving rise to a view among Japanese leaders that the United States "was endeavoring to utilize the conversations as a means of concealing the preparations…to complete the encirclement of Japan." Togo, Kase said, was not trying to threaten the United States. But the United States did not seem to appreciate the dynamics underlying Japan's effort. The Foreign Minister, the secretary observed, "entirely realizes that his own life is at stake, to say nothing of his official position, but that nevertheless he has had the courage to make this final attempt…."

Grew was again handicapped in responding to Kase's complaint because he had not received any summary of Nomura's meeting with Roosevelt and Hull. Still, the Ambassador sent Hull a summary of his conversation with Kase along with a separate comment. "While it would appear obvious," he told the Secretary of State, "that a continuation of the talks is greatly to be preferred to a complete break-down, nonetheless for the conversations to drag on for a considerable time with no definite progress…may well accelerate the creation of the dangerous situation referred to in my various reports of recent months, particularly in my [telegram of November 3]." Grew added an observation directed at Japan's characterization of its most recent proposals as the "final" effort. He could not say, said the Ambassador, whether those proposals did in fact "constitute the maximum Japanese concessions."

Grew's last comment cried out for some response from his State Department—if, of course, the United States was interested in using the Washington conversations to reach an agreement. The Secretary of State could have directed his ambassador to ask the Foreign Minister whether, as Hull believed, Plans A and B were ultimatums or whether the Japanese were prepared to make further concessions. But there was no such request from Hull, and Grew never made that inquiry. And so, when Nomura met with the Secretary of State at his apartment on November 15, the conversation continued to meander in an aimless direction.

The two men had met a few days earlier, but that conversation, like the others before it, had ended inconclusively. Hull had given Nomura a general statement of how Japan and China might pursue his suggestion of friendship but added that the United States could not approach China about the matter until he and Nomura had "reached a good basis in our exploratory conversations...." Hull also gave Nomura a summary of Japan's statements on its positions and asked the Japanese ambassador to let him know whether that summary was accurate. Another principal focus of the conversation had been the Tripartite Pact, but Hull indicated that there was no need for Japan to formally renounce the agreement. The pact "ought not be a problem," the Secretary told the Japanese ambassador, ". . . if we could work out our proposed agreement in other ways."

There was no reason for Nomura to question the Secretary's assurance. The Tripartite Agreement had been in effect when the conversations started the previous April. Hull had raised many questions about the pact, and the United States' draft proposals had tried to insulate the United States from any adverse decision Japan might make under the pact. But never before had Hull asked that Japan renounce the agreement.

All that changed when the two men met on the fifteenth of November in Hull's apartment. The Secretary made it clear that it was no longer enough for the parties to enter into an agreement that acknowledged that the United States' entry into the European war would be based on self-defense and thus outside the scope of the Tripartite Pact. Now the Secretary asked Nomura whether the pact "would be automatically abandoned" or otherwise "become a dead letter" if the United States and Japan entered into an agreement. Hull said that "it would be very difficult for him" to convince the American public "that Japan was pursuing a peaceful course so long as Japan was tied in an alliance with the most flagrant aggressor who has appeared on this planet in the last 2,000 years." As he was talking, Hull no doubt searched for a frame of reference to make Nomura understand that perceived difficulty. So the Secretary reached back into his state's history. If the United States entered into an agreement "while Japan had an outstanding obligation to Germany," said Hull, "he might well be lynched." It was an unmistakable sign of the Secretary's resistance to forging any agreement with the Empire of the Rising Sun.

Nomura did not give any response to indicate that he understood Hull's reference to lynching, but the Ambassador certainly understood that the United States was now taking the position that Japan had to renounce the pact. The Japanese ambassador also understood that Hull would not be rushed into making any decisions. The Secretary of State closed the conversation—with apparent reference to Kase's comment to Grew—by saying that the United States did not want to "be receiving ultimatums...from the Japanese Government" about the need for urgent action. The United States, he said, was "working as hard" as it could to fashion "a wholly satisfactory and broad settlement."

There continued to be much public sentiment to support Hull's approach to the discussions in general and the Tripartite Pact in particular. The American press routinely referred to an agreement with Japan as appeasement. At a Cabinet meeting on October 24, Roosevelt told the assembled group that he had pointed out to a magazine editor "how widespread and deep was anti-Japanese sentiment in this country and that, however much we didn't want to go to war, we might have to do so...." Symptomatic of that perspective was Interior Secretary Ickes. He confided to his diary in late November that, if the United States had entered into an agreement with Japan, he "would have promptly resigned from the Cabinet with a ringing statement attacking the arrangement and raising hell generally with the State Department and its policy of appeasement."

Grew was told nothing about Hull's conversation with Nomura on November 15, and he had only a general sense of the anti-Japanese sentiment referenced by the President. But the Ambassador knew that the noose around Japan's neck was getting tighter and that the prospect of war was becoming more imminent.

On November 13, the Ambassador forwarded to Hull a report by the Embassy's commercial attaché which explained that "military leaders of Japan decided months ago that it would be far better for the Japanese Army to go down fighting a major power than to withdraw from China for any other reason." This decision, said the attaché, was premised on an assessment that a failure to wage war would result in Japan expending her stockpile of resources and then being reduced to "a weakling from both a military and economic standpoint." Grew told Hull that he concurred in the attaché's report and that it should be read in conjunction with his telegram of November 3.

The attaché's report was followed up by another dispatch to Hull on November 17. Grew wanted to emphasize "the need to guard against sudden Japanese naval or military actions" outside China. Such actions, the Ambassador continued, included "the probability of the Japanese exploiting every possible tactical advantage, such as surprise and initiative." While he obviously hoped this insight would be useful, Grew cautioned the Secretary of State that he should not count on the Embassy "to give substantial warning" about any Japanese attack. The Embassy's assessment of military matters, he said, was "restricted almost literally to what could be seen with the naked eye," and there could obviously be developments that would escape the Embassy's attention.

Although he was not privy to Grew's telegrams, Kurusu was mindful of the limited time he had to orchestrate an agreement when he reached the San Francisco airport on Friday, November 14. "I realize the difficulty of my task," he told the crush of reporters, "but I wish I could break through the line and make a touchdown." The Special Envoy soon left to travel to Washington. By Monday morning, dressed in the formal diplomatic garb of a black cutaway jacket with black-stripped gray trousers, Kurusu and Nomura (who was similarly attired) entered Hull's office at the State Department. The Special Envoy told the Secretary of State that he had talked with Tojo immediately before departing Japan and that he was "agreeably surprised" that the Prime Minister, despite his military background, was "sincerely desirous of reaching an agreement with the United States."

After about twenty minutes, the three men put on their dark overcoats, grabbed their hats (Nomura's and Kurusu's being black, with Hull's a beige color), and, with Kurusu using a walking cane, strolled across West Executive Avenue for their meeting with the President in the White House. The men were received by Roosevelt in the Red Room at 11:10 a.m. The room featured doors that opened into the south portico (facing the Washington Monument and the Potomac River), along with red damask wallcovering, white wainscoting, red draperies, and a large painting of Theodore Roosevelt.

The President was his usual cordial self, saying that he "accepted" Kurusu's statement that Japan was eager "to avoid war" and "bring about a settlement...." In apparent recognition of Nomura's most recent conversation with Hull, Kurusu tried to explain why the Tripartite Pact should not be an obstacle to any settlement. Hull regarded the effort as "specious" and bluntly told the Special Envoy that he and the President would "be denounced in immeasurable terms" if Japan was "still clinging to the Tripartite Pact" when they reached any settlement.

At one point, the conversation veered toward the retention of Japanese troops in North China after settlement of the China Incident. Perhaps reflecting on the three paragraphs that Grew sent to Welles, Roosevelt said that the United States did not want to mediate the dispute between Japan and China but, "at a suitable stage,...might, so to speak, introduce Japan and China to each other" so that they could work out the "detailed adjustments" by themselves. Nomura later told Tokyo that the President said he would like to be the "introducer," although he was not sure that was appropriate "diplomatic phraseology."

Kurusu did not offer any specific proposal on any issue, and Hull later commented that "nothing new was brought out" by the Japanese representatives. The only hopeful sign for Nomura and Kurusu came when the Special Envoy commented that the "time element" was particularly important. If the discussions became "prolonged," said Kurusu, the Japanese people would become "anxious" that their country could be weakened from both a military and economic perspective. In response, Roosevelt said, "There are no last words between friends." It was a reiteration of a statement made almost three decades earlier by William Jennings Bryan, then Secretary of State under President Wilson, to a different Japanese ambassador who was complaining about California's discriminatory land law. Roosevelt's comment gave the two Japanese representatives hope that they might draw upon the President's goodwill down the road. Otherwise, the two Japanese representatives had no words of encouragement for Tokyo, and it was reported that they "appeared far from happy as they hurried out" of the front portico of the White House on Pennsylvania Avenue, with their car speeding off before the doors were closed.

The appointment with the President did not end the discussions. Hull had offered to discuss the issues further at the State Department, and the two representatives returned to Hull's office the following morning for a meeting that lasted about three hours. Hull stated at the outset that he "did not know whether anything could be done...in reaching a satisfactory agreement with Japan" and that, "rather than go beyond a certain point, it would be better" for the United States "to stand and take the consequences." Neither Nomura nor Kurusu pressed Hull on that point. Instead, they moved on to the Tripartite Pact. Kurusu explained that he could make no promise that Japan would "abrogate" that agreement but that Japan might do something "which would 'outshine' the Tripartite Pact." That did not satisfy the Secretary of State, and so the Special Envoy asked Hull whether he "had a concrete formula for dealing with Japan's relations with the Axis alliance." Hull was not willing to provide any such formula. He said only that "it would be difficult to get public opinion" in the United States "to understand" a situation where Japan remained allied with Germany.

The discussion on China was equally inconclusive. Hull reminded the Japanese representatives that they were still engaged in "exploratory conversations" and had not yet reached "a real basis for negotiations." Until they did, Hull continued, he could not initiate conversations with the Chinese or the British about a resolution of the China Incident. He added that "the present situation was one of Japan's own making" and that it "was up to the Japanese Government to find some way of getting itself out of the difficulty in which it had placed itself."

There was much discussion of Japan's need for an expeditious resolution of these and other issues. Nomura mentioned that "the situation in Japan was very pressing and that it was important to arrest a further deterioration of the relations between the countries." Kurusu added that the United States' "freezing regulations had caused impatience in Japan and a feeling that

Japan had to fight while it still could." The situation was "so pressing," said the Special Envoy, "that it might get beyond our control."

None of those statements troubled Hull. He rejected any notion that the United States had been responsible for any "delay," saying that he had met with Nomura "promptly every time" that Nomura had requested a meeting. The Japanese representatives did not argue with the Secretary of State on that point. But they did have a proposal—loosely based on Plan B but conjured up on their own initiative—to address the timing issue. Kurusu suggested that they could restore the situation to what it was previously so that the parties would have more time to resolve the outstanding issues. Nomura explained that they could go back "to the status which existed before the date in July" when the United States initiated its freezing order. The proposal would include Japan's withdrawal of the troops it had placed in southern Indochina.

The Secretary of State appeared skeptical, saying that any Japanese troops withdrawn from Indochina could "be diverted to some equally objectionable movement elsewhere." But there was a certain irony in the Japanese representatives' proposal. Roosevelt had told Stimson on November 6 that he was thinking of proposing a six-month truce when Kurusu arrived as a means to delay any hostilities in the Pacific. Although the Secretary of War opposed that proposal, Max Hamilton and Max Schmidt gave Hull a *modus vivendi* proposal on November 11. "If, as seems almost certain," they explained in a cover memo to the Secretary of State, "there is no possibility at the present time of reaching" a comprehensive agreement with Japan, "it is highly probable" that there would be "a rupture in the conversations" and "perhaps a sudden deterioration of relations." Their draft proposal, they said, could facilitate a continuation of the conversations and, perhaps, "an eventual comprehensive settlement...."

Hull made no mention of Hamilton and Schmidt's proposal in response to Nomura and Kurusu's suggestion about restoring the *status quo* prior to the July freezing order. The Secretary said only that he would discuss the suggestion with the British and Dutch.

There was nothing in the meetings with Roosevelt and Hull to indicate that Kurusu was doing anything more than trying to assist Nomura in reaching a resolution of the outstanding issues. But Hull came away with a decidedly negative view of the Special Envoy that Kurusu later attributed, in part at least, to American mistranslations of cables from Tokyo. "Neither his appearance nor his attitude," the Secretary later said, "commanded confidence or respect. I felt from the start that he was deceitful." Much of that perspective was based on Hull's view of Tojo and the reading of Togo's cables to Nomura—all of which suggested to Hull that Japan would soon initiate an armed attack somewhere. The Secretary concluded that Kurusu had two malevolent purposes in coming to the United States: to "induce" the United States "to accept Japan's terms," and, failing that, to "lull" the United States "with talk until the moment Japan got ready to strike." (It was a view shared by Sumner Welles. Kurusu, the Under Secretary of State later said, was on a "mission of deceit," and no administration official was "ingenuous enough to believe for an instant that any practical benefit would be gained from Mr. Kurusu's mission.")

Hull made no mention of his assessment of Kurusu when he sent Grew a summary of the conversation on November 18. The American ambassador might have taken special note of Nomura's comment in that summary that "it might be helpful" if the United States "could give the Japanese some hope…." Only days earlier, a Japanese friend had told Grew that the "trouble with you Anglo-Saxons is that you regard and deal with the Japanese as grown-up people" when in fact they "are but children and should be treated like children." For that reason, said Grew's friend, it would be useful to remember that an "encouraging word or gesture immediately inspires confidence"—a trait, he added, that the Germans understood and had played upon "with marked success."

All of that must have heightened the despair that Grew undoubtedly felt—and probably caused him to think about the letter he had written to Konoye upon the Prime Minister's resignation. The letter praised Konoye for his "long, arduous and most distinguished official service" to Japan. The Ambassador now wondered whether it was appropriate to praise a man who had been largely responsible for Japan's predicament. Konoye "alone tried to reverse the engine," Grew confided in his diary on November 21, "and tried hard and courageously, even risking his life and having a very close call as it was. Whatever mistakes he made in directing Japan's policy," the entry continued, "he had the sense and the courage to recognize those mistakes and to try to start his country on a new orientation of friendship with the United States." Grew recognized that it would be "difficult for anyone not living in Japan" to understand "the forces and stresses loose in this misguided country" and to "appreciate what Konoye was up against...." But the Ambassador understood those forces and stresses. And, after giving it further thought, he concluded that he "would not change" any word in the letter even if he were "to write it again." It was now, Grew surely knew, only a matter of time.

CHAPTER 20

The Hull Note

I t had been a long day for the President. He had spent about an hour and a half in the afternoon of Tuesday, November 25, "motoring" with Crown Princess Martha of Norway. That was followed by a dinner and conversation with her that lasted until shortly after midnight.

The forty-year-old Princess had fled her country after its occupation by Germany in the spring of 1940. She was now living in the United States with her children while her husband and his father, the king, had taken up residence in England. The President had taken an immediate liking to Princess Martha when she and her husband had met the Roosevelts on an earlier trip to the United States. She and her three children had spent a short time in the White House after she had left Norway but had then moved to the Pooks Hill estate in Bethesda, Maryland.

Roosevelt enjoyed her company. The statuesque Princess, with short brunette hair and fine features, had the appearance and charm of royalty. And more than that, she catered to the President's ego. "He loved her and being admired by her," said Roosevelt's daughter Anna.

Henry Morgenthau, Jr. may or may not have known about the President's dinner companion the prior evening, but Roosevelt was still in bed when the Treasury Secretary came to see him at 9:40 in the morning on Wednesday, November 26. The breakfast tray of kippered herring and coffee was still there as Morgenthau explained the purpose of his visit. The fifty-year-old Morgenthau was a member of a prominent New York family that operated a large farm near Roosevelt's estate in Hyde Park. Unlike Roosevelt, Morgenthau was Jewish, and he wanted to talk to the President—"as one friend to another"—about a remark Roosevelt had made at an earlier Cabinet meeting about "there being too many Jews employed [in the government] in Oregon."

The President was very open and matter-of-fact about the comment. The remark was not, he made clear, a sign of prejudice. Rather, said Roosevelt, it was a question of recognizing that the government payroll could not have a "disproportionate amount of any one religion." As a reference point, Roosevelt recounted to Morgenthau how he and the Treasury Secretary's father had talked with the Board of Overseers at Harvard many years earlier to gradually reduce the number of Jews entering the prestigious college from about a third "until it was down to 15%."

While the President was explaining his position on religious quotas and other matters, the Secretary of State called. Hull was disappointed because the Chinese representatives—and Chiang Kai-Shek in particular—had expressed outrage over the State Department's proposal for a *modus vivendi* agreement with Japan. The State Department's proposal was an alternative to the *modus vivendi* proposed in Japan's Plan B and would have been far less generous, but that was of no consolation to the Chinese. They could not abide any agreement that would relax the pressure on their adversary. ("The morale of the entire [Chinese] people will collapse," said Chiang Kai-Shek's telegram, "and every Asiatic nation will lose faith....") Hull was also annoyed because the British seemed reluctant to support the *modus vivendi* proposal.

It was the cap of a tortuous week for the Secretary of State as well as the Japanese. As he reviewed reports from Nomura and Kurusu during that week, Togo was mindful that there was no real progress even though his government's deadline for completion of the discussions was fast approaching. Nomura and Kurusu had visited with Postmaster General Frank Walker on the evening of November 17—the very day on which Kurusu had been introduced to Roosevelt. "The President," said Walker, "is very desirous of reaching an understanding between Japan and the United States." All that was needed, said Walker, was for Japan to "do something real, such as evacuating French Indochina, showing her peaceful intentions...."

Walker did not say whether Roosevelt had asked the Postmaster General to make that overture, but that was of no moment. As Grew had predicted, the Japanese were not prepared to move troops or take other definitive action without an agreement. Togo advised Nomura that the United States could introduce "complicated terms" if Japan acceded to Walker's suggestion. Beyond that, said the Foreign Minister, the "internal situation" in Japan precluded any withdrawal from Indochina "merely on assurances that conditions prior to this freezing act will be restored."

Togo also conveyed his disappointment with the initiative taken by his representatives in proposing their own standstill proposal to Hull on November 18. The Foreign Minister believed the initiative was "unfortunate" and would only "prolong" the discussions. He therefore instructed his representatives to present the *modus vivendi* proposal in Plan B immediately to the Secretary of State (modified to incorporate an express commitment for Japan to move its troops from southern Indochina to northern Indochina). The Foreign Minister explained that "no further concessions can be made" and that the discussions will "have to be broken off" if the United States did not respond favorably.

Nomura and Kurusu did as they were told. They convened at noon in Hull's State Department office on Thursday, November 20. They had no concern about unwanted publicity because it was Thanksgiving, and no reporters were around. By the time the Japanese representatives arrived, the Secretary of State had already seen intercepts of Togo's cables to the Japanese representatives that, according to American translators, identified Plan B as "Japan's absolutely final proposal"—even though Kurusu said that a correct translation would have interpreted the words to say that Plan B was "a means of overcoming final barriers." Relying on the American translation, Hull later told the congressional committee investigating the Pearl Harbor attack that he regarded Plan B as an "ultimatum" with "the most extreme demands and proposals" that Japan had advanced during the entire course of the discussions.

To Hull, it was "clearly unthinkable" that the United States would ever agree to the *modus vivendi* proposal in Plan B. But Hull could not express that sentiment to the Japanese representatives. At least not now—not when the United States needed time to build up its defenses. To do so might have resulted in an immediate termination of the discussions. And so, while

Kurusu felt the Secretary of State was "very cold" to Plan B, Hull said he would give the proposal a "sympathetic study...."

In the meantime, said the Secretary, he did have some comments on the status of matters. Although the Japanese public had virtually no role in the formulation of government policy, Hull explained that the United States wanted Japan to "develop public opinion in favor of a peaceful course." But even if Japan should succeed in that endeavor, it would not be enough for the Secretary of State. The Tripartite Pact remained a formidable obstacle to any agreement. The problem, said Hull, is that "the public in this country thinks that Japan is chained to Hitler." Kurusu asked the Secretary whether anything could be done to "eradicate such a belief" because Japan "could not abrogate the Tripartite Pact." The meeting ended without any response to Kurusu's inquiry.

Still, the Special Envoy understood the difficulty posed by the Tripartite Pact. And so he made an appointment to see Hull at the Secretary's apartment the next evening. The Special Envoy later said that Hull was "very friendly" and even joked about inviting Kurusu to dinner or a game of golf but said that "golfing takes up too much time...." The purpose of the visit, said the Special Envoy, was to give Hull a draft of a letter that Kurusu could sign to demonstrate that the Tripartite Pact would not be an obstacle to an adjustment in Japanese-American relations.

The letter recalled that Kurusu was the one who had signed the Tripartite Pact on behalf of Japan and was thus in a position to explain its meaning. The letter said that the pact "does not infringe, in any way, upon the sovereign right of Japan as an independent state," that Japan could "interpret its obligation freely and independently," and that Japan would not enter "into war at the behest of any foreign Power...." Hull glanced at the document and asked if he could keep it "because he wanted to show it to someone else." The two men shook hands as Kurusu prepared to leave, with the Special Envoy noticing that the Secretary "appeared to have a slight cold" and that his hand felt "feverish." As he left, Kurusu told Hull to "take care of his health."

Whatever hope the Special Envoy took from the meeting disappeared when he and Nomura met with Hull at this apartment at 8 p.m. the following day—Saturday, November 22. By then, Hull had seen the American translation of a telegram from Togo advising Nomura and Kurusu that the deadline for completion of the discussions had been extended to November 29. "There are reasons beyond your ability to guess why we wanted to settle Japanese-American relations by the 25th," said the telegram. "[I]f the signing can be completed by the 29th...we have decided to wait until that date. This time we mean it," the telegram added. "After that, things are automatically going to happen."

To Hull, the telegram signaled that Japan planned to take military action if an agreement was not reached by November 29. He was seething. "It was almost unreal," he later recounted in his *Memoirs*. "There they sat," he wrote of the two Japanese representatives, "bowing agreeably, Nomura sometimes giggling, Kurusu often showing his teeth in a grin, while through their minds must have raced again and again the thought that, if we did not say Yes to Japan's demands, their Government in a few days would launch new aggressions that sooner or later would inevitably bring war with the United States...."

Despite his anger, Hull was not prepared to advise the Japanese representatives that there was no hope for Plan B. He told them instead that he had had discussions with other governments' representatives about "a relaxation to some extent of freezing" and that "there was a general feeling that the matter could all be settled if the Japanese" could provide "some satisfactory evidences that their intentions were peaceful." One possibility, said Hull, was Japan's complete withdrawal from Indochina. He then asked whether the Japanese proposal "was intended as a temporary step to help organize public opinion in Japan" with an eye toward "the conclusion of a comprehensive agreement." Kurusu responded affirmatively to that question. That response may have satisfied Hull, but the Secretary of State was elusive when Nomura asked if Hull "could say what points in the Japanese proposal" were acceptable and "what points" he "desired to have modified." The Secretary said that he could not have an answer before Monday because he was obliged to confer with representatives of other governments. Nomura was quick to say that "the Japanese would be quite willing to wait until Monday." Hull closed the meeting by saying that he would soon discuss with Nomura "a general and comprehensive program" that was being developed with other countries.

Hull did not bother Grew with the details of these discussions. Not that the Ambassador was isolated from the growing likelihood of armed conflict between Japan and the United States. By the beginning of November, many Japanese citizens were writing to Grew, urging him to do something, anything, to forestall the looming crisis. "If things are allowed to pass as they are now," said one letter, "it is a foregone conclusion that hostilities would occur between the two countries and the consequences will be that the whole world would be enveloped in conflagration....I pray that you will do your best for the benefit of the two people."

The tension was readily apparent to American journalists in Tokyo as well. *New York Times* correspondent Otto Tolischus took particular note of speeches made to the Diet, which had convened for a special session on November 15 to address financial issues. "The policy speeches delivered before the Diet by Tojo and Togo," Tolischus reported, "make it evident that a final showdown between Japan and the United States is at hand...." And on November 22, the press reported that the Executive Vice President of the Imperial Rule Assistance Association had told a conference of business executives that "the international situation was becoming so tense that it was on the point of explosion."

In light of the rising tensions, Grew could not have been surprised when Togo asked him to come to the Foreign Office on the afternoon of Monday, November 24. The Ambassador was recovering from a cold that had left him "totally without energy and feeling generally on the blink" (despite the continued daily ingestion of the same Vitamin B complex he had given to Matsuoka months ago). But it was not enough to dissuade him from keeping the appointment with the Foreign Minister.

In response to Togo's inquiry, Grew said that he had had no report on Hull's conversation with Nomura and Kurusu on November 22. Togo then informed the Ambassador that Hull believed Japan's proposal to move troops from southern Indochina to northern Indochina was "unsatisfactory." That perplexed the Foreign Minister because the American freeze on Japanese assets had been triggered by "the presence of Japanese armed forces in southern Indochina...." The Foreign Minister also talked at length about Hull's objection to the cessation of American aid to China while China and Japan were—hopefully—engaged in direct talks to settle their differences.

Togo did not understand the American objection because, if peace talks had commenced, all hostilities "would cease immediately" and American support of "the Chinese military effort would be superfluous."

It was all very frustrating to Togo. He told Grew that "he had personally drawn up and assumed responsibility for the Japanese proposal" and he hoped that the United States would recognize Japan's desire to pursue "peaceful objectives."

Togo apparently recognized that his conversation with the American ambassador was not likely to advance the ball very much, if at all. Other measures were needed to persuade American decision-makers of Japan's peaceful intent. And so Kase scheduled a meeting at the Imperial Hotel with Tolischus on Wednesday, November 26 (November 25 in Washington time). The Foreign Minister's secretary told the *New York Times* correspondent that he had "an important story." Plan B, Kase explained, was "Japan's last word," and a rapid resolution was needed because "[t]ime was running short...." Still, said the secretary, "Japan was willing to do everything 'compatible with decency' to satisfy America on the Axis alliance."

Tolischus agreed that it was an important story, and he wrote an article that could be dispatched to the *Times*. He then encountered an unexpected impediment. The article attributed the information to "highest authoritative quarters in Tokyo." That may have been an accurate description of Tolischus' source, but it was not acceptable to the Japanese censors. They would allow the dispatch of the story only if Tolischus attributed the information to "diplomatic quarters." Tolischus refused to make the change because it would be interpreted to mean the American ambassador—which would not only be inaccurate but might also undermine the impact of the story. Kase could not get the censors to retreat from their position, and Tolischus could do nothing more than give the unpublished article to the American ambassador on November 27. By then, however, the dispatch had been overtaken by events in Washington.

Before Kase's meeting with Tolischus, the Far Eastern Division staff was continuing to work feverishly on a *modus vivendi* proposal that would be an alternative to the one proposed by Japan in Plan B. Roosevelt himself—no doubt motivated by his military's desire to avoid any conflict in the Pacific—had sent a penciled note to Hull sometime after November 20 proposing terms that probably would have been acceptable to Japan: resumption of economic relations with some oil and rice for Japan now with "more later;" Japan to agree to send no more troops to Indochina, Manchuria, or other points in South Asia; Japan to agree not to invoke the

Tripartite Pact if the United States entered the European war; and the United States "to introduce [the] Japs to Chinese to talk things over but US to take no part in their conversations."

To be sure, any agreement would have to include details that might prove to be a stumbling block. But Hull understood the importance of at least trying to reach some kind of standstill agreement with Japan. That goal was reinforced by a memo that Hull received from the Chief of the Army's War Plans Division. The Chief thought the State Department's draft *modus vivendi* proposal could be used as "a basis for discussion" and, if successful, would serve one of the Army's "major objectives—the avoidance of war with Japan."

Hull discussed the Far Eastern Division's draft *modus vivendi* (which would be for three months instead of the six mentioned by Roosevelt) with the British, Chinese, Dutch, and Australian representatives. They did not make it easy for him. The British and Chinese representatives objected to a provision that would allow Japan to retain 25,000 troops in northern Indochina (because Marshall had told Hull that retention of 25,000 troops "would be no menace....."). The Dutch and Australian representatives were equally slow to provide their countries' approval. On November 24, Roosevelt sent the British Prime Minister a telegram describing the American proposal. "I am not very hopeful," said the President, "and we must all be prepared for real trouble, probably soon."

Hull was not much more hopeful when he met with the President and the other members of the War Council at the White House at noon on the following day. "There is practically no possibility of an agreement being achieved with Japan," he explained. The Secretary of State added that the Japanese "are likely to break out at any time with new acts of conquest by force." Hull's commentary was followed by animated discussion. The President remarked that "the Japanese were notorious for making an attack without warning" and stated that "we might even be attacked, say next Monday...." Despite the risk "in letting Japan fire the first shot," they agreed that, "in order to have the full support of the American people," it was better for "the Japanese be the ones to do this so that there should remain no doubt in anyone's mind as to who were the aggressors."

The skepticism of a peaceful resolution expressed by Hull and his colleagues was reinforced by public commentary. Senator Claude Pepper of

Florida—often viewed as a spokesman for the administration's perspective—had asserted on November 19 that the Senate would not consent to
any treaty that would "make this country a party to any crime that Japan
has committed." James B. Reston, a Washington correspondent for the *New
York Times*, did report on November 24 that there remains hope "for a
limited agreement that would be mutually beneficial to both sides." But
Reston conceded that the outcome was far from certain. "Meanwhile," his
report continued, "the possibility of war with the Japanese continues to
provoke much discussion in the capital."

There was at least one government employee concerned about the execution of a standstill agreement between the United States and Japan: Harry
Dexter White, an alleged Soviet agent who happened to be one of Morgenthau's senior advisors in the Treasury Department. Morgenthau, an advocate
for China, had long tried to inject himself into the formulation of State
Department policy (which Hull resented). White, a bespectacled man with
a receding hairline and a scraggly toothbrush moustache, was a willing
accomplice to Morgenthau's designs. On November 18, the Treasury Secretary forwarded to Roosevelt and Hull a memo authored by White that
incorporated a detailed proposal to adjust American-Japanese relations. On
its face, the proposal appeared to be a vehicle to avoid war with Japan. But
many later wondered whether the proposal was intentionally designed to
include extreme demands that Japan would reject and thus precipitate a war
with the United States—all of which could be to the advantage of the Soviet
Union. A war with the United States would reduce the likelihood of a Japanese attack on the Soviet Union's eastern front.

"Virtually surrounded by a world ablaze," said White's November 17
cover memo to Morgenthau, "and with the fire growing hotter, and nearer
and more dangerous, our diplomatic machinery concerns itself chiefly with
maintaining a façade of important goings-on, an appearance of assured
and effective functioning, whereas behind that front is largely hesitation,
bewilderment, inaction, petty maneuvering, sterile conversations, and
diverse objections." White therefore outlined a broad-based proposal that
could be submitted to Japan. Among other provisions, the proposal said
that the United States would "withdraw the bulk of American Naval forces
from the Pacific," sign a twenty-year non-aggression pact with Japan, surrender all extra-territorial rights in China, remove the freeze on Japanese

funds in the United States and restore trade relations, place Indochina under the control of numerous countries (including the United States and Japan), and provide Japan with a $20 billion twenty-year credit. For its part, Japan would withdraw all of its military resources from China, surrender all extra-territorial rights in China, withdraw all troops from Manchuria except for "a few divisions necessary as a police force," and enter into a ten-year non-aggression pact with the United States and other countries (which seemed inconsistent with the twenty-year non-aggression pact to be signed by the United States and Japan).

Hull regarded the White proposal as "a further example" of Morgenthau's "inclination to try to function as a second Secretary of State." But the Secretary of State acknowledged that "some of its points were good," and Max Hamilton advised Hull that it was "the most constructive [proposal] which I have yet seen." Ironically, the Far Eastern Division had already been at work on a substantive agreement that would address all the issues and that could be added as an exhibit to the *modus vivendi* proposal then being discussed with the allies. Some of the statements and proposals in the White draft were incorporated into the State Department's substantive agreement.

By the time Hull placed that call to the President on the morning of November 26, the State Department's alternative *modus vivendi* proposal was no longer a viable option. Shortly after midnight, the United States had received Churchill's reply to Roosevelt's November 24 telegram. The British Prime Minister did not expressly object to execution of the *modus vivendi* proposal. But his questions and comments reflected a negative posture. "What about Chiang Kai-Shek?" said Churchill's telegram. "Is he not having a very thin diet? Our anxiety is about China. If they collapse, our joint dangers would enormously increase." Hull assumed—mistakenly—that Churchill's comments reflected England's "half-hearted support" of the alternative *modus vivendi* proposal. The Secretary of State would not proceed without the full support of China and Great Britain. And so he decided that he would give the Japanese representatives only the substantive proposal.

Hull met with Roosevelt in the Oval Study at 3:45 p.m. that afternoon and read to him a memorandum that explained his proposed course of action. The memorandum said that Hull proposed to give the Japanese representatives only the substantive agreement and not the *modus vivendi* proposal that he and his staff had been working on for weeks. In deciding to abandon the *modus vivendi* proposal, the Secretary of State cited the "opposition of the Chinese Government and either the half-hearted support or the actual opposition of the British, the Netherlands and the Australian Governments...." It was not only the allies' failure to support the *modus vivendi* that concerned Hull. He was equally concerned about the "wide publicity" that their opposition would receive—not to mention "the additional opposition that will naturally follow...." Roosevelt "promptly agreed" to his Secretary's recommendation.

Hull met with Nomura and Kurusu at the State Department shortly after he left the White House. The Secretary handed the Japanese representatives an Oral Statement and a proposed agreement (later identified as the "Hull Note") that had two sections: a preamble that referenced the four principles Hull had mentioned to Nomura at their meeting on April 16, and a ten-point program of actions to be taken by the United States and Japan.

In his later testimony before the congressional committee investigating the Pearl Harbor attack, the Secretary of State said that the Hull Note "was essentially a restatement of principles which have long been basic in this country's foreign policy" and "was really nothing new to the Japanese." In fact, that was not so.

There was no better example than the fate of Manchukuo, the puppet state created by Japan in Manchuria. The American drafts of May 31 and June 21 had stated that the fate of Manchukuo would be decided by "[a]micable negotiation." That perspective was still intact on October 6 when Hull met with Stimson to discuss a possible agreement with Japan. The War Secretary insisted that Japan's evacuation of all of China had to be a condition of any such agreement, but Hull responded that "he wanted to discuss Manchuria afterwards." That posture was not reflected in the Hull Note. The third point stated that Japan would "withdraw all military, naval, air and police forces from China and from Indochina." No exception was made for Manchukuo.

It was not an inadvertent omission. In accordance with the position of the prior American proposals, drafts of the Hull Note initially stated that the United States would suggest that China and Japan "enter into peaceful negotiations with regard to the future status of Manchuria." On November

24, Stanley Hornbeck suggested that the provision on Manchuria's status be deleted. "Leave this to be brought up by the Japanese," said the Political Relations Adviser. And so the provision was removed.

The Hull Note included other provisions that had no counterpart in earlier American drafts. Although Japan had indicated a willingness to sign an agreement with the British and other countries simultaneously with the execution of an agreement with the United States, the Hull Note now proposed that Japan enter into "a multilateral non-aggression pact" with the United States and other countries that would undoubtedly include provisions very different from those that had been discussed over the prior seven months. The Hull Note also proposed a new multilateral agreement with the same nations (other than the Soviet Union) to "protect the territorial integrity of French Indochina." Another point would require Japan (as well as the United States) to surrender all "extra-territorial rights in China," including those provided under the Boxer Protocol. And while it did not expressly require Japan to abrogate the Tripartite Pact, the Hull Note did say that "no agreement which either [the United States or Japan] has with any third power" would be interpreted in a way to "conflict with the purpose of this agreement...." That provision was not very dissimilar to prior American proposals, but the Japanese regarded it as a demand that the Tripartite Pact be renounced.

To be sure, there were provisions in the Hull Note that would be beneficial to Japan, including the lifting of the freeze and a commitment by the United States to negotiate a new trade agreement. But the time required to negotiate new multilateral agreements, not to mention the new trade agreement, removed any hope for an imminent resolution of the issues that divided Japan and the United States.

The Secretary of State later told the congressional committee investigating the Pearl Harbor attack that the Hull Note's ten-point program was merely "one practical example of a program to be worked out" and that the Japanese "could at any time have said, 'Let us see if we cannot narrow this somewhat.'" That was not, however, the posture he advanced to Nomura and Kurusu on that last Wednesday in November. He told the Japanese representatives that the proposal "was as far as [the United States] could go at this time...." And as for the provision in Plan B to give Japan the oil it needed, the Secretary of State said that "public feeling on that question was so acute that he might almost be lynched if he permitted oil to go freely to Japan."

The Japanese representatives knew from a quick review that the Hull Note would be unacceptable to their government. To them, it reinforced the perception that the United States was unwilling to yield on any point. Kurusu took particular note of the requirement that Japan abandon its puppet state in Nanking and agree to recognize Chiang Kai-Shek as the leader of all China. The Special Envoy told the Secretary of State that Japan could not "sell the Nanking government down the river" any more than the United States could abandon Chiang Kai-Shek. But, as Kurusu later commented, Hull made it clear "that to argue was practically useless...." Kurusu explained to the Secretary of State that his government "would be likely to throw up its hands" and regard the American proposal "as tantamount to meaning the end...." Nomura then reminded Hull of Roosevelt's comment that "there is no last word between friends" and asked if the Secretary could arrange a meeting with the President. Hull acceded to that request, and they all met with Roosevelt in the Oval Office at 2:30 p.m. the following day.

The meeting began with a gracious gesture. Roosevelt offered Nomura one of his Camel cigarettes and tried to light it for the Ambassador, but, having only one good eye, Nomura could not bring the cigarette to the light. The President laughed good-naturedly and extended his hand further to accomplish the task. But Roosevelt gave the Japanese representatives no other satisfaction. Stimson had recently advised the President of a large Japanese "expeditionary force of 30, 40 or 50 ships" proceeding south along the China coast. The President was outraged by the news, believing that it showed a breach of faith by Japan. So, relying on a memorandum he had received from Hull, Roosevelt lectured the Japanese representatives on the failure of their leaders to make statements in support of peaceful pursuits and said there could be no relaxation of "economic restrictions" against Japan unless the country provided "some clear manifestation of peaceful intent." For his part, Hull referred to the "250,000 carpetbaggers" who had descended from Japan into North China and complained that "they had seized other peoples' rights and properties located there as the carpetbaggers had done in the south after the Civil War...." The President then explained that he was going to Warm Springs, Georgia, for a few days and that he wanted to see the Japanese representatives the following Wednesday after he returned.

Roosevelt recognized the possibility of Japanese military action before that next meeting, but Hornbeck, for one, had no concern that the Hull

Note would precipitate war with Japan. In a memorandum to Hull on November 27, the Political Relations Adviser expressed his opinion that "the Japanese Government does not desire or intend or expect to have forthwith armed conflict with the United States" and that he would "give odds of five to one that the United States and Japan will not be at 'war' on or before December 15...."

It was a bold prediction that would soon prove to be unfounded. Unbeknownst to Hornbeck, while the Secretary of State was delivering the Hull Note to Nomura and Kurusu, the Japanese attack task force—with six aircraft carriers and numerous support vessels—was departing Hitokappu Bay in northern Japan for the trek across the North Pacific to the launch point for the attack on Pearl Harbor (with Yamamoto's promise to turn the task force around if a settlement was reached before December 7 local time).

Neither Grew nor Dooman knew about Hornbeck's memo or the departure of the Japanese task force. But they knew their days were numbered when they received a copy of the Hull Note on November 27. "So far as we were concerned in Tokyo," the Embassy Counselor later said, "the moment that note arrived, we were well aware that it was touch and go." Although the Hull Note was not published in Japan, the Tokyo press reported on November 28 that "there is little hope of bridging the gap between the opinions of Japan and the United States," and the United States issued a warning for all American nationals to leave the country.

As Kurusu had predicted, Japanese leaders were aghast at the Hull Note. Later there would be much debate on whether the Hull Note was or was not an ultimatum to Japan (as Tojo claimed). The Secretary of State denied that the Hull Note was an ultimatum—but he recognized, as did other administration officials, that the Hull Note was little more than a statement for the record. Hull himself told the congressional committee investigating the Pearl Harbor attack that he "had no serious thought that Japan would accept our proposal of November 26." Stimson later said that Hull had told the War Secretary on the morning of November 27 that "he had broken the whole matter off" with Japan. According to the War Secretary, Hull said, "'I have washed my hands of it and it is now in the hands of you and Knox—the Army and the Navy.'" And a few days later, Max Hamilton advised the Secretary of State that there was at least one disadvantage to allowing publication of the Hull Note and the related Oral Statement. "The press in this country and the American public," said the Chief of the Far Eastern Division, "would construe the documents as something in the nature of an ultimatum to Japan...."

In the end, the characterization of the Hull Note was of no moment. Japanese leaders received the document at the commencement of a Liaison Conference on November 27, and the participants were "dumbfounded." "I was utterly disheartened," Togo later said, by the "uncompromising tone" of the document and "the extreme nature of the contents." For the Foreign Minister, it was the end of the fight. The Prime Minister had a similar reaction. To him, it was significant that the Secretary of State had delivered the Hull Note "knowing that Japan could not accept these conditions." It was a signal that the United States had "already resolved on war against Japan."

Grew, ever the optimist (and perhaps the victim of wishful thinking), confided to his diary that the Hull Note was "a broad-gauge, objective and statesman-like document" that offered Japan "practically everything that she has ostensibly been fighting for...." Nowhere did Grew record in his diary any comparison of the Hull Note with the earlier American drafts of May 31 and June 21. That was not possible because he had never been sent copies of those drafts. Nor was the American ambassador able to square the Hull Note with all the comments that Nomura and Kurusu had recently made to Roosevelt and Hull because, aside from the Japanese representatives' conversations with Hull on November 18 and November 26, Grew had not received summaries of those meetings.

No matter. Grasping at straws, Grew ventured out to the Tokyo Club—perhaps the only remaining venue where he could find Japanese contacts of some prominence—and "regularly" and with much vehemence tried to convince people that the Hull Note offered a basis for compromise. His contacts were unconvinced and remained "very pessimistic" about the prospects for settlement. "I saw one of my old Japanese friends at the Tokyo Club tonight," Joe recorded in his diary on December 1. "He looked gray and worn and he told me that the cabinet had decided to break off the conversations...." The friend did not have to explain the ramifications to the American ambassador. "[I]n that case," Grew responded, "I feared that everything was over and that I would soon be leaving Japan."

CHAPTER 21

War

I t was not a novel idea. In December 1937, the President had asked Hull
to give Japan's ambassador his personal message to Hirohito to protest
Japan's sinking of the *Panay* in China's Yangtze River. But something
more direct and more extensive was required now. In Roosevelt's view,
delivery of the Hull Note on November 26 signified that "the talks [with
the Japanese] had been called off...." That could have serious consequences
for the United States. He had received another memorandum from George
Marshall and Harold Stark on November 27, this one stating that termination of the discussions could result in a Japanese attack somewhere in
Southeast Asia, including the Philippines. At this point, said the Army and
Navy Chiefs, the United States' highest military priority was "to gain
time...." A new initiative was needed to serve that goal. And so, when the
President met with his War Council in the Oval Office at noon on Friday,
November 28, he "suggested a special telegram from himself to the Emperor
of Japan." It might break the stalemate or, at a minimum, delay military
action by Japan.

Roosevelt had considered sending a telegram to Hirohito in October
after Konoye had resigned. Hull had opposed the overture then because Tojo
was regarded as a "moderate," and it would be "premature" to send a telegram until they had a better idea of the "probable attitude of the new

government." The circumstances had changed, but the Secretary of State's opinion had not. He opposed sending a telegram to Hirohito now as well—not because of any advice he had solicited from Grew (who knew nothing of Roosevelt's proposal). No, he opposed the dispatch of any telegram because of his assumption that Hirohito "was a figurehead under the control of the military" and because a direct appeal to the Emperor would cause Tojo's cabinet to feel "that they were being short-circuited...."

Hull's view was not shared by Nomura and Kurusu. Ironically, they had advanced a proposal to Togo on November 26 for an exchange of messages between the American President and the Japanese Emperor. It was, they thought, the only way to avoid war with the United States and Great Britain. "I believe it advisable," Nomura said in the telegram to the Foreign Minister, "to have the President wire to His Majesty the Emperor his desire for Japanese-American cooperation." Hirohito, they said, could give a reply that would create "sufficient time for Japan to propose the establishment of a neutral zone comprising French Indochina and Thailand...." The Foreign Minister quickly rejected the idea after consulting Tojo and other government leaders. (Kido said the proposal "would result in rebellion.")

Togo's rejection of the representatives' proposal did not reflect the Emperor's indifference to war. Quite the contrary. Hirohito, like Roosevelt, was troubled by the imminence of armed conflict between Japan and the United States (who would undoubtedly be joined by Great Britain). The pleasant memories of his trip to England decades earlier remained fresh in his mind. But he could not ignore the realities of the situation that confronted him. Kido, as well as Tojo and Togo, agreed that "there was nothing further" they could do. It appeared to them that the United States "had no sincere desire to make a peaceful settlement" and that acceptance of the demands in the Hull Note would be "tantamount to suicide." To them, war was the only acceptable alternative.

Tojo wanted to proceed with an Imperial Conference to secure Hirohito's approval for that alternative, but the Emperor did not want to be rushed. On November 29, he consulted with the Senior Statesmen, the former Prime Ministers. They agreed that Japan was facing a "grave" crisis, but the Senior Statesman expressed mixed feelings on whether war was necessary. Konoye's reaction was typical. "I have no choice but to judge that further diplomatic negotiations will be hopeless," said the former prime minister, but he wondered "if it is necessary to immediately resort to war...."

The ambivalence of the Senior Statesmen was compounded by doubts about the Navy's confidence in its ability to wage war against the United States and Great Britain. Prince Takamatsu, Hirohito's younger brother, visited with the Emperor on the morning of November 30 and told him that "the Navy had their hands full" and were "inclined to avoid war" with the United States and Great Britain. Kido advised Hirohito to "use every possible precaution until he was certain" about the action to be taken. So the Emperor summoned the Navy Minister and the Chief of the Navy's General Staff. They expressed "considerable confidence" in response to Hirohito's inquiries. The Emperor was satisfied and told Kido that they could proceed with the Imperial Conference.

The outcome of the conference on December 1 was a foregone conclusion. "The United States has not only refused to make even one concession," Tojo told the assembly, "...but also stipulated new conditions....Under the circumstances, our Empire has no alternative but to begin war against the United States, Great Britain, and the Netherlands...." Hirohito, dressed in his naval uniform, remained silent throughout the proceedings, but he "nodded in agreement with the statements being made," "...displayed no signs of uneasiness," and appeared "to be in an excellent mood." There was no reference to an attack on Pearl Harbor—an operational matter that would not be disclosed to Hirohito until the next day and would not be disclosed to Tojo and Togo until after the attack had commenced.

Still, the Cabinet knew that the Navy was planning a surprise attack of some kind. Togo demanded to know at the Liaison Conference on November 29 when it would occur. He could not conduct diplomacy, said the Foreign Minister, unless he knew the timing of the attack. Nagano leaned over and, in a soft whisper, said, "December 8." The date was critical to Togo. International law, he said, required some prior notification to the United States that the discussions were terminated. It was therefore decided that a message formally terminating the discussions would be delivered to the American Secretary of State at 12:30 p.m. on December 7 local time (although later the delivery time was postponed to 1 p.m.). Togo was assured that delivery at the suggested time would ensure "a proper interval between notification and attack."

Neither Nomura nor Kurusu were told of these plans. They were told only that further discussions would be fruitless. "Well, you two Ambassadors have exerted superhuman efforts," said Togo's telegram of November 28, "but, in spite of this, the United States has gone ahead and presented this humiliating proposal. The Imperial Government can by no means use it as a basis for negotiations....However, I do not wish you to give the impression that the negotiations are broken off. Merely say to them you are awaiting instructions...."

Hull read the intercept of Togo's telegram, but Grew remained in the dark about Japan's plans and Washington's strategy. Still, he continued to see signs in Tokyo of a downward spiral toward war. "[T]he Japanese were pouring more troops and supplies into southern Indochina," he confided to his diary on November 29, "and giving every indication of an intention to invade Thailand." And then the Japanese press reported a "bellicose" speech that had been delivered by Tojo. The Prime Minister allegedly said that the United States and Great Britain "were pitting the peoples of East Asia against each other" and that "'we must purge this sort of practice from East Asia with a vengeance.'" Grew confided to his diary that it was "the height of stupidity to continue [to] enflame public opinion" against the United States and that Tojo's speech merely confirmed his friend's earlier comment that "when dogs are frightened, they bark, and the more they are frightened the louder they bark."

Hull had a different reaction when he read about Tojo's speech in the American press. The virulent nature of the comments attributed to the Prime Minister, coupled with reports from British intelligence of an imminent Japanese attack on Thailand, convinced the Secretary of State that they stood on the brink of war. He called Roosevelt, then in Warm Springs, and said that the President needed to return to Washington immediately. Roosevelt agreed, and there was, as the *New York Times* reported, "bedlam" the next day—Sunday, November 30—when Roosevelt and the large contingent of aides, reporters, and photographers were rushed in automobiles for the forty-three-mile ride from Warm Springs to the train station in Newnan, Georgia. In prior trips, Roosevelt usually displayed a "light-hearted attitude" as he passed the "hastily assembled crowds" in the "back country villages" of Georgia. But not today. The President, said the *Times*, "looked grim and intent as he silently boarded his private car" at the train station. To the traveling press, the message was clear: "the showdown had come."

Kurusu was curious about the reason for Roosevelt's sudden return to Washington when he and Nomura met with Hull at the State Department on the morning of Monday, December 1. The Secretary of State mentioned Tojo's speech as well as the build-up of Japanese forces in Indochina. For some reason, he then asked the Japanese representatives "how they felt about the general trend in the world situation, especially the situation in Libya and Russia." Kurusu responded that "their attention had been largely engrossed in the situation between the United States and Japan." He and Nomura tried to steer the Secretary of State back to that situation and said that the Prime Minister's "utterances" did not warrant the attention given to them by the United States.

However vigorous their defense of Tojo, the Japanese representatives could not draw any satisfaction from Hull's responses. He emphasized that the United States "would not go into partnership with Japan's military leaders." For his part, Nomura explained that "the Japanese people feel that they are faced with the alternative of surrendering to the United States or fighting." It was not an observation that could move the Secretary of State. "[T]he American people," he responded, "are going to assume there is real danger to this country in the situation," and "there is nothing he can do to prevent it."

The President did not share his Secretary of State's fatalism. Hull was feeling ill and left for his apartment shortly after meeting with the Japanese representatives. Later that day, Roosevelt sent a memorandum to Sumner Welles, directing the Under Secretary of State to summon the Japanese representatives and ask them to explain the build-up of Japanese forces in southern Indochina. "The stationing of these forces in Indochina," said the President's memorandum, "would seem to imply the utilization of these forces by Japan for the purposes of further aggression...." Roosevelt wanted Welles to pose a basic question to Nomura and Kurusu: "what am I to consider is the policy of the Japanese Government by this recent and rapid concentration of troops in Indochina?" Roosevelt was pleased with himself for having made the inquiry. He believed Japanese leaders would have some anxiety in deciding how to respond, and he later told Henry Morgenthau, Jr. that he "had the Japanese running around like a lot of wet hens...."

Grew remained unaware of the President's inquiry to the Japanese representatives, but the Ambassador realized that the situation was rapidly deteriorating. The futility was captured in a fleeting moment on Wednesday, December 3, at the funeral of Dowager Princess Kaya, who was related to Hirohito's wife. It was a bitterly cold day, but etiquette for an imperial event prohibited the wearing of overcoats. So Grew donned two pairs of underwear and a sweater underneath his suit. After the ceremonies, the Ambassador was waiting for his car to take him back to the Embassy when Togo approached him. "I am very much disappointed," said the Foreign Minister. Grew made some remark about trying to continue the conversations, but the import of Togo's comment was clear.

A couple of days later, Grew received a forlorn letter from a friend. "The situation is most deplorable," said the friend. He did not know the specifics of the Hull Note (which had still not been published in Japan or the United States), but he said that people were saying it constituted an "ultimatum" and that "the only way out" was some kind of *modus vivendi* so that the parties would have time to "work out a final agreement...." That dark foreboding was reinforced by a meeting Grew and Dooman were scheduled to have with another friend at the Tokyo Club in the afternoon on Friday, December 5. The friend gave them only a cursory greeting when he arrived. His mind was obviously preoccupied with other matters. "I have just heard something which has made me sick," he commented, "and I am going home and going to bed."

Not surprisingly, a sense of doom enveloped the American Embassy. When one of the file clerks asked about having the grand piano in the American School (which was closed) moved to her apartment for safe keeping, Dooman replied that might be possible—if they made it through the weekend. And those members of the staff planning to leave for the weekend were advised to be somewhere nearby so that they could "return readily to Tokyo."

Later that same Friday, Nomura and Kurusu returned to Hull's office with a response to Roosevelt's inquiry about troop concentrations in Indochina. They handed the Secretary a short statement about Japan's need to guard against movements of Chinese soldiers along the northern frontier of Indochina. Hull questioned the credibility of that explanation, and the Japanese representatives' comments did nothing to erase that skepticism (causing Nomura to utter under his breath to Kurusu, "[T]his isn't getting us anywhere").

In the meantime, Roosevelt continued to toy with the idea of sending a message to Hirohito. He had delayed any action because he accepted Hull's view that a message to the Emperor would offend Japan's leaders. Neither the President nor the Secretary of State bothered to ask Grew whether that concern was well-founded. But Kurusu had no qualms about the wisdom of that kind of direct communication. In his view, it was the only thing that could make a difference.

There was, however, a problem. Kurusu could not approach Roosevelt to suggest a message to Hirohito—that would be viewed in Tokyo as a flagrant disregard of Togo's rejection of the proposal he and Nomura had already made. So the Special Envoy reached out to Terasaki Hidenari, the First Secretary in the Japanese Embassy in Washington. A few days earlier, Terasaki had suggested to Kurusu (a little tongue-in-cheek) that he should "become a national traitor" by taking the initiative to make a proposal to Roosevelt that would break the stalemate in the discussions. The Special Envoy now approached the First Secretary, recalling Terasaki's suggestion that Kurusu become a "traitor," and said, "How about becoming one yourself?" Someone needed to use an intermediary to urge the President to send a message directly to the Emperor. That someone, said Kurusu, should be Terasaki.

The First Secretary agreed to do it. After a night of deliberations with his wife, Terasaki decided to convey the proposal through Stanley Jones, a Methodist missionary who knew Roosevelt and had been trying to orchestrate some kind of settlement between Japan and the United States.

It was a daring tactic. Both Kurusu and Terasaki understood the dire consequences to themselves and their families if their disregard of the Foreign Minister's decision should be disclosed. At the end of November, Terasaki discussed the proposal with Jones, and the theologian relayed the request to Roosevelt at an Oval Office meeting on Wednesday, December 3. The President embraced the idea immediately, telling Jones that he had been reluctant to send a message to the Emperor for fear of offending the Japanese leaders but that the request from a Japanese embassy official "wipes my slate clean. I can send the cable." When told not to disclose the involvement of Terasaki, Roosevelt replied, "You tell that young Japanese he is a brave man."

Hull had already assisted Roosevelt in the preparation of a message, but the State Department was not an enthusiastic participant in the drafting process. As Stanley Hornbeck later remarked, the State Department staff was prepared to review and revise drafts "intermittently" but was "pressing neither for nor against the making use of [the drafts]." The State Department's revision of the first draft prepared by Stimson at the end of November reflected that indifference. The draft referenced developments in the Pacific area "which threaten to deprive each of our nations and all humanity of the beneficial influence of the long peace between our countries." But the message did not make any specific inquiry or propose any specific action. It merely urged the Emperor to "give thought to ways of dispelling the dark clouds which loom over the relations between our two countries...."

By early Saturday, December 6, the State Department had revised the message to include a "stand-still" agreement that Roosevelt had decided to propose. The arrangement would involve the cessation of hostilities between Japan and China, the initiation of direct talks between Japan and China to settle their differences, Japan's commitment to reduce the number of forces in Indochina to the level that existed as of July 26 (the date when the freeze was announced), and a promise to continue the conversations while exploring a comprehensive settlement. That version was eclipsed later that same day by another draft prepared by the White House that focused on the removal of all Japanese military resources from Indochina.

Hornbeck reviewed the White House draft and told Hull about the need for changes. Hull agreed with the changes and then asked the Political Relations Adviser to take the revised document to Roosevelt. Upon arrival at the White House around 3 p.m., Hornbeck was immediately ushered into the Oval Study to see the President. Roosevelt reviewed the State Department's changes and "expressed [his] appreciation." As Hornbeck was leaving, the President remarked that, "had this been a private transaction" and the State Department had been his "lawyers," they could have charged him "a handsome fee for having saved him" from making errors.

"Almost a century ago," began Roosevelt's message, "the President of the United States addressed to the Emperor of Japan a message extending an offer of friendship of the people of the United States to the people of

Japan. That offer was accepted, and in the long period of unbroken peace and friendship which has followed, our respective nations…have prospered and have substantially helped humanity." Roosevelt said he was now compelled to address Hirohito "because of the deep and far-reaching emergency which appears to be in formation." The emergency revolved around Japan's deployment of additional military resources in Indochina. "During the past few weeks," the message continued, "it has become clear to the world that Japanese military, naval and air forces have been sent to Southern Indochina in such large numbers as to create a reasonable doubt on the part of other nations that this continuing concentration in Indochina is not defensive in its character." Japan could dispel that doubt, said the President, "if every Japanese solider or sailor were to be withdrawn" from Indochina. "I address myself to your Majesty," the message concluded, "so that your Majesty may, as I am doing, give thought in this definite emergency to ways of dispelling the dark clouds."

Grew could have told the President that the proposed withdrawal of all Japanese forces from Indochina—without any agreement—was a futile exercise. But the Ambassador's opinion was not solicited. The President merely sent a handwritten note to his Secretary of State on the evening of December 6. "Shoot this to Grew," said the note, adding that message could be sent through the less secure "gray code" because Roosevelt did not care "if it gets picked up."

Sunday, December 7, was a bright and warm day in Tokyo. Grew was in the Embassy residence when he received the call from Otto Tolischus around noon. The *New York Times* reporter had been working on a profile of the American ambassador for the *New York Times Sunday Magazine* and had received a call from Joe and Alice the previous evening with a small correction to the draft Tolischus had given them. But that was not the purpose of Tolischus' call now. San Francisco radio station KGEI—which could be picked up in Tokyo by short-wave radio—had announced that the President of the United States had sent a message to the Emperor of Japan. As Grew would later learn, delivery of all incoming cables were to be delayed for ten hours. The telegram would not reach the Chancery until 10:30 p.m. that evening.

Hull's cover telegram to Grew requested that the message be delivered "at the earliest possible moment in such manner as you deem most appropriate...." Sometime around nine o'clock that evening, Grew telephoned Dooman and asked the Embassy Counselor to come to the residence at once to help handle "an urgent matter...." Almost as soon as he arrived, Dooman telephoned Togo's private secretary to alert him to the possibility that the American ambassador might want to see the Foreign Minister as soon as they could decode the President's message. The secretary was not pleased when Dooman later informed him that the message was almost decoded and that Grew expected to be at the Foreign Minister's official residence by midnight. The secretary explained that Togo "wished to retire as soon as possible" and "wondered whether it would not be possible for the Ambassador to defer his call until the following morning." Dooman said that the Ambassador "would not think of disturbing the Foreign Minister at that late hour unless the matter in hand were of extreme importance." The secretary relented and said he hoped that Grew would get there before midnight.

The next challenge was transportation. All the Embassy chauffeurs had left for the evening. Second Secretary Merrill Benninghoff proved to be the answer. He had been out for the day but pulled into the Embassy compound earlier that evening in his Ford coupe. It was smaller than the Embassy vehicles, but it had four wheels and could take the Ambassador wherever he needed to go. Around 11:45 p.m., Grew got into the passenger seat, his long legs pushed against the dashboard, and traveled with the Second Secretary along empty streets to the Foreign Minister's official residence. Grew quickly ascended the crimson-carpeted stairs to the second-floor reception room, where Kase was waiting for him. It was about 12:15 a.m. on Monday, December 8. Togo entered almost immediately afterwards, dressed in formal diplomatic attire, and Kase directed them to two blue plush overstuffed chairs.

Grew explained that he had a message for the Emperor from the President of the United States. He gave Togo a copy and said that he wished to have an audience with Hirohito. It was the only way, Grew thought, to afford the message the "maximum weight." When Togo responded that he would study the matter, the Ambassador pointedly asked the Foreign Minister whether he would honor the request for an audience with the Emperor. Togo did not quarrel with Grew. He said "he would present the matter to the Throne." The Ambassador left the Foreign Minister's residence around 12:30 a.m. for the ride back to the Embassy.

Togo had the President's message translated and immediately took it to Tojo. The Prime Minister's only question was whether the message included any concession by the United States. The answer, of course, was no. The two ministers crafted a short reply for Hirohito, and the Foreign Minister took the draft to the Palace. When Togo explained the situation to Kido, the Lord Keeper of the Privy Seal was equally laconic. "That's no use, is it?" he rhetorically asked the Foreign Minister. Togo presented the draft reply to Hirohito, who quickly approved it. The Foreign Minister was back in his residence by 4:30 a.m. when the Navy Ministry called to say that the Japanese Navy had "successfully attacked the American fleet at Pearl Harbor."

As Togo was learning about the Pearl Harbor attack, it was about 2:30 p.m. on Sunday, December 7, in Washington, and Hull was reviewing the fourteen-part memorandum that Nomura and Kurusu had brought to him at the State Department. Delivery of the memorandum had been delayed because of difficulties in the Japanese embassy's transcription of the memorandum. The Secretary of State already knew about the Pearl Harbor attack, and his hands shook with rage as he glanced over the memorandum (which he had already seen through the intercepts). The memorandum said nothing about the Hull Note being an ultimatum. It recounted the history of the conversations and then concluded that the Japanese Government "cannot accept [the Hull Note] as a basis for negotiation" and that the "Japanese Government regrets to have to notify the American Government hereby...that it is impossible to reach an agreement through further negotiations." Hull did not shrink from expressing his anger. "In all my fifty years of public service," he said, his voice rising, "I have never seen a document so crowded with infamous falsehoods and distortions...." And with that, he motioned for the Japanese representatives to leave his office.

No one at the State Department bothered to advise Grew that Japanese planes had attacked Pearl Harbor. He was still asleep in the Embassy residence when his phone rang at 7 a.m. (5 p.m. on December 7 in Washington). Togo's secretary explained that he had been trying to reach the Ambassador since 5 a.m. and that Togo wanted him to come to the Foreign Minister's residence as soon as possible.

Grew jumped out bed and, without shaving or eating anything, had one of the Embassy's cars take him and Bob Fearey, his private secretary, to the

Foreign Minister's official residence. Grew arrived at 7:30 a.m. and again ascended the crimson-carpeted stairs to the reception room on the second floor while Fearey waited at the entrance.

As soon as Grew walked into the room, he saw Togo standing behind a table, still dressed in formal attire and looking "grim." The Foreign Minister then "slapped" a document on the table and said it was "the Emperor's reply to the President." It was the same fourteen-part memorandum that Nomura and Kurusu had delivered to Hull. Togo asked the Ambassador to take particular note of the last paragraph. "In view of the fact the conversations in Washington had made no progress," said the Foreign Minister, "it had been decided to call them off." Togo then read the separate statement that he and Tojo had prepared for Hirohito only a few hours earlier. "His Majesty has expressed his gratefulness and appreciation for the cordial message of the President," Togo said. As Grew could have predicted, Hirohito saw no reason to honor Roosevelt's request for a complete withdrawal of Japanese forces from Indochina. He merely referenced the response that Nomura and Kurusu had given Hull on Friday, December 5. The reply concluded with a statement that the "[e]stablishment of peace" had been the Emperor's "cherished desire" and that Hirohito trusted that the President "is fully aware of this fact."

The formalities completed, Togo gave "a little speech" thanking Grew for his cooperation "during the conversations." He then escorted the Ambassador down the stairs to his waiting Embassy car. Nothing was said about Pearl Harbor.

Grew, still unaware of the attack on Pearl Harbor, returned to the Embassy and prepared his report to Hull. He was not entirely surprised by the termination of the discussions but saw no need for alarm—they had been broken off before and then resumed. So he decided that he would change into golf attire for the tournament that was to be played later that morning. And then he received the telephone call from Henri Smith-Hutton, who was in the Chancery. KGEI, the Naval Attaché told the Ambassador, was reporting a Japanese attack on Pearl Harbor. Grew responded that "he couldn't believe it." He had just left the Foreign Minister, he told Smith-Hutton, and Togo had said nothing about the attack.

Dooman arrived shortly thereafter. He and Grew decided that it would be useful for the Embassy Counselor to visit with the Vice Minister at the

Foreign Office to confirm the reports. Dooman left the compound in an Embassy car around 9:15 a.m.

In the meantime, Sir Robert Craigie had had his own meeting with Togo that morning and was eager to talk with the American ambassador. He was driven through the streets to the American embassy. "The demeanor of the people," the British ambassador later said, "was calm...." Dooman likewise noticed that there was "nothing unusual" in the streets of Tokyo—"people were getting out of streetcars, out of buses, out of trains, walking along," with "absolutely nothing" to indicate that Monday, December 8, was "different from any other day...."

When he arrived at the American embassy, Craigie "found the whole compound surrounded by police and a large crowd of spectators opposite the main entrance of the Chancery." Craigie tried to enter the compound, but the police grabbed him by the arms and refused to allow him to proceed. He shook them off and finally approached the police officer in charge with an explanation of who he was. After some tense moments, Craigie was allowed to enter the compound, but by the time he reached Grew at the residence, the British ambassador was "trembling"—so much so that Joe gave him some whiskey.

While Craigie and Grew were meeting, Mr. Ohno, Chief of the Second Section of the American Bureau in the Foreign Office, arrived at the Chancery with about a dozen plain clothes policemen. Ohno asked to see the Ambassador, and a call was made to the residence. Alice answered the phone, said the Ambassador was preoccupied, and inquired whether someone else in the Embassy could handle the matter. Dooman, the most senior staff member, was still at the Foreign Office. An overzealous policeman had prevented Dooman from entering the Embassy compound when he had returned from his first visit to the Foreign Office, and the Embassy Counselor went back to the Foreign Office to file a protest. So the task of receiving Ohno fell to Ned Crocker, the Embassy's First Secretary.

Ohno and his companions were escorted to the Chancery office of the First Secretary. After an exchange of greetings, Ohno pulled a piece of paper from his pocket, and, with trembling hands, read to Crocker a statement that Togo had prepared for Grew: "I have the honor to inform Your Excellency that there has arisen a state of war between Your Excellency's country and Japan beginning today." After a brief silence, Crocker responded, "This is a very tragic moment." "It is," Ohno replied, "and my duty is most distasteful."

Ohno's duties were not completed. He explained that the police would have to search the Embassy compound for radios that could transmit or receive communications. All sixty-five of the Embassy personnel were then placed under arrest and interned in the Embassy compound. They would not be repatriated to the United States until August 1942.

CHAPTER 22

Coming Home

The morning of Wednesday, August 26, 1942, was sunny and cool in Washington. Joe Grew and Bob Fearey emerged from the front door of the Ambassador's home on 2840 Woodland Drive in the northwest quadrant of the city. It was a large brick house situated slightly below the street and almost completely shielded from view by tall bushes along the street line. The property of almost two acres continued to slope downward toward a backyard populated by large trees that provided the kind of privacy that Grew had enjoyed in Tokyo.

The two men got into the backseat of Grew's black Cadillac. The driver maneuvered the car up the circular driveway and then turned left for the short trip to the State, War and Navy Building for Grew's appointment with the Secretary of State. The meeting would mark his first personal encounter with Hull since his return from Tokyo.

The United States and Japan had completed the details of an exchange of diplomatic personnel, journalists, and other prisoners the previous June. Grew and the other Embassy personnel (as well as everyone else returning to the United States) had boarded the *Asama Maru*, a Japanese ship, on June 17 for a scheduled departure on June 18. The departure was then delayed because the United States had insisted on the release of several American teachers in northern Japan who had been arrested as spies. That information was not shared with all the passengers, and the uncertainty created consternation among some that the exchange might be cancelled. "I'll jump off the ship and try to drown myself," said one man who had been imprisoned and tortured in the prior months, "rather than go back to what would face us on shore."

The American teachers were finally released, and the *Asama Maru* slipped out of Yokohama's harbor around midnight on June 24 for the trip to Lourenco Marques in the Portuguese colony of Mozambique on the east coast of Africa. There the passengers were transferred to the SS *Gripsholm*, a Swedish American Line ship that had brought Japanese diplomats and other Japanese personnel from the United States (who then boarded the *Asama Maru* for the return to Japan). The *Gripsholm* transported its new passengers around the Cape of Good Hope to Rio de Janeiro for a brief respite. The ship then departed for New York on August 11.

Alice decided to remain in Brazil for a visit with Elsie, who had flown in from Chile, where she was stationed with her husband (who was also in the Foreign Service). Grew asked Fearey to share the cabin with him on the trip from Rio de Janeiro to New York. The ship arrived in New York on August 25, and the two men took the train back to Washington that afternoon.

In that two-week voyage from Rio de Janeiro, the Ambassador and his private secretary spent considerable time discussing the report that Grew planned to give to Hull upon his return. It was not a routine matter. The Ambassador had spent a good portion of his time during internment drafting and polishing the report on legal-sized paper (after receiving comments from Fearey, Dooman, and other Embassy personnel with whom he had shared the drafts). By the time they were ready to board the *Asama Maru*, the report filled sixty of those legal-sized pages (and would eventually include telegrams and other documents in an addendum of more than a hundred pages).

Removing the report from Japan was no easy matter. Grew was concerned that Japanese custom officials would seize the report if they became aware of it. Secrecy was therefore required, but the logistics were challenging. Grew initially decided to have copies given to seven different Embassy personnel in the hope that at least one copy would make it through inspection. However, sixty pages of legal-sized paper could not be folded without creating a bulge in the coat pocket. And so, as Fearey later explained, it was decided to punch two holes at the top of each copy, place a string through the two holes, and hang the copies "down our backs inside our shirts, suspended by concealed strings around our necks."

The importance that Grew attached to the report was not surprising. He was bitter about his experience in those last months before the attack on Pearl Harbor, and the report recounted his disappointment in great detail. A few days after the *Gripsholm* left Rio de Janeiro, Grew drafted a letter to the President that would attach a copy of the report and be given to Roosevelt upon Grew's return to the United States. The letter said that the Ambassador's "final political report" was something that warranted the President's perusal because "it will presumably be carefully weighed by future historians" on the question of whether "war with Japan could have been avoided."

The bulk of the letter focused on Roosevelt's failure to meet with Konoye. "For the first time in ten years," said the letter, American policy "had created in Japan a soil fertile for the sowing of new seeds...." Grew explained that Konoye had told him—"with unquestionable sincerity"—that "he was prepared at that meeting to accept the American terms whatever they might be." Japan's leaders, said the Ambassador, understood that any agreement with the United States would entail a withdrawal of all forces from China and Indochina "with the mere face-saving expedient of leaving garrisons in Mongolia and North China, which in fact was what other nations had done up to that time." As for the Tripartite Pact, said Grew, "it could not have been immediately and overtly disavowed," but any agreement with the United States would have rendered it "a dead letter...."

Grew could not resist criticism of Hull's insistence that Japan's commitment to a comprehensive agreement be a condition to any meeting between Roosevelt and Konoye. "I told the Department," the letter advised the President, "that this problem could never be solved by formulas" because "the Japanese Government was constantly afraid of written records which would have inevitably come to the attention of the political and military extremists" and would almost certainly have caused the fall of the government "through overthrow or assassinations...."

Grew understood that other factors—"of which [he] was kept in ignorance"—could have influenced the decisions of Roosevelt and his Secretary of State. Grew nonetheless felt compelled to mention in the letter three questions that had "bewildered" him.

The first question concerned the administration's failure to give "any encouragement whatsoever" to Konoye with respect to his proposed meeting with the President. "Was the transcendent importance to our country of preserving peace," the letter rhetorically asked Roosevelt, "to depend on the utterly futile effort to find mutually satisfactory formulas?"

The second question concerned the President's failure to follow the recommendation in Grew's telegram of August 30—namely, that Roosevelt include in his Labor Day speech, or in any other speech, "a clear conception of the concrete advantages" Japan would secure through an agreement with the United States. Grew said he had told Hull that he would have had the speech widely published in Japan because "it would have immeasurably strengthened Prince Konoye's hand at a moment when he terribly needed strengthening...."

The last question concerned Hull's refusal to respond to Konoye's and Toyoda's repeated pleas for the State Department to set forth the terms that the United States wanted Japan to accept. That refusal, said the letter, "inevitably conveyed to [Konoye] and his associates the unfortunate impression that our Government was merely playing for time and had no real intention to come to an agreement with Japan." Grew acknowledged that the Hull Note did finally set forth the terms that the United States wanted to include in any agreement, but the delay in providing those terms caused the Hull Note to be "interpreted in Japan as an ultimatum" that could not be the basis for further negotiation. "My own belief," said the Ambassador, "although this can only be a matter of speculation, is that war, while all the plans had been long prepared, was definitely determined upon only after the receipt of the [Hull Note]."

Grew was not prepared to share his report or his letter to the President with the many reporters who hurled questions at him as he and Fearey entered the outer office of the Secretary of State's suite in the southwest corner of the State, War and Navy Building. The exchanges with the journalists did not last long, and the Ambassador was soon ushered into Hull's office while Fearey waited in the reception area.

It was not a pleasant meeting. Grew handed the report to Hull, and, as the aged Tennessean began to leaf through it, his face became flushed and his anger evident. As Grew later told Fearey, Hull "half threw the report back across the desk" toward him, saying, "Mr. Ambassador, either you promise to destroy this report and every copy you may possess or we will publish it and leave it to the American people to decide who was right and who was wrong." Fearey could not make out Hull's comments, but he could hear the Secretary of State's raised voice through the closed office door. For his part, Grew protested that the document was "his honest, confidential report to his superiors in Washington, and that he could not in good conscience agree to destroy it." Nor was Grew willing to accept the alternative of having his report—which was critical of the President and his administration—disseminated to the public. It was not appropriate, he told Hull, for him to be involved in "a public controversy in time of war when national unity was essential."

Hull remained adamant about the destruction of the report, and, after about thirty minutes, Grew walked out of Hull's office, clearly shaken by the encounter. He suggested to Fearey that they walk over to the nearby Metropolitan Club on H Street for lunch even though it was well before noon. As the two of them sat at a table adorned with a white linen tablecloth and fine silverware, Grew related the details of the meeting to his young protégé, including Hull's request that Grew return the next morning at ten o'clock with a response to the Secretary of State's demand that the report be destroyed or that it be made public. Grew and Fearey reviewed the alternatives, but, in truth, there were really none. And so Grew and Fearey returned to the State, War and Navy Building the next morning for the second meeting with the Secretary of State.

The Ambassador went into Hull's office alone while Fearey again waited in the outer office. This time, there were no raised voices, and, after a short while, the two men emerged, smiling and obviously on friendly terms. Grew again suggested to his private secretary that they adjourn to a lunch at the Metropolitan Club. The Ambassador did not volunteer what had been said in the meeting with the Secretary of State, and so Fearey eventually posed a question about the fate of the report. Grew cryptically replied that "the Secretary had not mentioned it, but that he had expressed strong support for Grew's planned nationwide speaking tour."

Fearey was thus left with the impression that the report on which Grew had doted so much time for so many months would not be destroyed. It proved to be a false impression. The Ambassador had in fact agreed to Hull's request that the report and all copies of the report be destroyed. In the absence of any report to give the President, Grew had also decided that the letter to Roosevelt would not be delivered.

There does not appear to be any written record of why Grew allowed Fearey to retain the mistaken impression about the report's continued existence. Perhaps Grew was leery of saying—especially when the wounds of the Pearl Harbor attack were still fresh—that he had agreed to destroy a report on American-Japanese relations that was critical of the President and his Secretary of State. Perhaps it also reflected Grew's sense of loyalty. More than just an ambassador, he saw himself as a patriot who placed his country's welfare above any selfish interest he might have. And, believing that, he may have wanted to avoid any possibility that his actions (whether through publication of the report or disclosure that he had destroyed the report) would sow division in a country that, as he said, required unity in facing another world conflict.

Whatever the reason, Fearey would devote untold hours over decades after that Metropolitan Club lunch searching in vain for the report—in conversations with the former ambassador and Gene Dooman, through review of the papers Grew had deposited with the Houghton Library at Harvard, and in discussions with members of the Ambassador's family. At one point in the late 1960s, Fearey took his teenage daughter Barbara (who was attending boarding school in Connecticut) to the home of Gene Dooman, then living in retirement in Litchfield. Fearey wondered whether a copy of the report might be in papers Dooman had stored in his attic. The former Embassy Counselor "was pretty negative about the possibility of there being a copy of the report," remembered Fearey's daughter, but he said, "'Feel free. Search the attic.'" But of course Dooman's pessimism proved to be well-founded.

Long before that search in Dooman's attic, Congress too had expressed an interest in seeing any report Grew may have given Hull upon his return to the United States. The American public's despair, anger, and frustration about the Pearl Harbor attack remained largely intact after the war had ended in 1945. There had been many investigations to explore how and why the United States Navy and Army were so unprepared for the surprise assault. One of them had been conducted by a commission Roosevelt had established in December 1941 under the chairmanship of Supreme Court Associate Justice Owen J. Roberts. The passage of time and the successful conclusion of the war had not dampened the interest in the inquiry, especially among Roosevelt's critics. "Never before in our history," said a September 1945 editorial in the *Chicago Tribune* (owned by Robert R. McCormick, a long-time Roosevelt nemesis), "did a President maneuver this country into a war for which it was unprepared, and then, thru insouciant stupidity, or worse, permit the enemy to execute a surprise attack costing the lives of 3,000 Americans...."

Shortly after publication of the *Tribune* editorial, Congress created a special committee—composed of three Democratic Senators, two Republican Senators, three Democratic Congressmen, and two Republican Congressmen—to investigate again the surprise attack on Pearl Harbor. The committee convened on November 15 in the cavernous, marble-floored Senate Caucus Room (which would later be the location of the Senate Watergate hearings and, after Senator Edward M. Kennedy's death in 2009, be re-named the Kennedy Caucus Room in honor of the three Kennedy brothers—John, Robert, and Edward—who had served in the Senate). One of the first witnesses was Joseph C. Grew, who appeared before the committee on November 26, 1945—the fourth anniversary of the Hull Note.

Grew had retired from the Foreign Service on August 15, 1945, but his meetings with Hull upon his return to the United States in 1942 had not impeded his career. He had served as a special assistant to the Secretary of State, and in May 1944, he had become Chief of the Far Eastern Division. Hull's health had continued to deteriorate, and he resigned in November of that year. Grew was then appointed Under Secretary of State under Edward R. Stettinius, the new Secretary of State. He retained that position when James F. Byrnes succeeded Stettinius in July 1945. The former ambassador to Japan was the Acting Secretary of State throughout much of those first eight months in 1945 because both Stettinius and Byrnes spent considerable time attending meetings and conferences outside of Washington.

The congressional committee had no interest in Grew's career after his return to the United States. The committee was focused instead on his opinions and writings during his ten-year service as America's ambassador to Japan, especially during the months preceding the Pearl Harbor attack. At one point, Homer S. Ferguson, the fifty-six-year-old, white-haired, first-term Republican senator from Michigan, asked the former ambassador whether he had made a "report in writing" to Hull when he returned to the United States in August 1942.

Grew could not have forgotten the report on which he had devoted so much time and energy while he was interned at the Embassy in Tokyo. But his response to Senator Ferguson was less than precise. "Everything had been written pretty well up to date," said Grew. "That wasn't quite my question," Ferguson replied. "No," said the former ambassador, "I don't recollect having submitted at that time any report in writing." Ferguson was not prepared to drop the matter. "Will you think about that?" he asked the witness. "That could be an important report." Grew did not want the matter to remain in suspension. "I can answer that question now," he told Ferguson. "I did not submit, I did not file any report, any written report."

Ferguson was not prepared to accept that vague response. "You said," the Senator persisted, "that you didn't file it, and that brought to my mind, 'what did you mean by you didn't file it?'" Grew responded that he had "notes" that he had used in his "talks with the Secretary." When asked if he still had those notes, Grew replied, "They have been destroyed long ago." When Ferguson continued to push Grew on the matter, the former ambassador asserted that he only had notes "to refresh" his memory.

The Michigan senator would not let the matter rest. "Did you suggest," he asked Grew, "that you wanted to make such a final report in writing?" To that question, the witness had a clear answer: "Of course I did not." Ferguson again reminded Grew that any such submission "would be an important report." And when Ferguson again asked about the notes he had used in his talks with Hull, Grew again responded that they "have been destroyed." In response to Ferguson's further questions, Grew hewed the same line, telling the Senator that "he had talked it over" with Hull, that "the whole thing was completely on the record," and that "no request was made for a written report because all the facts were already on file in the State Department."

When the committee recessed for lunch, Grew undoubtedly realized that his testimony was not entirely accurate. He surely felt squeezed between the horns of a dilemma. He understood the importance of the truth. But he probably recognized that the Republican members of the committee, as well as other critics of Roosevelt and his administration, would squeal with delight if the administration's ambassador to Japan revealed that he had honored the Secretary of State's request to destroy a report that was critical of the Secretary as well as the President in their handling of Japanese-American relations prior to the Pearl Harbor attack. There was no clear path to reconcile those alternatives, but Grew decided over the lunch break that he could not let his testimony stand as it was. Something more had to be said. So, when the committee re-convened after lunch, Grew said he wanted to "correct one misstatement of this morning for the record."

The committee was obviously prepared to let the former ambassador make the correction. But even then, Grew could not bring himself to disclose that Hull had asked him to destroy his report and that he had complied with the request. "Well," said Grew, "[three] years have gone by since that time and, frankly, I had forgotten the fact that I did submit to Mr. Hull a series of dispatches, quite a number of reports, covering the whole story of the last days before Pearl Harbor, the events as they occurred in Japan, all of which is on the record, completely on the record, and has been brought out, I think before this committee...." He added that the reports were "turned in to the State Department" and "are all available...."

Senator Alben Barkley of Kentucky, the committee chairman, asked Grew to confirm that he was referencing "reports made to Secretary Hull after the Ambassador returned from Japan in August 1942...." Grew gave an affirmative response. Ferguson then asked the committee's counsel to obtain those reports. And there the matter was left. But the committee's hearing transcripts do not include a copy of the report.

Grew had no trouble remembering the report when Walter Johnson, a University of Chicago history professor, contacted him in November 1950 about material for book that would have a section on Japan. Johnson, apparently referencing Grew's testimony, said he planned to use "the documents prepared for Mr. Hull dealing with the months just before Pearl Harbor." In his letter to Johnson on November 23, Grew responded that he was "not sure precisely" what documents the history professor had in mind. "As I have told you," Grew continued, "I gave Mr. Hull a promise that I would destroy the dispatch which I had intended to hand him on my return from Japan, and all copies thereof, adversely criticizing the Administration for its failure to allow the meeting between President Roosevelt and Prince Konoye." Grew assured Johnson that he did not want "to tamper with the facts of history" but, he added, "I want to be very careful to avoid any future charge from [Hull] that I had quibbled on the word of honor which I gave him in August 1942 on returning from Japan that I would destroy that dispatch and all copies thereof."

Not that Grew was deprived of telling his story and expressing his views without restraint. In 1952, Houghton Mifflin published his two-volume, 1,560-page memoir—*Turbulent Era*—which included a 132-page section entitled "Pearl Harbor: From the Perspective of Ten Years." He had already had selected portions of his diary from the Tokyo period published in 1944 (*Ten Years in Japan*); in July 1952, he deposited his voluminous papers with the Houghton Library at Harvard; and a substantial portion of his Tokyo telegrams had been published by the State Department in a multi-volume series entitled *Foreign Relations of the United States* (which included a multitude of other telegrams and documents as well). And so, when people asked him during his retirement—as they often did—what he thought about Pearl Harbor, the former ambassador to Japan would invariably respond that "everything he has to say on the subject is in his papers...."

It was the kind of modesty that had been the hallmark of Joe Grew's career. But it could not mask the contribution he had made—and had tried to make—in protecting his country's interests during a time of unprecedented turmoil.

ACKNOWLEDGMENTS

A bout six years ago I considered doing a book about America in 1941. It was a pivotal year for the country. Franklin D. Roosevelt became the first president to be inaugurated for a third term. In June of that year Ford Motor Company signed its first contract with the United Automobile Workers, thus signaling the emerging power of labor unions. Roosevelt signed an executive order in that same month to ban racial discrimination in employment in the federal government and in defense industries – a gesture designed to remove the prospect of a march of more than 100,000 people on Washington, DC being organized by the NAACP and A. Philip Randolph's Brotherhood of Sleeping Car Porters. The New York Yankees' Joe DiMaggio hit safely in fifty-six consecutive games—a record that still stands—while the Boston Red Sox's Ted Williams hit .406, making him the last Major League player to hit over .400. And then of course, there was the Japanese attack at Pearl Harbor.

In the course of my research, I came across the name of Joseph Grew, America's ambassador to Japan. There were references to his effort in 1941 to orchestrate an agreement to avoid war with Japan. I was intrigued. The more I looked, the more I realized that there was no detailed examination of that effort in any book. Waldo Heinrichs, a young Harvard PhD, had written a biography of Grew that was published in 1966, but as good as that book was, it gave only limited space to Grew's struggles in the months before the Pearl Harbor attack. And so it soon became clear to me that there was a need to tell the full story of Grew's effort to forestall the armed conflict he saw coming.

A word should be said here about Waldo Heinrichs. I contacted him in the course of my research, and he could not have been more helpful. Although in declining health, he was always available to answer my many questions about his long-ago research and, more importantly, his interactions with Grew and other members of Grew's embassy staff. All of which attests to that oft-stated aphorism that people who write history stand on the shoulders of those who came before them.

That is certainly true of those like me who write about Pearl Harbor. There is an untold number of books and articles about the Japanese attack and the circumstances leading up to that cataclysmic event. I was indeed fortunate to be able to profit by the research, analysis, and musings of the many scholars who came before me.

Still, much of Grew's story is unique to him, and there was no better resource on that story than the former ambassador himself. Grew was incredibly disciplined and maintained a daily diary throughout almost all of his long diplomatic career. His voluminous papers—which include not only his diary but also an abundance of letters, telegrams, and other material—are housed at Harvard's Houghton Library. They provide an almost daily picture of Grew's experiences and thoughts in the months before the Pearl Harbor attack, and they were invaluable in writing this book.

Grew's papers are complemented by the diaries and memoirs penned by many of the other people with whom Grew interacted in those months before the Pearl Harbor attack. In some cases those diaries and memoirs were published as books (and are identified in the Bibliography); in other cases they are housed in libraries around the country. Those libraries also include interviews, memos, and other material generated or collected by participants as well as authors, and I have been able to harvest that material as well in writing the book.

I could not have done this alone. The archivists and librarians who assisted me are many and include David Olson at the Columbia Center for Oral History in New York City; Michelle Frauenberger, Virginia Lewick, and especially Matthew Hanson at the Franklin D. Roosevelt Library in Hyde Park, New York; Jim Armistad at the Harry S. Truman Library and Museum in Independence, Missouri; Mary Haegert, Abraham Moffat, Alessandra Seiter, and Emily Walhout at the Houghton Library in Cambridge, Massachusetts; Jason G. Speck and Anne Turkos at the Hornbake Library at the University of Maryland in College Park, Maryland; Christa Cleeton at the Seeley G. Mudd Manuscript Library at Princeton University in Princeton, New Jersey; Amy Reytar at the National Archives and Records Administration in College Park, Maryland; Eric Mills at the US Naval Institute in Annapolis, Maryland; and Genevieve Coyle at the Yale University Library in New Haven, Connecticut.

Special thanks also go to Tiffany Cabrera in the Public Affairs Office of the State Department in Washington, DC, and to Carolann Adams at the

Collier County Library in Naples, Florida, each of whom was prompt in providing books and other materials that were not readily accessible. Jenny Fichman provided valuable research assistance at the Hoover Institution at Stanford University in Stanford, California, and John Ulrich with Harvard Student Agencies Research in Cambridge, Massachusetts was extremely helpful in ferreting out documents at the Houghton Library.

One goal in writing the book was to bring Grew alive to readers who may not have heard of him and certainly never met him. In pursuit of that goal I benefitted greatly not only from my discussions with Waldo Heinrichs but also from the time and assistance of many members of Grew's extended family. Peter Moffat and Lilla Cabot Lyon—two of Grew's grandchildren—were especially helpful, responding to my multiple visits, calls, and emails with insight, documents, and books (including a book by the daughter of Ned Crocker, the Embassy's First Secretary, that was privately published). Rob English, a great grandson, not only provided useful background on family history but also supplied me with an abundance of photos located in the family home in Hancock, New Hampshire. Jane Moffat, a cousin who spent considerable time with the family at the Hancock compound and in Washington, DC, was equally responsive with stories, articles, and photos. Some of Grew's other great grandchildren—Lilla Cabot Spenser, Jay Spenser, and Jon Spenser—were also helpful in answering my many questions about their great grandparents.

Family members of Grew's embassy staff made contributions that were equally valuable. Those family members offered memories, documents, and photos that helped bring the staff to life. They include Russ Dooman, Eugene Dooman's grandson; Barbara Fearey West and Seth Fearey, the children of Robert Fearey; Ted Green, the son of Marshall Green and Lipsenard Crocker (Ned Crocker's daughter); and Cynthia Smith-Hutton Bowers, Henri Smith-Hutton's daughter.

Pulling together all the strands of Grew's experience in Japan was challenging, and I sought comment from numerous people to assess the product of my labors. Mark Gitenstein, Doug Katz, Pete Koenig, Charley Phelps, and Ira Shapiro reviewed the entire manuscript with care and provided many useful observations and suggestions. I was also fortunate to receive feedback from Robbyn Swan, Professor Sidney Pash, and Professor Noriko Kawamura, each of whom has done extensive research into the people and events covered by the book (although I alone am responsible for any errors or omissions in the book).

Thanks too to Orlando Ferrer and Johann Saurbier, who helped translate Spanish-language news articles by and about Ricardo Rivera Schreiber.

Words are inadequate to express my appreciation to Rob Wilson, my literary agent. He had faith in the project from the beginning, made many useful suggestions in framing the proposal, engineered the contract with Regnery History, and then reviewed the entire manuscript with the same attention to detail he showed at the beginning of the project. None of this would have been possible without him.

The people at Regnery History have made the publishing experience both productive and enjoyable. Alex Novak, the Associate Publisher, was not only prompt in responding to my inquiries; he also made considerable efforts to accommodate requests both large and small. Anne Mulrooney made many edits that improved the book immeasurably. And other members of the Regnery team—including Margaret Vander Woude, Nicole Yeatman, and Kylie Frey—were equally helpful in editing, marketing and publicity.

As with my prior books, my wife Jan proved to be an invaluable partner. She was always available for endless discussions on points minor and significant, was there to review the manuscript as it was written (sometimes reading individual chapters more than once as they were revised), and offered insight and advice on the many issues that arose in the course of the research and writing. Her name may not be on the cover, but her imprint is suffused throughout these pages.

NOTES

The following acronyms and terms are used to denote sources:

ADST	Association for Diplomatic Studies and Training, Foreign Service Institute, Arlington, Virginia
Bullitt Papers	Papers of William C. Bullitt, Sterling Memorial Library, Yale University, New Haven, Connecticut
CCOH	Columbia Center for Oral History, Columbia University, New York, New York
Dooman Papers	Papers of Eugene H. Dooman, Hoover Institution, Stanford University, Stanford, California
Fearey Papers	Papers of Robert A. Fearey, Hoover Institution, Stanford University, Stanford, California
FRUS	*Foreign Relations of the United States*, United States Department of State, Washington, DC
Gellman Papers	Papers of Irving Gellman, Franklin D. Roosevelt Library, Hyde Park, New York
Grew Diary	Diary of Joseph C. Grew, Houghton Library, Harvard University, Cambridge, Massachusetts
Grew Papers	Papers of Joseph C. Grew (other than Diary), Houghton Library, Harvard University, Cambridge, Massachusetts
Hornbeck Papers	Papers of Stanley K. Hornbeck, Hoover Institution, Stanford University, Stanford, California
Hull Papers	Papers of Cordell Hull, Library of Congress, Washington, DC
Krock Papers	Papers of Arthur Krock, Seeley G. Mudd Manuscript Library, Princeton University, Princeton, New Jersey
Moffat Papers	Papers of Jay Pierrepont Moffat, Houghton Library, Harvard University, Cambridge, Massachusetts
Morgenthau Diaries	Diaries of Henry Morgenthau, Jr., Franklin D. Roosevelt Library, Hyde Park, New York
Morgenthau Presidential Diaries	Presidential Diaries of Henry Morgenthau, Jr., Franklin D. Roosevelt Library, Hyde Park, New York

Peter Moffat Papers	Papers of Jay Pierrepont Moffat, Jr., Washington, DC
PHA	Hearings before the Joint Committee on the Investigation of the Pearl Harbor Attack, 79th Congress, Ist Session (GPO 1945)
Prange Papers	Papers of Gordon Prange, University of Maryland, College Park, Maryland
Roosevelt Papers	Papers of Franklin D. Roosevelt, Franklin D. Roosevelt Library, Hyde Park, New York
Schuler Papers	Papers of Frank A. Schuler, Jr., Franklin D. Roosevelt Library, Hyde Park, New York
Stimson Diary	Diary of Henry L. Stimson, Sterling Memorial Library, Yale University, New Haven, Connecticut
Toland Papers	Papers of John Toland, Franklin D. Roosevelt Library, Hyde Park, New York
USNI	United States Naval Institute, Annapolis, Maryland
Wickard Diary	Diary of Claude R. Wickard, Franklin D. Roosevelt Library, Hyde Park, New York

The Notes also reference or otherwise rely on interviews conducted with Waldo Heinrichs and the following members of the families of Joseph C. Grew, Eugene H. Dooman, Robert A. Fearey, Marshall Green and Edward Crocker, and Henri Smith-Hutton: Cynthia Smith-Hutton Bowers, Lilla Cabot, Russell Dooman, Robert English, Seth Fearey, Edward C. Green, Lilla Cabot Lyon, Jane K. Moffat, Peter Moffat, Jay Spenser, Jon Spenser, and Barbara Fearey West.

A word should be said about the resources used in the writing of the book. Principal reliance was placed on diaries, letters, memoirs, interviews, testimony, and other primary source material. Despite that reliance, there were occasional conflicts or inconsistencies, even when individuals participated in the same meeting or conversation. In some other instances there were conflicts or inconsistencies between my findings and comments in other books. In all those situations, I tried to reconcile the conflict or inconsistency. In cases where reconciliation was not possible, the notes include a statement to that effect.

The Select Bibliography following the Notes identifies the books most frequently used. The Notes identify additional books as well as periodicals, websites, and other resources utilized in the writing process.

Weather information for Washington, DC was secured from the National Climatic Data Center.

Chapter 1: Anticipation

Page

1   "The high ceilings"—The description of the Oval Study is based on photos and comments from an archivist with the Franklin D. Roosevelt Library. Emails from Michelle Frauenberger (May 24 & May 25, 2017). At one point there was a tiger skin on the floor, but a photo taken in September 1940 (and used in the Franklin D. Roosevelt Library's "Day of Infamy" exhibit in 2016) shows a lion skin. The archivist at the library assumed the lion skin was there on DDecember 7, 1941. Email from Michelle Frauenberger (May 26, 2017). In her   memoir, White House housekeeper Henrietta Nesbitt says that she had stored the lion skin in the basement of the Garfinkel department store and that sometime after December 7, 1941 the President had asked for its return because he wanted it in the office when Winston Churchill arrived for a visit on December 22, 1941. *White House Diary* (1948), pp. 269-70. Nesbitt does not say whether she placed the lion skin in Garfinkel's before or after December 7, 1941. In light of the comments from the archivist and the exhibit at the Franklin D. Roosevelt Library, I have assumed that the lion skin was there on December 7, 1941.

"struck down by polio"—a 2003 article suggested that the cause of Roosevelt's paralysis might have been Guillain-Barre syndrome rather than poliomyelitis. *See* https://www.ncbi.nlm.nih.gov/pubmed/14562158.

2   "amiable, sweet disposition"—Max Hall, "A Hero to His Valet: McDuffie's Twelve Years with Roosevelt," *Emory University Quarterly* (October 1947), pp. 154, 155.

"lady killer"—www.americanheritage1.com/presidents/franklin-d-roosevelt.htm (May 6, 2014), p.4.

"didn't talk"—Barbara Gamarekian, "Reunion Echoes Bygone Years at White House," *N.Y. Times* (June 25, 1983), p. 5.

3   "This means"—PHA, Part 10, p. 4662.

"even the madness"—Ross T. McIntire, *White House Physician* (1946), p. 136.

"more acute"—"New Troop Moves," *N.Y. Times* (December 7, 1941), p. 1.

4   "work out"—Robert E. Sherwood, *Roosevelt and Hopkins* (Enigma Books ed. 2008), p. 42.

"[S]omeday" –*Id.*, p. 4.

5   "it is impossible"—*FRUS, Japan, 1931-1941, Vol II*, p. 792.

"It looks like"—PHA, Part 11, p. 5283.

"While he laid flat on his back"—*See* "Simple Acts of Strength and Courage," (January 15, 2012), www. lenbrzozowski.wordpress.com. Roosevelt did not like wearing the braces. *See* "Report of President Roosevelt," *N.Y. Times* (March 2, 1945), p. 12 (Roosevelt making a report to Congress on the Yalta Conference while sitting down, explaining that it was "a lot easier" if he did not have "to carry about ten pounds of steel around on the bottom of my legs"). Consequently, it is doubtful that Prettyman would have placed braces on Roosevelt's legs unless his schedule required him to go somewhere where he might have to stand up.

6   "nasty"—Herbert Feis, *The Road to Pearl Harbor* (Atheneum ed., 1965), p. 340.

7-8   "There is no need"—Interview with Mitsuo Fuchida (Prange Papers), p. I.2.

8   "All of"—*Id.*, p. I.8.

"Your nature"—Douglas T. Shinsato & Tadanori Urabe (Translators), *For That One Day: The Memoirs of Mitsuo Fuchida Commander of the Attack on Pearl Harbor* (2011) (hereafter *One Day*), p. 24.

8-9   "not to volunteer"—*Id.*, pp. 31, 33.

9   "What I"—*Id.*, p. 27.

"hostile riots"—Interview with Ambassador Jay Pierrepont Moffat (ADST), p. 41. Moffat references the "American Legation," which had been elevated to an embassy shortly after the signing of the Treaty of Portsmouth. For ease of understanding, reference is made here to the American embassy.

10   "The Japanese people"—*The Reminiscences of Capt. Henri Smith-Hutton, USN (Ret.), Vol. I* (1976) (hereafter *Smith-Hutton Reminiscences*), p. 71.

"cast a dark shadow"—Grew letter to Japanese friend (September 1, 1941), attached to Grew letter to Count Michimasa Soyeshima (September 4, 1941) (Grew Papers).

"the yellow and brown races"—United States Senate, Hearings on S.2576, Japanese Immigration Legislation, 68th Cong., lst Sess.

(1924). *See* Masayo Umezawa Duus, *The Japanese Conspiracy: The Oahu Sugar Strike of 1920* (1999), p. 303.

11   "decide the fate"—Quoted in Gordon W. Prange, *At Dawn We Slept* (1981), p. 16.

"so difficult"—Quoted in *id.*, p. 19.

"He had"—Quoted in *id.*, p. 13.

"Genda was"—Quoted in *id.*, p. 22.

12   "The plan"—Quoted in *id.*, p. 20.

"The fact is"—*One Day*, p. 61.

"Glorious dawn"—*Id.*, p. 89.

13   "one of the finest" and "Hoover's folly"—"Japan: Tokyo Team," *Time* (November 12, 1934); John K. Emmerson, *The Japanese Thread: A Life in the U.S. Foreign Service* (1978) (hereafter *The Japanese Thread*), p. 27.

14   "reporting"—Joseph C. Grew, *Turbulent Era: A Diplomatic Record of Forty Years 1904-1945* (1952) (hereafter *Turbulent Era*), Vol. II, p. 1273.

"It was especially"—*See* Waldo H. Heinrichs, Jr., *American Ambassador: Joseph C. Grew and the Development of the United States Diplomatic Tradition* (1966) (hereafter *American Ambassador*), p. 341.

15   "pull their"—Max Hill, *Exchange Ship* (1942), p. 123.

"Many a Japanese"—Joseph C. Grew, *Report from Tokyo* (1942), p. 32.

"Nobody can"—PHA, Part 2, p. 717.

"was almost"—*Turbulent Era*, Vol. II, p. 1334.

"there was a certain irony"—*See* Sidney Pash, *The Currents of War: A New History of American-Japanese Relations, 1899-1941* (2014) (hereafter *The Currents of War*), p. 144 (in the four-year period between the China Incident and the American freeze on Japanese assets in July 1941, neither Hull nor Stanley K. Hornbeck, his principal adviser, "saw any need to conclude a bargain with what both believed was an inherently untrustworthy Japan").

Chapter 2: The Diplomat

18   "forty-odd villagers"—J.C. Grew, *Sport and Travel in the Far East* (1910) (hereafter *Sport and Travel*), pp. 123, 125.

"smoothly"—Grew Diary (October 24, 1941), p. 5869.

18-19   "freely predicting"—Address by Joseph C. Grew, "Faith and the Church" (National Cathedral Association) (Aug. 15, 1948). Although Grew does not expressly identify the boy in the speech, it is clear that he is speaking of himself. Email from Jane K. Moffat (July 11, 2014).

19   "devotion"—Letter from Joseph C. Grew to The Reverend John Crocker (March 3, 1941), Appendix 1, Robert A. Fearey, "My Year with Ambassador Joseph C. Grew" (1991) (hereafter "Fearey"), Box 6, Folder 6, Fearey Papers (reprinted in 1 Journal of American-East Asian Relations 99 (1992)).

"Mr. John Harvard"—J. Pipkin and C. Lewis (eds.), The Metropolitan Club of Washington: The First 150 Years (2012), p. 71.

19-20   "very large" and "He lay"—Sport and Travel, pp. 241, 243.

20   "wanderlust"—Letter to Mrs. Waller (November 19, 1931) (Grew Papers).

"crazy"—Interview with Elizabeth Sturgis Grew Lyon (ADST April 17, 1987) (hereafter "Elizabeth Lyon Interview"), p. 7.

"especially his left ear"—Email from Rob English (March 12, 2019); Elizabeth Lyon Interview, p. 4 ("one ear was absolutely deaf"); "Joe Grew, Ambassador to Japan," Life Magazine (July 15, 1940), p. 82

21   "stuffed dolls"—Alfred L.P. Dennis, "The Foreign Service of the United States," North American Review (Feb. 1924), p. 178.

"I never had"—T.R. Roosevelt to G.O. Trevelyan (Oct. 1, 1911), Elting E. Morison, et al., Letters of Theodore Roosevelt, Vol. VII (1954), p. 392.

"I cannot imagine"—Sport and Travel, Foreword.

"You young men"—"Joseph C. Grew," N.Y. Times (May 27, 1965), p. 37.

21-22   "their marvelous"—Quoted in American Ambassador, p. 21.

22   "the dreadfulness"—Turbulent Era, Vol. I, p. 190.

"the most discouraging"—House Diary, December 14, 16, 1918 (Papers of Colonel Edward House, Yale University) (hereafter "House Papers). See American Ambassador, pp. 36, 38.

"gentleman"—quoted in American Ambassador., p. 41.

23   "got right down"—Letter to Ellis Dresel (January 1, 1921) (Grew Papers).

"I am rather"—*Turbulent Era, Vol. I*, p. 608.

"informally"—*Id.*, p. 615.

"not only"—Letter from Hughes to Kellogg (January 23, 1925) (Papers of Charles Evans Hughes, Library of Congress).

24   "like a petulant child"—*Turbulent Era, Vol. I*, p. 704.

"returns"—"Diplomatic Promotions," *N.Y. Times* (May 20, 1927), p. 18.

"[o]ne of the"—"Footnotes on a Week's Headliners," *N.Y. Times* (January 24, 1932), p. 2.

"unusually"—*Turbulent Era, Vol. II*, p. 910.

25   "won or lost"—*Smith-Hutton Reminiscences*, p. 347.

"John Pierpont Morgan's"—*Time* (August 15, 1928). *See American Ambassador*, p. 155.

"the opportunity"—*Turbulent Era, Vol. II*, p. 910.

27   "recognize"—*FRUS, Japan, 1931-1941, Vol. I*, p. 76. There is some debate on whether the Nine Power Treaty did or did not recognize Japan's special interest in Manchuria. *See The Currents of War*, pp. 55-56. The State Department's Office of the Historian says that the "treaty recognized Japanese dominance in Manchuria but otherwise affirmed the importance of equal opportunity for all nations doing business in the country." The Washington Naval Conference 1921-22, Office of the Historian, history.state.gov.

"He has"—Lispenard Green, *A Foreign Service Marriage* (1985) (hereafter *A Foreign Service Marriage*), p. 412.

"his eyes"—Interview with Cynthia Smith-Hutton Bowers (May 18, 2017).

28   "Joe hasn't"—Gordon Auchincloss Diary (Nov. 14, 23, 1918) (House Papers).

"That was"—Interview with Waldo H. Heinrichs, Jr. (February 25, 2017).

"steadily"—Joseph C. Grew, *Ten Years in Japan: A Contemporary Record Drawn from the Diaries and Private and Official Papers of Joseph C. Grew* (1944) (hereafter *Ten Years*), p. 295.

"To threaten"—*Id.*, p. 296.

"What I shall say"—*Id.*, p. 289.

"[T]his was"—*Smith-Hutton Reminiscences*, p. 273.

29   "All he wants"—Interview with Jane K. Moffat (October 24, 2016).

Chapter 3: Alice

31   "lovely creature" and "I didn't intend"—Grew Diary (January 4, 1929), p. 915.

33   "[W]e are so"—Grew letter to Lilla Grew Moffat (September 3, 1941) (Grew Papers).

34   "really recovered"—Interview with Jane K. Moffat (October 24, 2016).

"I am so built"—Grew letter to Elsie Grew Lyon (September 3, 1941) (Grew Papers).

"Whom are you"—Interview with Ambassador Marshall Green (ADST December 13, 1998) (hereafter "Green Interview"), p. 6.

35   "a splendid type"—Grew Diary (April 29, 1941), p. 5004.

"Grew is"—Letter from James W. Gerard to Edward M. House (May 10, 1916)(House Papers).

"[O]ne of the things"—Grew letter to William R. Castle (April 22, 1941) (Grew Papers).

"She knew how"—Interview with Jon Spenser (June 3, 2014).

"a formidable"—*Feary*, p. 6.

"utterly nasty"—Grew Diary, (May 14, 1941), p. 5149.

"Isn't it unfortunate"—*Fearey*, p. 6.

36   "Ach"—Helen Essary, "Dear Washington," *Evening Independent Newspaper* (June 21, 1944).

"She was"—Interview with Peter Moffat (September 12, 2016).

"ferocious"—*A Foreign Service Marriage*, p. 362.

"She wasn't"—Interview with Cynthia Smith-Hutton Bowers (May 18, 2017).

37   "[A]fter recovering"—*Fearey*, p. 18.

Chapter 4: Japan

40   "knowing"—Hugh Byas, *Government Assassination* (1942), p. 25.

"No use"—*Id.*

"The Japanese" and "his attention"—*Smith-Hutton Reminiscences*, p. 145; Sir Robert Craigie, *Behind the Japanese Mask* (1945), p. 30.

41   "There must be"—*Ten Years*, p. 4.

        "ugliness"—*Id.*, p. 7.

42   "wanted them"—*Id.*, p. 12.

        "be personally"—*Fearey*, Appendix 1.

        "had an infinite"—Green Interview, p. 9.

        "generally"—*Ten Years*, p. 81.

        "promoted"—Reminiscences of Eugene Hoffman Dooman (CCOH May 1962) (hereafter "Dooman Reminiscences"), p. 60.

43   "Japanese is"—*Smith-Hutton Reminiscences*, pp. 59-60.

        "It was"—*See* John Toland, *Infamy: Pearl Harbor and Its Aftermath* (1982), pp. 275-76; Hilary Conroy & Harry Wray, *Pearl Harbor Reexamined: Prologue to the Pacific War* (1990) (hereafter *Pearl Harbor Reexamined*), pp. 92-93. *But see* Robert J.C. Butow, *Tojo and the Coming of the War* (1961), p. 335.

        "feared that"—*The Japanese Thread*, p. 28.

44   "a reasonable sense"—Grew letter to Anita Grew English (June 12, 1941) (Grew Papers).

        "Why, Mr. Ambassador"—*Ten Years*, p. 373.

45   "that evening"—Grew Diary, Entertainment (October 26, 1941), p. 5870.

45-46   "was the most"—*A Foreign Service Marriage*, p. 366.

46   "a condition exemplified"—Noriko Kawamura, *Emperor Hirohito and the Pacific War* (2015), p. 27.

        "like a bird"—Quoted in Herbert P. Bix, *Hirohito and the Making of Modern Japan* (Perennial ed. 2000), p. 117.

47   "His Majesty"—Quoted in Eri Hotta, *Japan 1941* (2013) (hereafter *1941*), p. 93.

        "[T]o die"—Otto Tolischus, *Tokyo Record* (1943) p. 216.

        "that man"—*Report from Tokyo*, p. 28.

48   "What the ordinary"—Dooman Reminiscences, p. 58.

49   "two-headed"—*Id.*, p. 42.

"reign"—Quoted in John Toland, *The Rising Sun: The Rise and Fall of the Japanese Empire 1936-1945* (1970) (hereafter *The Rising Sun*), p. 24.

"even if"—quoted in *Emperor Hirohito and the Pacific War*, p. 35.

50   "Their traditional"—*Ten Years*, p. 207.

"the streets"—*Fearey*, p. 18.

51   "will not crack"—*Report from Tokyo*, p. 28.

"Mrs. Grew"—Interview with Cecil B. Lyon (ADST October 26, 1988) (hereafter "Lyon Interview"), p. 14.

"This is certainly"—*Id.*

52   "struggling"—*Ten Years*, p. 112.

"How is"—Lyon Interview, p. 14.

"Groton, Harvard"—Grew letter to Roosevelt (November 12, 1932) (Grew Papers); *Ten Years*, p. 55.

53   "This situation"—Grew letter to Henry L. Stimson (August 13, 1932) (Grew Papers). *See* PHA, Part 2, p. 564.

"two-faced"—Quoted in Peter Alexander Adams, "Eugene H. Dooman: 'A Penny a Dozen Expert' (University of Maryland Master Thesis 1976) (hereafter "Eugene H. Dooman"), p. 86.

54   "that we"—Dooman Reminiscences, p. 64.

"a courteous"—Unpublished autobiography (hereafter "Hornbeck Autobiography"), Box 497 (Hornbeck Papers), p. 47 (not all pages are numbered on document and so page numbers have been inserted).

"a bright-eyed"—*Id.*, p. 48.

"talked most"—*Id.*

55   "a very unpleasant"—Dooman Reminiscences, p. 108. Dooman was not alone   in expressing those views. Breckinridge Long, a Roosevelt friend who was a Special Assistant to Hull in 1939 and then an Assistant Secretary of State as of 1940, advised Hull to disregard Hornbeck's comments because they were shaped by a deep-seated hatred for Japan. *See* Kenneth G. McCarty, Jr., "Stanley K. Hornbeck and the Far East, 1931-1941" (Duke University Dissertation 1970) (hereafter "Stanley K. Hornbeck"), pp. 227-28; Fred Israel (ed.), *The War Diary of Breckinridge Long: Selections from the Years*

1939-1944 (1966) (hereafter *The War Diary of Breckinridge Long*), p. 139. For his part, Hornbeck rejected any notion that he had any bias in favor of China or against Japan. "[I]f...I advocate action by the United States which happens to be 'in support of' China and 'in opposition to' Japan," he told Hull at one point, "....et not my friends and associates injure me and impair my influence by affirming me to be 'pro' or 'anti' anything—except 'pro' the United States." Memorandum by the Political Relations Adviser (June 8, 1940), Hornbeck Papers, quoted in "Stanley K. Hornbeck," p. 228.

"very dictatorial"—Interview with Eugene Dooman, Box 3 (Toland Papers).

"in regard to"—Interview with Max W. Bishop (hereafter "Bishop Interview"), *id.*, p. 9.

"For an officer"—*The Japanese Thread*, p. 104.

"I never"—Reminiscences of Joseph Ballantine, (CCOH April 28, 1961) (hereafter "Ballantine Reminiscences"), p. 38.

Chapter 5: Turmoil

57   "it was full"—*Ten Years*, p. 175.

58   "had loved"—*Id.*, p. 171.

        "national glory"—Quoted in *Government Assassination*, pp. 123-24.

58-59   "as the head"—Quoted in *Id.*, p. 272.

59   "an impulse"—Quoted in *Id.*, p. 95.

        "I assassinated"—Quoted in *Id.*, p. 115.

        "outside influences"—Quoted in *Id.*, p. 106.

60   "You shall not"—Quoted in *Id.*, p. 121.

        "because the woman"—Quoted in *Tojo and the Coming of the War*, p. 66.

        "looked peaceful"—*Ten Years*, p. 171.

60-61   "to the military"—Wilfrid Fleisher, *Volcanic Isle* (1942), p. 95. See *Ten Years*, p. 174; email from Rob English (July 5, 2017).

61   "[N]ever have I"—Quoted in *Emperor Hirohito and the Pacific War*, p. 64.

"I will give you"—Quoted in Richard Storry, *The Double Patriots: A Study of Japanese Nationalism* (1957), pp. 187-88.

"the city"—*Government Assassination*, p. 125.

"The Emperor himself"—Quoted in *Tojo and the Coming of the War*, p. 68.

62   "military are too"—*Ten Years*, p. 207.

63   "[S]warthy"—*The Japanese Thread*, p. 96.

"He was"—*Smith-Hutton Reminiscences*, p. 288.

"that the clarity"—*The Japanese Thread*, p. 97.

"I try"—Grew letter to Lilla Grew Moffat (October 21, 1941) (Grew Papers).

"to be remembered"—Grew Diary, Entertainment (October 1941), p. 5866.

"came from"—Dooman Reminiscences, p. 6.

64   "I made up"—Letter from Eugene H. Dooman to Herbert Feis (July 8, 1949), Box 1, Folder 2 (Dooman Papers).

"extremely severe"—Dooman Reminiscences, p. 3.

"entirely favorable"—Grew letter to Stanley K. Hornbeck (June 22, 1936) (Grew Papers).

"magnificent presence"—Interview with Eugene H. Dooman, pp. 463-1 and 463-6 (Toland Papers).

"You and I"—Grew letter to Eugene H. Dooman (February 9, 1937) (Grew Papers).

65   "Another"—Grew letter to Elizabeth Grew Lyon (September 3, 1941) (Grew Papers).

"I've changed"—Interview with Eugene H. Dooman, p. 463-6 (Toland Papers).

65-66   "The present hostilities"—Ambassador in Japan to Secretary of State (August 27, 1937), *FRUS, The Far East, 1937, Vol. III*, pp. 485-88.

66   "will be guided"—Secretary of State to Ambassador in Japan (September 2, 1937), *id.*, p. 507.

"two points"—Cordell Hull, *Memoirs* (1948) (hereafter "*Hull Memoirs*"), *Vol. I*, p. 270.

"The unfortunate fact"—Dooman Reminiscences, p. 48.

67 "I saw"—*Tokyo Record*, pp. 203, 206.

68 "reign of terror" and "an epidemic of world lawlessness"—*Public Papers and Addresses of Franklin D. Roosevelt, Vol. 1937* (1941), pp. 406-11.

"The Old Man"—Quoted in *The Japanese Thread*, pp. 77-78.

"This was"—Grew Diary (October 7, 1937), pp. 3485-87.

"delighted"—Nancy Harvison Hooker, *The Moffat Papers* (1956), p. 153. Jay Pierrepont Moffat acknowledged that Hull's delight with the speech was "short-lived." In his *Memoirs*, Hull never referenced his initial delight at the speech—only that it "had the effect of setting back for at least six months our constant educational campaign intended to create and strengthen public opinion toward international cooperation." *Memoirs, Vol. I*, p. 545. For their part, William L. Langer and S. Everett Gleason say only that Hull was "shocked beyond words" by the President's reference to a quarantine. *The Challenge of Isolation 1937-1940* (1952) (hereafter *The Challenge to Isolation*), p. 19.

"outlaw"—Quoted in"Eugene H. Dooman," p. 51.

"It's a terrible thing"—Samuel I. Rosenman, *Working with Roosevelt* (1952), p. 167.

69 "the President" and "I am waiting"—Morgenthau Diaries (May 14, 1941), Vol. 397, p. 301-B; Morgenthau Presidential Diaries (May 17, 1941), Vol. 4, p. 929. *See* William S. Langer and S. Everett Gleason, *The Undeclared War, 1940-1941* (1953) (hereafter *Undeclared War*), p. 456.

"Your boys"—*E.g.* New York Times (October 31, 1940), p. 14. On many occasions, Roosevelt added "except in case of attack." In the speech in Boston on October 31, however, the President did not add that qualification. "It's not necessary," he told speechwriter Sam Rosenman. "It's implied clearly. If we're attacked, it's no longer a foreign war." *Working with Roosevelt*, p. 242.

"a black day"—*Ten Years*, p. 232.

"an unprecedented"—*Id.*, p. 233.

70 "really incredible"—*Id.*, p. 235.

"a new Far East"—"Radio Speech by the Japanese Prime Minister (Prince Konoye)" (November 3, 1938), *FRUS, Japan, 1931-1941, Vol. I*, pp. 478-81. The new policy was later identified as the "New Order." *See* Kenneth Colegrove, "The New Order in East Asia," 1

The Far Eastern Quarterly (Nov. 1941), p. 5. William L. Langer and S. Everett Gleason cite that radio address as the basis for Konoye's establishment of "a Greater East Asia Co-Prosperity Sphere based on a league of Japan, Manchukuo and China...." *The Challenge to Isolation*, p. 42. However, Konoye did not reference a "Greater East Asia Co-Prosperity Sphere" in that radio address. The term later evolved from a radio address by Foreign Minister Arita Hachiro on June 29, 1940. *See The Challenge to Isolation*, p. 603 (on June 29, 1940, "Foreign Minister Arita openly espoused the idea of a Greater East Asia Co-Prosperity Sphere"); Hugh Byas, "Japan Demands Vast Sphere," *N.Y. Times* (June 30, 1940), p. 1; Kazuo Yagami, *Konoe Fumimaro and the Failure of Peace in Japan 1937-1941* (2006) (hereafter *Konoe Fumimaro and the Failure of Peace in Japan*), p. 68 ("on November 3, [1938],...Konoe made an official statement called *Establishment of New Order for the Far East*"); *Tokyo Record*, p. 22 (a February 1941 issue of a Japanese periodical stated, "The new situation created in Europe by German military successes made it imperative for Japan to establish the Greater East Asia Sphere of Common Prosperity by enlarging her program for the construction of a New Order in East Asia").

"a comprehensive"—Memorandum of Adviser on Political Relations (December 22, 1938), *FRUS, The Far East, 1938, Vol. III*, pp. 425-27.

70-71   "I know"—*Ten Years*, p. 272.

71   "strongly opposed"—Letter from the Chief of the Office of Arms and Munitions Control (July 1, 1938), *FRUS, Japan 1931-1941, Vol. II*, p. 201.

"And in July 1940"—*See* "President's Proclamation on Control of Exports," *N.Y. Times* (July 3, 1940), p. 11.

"be free"—quoted in W.H.M., "Economic Warfare with Japan or a New Treaty," *Foreign Affairs* (January 1940).

72   "good relations"—Ambassador in Japan to Secretary of State (December 1, 1939), *FRUS, The Far East, 1939, Vol. III*, p. 605.

"Japan is"—*Id.*, pp. 606-07.

"complete intransigence"—*Id.*, p. 612.

73   "put the screws"—quoted in *Pearl Harbor Reexamined*, p. 38.

"We should not"—Personal Notes, Grew Diary (November 1939) (Hornbeck Papers). *See The Japanese Thread*, pp. 83-84.

"We obviously"—*Hull Memoirs, Vol. I*, pp. 725-26.

"The simple fact"—Ambassador in Japan to Secretary of State (December 18, 1939), *FRUS, The Far East, 1939, Vol. III*, pp. 620-22.

73-74   "The German military"—*Ten Years*, p. 325.

74   "substantially"—Memorandum of Adviser on Political Relations (May 11, 1939), *FRUS, The Far East, 1939, Vol. III*, p. 37.

"would force"—quoted in *The Rising Sun*, p. 63.

75   "You must"—Quoted in *id. See Konoe Fumimaro and the Failure of Peace in Japan*, p. 95 (which has slightly different wording of Hirohito's statement to Konoye). *See also Hirohito and the Making of Modern Japan*, p. 381 (Hirohito telling the Lord Keeper of the Privy Seal on September 15, 1940, "When matters come this far Konoe should really share the joy and suffering with me").

"a well substantiated story"—*Behind the Japanese Mask*, p. 109.

"New Order"—*See Turbulent Era, Vol. II*, pp. 1221-23; sources cited on page 85 for "a new Far East."

75-76   "[T]he time"—Ambassador in Japan to Secretary of State (September 12, 1940), *FRUS, The Far East, 1940, Vol. IV*, p. 603. *See Turbulent Era, Vol. II*, pp. 1223-29.

76   "My thought"—PHA, Part 2, p. 640.

"When you"—*Id.*, p. 619.

"After eight years"—*Ten Years*, pp. 359-61.

77   "absurd"—Quoted in R.J.C. Butow, *The John Doe Associates: Backdoor Diplomacy for Peace 1941* (1974) (hereafter *The John Doe Associates*), pp. 94-96.

"This is"—Grew Diary (November, 1940), p. 4659.

"what counts"—Introductory Address at the Luncheon of the American-Japan Society (December 19, 1940), MS AM 1687(101) (Grew Papers). *See* Remarks by Ambassador in Japan (December 19, 1940), *FRUS, Japan, 1931-1941, Vol. II*, pp. 129-30.

77-78   "forthright"—Quoted in *The John Doe Associates*, pp. 99-102.

78   "I find myself"—*Ten Years*, pp. 361-63.

"confidential"—Grew Letter to Stanley K. Hornbeck (February 25, 1941), Box 188 (Hornbeck Papers).

"Dear Frank"—Quoted in Dooman Reminiscences, p. 64.

"possessed"—Grew Diary (January 23, 1941), p. 4736.

"a long harangue"—Quoted in *The John Doe Associates*, p. 128.

Chapter 6: The First Warning

81   "Felipe Akakawa"—It is not clear from Schreiber's post-war state-
ments whether the interpreter was an employee of the Peruvian
Embassy or perhaps a member of the Foreign Office on loan to the
Peruvian embassy. *See* "Peruvian Ambassador's Account of Pearl
Harbor Rumor," *El Comercio* (February 5, 1949) (hereafter "*El
Comercio* Article"); interview with Mrs. Teresa Kroll de Rivera
Schreiber (July 2, 1997), RichardSorge.com. Richard Sorge was a
Soviet spy who was arrested in Tokyo in 1941.

"Japanese squadron"—Affidavit of Teresa K. de Rivera Schreiber
(May 3, 1983) (Schuler Papers) (hereafter "Schreiber Affidavit").
Schreiber's wife explained that the affidavit was "based on a transcript of what [her] husband wrote." Schreiber himself discussed
his meeting with Grew in an interview in 1949 after he returned
from overseas diplomatic service. *See* "*El Comercio* Article. In that
interview, Schreiber refers to his chief of staff as his "valet." *See*
"The Peruvian Who Warned the United States of the Attack on
Pearl Harbor," *El Comercio* (December 7, 2016). A copy of the
translation of a portion of the *El Comercio* Article was attached to
a State Department dispatch from the American Embassy in Lima,
Peru. Dispatch No. 148, American Embassy, Lima, Peru (February
7, 1949). *See also* Interview of Mrs. Teresa Kroll de Rivera Schreiber with Giovanni Volpiin in RichardSorge.com.

82   "carried out"—Schreiber Affidavit.

"steaming"—*Id.*

"great excitement"—*El Comercio* Article.

"had already"—*Id.* The Schreiber Affidavit states that Schreiber
met with Yoshuda "about January 26" and that Schreiber met with
Grew on the same day he was visited by Yoshuda. Schreiber's son
had a more definitive recollection, saying that his father told him
that he had met with Grew on Sunday January 26. Letter from
Jorge Rivera Schreiber to Giovanni Volpi (August 1, 2005), in Rich-
ardSorge.com. It therefore appears that Rivera met with Yoshuda
on that Sunday.

83   "the Japanese people"—Grew Diary (January 7, 1941), p. 4724.

"is the public's"—"Japan Shows Anxiety on Relations with U.S.,"
N.Y. Times, (January 15, 1941), p. 1.

"With all"—*Ten Years*, p. 358.

"As for"—Grew letter to William R. Castle (January 7, 1941)
(Grew Papers).

84   "[I]t was"—*Report from Tokyo*, p. 49.

"national situation"—"Japan to Conduct Emergency Talks," *N.Y.
Times* (January 9, 1941), p. 10.

85   "The odor"—*Exchange Ship*, p. 11.

"It seemed"—*Smith-Hutton Reminiscences*, p. 269.

"Both sides"—*Tokyo Record*, pp. 6, 8.

86   "gave"—*Behind the Japanese Mask*, p. 59.

"smother"—Richard H. Mitchell, *Thought Control in Prewar
Japan* (1970) (hereafter *Thought Control*), p. 161.

"to be careful" and "to refrain"– *Tokyo Record*, pp. 121-22. Tolischus refers to   the law as the "State Secrets Defense Law," but he
is presumably referring to the National Defense Security Law. *See
Thought Control*, pp. 162, 170.

"to foreign agents"—*Tokyo Record*, p. 323.

"[O]ur Japanese contacts"—PHA, Part 2, p. 625.

"For the most part"—Green Interview, p. 13.

86-87   "These Gestapo agents"—*Behind the Japanese Mask*, p. 110.

87   "growing activity"—*Ten Years*, p. 381.

"an economical"—*Id.*, p. 327. Shigemitsu Mamoru, who served in
various diplomatic posts, including service as ambassador to the
Soviet Union and United Kingdom, called the IRAA the "Imperial
Rule Aid Association." Mamoru Shigemitsu, *Japan and Her Destiny: My Struggle for Peace* (1958) (hereafter *Japan and Her Destiny*), p. 199. This different terminology may reflect nothing more
than the challenges of translating Japanese terms into English.

"It has been"—"Secretary of State Hull's Statement," *N.Y. Times*
(January 16, 1941), p. 8.

88   "merely"—"Japanese Angered by Hull Testimony," *N.Y. Times* (January 17, 1941), p. 5.

"a new order"—"Japan Defies U.S. to Upset Her Plan," *N.Y. Times* (January 22, 1941), p. 8.

"I have worked"—Grew letter to Professor Asataro Miyamori (January 13, 1941) (Grew Papers).

"[t]he outlook"—Grew Diary (January 1941), p. 4716. *See Ten Years*, p. 369.

"a close"—PHA, Part 29, p. 2146.

"I trusted"—*Id.*, Part 2, p. 572.

88-89   "One has to"—Grew Diary (August 1, 1941), p. 5509.

89   "appeared"—Schreiber Affidavit.

"very unlikely"—PHA, Part 2, pp. 573, 626.

"whose continued"—Grew Diary (February 12, 1941), p. 4802.

90   "[W]ar"—*The Japanese Thread*, p. 95.

"jointly agree"—Schreiber Affidavit.

"strong-armed"—*Ten Years*, pp. 367-68.

"a young man"—Dooman Reminiscences, pp. 106-07

91   "over"—Bishop Interview, p. 1.

"side alcove"—Quoted in Robert B. Stinnett, *Day of Deceit: The Truth about FDR and Pearl Harbor* (1999), p. 30 (based on a letter dated September 19, 1988 from Bishop to Stinnett).

"the Japanese"—Bishop Interview, p. 1.

"did not name"—Interview with Max W. Bishop (ADST February 26, 1993), p. 9. Gordon W. Prange and John Toland stated in their respective books that Schreiber had conveyed the information about the Pearl Harbor attack to Edward S. Crocker, the First Secretary of the Embassy. *See The Rising Sun*, p. 151, and *At Dawn We Slept*, p. 31. However, neither Toland nor Prange identified the source for those representations. It does not appear that either author interviewed either Grew or Crocker. I interviewed Ted Green, Crocker's grandson (and Marshall Green's son), and he could not recall his grandfather ever saying that he had received the Pearl Harbor information from Schreiber. In a brief telephone conversation, Mr. Bishop's son told me that his father talked with his family about receiving the information from Schreiber. Toland interviewed Bishop in 1979, and the former Third Secretary said that he had received the information from Schreiber. *See* Bishop Interview. In his later book about Pearl Harbor, Toland therefore wrote that it was Bishop and not Crocker who had received the information from Schreiber. *See* John Toland, *Infamy: Pearl Harbor and Its Aftermath* (1982), p. 263.

"heard the rumor"—*Smith-Hutton Reminiscences*, p. 323.

"whispered"—*The Japanese Thread*, p. 109.

92   "My Peruvian colleague"—Ambassador in Japan to Secretary of State   (January 27, 1941), *FRUS, The Far East, 1941, Vol. IV* (1941), p. 17

"There is"—Grew Diary (January 27, 1941), p. 4740. When he published portions of the diary in 1944, Grew changed the second sentence to read as follows: "Of course I informed our Government." *Ten Years*, p. 368.

"the basis"—PHA, Part 29, p. 2145.

"was based"—*Id.*, Part 2, p. 561 (emphasis added).

93   "a subordinate"—Schreiber Affidavit. *See El Comercio* (February 5, 1949).

"should be"—"Pearl Harbor: A Tangled Web of Lies" (Schuler Papers), pp. 2-3. Schuler claims that Grew sent another telegram to the State Department on January 31, 1941 in which the American ambassador stated, "The Embassy places no credence in these rumors." *Id.* As Schuler acknowledged, there is no record of that second telegram in the *Foreign Relations of the United States* or other official records of the State Department. Nor is it referenced in Grew's papers. Even if it did exist, that second telegram would not have had any impact on subsequent events. As discussed below, the Army and Navy intelligence offices discounted any credence in the telegram of January 27 without any reference to that second telegram.

94   "The Japanese"—87 *Congressional Record, Part 2* (February 19, 1941), p. 1198. *See At Dawn We Slept*, p. 36.

"I thought"—PHA, Part 24, p. 1363.

"insane"—"Memorandum by Stanley K. Hornbeck (January 12, 1940), Hornbeck Papers. *See The Japanese Thread*, p. 117.

"keep all the time"—Memorandum of the Political Relations Adviser (January 28, 1941), p. 4, State Department File 894.00/1008. *See* Chihiro Hosoya, "Miscalculations in Deterrent

Policy: Japanese-U.S. Relations, 1938-1941," 5 *Journal of Peace Research* 99, 111 (1968); *The Undeclared War*, p. 322.

"[T]hat those"—Memorandum by Adviser on Political Relations (April 5, 1941), *FRUS, The Far East, 1941, Vol. IV*, p. 120.

95   "If war"—PHA, Part 4, pp. 1939-40, Part 23, p. 1114. *See At Dawn We Slept*, p. 45.

"[t]he Division"—PHA, Part 14, p. 1044. Ironically, on February 18, 1941, Kimmel sent a communication to Harold R. Stark, the Chief of Naval Operations, saying, "I feel that a surprise attack (submarine, air, or combined) on Pearl Harbor is a possibility." *Id.*, Part 16, p. 2228.

"was inconceivable"—*Id.*, Part, 2, pp. 876-77, corrected by Part 5, p. 2488.

Chapter 7: Matsuoka

97   "Young as I was"—Quoted in David J. Lu, *Agony of Choice: Matsuoka Yosuke and the Rise and Fall of the Japanese Empire, 1880-1946* (2002) (hereafter *Agony of Choice*), p. 1.

98   "loving hands"—"Matsuoka Honors Woman Kind to Him," *Nevada State Journal* (April 10, 1933), p. 2.

"gave him"—Dooman Reminiscences, p. 78.

98-99   "There seemed"—*Id.*

"Dooman's assessment"—Kase Toshikazu, who served in the Foreign Office for many years and knew Matsuoka well, said that "he entertained a genuine affection for America." Toshikazu Kase, *Journey to the Missouri* (1950), p. 43.

"If you stand"—Quoted in *The Rising Sun*, p. 64.

"as a man"—Matsuoka Yosuke letter to Grew (May 14, 1941), Grew Diary, p. 5119.

"Its report"—*See* "Lord Lytton's Broadcast," *N.Y. Times* (November 21, 1932), p 16; "Lytton Board's Plan," *N.Y. Times* (February 7, 1933), p. 12 (stating that "[t]he Manchurian Government should be modified to secure, consistently with the sovereignty of China, a large measure of autonomy").

100   "to preserve"—"Address of Yosuke Matsuoka," *N.Y. Times* (February 25, 1933), p. 2.

"withdrawal"—Quoted in *Agony of Choice*, p. 93.

"not to accept"—"Japan Walks Out of Geneva Assembly," youtube.com.

"a passionate conviction"—Hugh R. Wilson, *Diplomat between Wars* (1941), pp. 279-81. *See* Thomas W. Burkman, *Japan and the League of Nations: Empire and World Order, 1914-1938* (2007), p. 173.

100-01   "profound regret"—"Advisory Body is Formed," *N.Y. Times* (February 25, 1933), p.3.

102   "the era"—Ambassador in Japan to Secretary of State (July 21, 1940), *FRUS, The Far East, 1940, Vol. IV*, pp. 966-67.

"more intensely"—*Id.*, p. 967.

"he had always"—*Ten Years*, p. 322.

"if at any point"—Grew telegram to Hull (February 27, 1941), Box 183 (Hornbeck Papers); *Ten Years*, p. 326.

103   "Yosuke Matsuoka"—"An Enigma named Matsuoka," *N.Y. Times Sunday Magazine* (March 23, 1941), p. 6.

"As usual"—*Ten Years*, p. 344.

"feeling like"—*Id.*, p. 374.

"intellectual and political"—Grew telegram to Hull (May 27, 1941), Grew Diary, pp. 5106, 5110; Ambassador in Japan to Secretary of State (May 27, 1941), *FRUS, The Far East, 1941, Vol. IV*, pp. 234-38.

"air of satisfaction"—Grew Diary (January 22, 1941), pp. 4734-35; "'New World Order' Only a Matter of Time," *N.Y. Times* (January 21, 1941), pp. 1, 14.

104   "indulges"—*Ten Years*, p. 389.

"These instructions"—PHA, Part 20, p. 4296; Elliot Roosevelt (ed.), *F.D.R.: His Personal Letters, 1928-1945, Vol. II* (1950), p. 1126.

"of a man"—Paraphrase of telegram from His Majesty's Ambassador (May 18 1941), Grew Correspondence, Box 188 (Hornbeck Papers).

"by all criteria"—Grew Diary (May 14, 1941), pp. 5097-98.

"The Foreign Minister"—Quoted in *The Rising Sun*, p. 77.

"the vital role"—*Ten Years*, p. 370.

105   "felt certain" & "There are indications"—President's Secretary Files, Box 41 (Roosevelt Papers); PHA Part 19, pp. 3447-49, 3452-53.

"had been planned"—Quoted in Joseph W. Ballantine, "Mukden to Pearl Harbor," 27 *Foreign Affairs* (July 1949), pp. 651, 660.

"Matsuoka's communication"—*See Tojo and the Coming of the War*, p. 206.

"firm intention"—*Ten Years*, p. 369; Grew Diary (February 2, 1941), p. 4799.

106   "alarming"—*Tokyo Record*, p. 20.

"tense"—Grew Diary (February 17, 1941), p. 4808.

"the reckless"—*Ten Years*, p. 370.

"Poor Dooman"—Grew Diary (January 4, 1941), p. 4722.

"You betcha"—Grew Diary (February 7, 1941), p. 4801. Heinrichs states in *American Ambassador* (at page 326) that Dooman returned on February 6, 1941, but Grew's contemporaneous diary for February 7, 1941 states that "Dooman returned today...." It may be that Heinrichs' reference was time in United States, where it would have been February 6.

"as originally drafted"—Grew Diary (February 7, 1941), p. 4801. Dooman later told Grew biographer Waldo Heinrichs as well as John Toland that the original draft telegram had proposed to send the fleet to the Singapore area and that Dooman had persuaded Grew to strike that recommendation. Dooman Interview, Box 3, "D," (Toland Papers), p. 463-3, and *American Ambassador*, pp. 326-27. However, Grew's contemporaneous diary says that "there was no disagreement as to the wording of the telegram and it went off as originally drafted." Grew Diary (February 7, 1941), p. 4801. It is possible that a suggestion was made in Grew's meeting with the Embassy staff for the fleet to be sent to Singapore, that Dooman successfully argued against that proposal, and that Grew agreed to send the telegram without adding that recommendation. The telegram was sent out at 11 pm on the night of February 7, 1941, providing further confirmation that Dooman returned on February 7.

106-07   "Japan has"—Ambassador in Japan to Secretary of State (February 7, 1941), *FRUS, The Far East, 1941, Vol. V*, pp. 62-64.

107   "Of course"—Grew Diary (February 19, 1941), pp. 4810-11.

"Whenever"—PHA, Part 2, p. 727.

"amazingly"—*Ten Years*, p. 355. *See id.*, p. 371.

107-08   "had seen"—Memorandum by Counselor (February 14, 1941), *FRUS, Japan, 1931-1941, Vol. II*, pp. 138, 139.

108   "He was"—Ballantine Reminiscences, p. 3.

"had no intention" & "Do you mean"—Memorandum by Counselor (February 14, 1941), *FRUS, Japan, 1931-1941, Vol. II*, p. 142 (emphasis added); Ambassador in Japan to Secretary of State (February 26, 1941), *id.*, pp. 137-38.

"he would be"—Ambassador in Japan to Secretary of State (February 26, 1941), *FRUS, Japan 1931-1941, Vol. II*, pp. 137-38. Grew said in the telegram that Ohashi was "greatly agitated and distrait" but presumably meant to say "distraught."

108-09   "volunteering"—Hornbeck letter to Grew (April 10, 1941), Box 188 (Hornbeck Papers). *See* Grew letter to Hornbeck (June 13, 1941), Box 188 (Hornbeck Papers), saying that he was unwilling to send the letter requested by Hornbeck because it would convey the inaccurate impression that "the likelihood of a Japanese descent on the East Indies or Singapore had either increased or remained unchanged...."

109   "axiomatic"—Hornbeck memo to Welles (May 19, 1941), Box 188 (Hornbeck Papers).

"we shall avoid"—Memo from Welles to Roosevelt (May 22, 1941), Box 188 (Hornbeck Papers); Memorandum from Under Secretary of State to President Roosevelt (May 22, 1941), *FRUS, The Far East, 1941, Vol IV*, p. 208.

"better news"—British Prime Minister to President Roosevelt (February 20, 1941), *FRUS, The Far East, 1941, Vol. V*, p. 83. *See* PHA, Part 19, p. 3454.

110   "to make puppets"—Quoted in Waldo Heinrichs, *Threshold of War: Franklin D. Roosevelt and American Entry into World War II* (1988) (hereafter *Threshold of War*), p. 32.

"reasonable and calm"—*Ten Years*, p. 381; *Exchange Ship*, p. 95.

"lectured"—*Ten Years*, p. 378.

111   "self-prepared"—*Tokyo Record*, p. 106. *See Japan and Her Destiny*, pp. 216, 245 ("[w]hen Stalin signed the neutrality pact with Matsuoka, he already knew the date set for the [German] attack").

"You Americans"—*Exchange Ship*, p. 96.

"[w]elcomed home"—*Tokyo Record*, p. 105. In his biography of Matsuoka, David J. Lu states that Baron Hiranuma, the Home Minister and one ofMatsuoka's adversaries in the Cabinet, persuaded Konoye that there should be "no pomp and circumstance befitting a national hero's return" for Matsuoka. According to Lu, Hiranuma reasoned that the Japanese government "should not create an impression that it rejoiced in the conclusion of the Neutrality Pact, as if to tolerate communism." *Agony of Choice*, p. 227. It may be that the airport ceremony was less flamboyant than Matsuoka would have liked, but Tolischus' contemporaneous account, along with the contemporaneous newspaper commentary, indicate that Matsuoka received commendations from both the public and the press in his accomplishment.

"It was"—Quoted in *The John Doe Associates*, p. 171.

"to put it"—*Exchange Ship*, p. 96.

112   "He had come back"—*Tokyo Record*, p. 114.

"badly"—Grew report of conversation with Matsuoka (May 14, 1941), Grew Diary, p. 5113. *See* Ambassador in Japan to Secretary of State (May 14, 1941), *FRUS, Japan, 1931-1941, Vol. II*, pp. 145-48; *Agony of Choice*, p. 228.

"serious colds"—Grew Letter to Anita Grew English (April 23, 1941) (Grew Papers); Grew Diary (May 19, 1941), p. 5144.

"bellicose"—Grew report on conversation with Matsuoka (May 14, 1941), Grew Diary, pp. 5113-14; *See* Ambassador in Japan to Secretary of State (May 14, 1941), *FRUS, Japan, 1931-1941, Vol. II*, pp. 145-48.

"was guilty"—Grew Diary, p. 5117.

113   "misapprehension"—*Id.*, p. 5119.

"I very often forget"—*Id.*, p. 5129.

"intimidated"—Report of conversation with Matsuoka (May 19, 1941), id. pp. 5137, 5139-40. *See* Ambassador in Japan to Secretary of State (May 27, 1941), *FRUS, The Far East, Vol., 1941, IV*, pp. 234-38.

113-14   "follows"—Grew letter to Hull (May 27, 1941), Grew Diary, pp. 5106-10. *See* Ambassador in Japan to Secretary of State (May 27, 1941), *FRUS, The Far East, 1941, Vol. IV*, pp. 234-38.

114   "It is not likely"—Grew Diary (May 2, 1941), p. 5091.

"wastepaper"—*Tokyo Record*, p. 229.

"to divulge"—Grew letter to Sumner Welles (May 8, 1941) (Grew Papers).

"I know"—Grew Diary (July 8, 1941), p. 5376. *See id.*, p. 5391.

"gone Western"—Quoted in *The John Doe Associates*, p. 88.

115   "[w]hite men"—Grew letter to Matsuoka (March 2, 1941) (Grew Papers). *See Exchange Ship*, p. 89.

"Japan's true aim"—Quoted in *Tokyo Record*, p. 71.

"Strike"—Grew letter to the Vice Minister for Foreign Affairs (March 25, 1941), Grew Diary, p. 4968.

"the Anglo-Saxons"—"'Anglo-Saxon' Plot to Encircle Japan Charged in Tokyo," *N.Y. Times* (February 22, 1941), p. 1.

115-16   "other recent cases"—Grew letter to Matsuoka (March 11, 1941) (Grew Papers).

Chapter 8: The Overture

117   "Nervy"—"The Hulls of Tennessee," *Life* Magazine (March 18, 1940), p. 79.

"slow-witted"—*Id.*

118   "Lord 'a mercy"—*Id. See Hull Memoirs*, Vol. I, p. 3.

"the wound"—*Hull Memoirs*, Vol. I, p. 3.

"Why, hello"—*Id.*, p. 4; *Life* Magazine (March 18, 1940), p. 79.

"He only did"—*Life* Magazine (March 18, 1940), p. 79.

"never forget"—"Hull is a little man," said Interior Secretary Harold Ickes at one point in 1938, "just a small mountaineer type, who is governed by his personal feelings and grudges." Harold L. Ickes, *The Secret Diary of Harold L. Ickes Diary* (hereafter *Ickes Diary*), Vol. II: *The Inside Struggle 1936-1939* (1954) (hereafter *Vol. II*), p. 418.

"one of the worst"—PHA, Part 2, pp. 556, 5395.

"I felt"—*Id.*, p. 453.

118-19   "as crooked"—*Hull Memoirs*, Vol. I, p. 902.

119   "Matsuoka"—Memorandum by Secretary of State (May 7, 1941), *FRUS, Japan, 1931-1941*, Vol. II, p. 413.

"real difficulty"—Memorandum by Secretary of State (May 11, 1941), *id.*, p. 416.

"more or less"—Memorandum by the Secretary of State (May 14, 1941), *id.*, p. 426.

"the war element"—Memorandum by Secretary of State (August 23, 1941), *id.*, p.566.

"Mr. Matsuoka kept"—Memorandum of Conversation (August 28, 1941), *id.*, p. 577.

"Mr. Matsuoka was"—Memorandum of Conversation (October 2, 1941), *id.*, p. 655. *See* Memorandum of Conversation (October 2, 1941), Box 60 (Hull Papers).

"removes"—Ambassador in Japan to Secretary of State (July 19, 1941), *FRUS, The Far East 1941, Vol. IV*, p. 332.

119-20   "[T]he elimination"—"New Tokyo Cabinet Expected to Ease Its Ties with Axis," *N.Y. Times*, (July 19, 1941), pp. 1, 4. This quotation corrects the spelling error of "rapprochement."

120   "In my first"—*Hull Memoirs, Vol. I*, p. 14.

"to read"—*Id.*, p. 5.

"studied"—*Id.*, p. 11.

121   "king of evils"—Quoted in Arthur M. Schlesinger, Jr., *The Coming of the New Deal* (1959), p. 189.

"economic wars"—Quoted in *id.*

122   "I am"—Quoted in Arthur M. Schlesinger, Jr., *The Crisis of the Old Order* (1957), pp. 379-80.

123   "did not want"—Arthur Krock, *Memoirs: Sixty Years on the Firing Line* (1968) (hereafter *Krock Memoirs*), p. 161.

"every help"—*Hull Memoirs, Vol., I*, p. 93.

"got a rather"—Stimson Diary (February 25 & 26, 1933).

"uncertain"—*Hull Memoirs, Vol. I.*, p. 134.

"diabetes" and "tuberculosis"—Cordell Hull, Medical (Gellman Papers).

124   "I want"—Quoted in *The Coming of the New Deal*, p. 230.

"Never" and "full share"—*Hull Memoirs, Vol. I*, pp. 191, 195.

"inherently"—Henry L. Stimson & McGeorge Bundy, *On Active Service* (1948), p. 333.

125   "was magnificent"—Quoted in Beatrice Berle and Travis Jacobs
(eds.), *Navigating the Rapids, 1918-1971: From the Papers of
Adolf A. Berle* (1973), p. 151.

"Hull was"—Morgenthau Presidential Diaries (June 4, 1941), Vol.
4, p. 932.

"wary"—*The War Diary of Breckinridge Long*, p. 210.

"If Hull"—*Ickes Diary, Vol. III, The Lowering Clouds 1939-1941*
(1955) (hereafter *Vol. III*), p. 537.

"We must"—Quoted in *The Coming of the New Deal*, p. 190.

"When"—"Washington Merry-Go-Round," *Indiana Gazette*
(May 28, 1941), p. 25.

"Hull was"—Grace Tully, *F.D.R. My Boss* (1949), p. 174. I have
changed the "Cwist" in Tully's rendition to "Chwist" to make it
consistent with Frances Perkins' description.

126   "If Cordell"—Interview with Francis Perkins, Part VIII (CCOH),
p. 30. Perkins says that Hull's comments were made at the November 14, 1941 Cabinet meeting. Although that is possible, it was at
the November 7, 1941 Cabinet meeting when Hull gave a full
report on the status of discussions with the Japanese representatives. *See Hull Memoirs, Vol. II*, p. 1057.

"abominably"—Henry A. Wallace, *The Price of Vision: The Diary
of Henry A. Wallace 1942-1946* (1973), p. 1182.

"I was never"—James A. Farley, *Jim Farley's Story: The Roosevelt
Years* (1948) (hereafter *Jim Farley's Story*), p. 233. *See* Julius Pratt,
"The Ordeal of Cordell Hull," 28 *The Review of Politics* (Jan.
1966), pp. 76, 92-93.

"that he could not"—*Krock Memoirs*, pp. 208-09. *See The War
Diary of Breckinridge Long*, pp. 386-88 (Hull telling Long that he
was "tired of being by-passed" and "tired of being relied upon in
public and ignored in private").

127   "eminently"—Grew Diary (January 5, 1941), p. 4722.

"the greatest"—Dooman Reminiscences, p. 51.

127-28 "a matter primarily"—Transcript of Conversation (June
5,1939),www.uscg.mil/history/faqs/HullMorgan1.asp. *See* Gordon
Thomas and Max Morgan-Witts, *Voyage of the Damned* (Sky-
horse ed. 2010), p. 251.

128   "a realistic"—Ambassador in Japan to Secretary of State (December 1, 1939), *FRUS, The Far East, 1939, Vol. III*, pp. 604, 611.

"that all"—Memorandum of Conversation (November 19, 1941), *FRUS, Japan, 1931-1941, Vol. II*, p. 753.

"when confronted"—Quoted in *The Coming of the New Deal*, p. 207 (emphasis in original).

"John Doe"—Memorandum by Adviser on Political Relations (April 5, 1941), *FRUS, The Far East, 1941, Vol. IV*, pp. 120-22. *See The John Doe Associates*, p. 19.

129   "Fifteen minutes"—In *The John Doe Associates*, R.J.C. Butow states that the fifteen minutes "allotted for the meeting grew into one hour and then into two...." *The John Doe Associates*, p. 10. This conclusion appears to be based on Drought's subsequent communication to Joseph P. Kennedy that "the interview [with Roosevelt] consumed *nearly* two hours." Quoted in *id.*, p. 119 (emphasis added). The President's daily logs and the White House Usher logs indicate that Roosevelt met with Walsh and Drought (along with Walker and Hull) at 10:45 am in "the White House," which, according to the archivist at the Roosevelt Library, could have been anywhere in the White House but probably meant the President's Oval Study. *See* http://www.fdrlibrary.marist.edu/daybyday (January 23, 1941); email from Matthew Hanson (September 26, 2017). The daily log states that Roosevelt went to the "Office" at 12:10 pm. *See The John Does Associates*, p. 118. According to the archivist, the "'Office' generally means the Oval Office." Email from Matthew Hanson (September 26, 2017). In short, it appears that the meeting with Walsh and Drought occurred in the Oval Study and lasted about one and half hours (when Roosevelt went to the Oval Office). This conclusion is consistent with Drought's contemporaneous comment to Kennedy that the meeting lasted "nearly" two hours.

"have been"—Memorandum Handed to President Roosevelt by Bishop James E. Walsh (January 23, 1941), *FRUS, The Far East, 1941, Vol. IV*, pp. 14-16.

"harsh talk"—Bishop James E. Walsh to Postmaster General (Walker), *id.*, pp. 17-18.

"What"—*Id.*, p. 17 n. 37.

130   "great misgivings"—Hornbeck letter to Grew (April 5, 1941), Box 188 (Hornbeck Papers).

"I am skeptical"—Secretary of State to President Roosevelt, (February 5, 1941), *FRUS, The Far East, 1941, Vol. IV*, p. 25.

"there was not"—*Hull Memoirs, Vol. II*, p. 985.

"Japan's past"—*Id.*

"he had made"—Memorandum of Conversation with Secretary of State Hull (December 11, 1941) (hereafter "Krock Memorandum"), Box 1, p. 2 (Krock Papers).

"were sincerely"—Ballantine Reminiscences, p. 206.

"was never"—Krock Memorandum, p. 1.

131   "We had"—*Hull Memoirs, Vol. II*, p. 986.

"had urged"—Krock Memorandum, p. 1.

131-32   "It is terribly"—*Ickes Diary, Vol. III*, p. 567.

132   "constantly"—PHA, Part 11, p. 5384.

"I had been striving"—PHA, Part 2, p. 428.

"Our whole"—Ballantine Reminiscences, p. 39.

132-33   "reluctantly"—Oral Statement (June 21, 1941), *FRUS, Japan, 1931-1941, Vol. II*, p. 486.

133   "should have"—Memorandum of Conversation (July 2, 1941), Id., p. 495.

"furnish"—Statement Handed by President Roosevelt to Japanese Ambassador (August 17, 1941), *id.*, p. 559; Box 60 (Hull Papers), p. 8.

"with certain"—Memorandum by the Secretary of State (April 14, 1941), *FRUS, Japan, 1931-1941, Vol. II*, p. 405.

"Unofficial"—*See*, for example, Draft Proposal Handed by the Secretary of State to the Japanese Ambassador (June 21, 1941), *id.*, p. 486.

"Well"—Krock Memorandum, p. 2.

Chapter 9: The New Ambassador

136   "very high opinion"—Memorandum of Trans-Atlantic Telephone Conversation (February 2, 1932), *FRUS, The Far East, 1932, Vol. III*, p. 180.

"high professional ability"—Josephus Daniels to U.S. Naval Attaché, Tokyo Embassy (February 5, 1919), Record Group 80,

General Correspondence 1916-1925, National Archives and Record Administration.

"skillful"—Quoted in Peter Mauch, *Sailor Diplomat: Nomura Kichisaburo and the Japanese-American War* (2011) (hereafter *Sailor Diplomat*), p. 51.

137   "shambles"—*Id.*, p. 82.

"pushed"—*Smith-Hutton Reminiscences*, p. 118.

138   "Matsuoka Hurricane"—Shigenori Togo, *The Cause of Japan* (1956), p. 45.

139   "Besides"—Quoted in *Sailor Diplomat*, p. 119.

"There is"—Quoted in *id.*

"sly fox"—Quoted in *id.*, p. 125.

"His Majesty"—Quoted in *id.*, p. 123.

140   "as a man"—*Ten Years*, p. 350.

"his determination"—*Id.*, p. 351. *See* Ambassador in Japan to Secretary of State (November 11, 1940), *FRUS, The Far East, 1940, Vol. IV*, pp. 546-47.

"improve"—*Ten Years*, p. 366.

"is clearly"—*Id.*, p. 367.

"bowing"—*Hull Memoirs, Vol. II*, p. 987.

"Nomura's command"—*Id.*, p. 996.

141   "northern troops"—Memorandum of Conversation (October 9, 1941), *FRUS, Japan, 1931-1941, Vol. II*, p. 672.

"a very, very"—Ballantine Reminiscences, p. 43.

143   "unhappy"—William Castle Diary (February 18, 1941), MS AM 2021.

"proposed"—Memorandum by Secretary of State (February 14, 1941), *FRUS, Japan, 1931-1941, Vol. II*, p. 387; Memorandum of Conversation (February 14, 1941), Box 60 (Hull Papers), p. 1.

"The general"—Ambassador in Japan to Secretary of State (January 22, 1941), *FRUS, 1941, The Far East, Vol. IV*, p. 10.

"the present relations" –Memorandum by Secretary of State (February 14, 1941), *FRUS, Japan, 1931-1941, Vol. II*, p. 388.

"to make peace"—Quoted in Wilfred Fleisher, *Our Enemy Japan* (1942), p. 74. *See Sailor Diplomat*, pp. 133, 145; *Japan and Her Destiny*, pp. 220-21.

144   "to promote"—Memorandum by Secretary of State (February 14, 1941), *FRUS, Japan, 1931-1941, Vol. II*, p. 389; Box 60 (Hull Papers), p. 5.

"did not believe"—Ambassador in Japan to Secretary of State (February 27, 1941), *FRUS, The Far East, 1941, Vol. IV*, p. 53.

"Japan rightly"—Grew telegram to Hull (February 27, 1941), Box 183 (Hornbeck Papers).

"Since"—Ambassador in Japan to Secretary of State (March 5, 1941), *FRUS, The Far East, 1941, Vol. IV*, p. 58.

"Plenipotentiary"—Postmaster General to President Roosevelt (February 28, 1941), *FRUS, The Far East, 1941, Vol. IV*, p. 54.

"Wikawa Tadao"—Wikawa's name is sometimes spelled "Ikawa." *See The John Doe Associates*, p. 23 n.*; *Sailor Diplomat*, pp. 151-54.

145   "any connection"—Quoted in *The John Doe Associates*, p. 146.

"wanted"—Ballantine Reminiscences, pp. 34, 41.

145-46 "good people"—Memorandum by Secretary of State (March 8, 1941), *FRUS, Japan, 1931-1941, Vol. II*, pp. 389-96.

146   "the threatening"—Memorandum by Secretary of State (March 14, 1941), *id.*, pp. 396-98.

147   "in the strictest"—Adviser on Political Relations to Ambassador in Japan (March 15, 1941), *FRUS, The Far East, 1941, Vol. IV*, p. 81.

"to forget"—Grew Diary (April 11, 1941), p. 4987. *See Our Enemy Japan*, p. 65 (with Fleisher saying that Nazis who gathered at the Karuizawa resort would give each other Nazi salutes when passing each other). It is assumed that Germans would follow that same practice at other Japanese resorts.

"With great reluctance"—*Ten Years*, p. 379.

"Duty first"—Grew letter to Godfrey Cabot (April 25, 1941) (Grew Papers).

"further evidence"—Hornbeck memo to Welles (May 24, 1941), Box 188 (Hornbeck Papers).

Chapter 10: Commencement of the Conversations

149   "Alice was"—Grew Diary (May 10, 1941), pp. 5094-96. *See Ten Years*, p. 386.

150   "It is"—"President Sharp," *N.Y. Times* (May 5, 1941), p. 1.

"FDR"—*Time* (May 19, 1941), p. 16. *See* Doris Kearns Goodwin, *No Ordinary Time—Franklin and Eleanor Roosevelt: The Home Front in World War II* (1994), p. 235.

"The report"—*See* Steven Lomazow and Eric Fettmann, *FDR's Deadly Secret* (Public Affairs: New York, 2009), p. 79; https://fdrs-deadlysecretblogpost.com/2010.

"But subsequent"—After Roosevelt's death, McIntire claimed that Roosevelt had a mild case of anemia that reflected bleeding hemorrhoids, but this explanation does not appear to square with the facts. *See FDR's Deadly Secret*, p. 80; https://fdrsdeadlysecretblog-post.com/2010 (according to Lomazow, "I've yet to find a single physician who doesn't chuckle when presented with the facts and the wholly untenable diagnosis....")

151   "an intestinal"—*Ickes Diary, Vol. III*, p. 511.

"What he's suffering"—*Roosevelt and Hopkins*, p. 293.

"through the medium"—Proposal Presented to the Department of State (April 9, 1941), *FRUS, Japan, 1931-1941, Vol. II*, p. 398.

"endangering"—Postmaster General to Secretary of State (March 17 & 18, 1941), *FRUS, The Far East, 1941, Vol. IV*, pp. 97, 111.

152   "aggressively attacked"—Proposal Presented to Department of State (April 9, 1941), *FRUS, Japan 1931-1941, Vol. II*, pp. 398-402.

"our disappointment"—*Hull Memoirs, Vol. II*, p. 991.

"The views"—Hornbeck Autobiography, p. 65.

152-53   "From the beginning"—*Id.*, p. 75.

153   "a super-colossal"—Hornbeck Memorandum (April 5, 1941), *FRUS, The Far East, 1941, Vol. IV*, p. 122.

"were endeavoring"—Hornbeck letter to Grew (April 5, 1941), Box 188 (Hornbeck Papers).

"pressing"—Hornbeck letter to Grew (April 10, 1941), *Id.*

"he did not"—Stimson Diary (April 24, 1941).

"in the background"—Hornbeck Autobiography, p. 75.

154   "precise"—*Hull Memoirs, Vol. II*, p. 1031.

"could be"—Hornbeck letter to Grew (April 10, 1941), Box 188 (Hornbeck Papers).

"Alice has"—Items, April 2, 1941 (Grew Diary), p. 4985.

"it was really"—Grew letter to Lilla Grew Moffat (September 3, 1941) (Grew Papers).

"it was not"—Items, April 2, 1941 (Grew Diary), p. 4985.

154-55   "he had collaborated"—Memorandum by Secretary of State (April 14, 1941), *FRUS, Japan, 1931-1941, Vol. II*, pp. 403, 405-06.

155   "contained"—Memorandum by Secretary of State (April 16, 1941), *Id.*, p. 407.

"The word"—*The Japanese Thread*, p. 80.

155-56   "would interfere"—Memorandum by Secretary of State (April 16, 1941), *FRUS, Japan, 1931-1941, Vol. II*, pp. 407-09.

156   "was not sure"—*Id.*, p. 409.

"[I]f the Japanese Government"—*Id.*, pp. 407, 410.

"is in real earnest"—*Id.*, p. 409.

"consider"—Secretary of State to Ambassador in Japan (April 24, 1941), *FRUS, The Far East, 1941, Vol. IV*, p. 163.

157   "continuing complaint"—*Smith-Hutton Reminiscences*, p. 163.

"felt"—Grew letter to Hornbeck (February 25, 1941), Box 188 (Hornbeck Papers).

"humiliated"—*The Japanese Thread*, p. 101.

"to receive"—Grew Diary (April 30, 1941), p. 5006.

"too seriously" and "difference"—Grew letter to Hornbeck (May 26, 1941) (Grew Papers), with attachments.

"in an intoxicated"—Ambassador in Japan to Secretary of State (May 2, 1941), *FRUS, The Far East, 1941, Vol. IV*, p. 175. *See Ten Years*, p. 385.

158   "an extraordinarily"—"Memoirs of Prince Konoye," PHA, Part 20, Exhibit 173 (hereafter "Konoye Memoirs"), p. 3987.

"it would be"—Quoted in *Sailor Diplomat*, p. 161.

159   "70%"—Konoye Memoirs, p. 3987.

"ill-feeling"—*Id.*, pp. 3987-88

"not comprehensible"—Memorandum by Secretary of State (May 7, 1941), *FRUS, Japan, 1931-1941, Vol. II*, p. 413.

"capitulation"—Quoted in *Sailor Diplomat*, p. 171.

159-60   "Very few"—*Hull Memoirs*, Vol. II, pp. 1000-01.

"aggressive measure"—Proposal Presented to Department of State (April 9, 1941) & Draft Proposal (May 12, 1941), *FRUS, Japan, 1931-1941, Vol. II*, pp. 399-400, 421-22. *See Hull Memoirs, Vol. II*, pp. 1000-01.

"without resorting"—Proposal Presented to Department of State (April 9, 1941), *FRUS, Japan, 1931-1941, Vol. II*, p. 401.

"aggressively attacked"—*Id.*, p. 400.

"will be"—Draft Proposal (May 12, 1941), *id.*, p. 421.

161   "appears"—Memorandum by Adviser on Political Relations (May 5, 1941), *FRUS, The Far East, 1941, Vol. IV*, p. 189.

" a little tight"—Grew Diary (June 10, 1941), p. 5219.

161-62   "Based"—Ambassador in Japan to Secretary of State (May 13, 1941), *FRUS, Japan, 1931-1941, Vol. II*, p. 187.

162   "is very much"—*Ten Years*, p. 393.

"the Axis ambassadors"—Ambassador in Japan to Secretary of State (May 19, 1941), *FRUS, The Far East, 1941, Vol. IV*, p. 202.

"trustworthy"—Ambassador in Japan to Secretary of State (May 16, 1941), *id.*, p. 195.

162-63   "aggressively attacked"—Draft Suggestion (May 16, 1941), *FRUS, Japan, 1931-1941, Vol. II*, pp. 432-34.

163   "still"—Stimson Diary (May 13, 1941).

"just fusses"—Quoted in Dorothy Berg and Shumpei Okamoto, *Pearl Harbor as History: Japanese-American Relations, 1931-1941* (1973), p. 88.

"is there"—Memorandum by Adviser on Political Relations (May 5, 1941), *FRUS, The Far East, 1941, Vol. IV*, p. 190.

"Japan has"—Memorandum by Adviser on Political Relations (May 23, 1941), *id.*, p. 214.

164   "judgment"—Secretary of State to Ambassador in Japan (May 24, 1941), *id.*, p. 224. That telegram was supplemented by another telegram to Grew and Dooman on Monday May 26 "urgently"

requesting their opinion whether the Japanese government "could or would in good faith carry out" any new agreement with the United States with respect to China, non-discrimination in trade, and "a policy of peace in the Pacific area...." Secretary of State to Ambassador in Japan (May 26, 1941), *id.*, p. 228. That second telegram was not received in Tokyo until after Grew had sent his response to the May 24 telegram.

"Grew was"—Interview with Eugene Dooman, Box 3, "D" (Toland Papers).

"survey"—Ambassador in Japan to Secretary of State (May 26, 1941), *FRUS, The Far East, 1941, Vol. IV*, pp. 228-31.

"the most"—Grew Diary (May 25, 1941), pp. 5100-01.

165   "There can be"—Ambassador in Japan to Secretary of State (May 27, 1941), *FRUS, The Far East, 1941, Vol. IV*, pp. 231-32.

"be released"—*id.*, p. 232."Unofficial"—American Draft (May 31, 1941), *FRUS, Japan, 1931-1941, Vol. II*, p. 446."clear-cut"— Memorandum of Conversation (June 6, 1941), *id.*, p. 466.

166   "a sharp"—PHA, Part 18, p. 3259.

"the Japanese Government"—Memorandum of Conversation (May 28, 1941), *FRUS, Japan, 1931-1941, Vol. II*, p. 441.

"had been"—PHA, Part 2, pp. 425, 559.

166-67   "defensive"—American Draft (May 31, 1941), *FRUS, Japan, 1931-1941, Vol. II*, p. 447.

167   "had become"—Memorandum of Conversation (May 20,1941), *FRUS, Japan, 1931-1941, Vol. II*, p. 435-36.

"perhaps"—Memorandum of Conversation (May 21, 1941), *id.*, p. 438.

"further consideration"—Memorandum of Conversation (May 30, 1941), *id.*, p. 445.

"subject"—*Id.*, p. 449. *See Currents of War*, p. 165 ("the last thing that Hull, Hornbeck, and [the Far Eastern Division] wanted was a draft agreement or an end to the war in China," and, "[b]y clearly delineating the American position on Japan's obligations to Berlin while remaining vague concerning China, Hull could achieve all that he wanted").

"with the exception"—Memorandum by Secretary of State (June 2, 1941), *FRUS, Japan, 1931-1941, Vol. II*, p. 454.

168   "that the potentialities"—Ambassador in Japan to Secretary of State (June 2, 1941), *FRUS, 1941, The Far East, Vol. IV*, p. 248.

"very slowly"—Memorandum by Secretary of State (June 2, 1941), *FRUS, Japan, 1931-1941, Vol. II*, p. 454.

"Japanese troops"—*id.*, p. 455.

Chapter 11: The Decision

171-72   "vision"—Grew Diary (June 1941), pp. 5260-72.

172   "displeasure"—Konoye Memoirs, p. 3992.

"[A]n important"—Quoted in *Sailor Diplomat*, p. 180.

172-73   "one would"—Diary of Nomura Kichisaburo (hereafter "Nomura Diary"), Donald M. Goldstein & Katherine V. Dillon (eds.), *The Pacific War Papers: Japanese Documents of World War II* (2004) (hereafter *The Pacific War Papers*), p. 140.

173   "some unilateral"—Memorandum of Conversation (June 17, 1941), *FRUS, Japan, 1931-1941, Vol. II*, p. 479.

173-74   "the principle"—Memorandum of Conversation (June 4, 1941) & Memorandum of Conversation (June 9, 1941), *id.*, pp. 457, 470.

174   "something"—Adviser on Political Relations to Secretary of State (June 10, 1941), *FRUS, The Far East, 1941, Vol. IV*, p. 263.

"carried"—Memorandum of Conversation (June 9, 1941), *FRUS, Japan, 1931-1941, Vol. II*, p. 468.

"a satisfactory"—Oral Statement Handed to Japanese Ambassador (June 6, 1941), *id.*, p. 467.

175   "would like"—Memorandum of Conversation (June 15, 1941), *id.*, p. 471.

"such a procedure"—*Id.*

"solely"—Memorandum of Conversation (June 21, 1941), *id.*, pp. 483-92.

175-76   "many Japanese leaders"—*Id.*, p. 485.

176   "does not"—*Id.*, pp. 485-86.

"the Secretary of State"—*Id.*, p. 486.

"wanted"—Nomura Diary, *The Pacific War Papers*, p. 144.

"in the dark"—Ambassador in Japan to Secretary of State (June 10, 1941), *FRUS, The Far East, 1941, Vol. IV*, p. 264.

176-77   "that most"—Memorandum by Chief of Division of Far Eastern Affairs (June 18, 1941), *FRUS, The Far East, 1941, Vol. IV,* pp. 269-70.

177   "he was"—Ambassador in Japan to Secretary of State (June 6, 1941), *id.,* p. 254.

"dangerous"—Quoted in Grew Diary (May 1941), p. 5103.

"the suppression"—*Id.* (June 19, 1941), p. 5231.

"totalitarian"—*Id.*

178   "ruthlessly"—*Id.,* p. 5230; "Japan Will Extend Thought Control," *N.Y. Times* (July 11, 1941), p. 1.

"almost"—*Ten Years,* p. 384.

"had long"—Grew Diary (June 22, 1941), pp. 5232-33.

"a war"—Quoted in James William Morley (ed.) & David Titus (trans.), *Japan's Road to the Pacific War—The Final Confrontation: Japan's Negotiations with the United States, 1941* (1994) (hereafter *The Final Confrontation*), p. 133.

"will have"—Quoted in *id.,* p. 84. *See The Road to Pearl Harbor,* p. 192.

"And in June"—*See Tojo and the Coming of the War,* p. 212; *Undeclared War,* p. 626.

179   "[I]t was obvious"—*Tokyo Record,* p. 139.

"Something"—"Japanese Stress Policy of 'Peace,'" *N.Y. Times* (June 24, 1941), p.1.

180   "must cooperate"—Konoye Memoirs, p. 3993.

"astonished"—*Id.*

"Matsuoka will"—Grew Diary (June 1941), unnumbered page.

"The police"—*Tokyo Record.,* p. 141. *See* "Emperor Consults on Japan's Course," *N.Y. Times* (July 8, 1941), p. 1 (police repeat warning against "loose talk").

181   "Japan is"—"Japanese Premier Seeks Our Amity," *N.Y. Times* (June 30, 1941), p. 1.

"different from"—Memorandum by Joseph W. Ballantine," (June 30, 1941), *FRUS, The Far East, 1941, Vol. IV,* p. 285.

"Only"—Grew Diary (July 2, 1941), p. 5338.

"seeing Matsuoka"—*Id.* (June 25, 1941), p. 5235.

"the United States"—Ambassador in Japan to Secretary of State (June 10, 1941), *FRUS, The Far East, 1941, Vol. IV*, p. 264. *See Ten Years*, p. 392.

181-82   "Today"—"Japan Gropes for a Policy," *N.Y. Times* (June 29, 1941), p. 6.

182   "[M]any"—Grew Diary (June 25, 1941), p. 5236. *See PHA*, Part 2, p. 747.

"As a matter"—Nobutaka Ike (ed. & translator), *Japan's Decision for War: Records of the 1941 Policy Conferences* (1967) (hereafter *Japan's Decision*) , p. 58.

"When Germany"—*Id.*, p. 60.

"Unlike the more formal"—*See Tokyo Record*, p. 145.

183   "no matter"—*Japan's Decision*, p. 78.

"various"—*Id.* This language ("will not be deterred") comports with Konoye Memoirs, Appendix III, p. 4019. Another translation of that section has been interpreted to read, "The Empire shall not flinch from war with Britain and the United States." *The Final Confrontation*, p. 129. *Accord 1941*, p. 131. The differing translations on this statement and other statements made at Imperial and Liaison Conferences presumably reflect the inherent challenge in converting the Japanese language to English.

183-84   "that it was"—Grew Diary (April 17, 1941), p. 4992.

184   "decide independently"—*Japan's Decision*, p. 79.

184-85   "abstinence" & "The danger"—"Roosevelt Moves," *N.Y. Times* (September 27, 1940), p. 1.

185   "[I]f you"—Nomura Diary, *The Pacific War Papers*, p. 147.

"relevant"—*Japan's Decision*, p 90.

185-86   "I want"—Quoted in *id.*, p. 87

186   "I cannot"—Quoted in *id.*, p. 88.

"occupation"—Quoted in *id.*

"I am convinced"—*Tokyo Record*, p. 104.

"the extremists"—Grew Diary (April 25, 1941), p. 5003.

187   "[a] decision"—Quoted in Ambassador in Japan to Secretary of State (July 2, 1941), *FRUS, The Far East, 1941, Vol. IV*, p. 287.

"the Foreign Minister's"—Konoye Memoirs, p. 3994.

"a serious problem"—Diary of Marquis Koichi Kido (hereafter "Kido Diary"), *The Pacific War Papers*, p. 116.

187-88   "sit on the fence"—Grew Diary (July 6, 1941), p. 5344.

188   "I don't know"—Grew letter to Elsie Grew Lyon (June 12, 1941) (Grew Papers).

Chapter 12: The Response

189   "The Secretary of State"—*See* "President Mourns at Bankhead Bier," *N.Y. Times* (September 18, 1941), p. 16.

190   "one of the most" –Quoted in Benjamin Welles, *Sumner Welles: FDR's Global Strategist* (1997) (hereafter *Sumner Welles*). *See Ickes Diary, Vol. II, The Inside Struggle* (1954), p. 351.

"butlers" –*Sumner Welles*, p. 8.

"Mr. Secretary"—Quoted in *id.*, p. 69.

191   "behind"—Sumner Welles, *The Time for Decision* (1944), p. 275.

"outstanding"—Quoted in *Sumner Welles*, p. 100.

"If Welles"—Interview with Robert H. Jackson, CCOH (hereafter "Jackson Interview"), p. 802.

"special aptitude"—David J. Danelski & Joseph Tulchin (eds.), *The Autobiographical Notes of Charles Evans Hughes* (1973) p. 269.

"fine work"—Quoted in *Sumner Welles*, p. 107.

192   "accomplishments"—Quoted in *id.*, p. 110.

"All O.K."—Quoted in *id.*, p. 114.

193   "since"—Roosevelt letter to Bryan (March 20, 1915), State Department Jacket (Sumner Welles).

"Mr. Welles"—Quoted in Orville Bullitt (ed.), *For the President: Personal and Secret* (1972) (hereafter *For the President*), p. 211.

193-94   "I don't"—*Jim Farley's Story*, p. 341.

194   "reasonable latitude"—*Hull Memoirs Vol. II*, p. 1227.

"Hull"—Quoted in Joseph Lash (ed.), *From the Diaries of Felix Frankfurter* (1975), pp. 204-05, 250.

"that he had"—*Ickes Diary, Vol. III*, p. 401.

"[E]very"—Quoted in James MacGregor Burns, *Roosevelt: The Soldier of Freedom, 1940-1945* (1970), p. 350.

"as the train" and "When the train"—*See* Attachment to Memorandum of Conversation with the President (April 23, 1941) (hereafter "Bullitt Memorandum"), Box 210, Folder 217 (Bullitt Papers).

195   "he had been"—Memorandum by J. Edgar Hoover (January 30, 1941), p. 4, Box 6 (Gellman Papers).

"Welles had"—*Id.*, p. 1. *See* Irwin F. Gellman, *Secret Affairs: FDR, Cordell Hull, and Sumner Welles* (1995), p. 237.

195-96   "on his deathbed"—Bullitt Memorandum.

196   "believed"—Elliot Roosevelt & James Brough, *A Rendezvous with Destiny: The Roosevelts of the White House* (1975), p. 263.

"The Secretary had discussed"—Memorandum of Conversation (January 5, 1943), Box 210, Folder 217 (Bullitt Papers).

"had been trying"—Welles letter to Mathilde Townsend Welles (August 12, 1943), quoted in *FDR's Global Strategist*, p. 347.

"I didn't speak"—William C. Bullitt, Confidential Memoranda of Conversations (April 23, 1941—June 21, 1944); quoted in *id.*

"on his own"—*Hull Memoirs, Vol. II*, p. 1230.

197   "he was leaving"—Memorandum of Conversation (June 21, 1941), *FRUS, Japan, 1931-1941, Vol. II*, p. 484.

"the intention"—Statement Handed by the American Ambassador in Japan (July 6, 1941), *FRUS, Japan, 1931-1941, Vol. II*, pp. 502-03.

"would be glad"—*Ten Years*, p. 397.

"are abundantly"—Statement Handed by the Japanese Minister for Foreign Affairs (July 8, 1941), *FRUS, Japan, 1931-1941, Vol. II*, pp. 503-04.

"to the advantage"—*Japan's Decision*, p. 79.

198   "southward advance"—*Hull Memoirs, Vol. II*, p. 1013.

"a prompt denial"—Memorandum of Conversations (July 5, 1941), *FRUS, Japan, 1931-1941, Vol. II*, pp. 501; Nomura Diary, *The Pacific War Papers*, pp. 148-49.

"recurrent rumors"—Memorandum of Conversation (July 15, 1941), *FRUS, Japan, 1931-1941, Vol. II*, p. 508; Nomura Diary, *The Pacific War Papers*, p. 153.

199   "rupture"—Nomura Diary, *The Pacific War Papers*, pp. 150-51.

199-200   "in the event"—Memorandum of Conversation (July 10, 1941), *FRUS, 1941, The Far East, Vol. IV*, p. 301.

"to do"—Morgenthau Presidential Diaries (July 18, 1941), Vol. 4, pp. 946-47 (after Cabinet meeting). The proposed freeze on Japan's use of assets in the United States could limit or entirely foreclose Japan's use of dollars in American banks for the purchase of oil or other American products. The freeze would reflect the President's invocation of powers accorded to him by Section 5(b) of the Trading with the Enemy Act, which had been enacted in November 1917 and amended in March 1933. *See* Edward S. Miller, *Bankrupting the Enemy: the U.S. Financial Siege of Japan before Pearl Harbor* (2007) (hereafter *Bankrupting the Enemy*), pp. 6-8. As reflected in regulations later adopted, the freeze contemplated that an export license would be issued by the State Department and that the Treasury Department would then issue a separate license to allow the release of Japanese funds from American banks after getting approval from the Foreign Funds Control Committee.

"to slip"—*Ickes Diary, Vol. III*, p. 588. *See Dean Acheson, Present at the   Creation: My Years in the State Department* (1969), pp. 25-26.

200-01   "the application"—Joseph E. Davies to Secretary of State (March 17, 1941), *FRUS, The Far East, 1941, Vol. IV*, p. 108.

201   "the British"—Ambassador in Japan to Secretary of State (July 22, 1941), *FRUS, The Far East, 1941, Vol. V*, pp. 222-23; Grew Diary (July 22, 1941), p. 5358.

"the Japanese Government"—Memorandum by Acting Secretary of State (July   23, 1941), *FRUS, Japan, 1931-1941, Vol. II*, pp. 522-24, 526.

201-02   "encirclement"—*Id.*, pp. 524-26.

Chapter 13: Deadlock

203   "the codes"—Hornbeck letter to Grew (June 26, 1941), Box 188 (Hornbeck Papers).

203-04   "usually"—Grew Diary (July 10, 1941), p. 5346.

204   "from the outset"—*Time for Decision*, p. 294.

"I feel"—Ambassador in Japan to Acting Secretary of State (July 10, 1941), *FRUS, The Far East, 1941, Vol. IV*, p. 299.

"I appreciate"—Acting Secretary of State to Ambassador in Japan (July 11, 1941), *FRUS, The Far East, 1941, Vol. IV*, pp. 305-06; Grew Diary (July 13, 1941), pp. 5348-49.

205 "the nation"—*Japan's Decision*, p. 79.

"sayonara"—Grew Diary (March 16, 1941), p. 4896.

"seize"—Grew Diary (May 29, 1941), p. 5104.

"engaged"—Quoted in *Tokyo Record*, p. 153.

"it was better"—*Id.*, p. 162.

206 "high nervous tension"—Ambassador in Japan to Secretary of State (July 17, 1941), *FRUS, The Far East, 1941, Vol. IV*, p. 1007.

"'startling'"—Ambassador in Japan to Secretary of State (June 27, 1941), *id.*, p. 283.

"Mr. Matsuoka"—Grew Diary (July 6, 1941), p. 5343.

"Japanese leaders"—Memorandum of Conversation (June 21, 1941), *FRUS, Japan, 1931-1941, Vol. II*, p. 485.

"outrageous statement"—*Japan's Decision*, p. 97.

207 "intention"—Kido Diary, *The Pacific War Papers*, p. 116.

"no hope"—*Japan's Decision*, p. 98.

"As the Foreign Minister"—*Id.*, p. 101.

"[I]n spite"—Konoye Memoirs, p. 3995.

"[A]t this point"—Quoted in *The Final Confrontation*, p. 149.

208 "interference"—Memorandum of Conversation (July 15, 1941), *FRUS, Japan, 1931-1941, Vol. II*, p. 507.

"hoping"—*Id.*, p. 514.

209 "He was"—*Smith-Hutton Reminiscences*, pp. 325-26.

"is a very good"—Grew Diary (July 18, 1941), p. 5356.

"had come"—*Ten Years*, p. 406.

209-10 "encirclement"—*Id.*, pp. 407-08.

210 "this move"—Memorandum of Conversation (July 24, 1941), *FRUS, Japan, 1931-1941, Vol. II*, pp. 527-29.

210-11 "would be"—*Id.*, pp. 529-30.

211 "somehow"—Quoted in *Sailor, Diplomat*, p. 192.

"The vicious"—Grew Diary (July 1941), pp. 5332-34.

"distressed"—*Ten Years*, pp. 409-10.

"reluctant"—*Id.*, p. 410.

211-12   "may well"—Memorandum by Adviser on Political Relations (July 28, 1941), *FRUS, The Far East, 1941, Vol. IV*, p. 346.

212   "no reason"—Grew Diary (July 24, 1941), p. 5364.

"stars"—*Ten Years*, p. 411.

"precisely"—*Id.*

"would wish"—*Id.*, p. 412.

212-13   "the strongest"—*Id.*; Memorandum by Ambassador in Japan (July 27, 1941), *FRUS, Japan, 1931-1941, Vol. II*, p. 535. In his biography of Nomura, Peter Mauch suggests that Toyoda lied when he told Grew he was unaware of Roosevelt's proposal "in the hope that he might dissuade Washington from further ratcheting up the pressure." *Sailor Diplomat*, p. 193. That may be so, but Toyoda would have had to know that Japan would have to respond to Roosevelt's proposal in due course (or that a failure to respond would be taken as a rejection). In that latter circumstance, whatever inclination the United States may have had to "ratchet up" the pressure would have bubbled to the surface in any event. In short, it is not clear what Toyoda would have to gain by lying to Grew—especially because the Foreign Minister could anticipate that the Americans would surely ask Nomura why he had not forwarded the proposal to his government. In fact, after reading Grew's report of the conversation with Toyoda, Welles did ask Nomura why he had not forwarded the proposal to his government. Nomura responded that he had in fact "immediately" telegraphed the summary to Tokyo. Memorandum by Acting Secretary (July 28, 1941), *FRUS, Japan, 1931-1941, Vol. II*, pp. 537-38.

213   "On the 26th"—Grew letter to Anita Grew English (July 28, 1941) (Grew Papers).

"entirely convinced"—*Ten Years*, p. 411.

214   "It was obvious"—"Japanese Bitter over U.S. Stand," *N.Y. Times* (July 26, 1941), p. 1.

"stung"—*Tokyo Record*, p. 175.

"There is no greater" & "Japan will not succumb"—Quoted in *id.*, pp. 175-76,   222.

"occupation"—*Japan's Decision*, p. 108.

"as strong as"—Third Secretary to Ambassador (July 31, 1941), *FRUS, The Far East, 1941, Vol. IV*, pp. 354-55. In *1941*, Eri Hotta references a letter that Arita Hachiro, the former Foreign Minister, had written to the Prime Minister on August 1 saying that Japan should not have moved into southern Indochina while Japan was engaged in negotiations with the United States. In response, Konoye appears to express his surprise at the American freeze, telling Arita "It was a mistake to think that [the move into] French Indochina would not inflict serious damage." *1941*, p. 152. There is a possible reconciliation of that statement with Ushiba's comment to Embassy staff members that Konoye was not surprised by the American freeze: it may be that Konoye thought it better to tell Arita he was surprised by the freeze rather than admit to Arita that he anticipated the American sanction and therefore knowingly took the risk of undermining the discussions with the United States.

"avert"—Kido Diary, *The Pacific War Papers*, p. 119.

215   "out of the question"—Quoted in *Emperor Hirohito and the Pacific War*, p. 91. *See Tojo and the Coming of War*, p. 234.

"As the *New York Times*"—*See* "Two-Thirds Cut Due in Oil Sales," *N.Y. Times* (July 27, 1941), p. 1.

"As de facto chairman"—In his biography of Dean Acheson, James Chace states that Acheson "chaired" the FFCC. James Chase, *Acheson: The Secretary Who Created the American World* (1998), p. 84. Edward S. Miller states that Acheson was the "de facto chief of the FFCC." *Bankrupting the Enemy*, p. 205. Acheson himself says nothing of being chairman or chief of the FFCC in his memoir of his State Department years. *Present at the Creation*, pp. 23-27. There is no question that, whatever the nomenclature, Acheson was the key figure on the FFCC. I have therefore resorted to calling him the "de facto chairman."

"policy of appeasement" and "in great triumph"– *Ickes Diary, Vol. III*, pp. 591, 608. *See* Under Secretary of State to President Roosevelt (July 31, 1941), *FRUS, The Far East, 1941, Vol. IV*, pp. 846-48; Michael A. Barnhart, *Japan Prepares for Total War, 1919-1941* (1987) (hereafter *Japan Prepares for Total War*), pp. 230-31; *Threshold of War*, pp. 177-78.

216   "hold without action"—*FRUS, The Far East, 1941, Vol. IV*, p. 848. *See Japan Prepares for Total War*, pp. 230-31; *Threshold of War*, pp. 177-78; *The Currents of War*, p. 184; *Bankrupting the Enemy*, pp. 195-204.

"Hull was in"—Hull was in White Sulphur Springs at the end of July and beginning of August when the freeze was announced and the regulations adopted. The Secretary of State apparently learned about the *de facto* total embargo at a meeting with Acheson on September 5, 1941. Hull had lunch with Roosevelt that same day and, as far as the record shows, did not register any objection with the President. *See Threshold of War*, p. 177; Jonathan G. Utley, *Going to War with Japan 1937-1941* (Fordham University Press ed., 2005), p. 156.

"Southwestern Pacific"—Memorandum of Conversation (August 6, 1941), *FRUS, Japan, 1931-1941, Vol. II*, 546-51.

217   "From now on"—*Hull Memoirs, Vol. II*, p. 1015.

"He has made up"—Stimson Diary (August 8, 1941).

"might care"—Memorandum of a Conversation (August 8, 1941), *FRUS, Japan, 1931-1941, Vol. II*, p. 551.

"[T]here is no mistaking"—Quoted in *The Final Confrontation*, p. 190. *See* Nomura Diary, *The Pacific War Papers*, pp. 162-63. The translations in both books are identical in substance but different in language.

218   "of a candidate"—PHA, Part 2, p. 566.

Chapter 14: The Meeting Proposal

220   "looked upon"—*Ten Years*, pp. 68-69.

"weathered, tired face"—*Exchange Ship*, p. 137.

"We looked"—*Smith-Hutton Reminiscences*, pp. 82-84.

"It was reported"—*Tokyo Record*, p. 96; *Exchange Ship*, p. 94.

221   "overcome"—Grew Diary (July 3, 1941), pp. 5383-84. *See* Stefano van Loë, "Nakano Seigo and the Politics of Democracy, Empire and Fascism in Pre-War and Wartime Japan" (Doctoral Dissertation, Harvard University: Cambridge, MA 2011), pp. 273-371. Grew was skeptical when he first heard the account of Hiranuma's telephone conversation with Nakano, but subsequent events appear to provide some confirmation. *See Ten Years*, p. 401.

"One of the first"—Grew Diary (information culled from British embassy bulletin on August 27, 1941), p. 5597.

"ripping"—*Exchange Ship*, p. 289.

"Harmed and bloody"—*See* "Cabinet Member Is Shot in Japan," *N.Y. Times* (August 14, 1941), p. 1; "Japanese Rally Around Hiranuma," *N.Y. Times* (August 15 1941), p. 1.

222   "saw the handwriting"—PHA, Part 2, p. 640.

222-23   "I have made"—Quoted in *1941*, p. 160.

"We can't say"—Quoted in *The Final Confrontation*, p. 180.

"a suitable move"—Konoye Memoirs, p. 4000.

"In view of this"—*Id.*

223-24   "In his heart-to-heart"—Quoted in *The Final Confrontation*, p. 180.

224   "If you push"—Quoted in *Konoe Fumimaro and the Failure of Peace in Japan*, p. 120.

"the easy gait"—*Behind the Japanese Mask*, p. 60.

"descended"—*Time* (July 22, 1940), pp. 31-32.

225   "He was only twelve"—*See 1941*, p. 33. Another source says Konoye's father died when he was thirteen. *See The Rising Sun*, p. 51. Other sources have said that his father died when Konoye was 14. *See Konoe Fumimaro and the Failure of Peace in Japan*, p. 14; "Synthesis of Japan," *N.Y. Times* (August 3, 1941), Sunday Magazine (hereafter "Synthesis of Japan"), p. 40. Konoye's father died sometime in 1904, and it is likely that Konoye, who was born on October 12, 1891, was not yet 13 at the time.

"I was"—"Synthesis of Japan." p. 40.

"I really have"—Quoted in *Konoe Fumimaro and the Failure of Peace in Japan*, p. 72.

226   "Few are"—"Synthesis of Japan," p. 39.

"a man of weak"—Grew Diary (August 1940), p. 4463.

"He uses"—*Time* (July 22, 1940), p. 32.

"there seems to be"—Quoted in "Prince Konoye 'Ill' Again," *N.Y. Times* (February 22, 1941), p. 4.

226-27   "patience"—Memorandum of Conversation (August 8, 1941), *FRUS, Japan, 1931-1941, Vol. II*, pp. 550-51.

227   "conveying"—Nomura Diary, *The Pacific War Papers*, p. 163.

"another example"—Stimson Diary (August 9, 1941).

"We knew"—PHA, Part 2, pp. 425-26. The spelling of the Prime Minister's name in Hull's testimony is "Konoe." For the sake of consistency, that has been changed to "Konoye."

228   "concrete and clear-cut"—*Id.*

Chapter 15: The Dinner

229   "The President advised"—*See* Memorandum of Trip to Meet Winston Churchill (August 23, 1941), PSF, Safe, Atlantic Charter, Roosevelt Papers. The memorandum was apparently dictated by Roosevelt after his return from the meeting with Churchill and references Roosevelt's proposal to meet Churchill at Argentia Harbor near the newly-established naval base.

"undertakes"—FRUS, *The Far East, 1941, Vol. IV*, p. 375.

230   "needed"—*Id.*

"a clearer statement"—Statement Handed by President Roosevelt to Japanese Ambassador (August 17, 1941), FRUS, *Japan, 1931-1941, Vol. II*, p. 559.

"olive branch"—FRUS, *The Far East, 1941, Vol. IV*, p. 372.

230-31   "if he had"—Memorandum by Secretary of State (August 17, 1941), FRUS, *Japan, 1931-1941, Vol. II*, p. 555.

231   "would be"—Memorandum by Embassy Counselor, *id.*, pp. 559-60.

"the longest"—Grew Diary (August 18, 1941), p. 5525.

232   "He is"—*Id.*

"hold the key"—Memorandum by Ambassador in Japan (August 18, 1941), FRUS, *Japan, 1931-1941, Vol. II*, pp. 562-63.

"only be guided"—*Id.*, p. 564.

233   "with all the force"—*Id.*, p. 565.

"shows a remarkable"—Ambassador in Japan to Secretary of State (August 19, 1941), FRUS, *The Far East, 1941, Vol. IV*, p. 382.

"Hornbeck did not"—Ballantine Reminiscences, pp. 46, 211.

"from the outset"—Hornbeck Autobiography, pp. 71-72.

234   "an all-out"—Memorandum by Adviser on Political Relations (August 21, 1941), FRUS, *The Far East, 1941, Vol. IV*, p. 387.

"Daily life"—Ambassador in Japan to Secretary of State (August 29, 1941), *id.*, p. 408.

"oil restrictions"—*Tokyo Record*, p. 185.

"taxicabs"—Memorandum of Conversation (August 27, 1941), *FRUS, The Far East, 1941, Vol. IV*, p. 403.

"In Japan"—Ambassador in Japan to Secretary of State (August 27, 1941), *id.*, p. 397.

"The Japanese Government"—Memorandum by Adviser on Political Relations (August 30, 1941), *id.*, p. 414.

"We are not"—Memorandum by Adviser on Political Relations (September 5, 1941), *id.*, p. 427. *See id.*, p. 419 ("Japan is in a weakened and perilous position," Hornbeck told the Secretary of State, and "is in no position to attack, with the expectation of success, either the Russians, the British and Dutch or the United States").

235   "What do you people"—*Pearl Harbor Reexamined*, p. 43. Emmerson says in this essay that he returned to Washington by "late October." In *The Japanese Thread*, he says he "reported for duty at the State Department in mid-November." *The Japanese Thread*, p. 116. Emmerson apparently had the conversation with Hornbeck before he reported for duty.

"Far from exhausting"—*Tokyo Record*, p. 153.

"great solicitude"—Memorandum by Adviser on Political Relations (August 30, 1941), *FRUS, The Far East, 1941, Vol. IV.*, p. 414.

235-36   "I don't quite know"—Grew Diary (September 1941), pp. 5630-33. *See* Ambassador in Japan to Secretary of State (September 12, 1940), *FRUS, The Far East, 1940, Vol. IV*, p. 603 (Grew's "Green Light" telegram).

236   "The present deterioration"—Memorandum by Secretary of State (August 28, 1941), *FRUS, Japan, 1931-1941, Vol. II*, pp. 572-73.

"highly commended"—Nomura Diary, *The Pacific War Papers*, p. 172.

"to accelerate"—Memorandum by Secretary of State (August 28, 1941), *FRUS,   Japan, 1931-1941, Vol. II*, pp. 574-75.

237   "in strictest"—Ambassador in Japan to Secretary of State (August 18, 1941), *FRUS, The Far East, 1941, Vol. IV*, p. 381.

"mutually agreed"—Nomura Diary, *The Pacific War Papers*, p. 173.

"proposed"—"Pacific Parley Doubted," N.Y. *Times* (September 3, 1941), p. 1. The article misspelled "Chesapeake," and that error has been corrected here.

"Mr. Hull"—Ballantine Reminiscences, p. 208.

237-38   "his appreciation"—Memorandum of Conversation (August 28, 1941), *FRUS, Japan, 1931-1941, Vol. II*, pp. 576-77.

238   "it would be unfortunate"—*Id.*, p. 577.

"was a man"—*Id.*, p. 579.

"[H]e is very careful"—Nomura Diary, *The Pacific War Papers*, p. 174.

238-39   "In liberal circles"—Ambassador in Japan to Secretary of State (August 30, 1941), *FRUS, The Far East, 1941, Vol. IV*, p. 418.

239   "There is no way"—Grew Telegram of August 30, 1941, Box 183 (Hornbeck Papers).

"there was no assurance"—Memorandum of Conversation (September 1, 1941), *FRUS, Japan, 1931-1941, Vol. II*, p. 585.

239-40   "the Government of Japan"—Memorandum by Secretary of State (September 3, 1941), *id.*, pp. 591-92.

240   "was still favorable"—*Id.*, p. 588.

"leave no stone"—Conversation (September 4, 1941), Grew Diary, p. 5678; Memorandum by Ambassador in Japan (September 4, 1941), *FRUS, Japan, 1931-1941, Vol. II*, p. 593.

240-41   "not make"—Draft Proposal Handed by Japanese Ambassador (September 6, 1941), *FRUS, Japan, 1931-1941, Vol. II*, pp. 608-09.

241   "a difference"—Comment by Ambassador in Japan (September 4, 1941), *id.*, pp. 594-95.

"would always"—Comment by Ambassador in Japan (September 5, 1941), *id.*, pp. 602-03.

"In various respects"—*Japan's Decision*, pp. 130-31.

242   "complete its preparation"—*Id.*, pp. 135-36.

"to give precedence"—Konoye Memoirs, p. 4004. In *1941*, Eri Hotta quotes another Japanese source in saying that Konoye rejected Hirohito's request that the resolutions of the proposed policy statement be reversed so that it would be clear that diplomacy would be "Japan's overwhelming priority." According to *1941*, the Prime Minister responded to the Emperor's request to reverse the order of the resolutions by saying, "'That would be impossible.'"

1941, p. 173. It may be, as *1941* suggests, that Konoye's response did not signal a refusal to give priority to diplomacy but was merely an indication that he could not change the wording of the policy statement. That posture may explain why Konoye proposed that Hirohito raise the matter of priorities directly with the military chiefs rather than with him. This appears to be the interpretation set forth in *Emperor Hirohito and the Pacific War*, pp. 93-94.

243   "the probable length"—Quoted in *1941*, p. 174. *See Hirohito and the Making of Modern Japan*, pp. 410-12, which includes a similar exchange.

"hinterland"—Konoye Memoirs, p. 4004.

"to cooperate"—Quoted in *Hirohito and the Making of Modern Japan*, p. 413. *See Tojo and the Coming of the War*, p. 257; *The Rising Sun*, p. 101.

"try to prevent"—*Japan's Decision*, pp. 138, 149.

244   "When Prime Minister Konoye"—Quoted in *The Final Confrontation*, pp. 175-76.

"The question"—Quoted in *id.*, pp. 176.

"All the seas"—*Japan's Decision*, p. 151, n.36.

"I always read"—quoted in *The Final Confrontation*, p. 176. In *1941*, Hotta agrees that Hirohito had read a "peace poem" but says that Tojo "did not think the emperor was objecting to war. To him, the poem represented imperial encouragement for the military in the face of long odds." *1941*, p. 178. However, *The Final Confrontation* (relying on a Japanese source) quotes Tojo as saying upon returning to his office after the Imperial Conference, "His Majesty is for peace, I tell you!" *The Final Confrontation*, p. 177. *The Final Confrontation* (again relying on a Japanese source) also quotes a member of the Military Affairs Bureau as saying, "War is absolutely out of the question!" *Id.* *See Emperor Hirohito and the Pacific War*, p. 96 ("[t]here was no doubt in anyone's mind at the conference that the emperor wanted the supreme command to pursue diplomatic means, not war preparation"). A possible reconciliation with *1941* may be that, while agreeing to give precedence to diplomacy, Tojo believed that Hirohito was also signaling his willingness to wage war if the conditions for peaceful settlement were not achieved. *See Hirohito and the Making of Modern Japan*, pp. 410-14.

"Ushiba told Dooman"—Memoir of Eugene H. Dooman (hereafter "Dooman Memoir"), Box 1, Folder 19 (Dooman Papers), p. 29. The pages of the Dooman Memoir are not paginated by Dooman and have been inserted. In that memoir, Dooman says that Ushiba called him on September 4 to convey the invitation. However, Grew's contemporaneous record says the invitation was conveyed on September 5. Ambassador in Japan to Secretary of State (September 5, 1941), *FRUS, Japan, 1931- 1941, Vol. II*, pp. 600-01. Reliance has been placed on that latter date because Dooman's Memoir was written in the winter of 1968 when the former Embassy Counselor was 78 years old.

245   "probably"—Grew Diary (September 6, 1941), p. 5643. Dooman's Memoir says that he and Grew were taken to the home of Baron Tokugawa, an army general, whose home had been placed at the disposal of Prince Tokugawa, an influential political figure. Dooman Memoir, p. 29. However, Grew's contemporaneous record—as well as his post-war memoir (published in 1952)—say that the men were taken to the home of Baron Ito. Grew Diary (September 6, 1941), p. 5643; *Turbulent Era, Vol. II*, p. 1325. Reliance has been placed on Grew's records because Dooman wrote his memoir in 1968 when he was 78.

"especially delicious"—Grew Diary (September 6, 1941), p. 5643.

"were splendid"—Konoye Memoirs, p. 4005.

"Konoye said"—Dooman Reminiscences, pp. 95-96. *See* Dooman Memoir, pp. 29-30; *The Rising Sun*, p. 102; *Turbulent Era, Vol. II*, p. 1331.

"conclusively and wholeheartedly"—Memorandum by Ambassador in Japan (September 6, 1941), *FRUS, Japan, 1931-1941, Vol. II*, p. 604-05.

246   "the present regrettable"—*Id.*, 604.

"certain elements"—*Id.*, p. 605.

"any inkling"—Dooman Reminiscences, p. 94; Dooman Memoir, p. 31.   Dooman visited Japan after the war and asked Ushiba whether he knew what the proposal was. Ushiba said that he did not and that the proposal was probably known only to Hirohito and Kido. Dooman Memoir, p. 31.

Grew's report to Hull on September 6—referenced in the next note—said that the military leaders, as well as the Navy and War

Ministers, had agreed to the proposal, and so presumably they knew as well.

"it might take"—Memorandum by Ambassador in Japan (September 6, 1941), *FRUS, Japan, 1931-1941, Vol. II*, p. 605.

"impossible"—Dooman Reminiscences, p. 94.

247   "abounded"—Dooman Memoir, p. 29.

"personally and confidentially"—Memorandum by Ambassador in Japan (September 6, 1941), *FRUS, Japan, 1931-1941, Vol. II*, p. 606.

"to the commander-in-chief"—Dooman Reminiscences, p. 95; Dooman Memoir, p. 31.

"Now"—In his 1962 interview, Dooman stated that, upon receipt of Konoye's radio report, the Emperor would "command the army to suspend hostilities." Dooman Reminiscences, p. 95. In his 1968 memoir, Dooman stated that, upon receipt of the radio report, the Emperor would "order thewithdrawal of our troops from China." Dooman Memoir, p. 31. There is no apparent way to reconcile the different language, but I have chosen to rely on Dooman's 1962 statement because (1) it is consistent with the other statement in Dooman's 1962 interview about the suspension of hostilities in China, (2) suspending hostilities posed far fewer logistical problems than withdrawing about a million troops from China, and (3) Dooman's memoir was written 18 years later when Dooman's recollection may have blurred. In either event, it is clear that Konoye told Grew and Dooman that an agreement with Roosevelt would result in the Emperor's termination of military combat in China.

"determined"—Memorandum by Ambassador in Japan (September 6, 1941), *FRUS, Japan, 1931-1941, Vol. II*, p. 606.

Chapter 16: Frustration

249   "[F]our men"—*Ten Years*, p. 459. Grew reported that the attempt was made on September 18, but *New York Times* correspondent Otto Tolischus learned of the attempted assassination on September 10 and said that it had happened a few days earlier. *See Tokyo Record*, p. 246.

"I don't like"—*Ten Years*, p. 459.

249-50   "I thought"—Grew Diary (October 19, 1941), p. 5845.

250   "owing to"—Grew Diary (October 10, 1941), p. 5860.

"suggested"—Grew Diary (September 16, 1941), p. 5650.

251   "I can't imagine"—*The Japanese Thread*, p. 115.

"redraft"—Memorandum of Conversation (September 4, 1941), *FRUS, Japan, 1931-1941, Vol. II*, p. 596.

"It was not until"—Memorandum of Conversation (September 10, 1941), *id.*, p. 615.

"satisfied"—Secretary of State to Ambassador in Japan (September 9, 1941), *FRUS, The Far East, 1941, Vol. IV*, p. 433.

252   "deadlock"—Memorandum by Ambassador in Japan (September 10,   1941), *FRUS, Japan, 1931-1941, Vol. II*, p. 611-12. *See id.*, p. 489.

"had narrowed"—Memorandum of Conversation (September 10, 1941), *id.*, pp. 613-14.

"obviate"—Memorandum by Ambassador in Japan (September 13, 1941), *id.*, pp. 620, 623-24.

253   "that no progress"—Ambassador in Japan to Secretary of State (September 20, 1941), *FRUS, The Far East, 1941, Vol. IV*, p. 465; Secretary of State to Ambassador in Japan (September 22, 1941), *id.*, p. 468. *See* Nomura Diary, *The Pacific War Papers*, p. 182.

"certain themes"—Note (September 6, 1941), Box 188 (Hornbeck Papers).

"The holding"—Memorandum by Adviser on Political Relations (September 5, 1941), *FRUS, The Far East, 1941, Vol. IV*, p. 426.

"a Gallup poll"—*At Dawn We Slept*, p. 206. *See The John Doe Associates*, p. 240.

254   "We are confident"—Quoted in *Turbulent Era, Vol. II*, p. 1365.

"a very carefully"—*Ickes Diary, Vol. III*, p. 608.

"communistic"—Memorandum of Ambassador in Japan (September 22, 1941), *FRUS, Japan, 1931-1941, Vol. II*, p. 633; *Ten Years*, pp. 431-33.

254-55   "is courageously"—Ambassador in Japan to President Roosevelt (September 22, 1941), *FRUS, The Far East, 1941, Vol. IV*, pp. 468-69.

255   "no prospect"—*Japan's Decision*, p. 135.

"no confidence"—Kido Diary, *The Pacific War Papers*, pp. 122-23. The actual quotation in Kido's diary is "15 October," but that has been changed to "October 15" for ease of reading.

255-56   "You cannot leave"—Quoted in *1941*, p. 188.

256   "the anxiety"—Memorandum by Ambassador in Japan (September 27, 1941), *FRUS, Japan, 1931-1941, Vol. II*, pp. 642-44.

"The counterproposal"—Japanese Ambassador to Secretary of State (September 27, 1941), *id.*, pp. 636-40.

"one of the longest"—Grew Diary (September 1941), p. 5629.

257   "Japan is now"—Ambassador in Japan to Secretary of State (September 29, 1941), *FRUS, The Far East, 1941, Vol. IV*, pp. 485-86.

257-58   "The question arises"—*Id.*, pp. 486-87.

258   "*narrowed* their position"—Exchange between Hull and Roosevelt, *FRUS, The Far East, 1941, Vol. IV*, p. 483 (emphasis in original). The original notes are found in Box 43, Diplomatic Correspondence - Japan (Roosevelt Papers).

"served to narrow"—Memorandum by Joseph W. Ballantine (September 23, 1941), *FRUS, The Far East, 1941, Vol. IV*, p. 475.

"no promises"—Stimson Diary (October 6, 1941). When he was chairman of the Democratic National Committee, Hull had expressed similar skepticism about Japan's willingness to honor agreements it had signed, in that case the disarmament agreements reached at the Washington Conferences of 1921-22. "Japan, as she has done for thirty years," said Hull, "will agree on paper and then proceed with her fixed policy of economic penetration of China, Siberia, Manchuria, and other portions of the Far East." *Hull Memoirs, Vol. I*, p. 117.

"reveal"—Memorandum by Joseph W. Ballantine (September 23, 1941), *FRUS, The Far East, 1941, Vol. IV*, p. 475.

259   "unmistakably clear"—*Id.*

"to exert pressure"—Secretary of State to Ambassador in Japan (October 15, 1941), *id.*, p. 510.

"Today"—"Hull on Birthday Urges Faith in Future," *N.Y. Times* (October 3, 1941), p. 5.

"just keep it"—Bishop Interview, p. 8.

259-60   "Japan's desire"—Memorandum of Conversation (October 2, 1941), *FRUS, Japan, 1931-1941, Vol. II*, p. 659.

260   "Southwest Pacific"—*Id.*, p. 660.

"to judge"—*Hull Memoirs, Vol. II*, p. 1028; Memorandum of Conversation (October 2, 1941), *FRUS, Japan 1931-1941, Vol. II*, p. 660.

"would be likely"—Memorandum of Conversation (October 2, 1941), *FRUS, Japan, 1931-1941, Vol. II*, p. 661.

261   "was overwhelmed"—Nomura Diary, *The Pacific War Papers*, p. 188.

"his Government"—Memorandum of Conversation (October 2, 1941), *FRUS, Japan, 1931-1941, Vol. II*, pp. 655-56.

"have finally"—Quoted in *The Final Confrontation*, p. 211.

"was the turning point"—Dooman Reminiscences, p. 112.

"[T]he Japanese"—Konoye Memoirs, p. 4008.

261-62   "It was true"—Memorandum by Ambassador in Japan (October 7, 1941), *FRUS, Japan, 1931-1941, Vol. II*, pp. 662-63.

262   "fully subscribed"—*Id.*, p. 664.

"unofficially and privately"—*Id.*, p. 665; *Turbulent Era, Vol. II*, pp. 1334 - 1339 (in Grew's view, the State Department's policy and attitude between August and November 1941 was "uncompromising" and "almost completely inflexible").

"I have the feeling"—Grew Diary (October 13, 1941), p. 5839.

"to assure itself"—Memorandum by Ambassador in Japan (October 7, 1941), *FRUS, Japan, 1931-1941, Vol. II*, pp. 664-65. *See FRUS, The Far East, 1941, Vol. IV*, p. 501 n. 97 (Grew telling Hull that adverse comment by an informant on the October 2 Oral Statement was unjustified because "the tone is excellent and the substance helpful").

263   "friendly in tone"—Memorandum of Conversation (October 7, 1941), *FRUS, Japan, 1931-1941, Vol. II*, p. 667. *See id.*, pp. 667-69.

Chapter 17: Resignation

265   "set forth"—*Ten Years*, p. 454. *See* Memorandum by Ambassador in Japan (October 10, 1941), *FRUS, Japan, 1931-1941, Vol. II*, pp. 677-78.

"considerably stiffened"—Nomura Diary, *The Pacific War Papers*, p. 178.

266   "needed three months"—Stimson Diary (October 6, 1941).

"to narrow down"—Memorandum of Conversation (October 9, 1941), *FRUS, Japan, 1931-1941, Vol. II*, pp. 670-72.

"to see"—*Id.*, p. 671.

267   "point-by-point"—Memorandum of Conversation (October 9, 1941), *id.*, pp. 672-77.

"of very valuable time"—Memorandum by Ambassador in Japan (October 10, 1941), *id.*, p. 678.

"would create"—*Id.*, p. 679.

268   "his impressions" & "unanimous"—Memorandum by Under Secretary of State (October 13, 1941), *id.*, pp. 680-81.

"been very clearly"—*id.*, p. 682.

"Welles—who already believed"—*See* PHA, Part 2, p. 496 (Welles testifying that it seemed to him, "from the middle of September, more or less, that there   wasn't the remotest possible chance of reaching a satisfactory and peaceful solution...and that consequently hostilities would probably be inevitable").

"because of assassination"—Memorandum of Conversation (October 13, 1941), *FRUS, Japan, 1931-1941, Vol. II*, pp. 682-86.

"Two days later"—Hull's telegram was sent at 6 pm on October 15, 1941. Secretary of State to Ambassador to Japan (October 15, 1941), *FRUS,   1941, The Far East, Vol. IV*, p. 509. That was 8 am on October 16 in Tokyo. It could take two hours or more for a telegram to reach the Embassy in Tokyo. So Grew would have been able to see Hull's telegram before Konoye tendered   the resignations of his cabinet on the afternoon of October 16.

268-69   "The American reply"—*Japan's Decision*, p. 180.

269   "The United States"—Quoted in *The Final Confrontation*, p. 216.

"What if"—Quoted in *id.*, p. 215.

"If the Navy"—Quoted in *id.*, p.216.

"a war"—Quoted in *1941*, p. 20. Nagano did not approve of the Pearl Harbor attack until October 19 or 20 at the earliest. *See At Dawn We Slept*, p. 299 n. 22. Langer and Gleason say the approval was given on November 3, 1941. *See The Undeclared War*, p. 854.

269-70   "The Navy"—Quoted in *The Rising Sun*, p. 109.

270   "We have indeed"—Konoye Memoirs, p. 4009.

"too extravagant"—Kido Diary, *The Pacific War Papers*, pp. 123-24.

"To change"—*See* Konoye Memoirs, p. 4010.

"I have"—*Id.*

"We as persons"—Quoted in *Konoe Fumimaro and the Failure of Peace in Japan*, p. 128.

"were so sudden"—Konoye Memoirs, pp. 4009-10.

271   "he was not sure"—Kido Diary, *The Pacific War Papers*, p. 126.

"there is"—Konoye Memoirs, p. 4010.

"To plunge"—*Id.*, Appendix VIII.

"lack"—Quoted in *Emperor Hirohito and the Pacific War*, p. 100.

"surprised"—Grew Diary (October 16, 1941), p. 5839.

"was normally"—Memorandum by Counselor (October 17, 1941), *FRUS, Japan, 1931-1941, Vol. II*, pp. 689-90.

272   "It is"—*Id.*, pp. 691-92.

"a prisoner"—*The Road to Pearl Harbor*, p. 275.

"There were many"—*See, for example, Hirohito and the Making of Modern Japan*, p. 404 ("[i]f a summit had taken place, Konoe's set of stale positions, already proven inadequate, could never had led to a modus vivendi, and might even have hastened the coming of war"); *Japan Prepares for Total War*, p. 242 (the Army's demand that Konoye adhere to the decisions of the   August 4 Liaison Conference—which reflected the Army's refusal to compromise on certain points—"ensured that a summit, had one been held, would have failed").

272-73   "absorbingly interesting"—Dooman letter to Feis (July 8, 1949), Box 1, Folder 2 (Dooman Papers).

273   "those documents"—Dooman Reminiscences, pp. 120-21.

"[H]e was somebody"—Interview with Waldo H. Heinrichs, Jr. (February 25, 2017).

"We in Tokyo"—*Turbulent Era, Vol. II*, pp. 1352, 1354, 1359 (emphasis in original). *See* Ambassador in Japan to Secretary of State (October 7, 1941), *FRUS, The Far East, 1941, Vol. IV*, pp.

500-01 (reporting on a conversation with former Prime Minister Hirota).

"There were some"—*See The Currents of War*, p. 204, and sources cited there.

Chapter 18: The Second Warning

275   "[Y]ou are always"—Grew letter to Anita Grew English (October 30, 1941) (Grew Papers).

"harmonize"—Kido Diary, *The Pacific War Papers*, p. 126.

276   "The prince"—Quoted in *The Final Confrontation*, p. 232.

"serious problems"—Quoted in *id.*, p. 234.

"He stood"—*See Tojo and the Coming of War*, p. 73. Max Hill said that Tojo was "a larger man than the average Japanese." *Exchange Ship*, p. 162.

"had a scraggy"—*Exchange Ship*, p. 163.

"certain pallor"—*Behind the Japanese Mask*, p. 127.

"sharp intellect"—*Tokyo Record*, p. 278.

"a sharp and cutting mind"—Edwin P. Hoyt, *Warlord: Tojo Against the World* (2001), p. xvi. *See Tojo and the Coming of the War*, p. 42.

"his insistence"—Quoted in *The Final Confrontation*, p. 246.

277   "the Japanese Gestapo"—*Tokyo Record*, p. 276.

"[T]he Emperor"—Quoted in *Emperor Hirohito and the Pacific War*, p. 103.

"From the way"—Quoted in *The Final Confrontation*, p. 237.

"We direct you"—Quoted in *Tojo and the Coming of War*, p. 301.

278   "Deep consideration"—Kido Diary, *The Pacific War Papers*, p. 128.

"the emperor's message"—Quoted in *The Final Confrontation*, p. 241.

"an increase"—"Japan Surprised by Call for Diet," *N.Y. Times* (October 25, 1941), p. 1.

279   "Get up"—Quoted in *Exchange Ship*, pp. 165-66.

"was held"—Grew Diary (October 18, 1941), p. 5842. *See* Ambassador in Japan to Secretary of State (October 20, 1941), *FRUS, The Far East, 1941, Vol. IV,* p. 542.

"be tantamount"—Togo Shigneroi, *The Cause of Japan* (1956), p. 45.

279-80   "the necessity"—*Id.,* p. 52.

280   "from the uncompromising"—*Id.,* pp. 54-55.

"an experienced"—Memorandum by Chief of the Far Eastern Affairs Division (October 18, 1941), *FRUS, The Far East, 1941, Vol. IV,* p. 523.

"it would be"—Ambassador in Japan to Secretary of State (October 20, 1941), *FRUS, The Far East, 1941, Vol. IV,* p. 542. In testimony before the congressional committee investigating the Pearl Harbor attack, Grew later said that "Japan had a totalitarian form of government after the Tojo cabinet came in." PHA, Part 2, p. 595. *See id.,* p. 626. Grew never reconciled his pre-Pearl Harbor attack memorandum with his post-Pearl Harbor attack testimony. While the military, and especially the Army, had considerable influence in the decision-making process in the final months before the Pearl Harbor attack, Tojo did not possess the powers of a dictator to unilaterally make decisions of war and peace. It may be that, in describing the Japanese government as totalitarian, Grew had in mind the control wielded by the government as a whole and not the power exercised by a single leader.

"informant"—Memorandum by Ambassador in Japan (October 25, 1941), *FRUS, Japan, 1931-1941, Vol. II,* p. 698.

280-81   "a wholly reliable source"—Ambassador in Japan to Secretary of State (October 26, 1941), *FRUS, The Far East, 1941, Vol. IV,* p. 554.

281   "possibility"—Grew Telegram of October 25, 1941, Box 194 (Hornbeck Papers).

"wholly reliable informant"—Note (November 5, 1941), Box 188, *id.*

"Hull thinks"—Stimson Diary (October 28, 1941). *See The Undeclared War,* p.   850.

"The entire purpose"—PHA, Part, 2, p. 462.

282   "two months' respite"—Roosevelt to Churchill (October 15, 1941), Warren F. Kimball (ed.), *Churchill and Roosevelt: The Complete Correspondence, Vol. I* (Princeton University Press: Princeton, NJ, 1984), p. 250.

"the delicate question"—Stimson Diary (October 16, 1941). *See* PHA, Part 11, p. 5426 (Stimson description of the "so-called War Cabinet").

"It is a matter"—Nomura Diary, *The Pacific War Papers*, pp. 192-93.

"conciliatory"—*Id.*, p. 193. *See* Memorandum of Conversation by Secretary of State (October 17, 1941), FRUS, *The Far East, 1941, Vol. IV*, pp. 516, 518 (attaching a memorandum from British ambassador of his conversation with Nomura).

283   "I am now"—Nomura Diary, *The Pacific War Papers*, pp. 194-95.

"without delay"—Memorandum by Under Secretary of State (October 24, 1941), FRUS, *Japan, 1931-1941, Vol. II*, pp. 692-97.

"On entering"—*Ten Years*, p. 465.

283-84   "What a difference"—*Id.*

284   "was a person"—Dooman Reminiscences, p. 71.

"The United States"—*The Cause of Japan*, p. 62.

"[T]he attitude"—Quoted in *The Undeclared War*, p. 851.

"progressively worsened"—Ambassador in Japan to Secretary of State (October 30, 1941), FRUS, *Japan, 1931-1941, Vol. II*, pp. 699-700.

285   "It seems"—President Roosevelt to Ambassador in Japan (October 30, 1941), FRUS, *The Far East, 1941, Vol. IV*, p. 560. A copy of the signed letter is found in Box 43, President's Secretary's File (Roosevelt Papers).

"If Tojo"—Grew Diary (October 1941), p. 5815.

"I don't want"—*Id.* (November 3, 1941), p. 5939.

286   "the greater part"—Ambassador in Japan to Secretary of State (November 3, 1941), FRUS, *Japan, 1931-1941*, Vol. II, pp. 702-03.

"constructive conciliation"—Ambassador in Japan to Secretary of State (September 29, 1941), *id.*, p. 647.

"any 'appeasement'"—Ambassador in Japan to Secretary of State (November 3, 1941), *id.*, p. 704.

"[I]t would be"—*Id.* The telegram published in FRUS is a paraphrase of the complete telegram, which was published in PHA, Part 14, p. 1045 *et seq.* Grew's reference to the Japanese attack at Port Arthur is found in PHA, Part 2, p. 566 (although Grew incorrectly stated that the attack occurred in 1905 when, in fact, it occurred in 1904).

287   "from foreign soil"—Grew Diary (November 1941), p. 5935.

"which would be"—*Id.*, pp. 5935-36.

"preliminary"—*Id.*, p.5936.

"the desire"—Stimson Diary (April 22, 1941).

288   "I believe"—Grew Diary (November 1941), p. 5936.

"If war"—*Id.*, p. 5930.

Chapter 19: Kurusu

289   "In Tennessee alone"—www.onlinelibrary.com. *See* Kathy Bennett, "Lynching," *Tennessee Encyclopedia of History and Culture* (Version 2.0 1998); "Hey, Boy, Do You Want to See a Hangin'," *Washington Post* (June 9, 2017) (177 blacks were reportedly lynched in Tennessee between 1882 and 1930).

"They have been"—www.jacksonsun.com/story/life/2017/06/05.

290   "the outset"—*Hull Memoirs, Vol. II*, p. 1101.

"The reasoning"—Memorandum by Adviser on Political Relations (November 5, 1941), *FRUS, The Far East, 1941, Vol. IV*, p. 568-69.

"was rapidly"—PHA, Part 11, p. 5380.

"restitution"—Grew Diary (November 5, 1941), p. 5941.

291   "widely circulated"—Secretary of State to Ambassador in Japan (November 5, 1941), *FRUS, The Far East, 1941, Vol. IV*, p. 569.

"nasty"—Grew Diary (November 5, 1941), pp. 5941-42.

"appeared"—Ambassador in Japan to Secretary of State (November 7 & 8, 1941), *FRUS, The Far East, 1941, Vol. IV*, pp. 574-75; Grew Diary (November 7 & 8, 1941), pp. 5949, 5952.

292   "there is"—Nomura Diary, *The Pacific War Papers*, p. 162.

"Immediately"—J. Garry Clifford and Masako R. Okura, *The Desperate Diplomat: Saburo Kurusu's Memoir of the Weeks before Pearl Harbor* (2016) (hereafter *Desperate Diplomat*), p. 168 n.3.

"the participation"—*Id.*, p. 53.

292-93   "While on the train"—*The Cause of Japan*, p. 150.

293   "The Navy"—*Japan's Decision*, p. 186.

"amid"—*Id.*, p. 199.

"it was not"—*The Cause of Japan*, pp. 130-31.

294   "act independently"—*Japan's Decision*, p. 210.

"to be used"—*The Cause of Japan*, pp. 133-34.

"except French Indochina"—*Japan's Decision*, pp. 210-11.

"Nagano had approved"—Langer and Gleason said in 1953 that Nagano approved Yamamoto's plan on November 3 and that the date for the attack was established on November 7. *The Undeclared War*, p. 854. John Toland similarly stated in 1970 that the date for the attack was approved on November 7. *The Rising Sun*, p. 169. However, Gordon Prange, relying on statements of numerous naval officers and other evidence, said in 1981 that Nagano approved Yamamoto's plan on October 19 or 20 and that the Navy General Staff had decided by October 30 that the attack would be made on December 8 (December 7 local time). *At Dawn We Slept*, p. 299 n. 22 & p. 325. Prange's statement is consistent with Noriko Kawamura's later statement in *Emperor Hirohito and the Pacific War* (based on Japanese sources) that Nagano and Sugiyama advised Hirohito about the timing of the attack on November 3. *Emperor Hirohito and the Pacific War*, p. 107.

294-95   "To adopt"—Quoted in *The Undeclared War*, p. 852.

295   "further concessions"—*The Cause of Japan*, p. 144.

"may be unavoidable"—Quoted in *Emperor Hirohito and the Pacific War*, p. 106.

"doggedly"—*Desperate Diplomat*, p. 57.

"Please do your best"—Quoted in *The Rising Sun*, p. 130.

"Togo wanted"—Grew Diary (November 4, 1941), pp. 5939-40.

296   "one of Japan's"—*Turbulent Era, Vol. II*, p. 1247.

"was going"—Grew Diary (November 4, 1941), pp. 5940, 5988.

"a new plan"—*Desperate Diplomat*, p. 58.

"I was"—*Id.*

"final effort"—*The Cause of Japan*, pp. 147-49.

297   "if the Chinese"—Memorandum of Conversation (November 7, 1941), *FRUS, Japan, 1931-1941, Vol. II*, pp. 706-09.

"We should be"—*Hull Memoirs, Vol. II*, p. 1058.

"[w]ar between"—Memorandum to the President (November 5, 1941), PHA, Part 14, pp. 1061-67.

298   "he wanted"—Wickard Diary (November 8, 1941); PHA, Part 27, p. 5420 (Stimson testimony).

"[T]he American Government"—Memorandum by Ambassador in Japan (November 10, 1941), *FRUS, Japan, 1931-1941, Vol. II*, pp. 710-14.

"understand the realities"—*Id.*, p. 713.

299   "[h]is present"—*Roosevelt and Hopkins*, p. 329.

"best"—Memorandum by Secretary of State (November 10, 1941), *FRUS, Japan, 1931-1941, Vol. II*, p. 718.

"not [his] wish"—Nomura Diary, *The Pacific War Papers*, p. 201.

"shocked"—Memorandum by Ambassador in Japan (November 12, 1941), *FRUS, Japan, 1931-1941, Vol. II*, pp. 719-21.

299-300   "While"—Memorandum of Comment (November 12, 1941), *id.*, p. 722.

300   "reached"—Memorandum of Conversation (November 12, 1941), *id.*, p. 723-24.

301   would be automatically"—Memorandum of Conversation (November 15, 1941), *id.*, pp. 731-34.

"be receiving"—*Id.*, p. 734.

"The American press"—*See, for example*, the headline of a page-one *New York Times* article on October 31, 1941: "U.S. Won't Move to Appease Tokyo."

"how widespread"—*Ickes Diary, Vol. III*, pp. 635-36.

"would have promptly"—*Id.*, p. 655. *See The Currents of War*, pp. 236-37 (Ickes' view was supported by public opinion polls which "revealed overwhelming support for a firm stand against Japan" and by "leading newspapers" which "continued their call for a strong stand").

302   "military leaders"—Ambassador in Japan to Secretary of State (November 13, 1941), *FRUS, The Far East, 1941, Vol. IV*, pp. 589-91.

"the need"—Ambassador in Japan to Secretary of State (November 17, 1941), *FRUS, Japan, 1931-1941, Vol. II*, p. 744.

"I realize"—"Kurusu Arrives," *N.Y. Times* (November 15, 1941), p. 5.

"agreeably surprised"—Memorandum of Conversation (November 17, 1941), *FRUS, Japan, 1931-1941, Vol. II*, p. 738.

303   "accepted"—Memorandum by Secretary of State (November 17, 1941), *id.*, pp. 740-43.

"introducer"—Nomura Diary, *The Pacific War Papers*, p. 203.

"nothing new"—Memorandum of Conversation (November 17, 1941), *FRUS, Japan, 1931-1941, Vol. II*, p. 742.

"time element"—*Desperate Diplomat*, p. 79. *See* Nomura Diary, *The Pacific War Papers*, p. 203 (quoting Roosevelt as saying, "There is no last word between friends").

304   "appeared"—"Kurusu and Roosevelt Talk," *N.Y. Times* (November 18, 1941), p. 1.

304-05   "did not know"—Memorandum of Conversation (November 18, 1941), *FRUS, Japan, 1931-1941, Vol. II*, 744-50.

305   "be diverted"—*Id.*, p. 750.

"If, as seems"—Documents Prepared in the Division (November 11, 1941), *FRUS, The Far East, 1941, Vol. IV*, p. 579.

"that Kurusu"—*See Desperate Diplomat*, pp. 47, 93-94.

306   "Neither his appearance"—*Hull Memoirs, Vol. II*, pp. 1062-63.

"mission"—*Time for Decision*, p. 295.

"it might be helpful"—Secretary of State to Ambassador in Japan (November 18, 1941), *FRUS, The Far East, 1941, Vol. IV*, p. 620.

"trouble with you"—*Ten Years*, p. 479.

"long, arduous"—Grew Diary (October 17, 1941), p. 5841.

306-07   "alone"—*Id.* (November 21, 1941), p. 5968.

Chapter 20: The Hull Note

309   "He loved her" –Quoted in Joseph E. Persico, *Franklin & Lucy: President Roosevelt, Mrs. Rutherford, and the Other Remarkable Women in His Life* (2008), p. 252.

310   "as one friend to another"—Morgenthau Presidential Diaries (November 26, 1941), Vol. 4, p. 1020.

"disproportionate"—*Id.*

"The morale"—*Id.*, p. 1029. *See Hull Memoirs, Vol. II*, pp. 1076-81.

"The President"—Telegram from Nomura to Tokyo (November 18, 1941), PHA, Part 12, p. 154.

311   "complicated terms"—Telegram from Tokyo to Nomura (November 19, 1941), *id.*, p. 155.

"unfortunate"—*The Cause of Japan*, p. 161.

"no further concessions"—Telegram from Tokyo to Nomura (November 19, 1941), PHA, Part 12, p. 155.

"Japan's absolutely"—*Desperate Diplomat*, p. 84 n.3.

"ultimatum"—PHA, Part, 2, pp. 430-32, 553.

"clearly unthinkable"—*Id.*, p. 432.

312   "very cold"—*Desperate Diplomat*, p. 84; Memorandum of Conversation (November 20, 1941), *FRUS, Japan, 1931-1941, Vol. II*, p. 753.

"develop public opinion"—Memorandum of Conversation (November 20, 1941), *FRUS, Japan, 1931-1941, Vol. II.*, pp. 753-54.

"very friendly"—*Desperate Diplomat*, p. 92.

"does not infringe"—Memorandum by Secretary of State (November 21, 1941), *FRUS, Japan, 1931-1941, Vol. II*, pp. 756-57.

"because he wanted"—*Desperate Diplomat*, p. 92. Hull later took a different view of the conversation, saying that he told Kurusu that the letter "would [not] be of any particular help, and so dismissed it." *Hull Memoirs, Vol. II*, p. 1071.

313   "There are reasons"—Telegram from Tokyo to Washington (November 22, 1941), PHA, Part 12, p. 165.

"It was almost"—*Hull Memoirs, Vol. II*, p. 1074.

"a relaxation"—Memorandum of Conversation (November 22, 1941), *FRUS, Japan, 1931-1941, Vol. II*, pp. 757-61. *See* Nomura Diary, *The Pacific War Papers*, p. 207 (Hull refused Nomura's request to identify which articles in Plan B were acceptable and which were not).

314   "If things"—Letter from Ninjin Matsuda, The State Construction Association, Grew Diary (November 5, 1941), p. 5944.

"The policy speeches"—*Tokyo Record*, p. 298.

"the international situation"—*Id.*, p. 301.

"totally"—Grew Diary (November 21, 1941), p. 5968.

314-15   "unsatisfactory"—Conversation (November 24, 1941), Grew Diary, pp. 6011-15. *See* Ambassador in Japan to Secretary of State, *FRUS, Japan, 1931-1941, Vol. II*, pp. 762-64.

315   "an important story"—*Tokyo Record*, pp. 304-05.

"highest"—*Id.*, p. 306.

"Kase could not"—*See* Grew Diary (November 27, 1941), p. 5970.

315-16   "more later"—President Roosevelt to Secretary of State, *FRUS, The Far East, 1941, Vol. IV*, p. 626.

316   "a basis"—Acting Assistant Chief of Staff to Secretary of State (November 21, 1941), *id.*, p. 630.

"would be"—Memorandum of Conversation (November 24, 1941), *FRUS, The Far East, 1941, Vol. IV*, p. 646.

"I am not"—From President to Former Naval Person (November 24, 1941), *id.*, p. 649.

"There is practically"—*Hull Memoirs, Vol. II*, p. 1080.

"the Japanese were notorious"—PHA, Part 27, p. 5421 (Stimson testimony). *See* Stimson Diary (November 25, 1941) (Stimson confided to his diary that the question "was how we should maneuver them into the position of firing the first shot without allowing too much danger to ourselves").

317   "make this country"—"Japanese Envoys Still Await Word," *N.Y. Times* (November 20, 1941), p. 1.

"for a limited agreement"—"U.S.-Japan Talks at Critical Point," *N.Y. Times* (November 24, 1941), p. 1.

"There was at least"—There is some debate on whether White was or was not a Soviet agent. *See* John Koster, *Operation Snow: How a Soviet Mole in FDR's White House Triggered Pearl Harbor* (2012); R. Bruce Craig, *Treasonable Doubt: The Harry Dexter White Spy Case* (2004).

"On November 18"—Memorandum by Secretary of Treasury (November 17, 1941), *FRUS, The Far East, 1941, Vol. IV*, pp. 606-13, with footnote stating that the memorandum was sent to the Secretary of State and the President on November 18, 1941.

"Virtually"—Memorandum from H.D. White to Secretary Morgenthau (November 17, 1941), Morgenthau Diaries, Vol. 462, p. 361.

317-18   "withdraw"—Memorandum by Secretary of the Treasury (November 17, 1941), *FRUS, 1941, The Far East, Vol. IV*, pp. 606-13; H.D. White to Secretary Morgenthau (November 17, 1941), Morgenthau Diaries, Vol. 462, pp. 364-73.

318   "a further example"—*Hull Memoirs, Vol. II*, p. 1073; Memorandum of Chief of the Far Eastern Division (November 19, 1941), *FRUS, The Far East, 1941, Vol. IV.*, p. 622.

"Ironically"—*See* Morgenthau Presidential Diaries (November 27, 1941), Vol. 4, p. 1032 (recounting a conversation between T.V. Soong, a Chinese representative, and Stanley Hornbeck, in which the Political Relations Adviser said that the division began preparing a substantive agreement "some time ago...in case the United States was ready to break off with Japan....").

"What about"—For the President from the Former Naval Person (November 26, 1941), *FRUS, The Far East, 1941, Vol. IV*, p. 665.

"Hull assumed—On November 27, the British ambassador told Welles that he was surprised by Hull's "sudden change" in strategy in not giving the Japanese the *modus vivendi* proposal. Welles responded that Hull had abandoned the proposal in part because the British had given only "half-hearted" support for it. Lord Halifax advised the Under Secretary that Hull's impression was mistaken and that "he had communicated to Secretary Hull the full support of the British Government." Memorandum of Conversation (November 27, 1941), *id.*, p. 667. *See Hull Memoirs, Vol. II*, p. 1080 (Hull continuing to insist that the British had only given "half-hearted" support for the proposal).

"Hull met"—Hornbeck later said that the State Department had learned of Churchill's comments on the afternoon of November 25 from the British ambassador and that the staff had convened with Hull that evening to draft a memorandum explaining the Secretary of State's decision to abandon the alternative *modus vivendi* proposal. Hornbeck Autobiography, pp. 83-84. According to Hull, he took that memorandum to the White House "early on November 26" and read it to Roosevelt. However, records at the FDR Library show that Hull met with Roosevelt at 3:45 p.m. and not in the morning. *See Hull Memoirs, Vol. II*, pp. 1081-82; http://www.fdrlibrary.marist.edu/daybyday/daylog/november 26th 1941. I have chosen to rely on that latter time because it reflects a contemporaneous record, and Hull's *Memoirs* were written many years later. It is also noteworthy that Hull's penciled note on his memorandum states only that he read it the President without any indication of the time. *See* Secretary of State to President Roosevelt, *FRUS, The Far East, 1941, Vol. IV* (November 26, 1941), p. 665 n. 97.

319   "opposition"—Secretary of State to President Roosevelt, *FRUS, The Far East, 1941, Vol. IV*, p. 666.

"promptly agreed"—*Hull Memoirs, Vol. II*, p. 1082.

"was essentially"—PHA, Part, 2, p. 437 & Part 11, p. 5413.

"[a]micable negotiation"—*FRUS, Japan, 1931-1941, Vol. II*, pp. 449, 490; Stimson Diary (October 6, 1941).

"withdraw"—Document Handed by Secretary of State *FRUS, Japan, 1931-1941, Vol. II.*, p. 769.

"enter into"—*FRUS, The Far East, 1941, Vol. IV*, pp. 629, 638, 646.

320   "Leave this"—*id.*, p. 646 n. 75.

"a multilateral"—Document Handed by Secretary of State, *FRUS, Japan, 1931-1941, Vol. II*, pp. 768-69.

"one practical example"—PHA, Part, 2, pp. 437, 556.

"was as far"—Memorandum of Conversation (November 26, 1941), *FRUS, Japan, 1931-1941, Vol. II*, p. 765.

321   "sell the Nanking government"—*Desperate Diplomat*, p 96.

"would be likely"—Memorandum of Conversation (November 26, 1941), *FRUS, Japan, 1931-1941, Vol. II*, pp. 765-66; Nomura Diary, *The Pacific War Papers*, p. 208.

"expeditionary"—PHA, Part 27, p. 5422.

"economic restrictions"—Memorandum by Secretary of State (November 27, 1941), *FRUS, Japan, 1931-1941, Vol. II*, p. 771. *See* Secretary of State to President Roosevelt (November 27, 1941), *FRUS, The Far East, 1941, Vol. IV*, pp. 670-71.

322   "the Japanese Government"—Memorandum by Adviser on Political Relations (November 27, 1941), *FRUS, The Far East, 1941, Vol. IV*, p. 673.

"So far"—Dooman Reminiscences, p. 123.

"there is little hope"—"Japan Sees End of Negotiations," *N.Y. Times* (November 28, 1941), p. 1.

"had no serious thought"—PHA, Part 27, p. 5392.

"he had broken"—*Id.*, p. 5422. Hull disputed that he said those words to Stimson. *See Hull Memoirs, Vol. II*, p. 1080 ("I did not make...the statement later attributed to me that I had 'washed my hands' of the matter"); Ballantine Reminiscences, p. 214 (Hull telling Ballantine "that wasn't his wording and he never would have said such a thing"). However, the Secretary of State used almost those precise words in describing the situation to the British ambassador on November 29. "I expressed the view," Hull said in his summary of the conversation, "that the diplomatic part of our relations with Japan was virtually over and that the matter will now go to the officials of the Army and the Navy...." Memorandum of Conversation (November 29, 1941), *FRUS, The Far East, 1941, Vol. IV*, p. 686. It is also noteworthy that Roosevelt told Stimson on the morning of November 27 that "the talks had been called off." PHA, Part, 27, p. 5422.

322-23   "The press"—Memorandum of Chief of the Division of Far Eastern Affairs (December 2, 1941), *FRUS, The Far East, 1941, Vol. IV.*, p. 710.

323   "dumbfounded"—*Tojo and the Coming of the War*, p. 343.

         "I was utterly"—*The Cause of Japan*, p. 176.

         "knowing"—Quoted in *The Final Confrontation*, pp. 319-20

         "a broad-gauge"—Grew Diary (November 29, 1941), p. 5973.

         "regularly"—*id.*, pp. 5973-74.

         "I saw"—*Id.* (December 1, 1941), p. 6097

Chapter 21: War

325   "In December 1937"—Memorandum handed to Secretary of State (December 13, 1937), *FRUS, Japan, 1931-1941, Vol. I*, p. 523.

         "the talks"—PHA, Part 11, p. 5422 (Stimson testimony of conversation with Roosevelt on November 27, 1941).

         "to gain time"—Memorandum for the President (November 27, 1941), *id.*, Part 12, p. 1083.

         "suggested"—*Id.*, Part 11, p. 5427.

325-26   "moderate"—Secretary of State to President Roosevelt (October 17, 1941), *FRUS, The Far East, 1941, Vol. IV*, p. 521.

326   "was a figurehead"—*Hull Memoirs, Vol. II*, p. 1092.

"I believe"—Nomura Diary, *The Pacific War Papers*, p. 208.

"would result"—*The Cause of Japan*, p. 166.

"there was nothing"—*Id.*, p. 178.

326-27   "grave"—Diary of Kido Koichi, p. 42 (Toland Papers).

327   "the Navy"—*Id.*, pp. 44-45.

"The United States"—*Japan's Decision*, p. 262.

"nodded"—*Id.*, p. 283.

"December 8"—*Id.*, p 261.

"a proper"—*The Cause of Japan*, p. 199.

328   "Well"—Telegram from Tokyo to Washington (November 28, 1941), PHA, Part 12, p. 195.

"[T]he Japanese"—Grew Diary (November 29, 1941), p. 5974.

328-29   "bedlam"—"President is Grim," *N.Y. Times* (December 1, 1941), p. 1.

329   "how they felt"—Memorandum of Conversation (December 1, 1941), *FRUS, Japan, 1931-1941, Vol. II*, pp. 772-77. The day after this meeting, an official with the Japanese Embassy advised Joe Ballantine and Max Schmidt that the "bellicose" speech allegedly delivered by Tojo had actually been written by the staff of the East Asia Restoration League, that it had been read by someone else, and that the Prime Minister had not even seen the speech before it was reported in the press. *See* Memorandum of Conversation (December 2, 1941), *FRUS, The Far East, 1941, Vol. IV*, p. 777.

"The stationing"—Memorandum for Secretary of State and Under Secretary of State (December 1, 1941), President's Secretary's File, Box 43 (Roosevelt Papers).

"had the Japanese"—Morgenthau Presidential Diaries (December 3, 1941), Vol. 4, p. 1037.

330   "I am"—*Ten Years*, p. 485.

"The situation"—*Id.*, pp. 485-86.

"I have just"—Dooman Reminiscences, p. 60.

"return readily"—*Id.*, p. 124.

331   "[T]his isn't"—Memorandum of Conversation (December 5, 1941), *FRUS, Japan, 1931-1941, Vol. II*, p. 782.

"become"—Gwen Terasaki, *Bridge to the Sun: A Memoir of Love and War* (Rock Creek Books ed. 2017) (hereafter *Bridge to the Sun*), pp. 61-63.

331-32 "wipes"—E. Stanley Jones, "An Adventure in Failure: Behind the Scenes before Pearl Harbor," 45 *Asia and the Americas* (1945), pp. 609, 614; *Bridge to the Sun*, p. 65. *See Desperate Diplomat*, p. 20; *At Dawn We Slept*, pp. 451-52.

332 "intermittently"—Hornbeck Autobiography, p. 93.

"which threaten"—Draft Message (November 29, 1941), *FRUS, The Far East, 1941, Vol. IV*, pp. 697-98.

"stand-still"—Draft Message (December 6, 1941), *id.*, pp. 722-23.

"Upon arrival"—Hornbeck described the meeting with Roosevelt in his unpublished autobiography. However, the logs of Roosevelt's visitors for December 6 do not include any notation of Hornbeck's meeting with the President. *See* http://www.fdrlibrary.marist.edu/daybyday/ (December 6, 1941). The logs do indicate that Cordell Hull met with Roosevelt between 3:10 and 4:10 p.m. Hull's *Memoirs* do not reference any meeting with Roosevelt on December 6. *See Hull Memoirs, Vol. II*, p. 1094. It is therefore assumed that the reference to Hull in the logs reflects an appointment Hull made for Hornbeck. This conclusion is reinforced by a note from Hull to Roosevelt on December 6 transmitting the revised message. *See* Secretary of State to President Roosevelt (December 6, 1941), *FRUS, The Far East, 1941Vol. IV*, p. 726. Hornbeck was presumably the person who delivered this note along with the revised draft.

"expressed [his] appreciation"—Hornbeck Autobiography, p. 95.

332-33 "Almost"—President Roosevelt to Emperor Hirohito (December 6, 1941), *FRUS, Japan, 1931-1941, Vol. II*, pp. 784-86.

333 "Shoot"—PHA, Part 14, p. 1238. *See* President Roosevelt to Secretary of State (December 6, 1941), *FRUS, Japan, 1931-1941, Vol. II*, p. 784.

333-34 "at the earliest"—Grew Diary (December 7, 1941), p. 6101. *See* Secretary of State to Ambassador in Japan (December 6, 1941), *FRUS, The Far East, 1941, Vol. IV*, p. 727.

334 "an urgent matter"—Dooman Diary (December 8, 1941), Box 2 (Dooman Papers).

All the Embassy chauffeurs"—*See id.*; Stanley Weintraub, *Long Day's Journey into War: Pearl Harbor and a World at War December 7, 1941* (Lyons Press ed. 2001) p. 189.

"maximum weight"—Grew Diary (December 7, 1941), p. 6101.

335   "That's no use"—*The Cause of Japan*, p. 221.

"cannot accept"—Memorandum of Conversation (December 7, 1941), *FRUS, Japan, 1931-1941, Vol. II*, p. 792. The entire Japanese memorandum is found at *id.*, pp. 787-92.

"In all my fifty years"—*Id.*, p. 787.

336   "grim"—Grew Diary (December 8, 1941), p. 6106.

"slapped"—PHA, Part 12, p. 570.

"His Majesty"—Ambassador in Japan to Secretary of State (December 8, 1941), *FRUS, The Far East, 1941, Vol. IV*, p. 734.

"a little speech"—Grew Diary (December 8, 1941), p. 6106.

"he couldn't believe"—Smith-Hutton Reminiscences, p. 328.

337   "The demeanor"—*Behind the Japanese Mask*, p. 135.

"nothing unusual"—Dooman Reminiscences, p. 126.

"found"—*Behind the Japanese Mask*, p. 135.

"trembling"—Grew Diary (December 8, 1941), p. 6107.

337-38   "I have"—*Fearey*, p. 12.

"All sixty-five"—*See Life* Magazine (September 7, 1942), pp. 24-25.

Chapter 22: Coming Home

340   "I'll jump"—Quoted in *Exchange Ship*, p. 78. *See Smith-Hutton Reminiscences*, pp. 357-58.

341   "down our backs"—*Fearey*, p. 25.

"He was bitter"—Interview with Jon Spenser (June 3, 2014); interview with Lilla Cabot Spenser (June 1, 2014). Although Grew did not use the word "bitter" in *Turbulent Era*, it is an apt inference from Grew's description of his frustration with State Department policy in those months before the Pearl Harbor attack. *See especially Turbulent Era, Vol. II*, pp. 1272-73 ("reporting to our Government was like throwing pebbles into a lake at night") & 1333-34 ("the policy of the Administration during this critical time was almost completely inflexible").

"final political report"—Letter to the President (August 14, 1942), p. 1, MS AM 1687 II (Grew Papers) (hereafter "Roosevelt Letter"). Fearey recalled in 1991 that the report described the terms which Konoye told Grew he planned to offer Roosevelt if their requested meeting had materialized. In exchange for a lifting of the freeze and the negotiation of a new commercial treaty, Japan, Fearey remembered, would agree "not to take hostile action" against the United States if war should arise between Germany and the United States, would withdraw its military forces from China and Indochina, and would leave the fate of Manchuria to be decided after the European war had ended. According to Fearey, the report also explained that Konoye hoped to keep the settlement agreement a secret from the public until he had returned to Tokyo. At that point, said Fearey, the Prime Minister expected to secure an Imperial Rescript from Hirohito approving the agreement, thus making it impossible for "the extremist elements....to prevail against it." *Fearey*, pp. 23-24. Grew himself never described the settlement terms in any detail in any of his cables to Hull or in his post-war memoir. His letter to Roosevelt—penned in 1942 and described below—included statements that appear to be inconsistent with Fearey's recollection (especially Konoye's statement to Grew that he would accept whatever terms Roosevelt proposed except for the retention of troops in North China and Mongolia). It is also worth noting that Konoye told Dooman at the dinner on September 6, 1941 that he would radio Hirohito immediately after reaching an agreement with Roosevelt (rather than waiting until he returned to Japan). Finally, it is worth mentioning that Dooman remained unaware of the settlement terms when he drafted his memoir in the 1960s. *See* Dooman Memoir, p. 31 (Ushiba telling Dooman in 1953 that, as far as the former secretary knew, Konoye's settlement terms were known only to Hirohito and Kido). If the report included the details of Konoye's settlement terms, Dooman presumably would have known about them because, as Fearey explained, Grew shared the draft with the Embassy Counselor. *See Fearey*, p. 22. There does not appear to be any way to make a definitive determination on what the report said about the settlement terms Konoye would have offered Roosevelt.

"For the first time"—Roosevelt Letter, pp. 3, 5. Grew's conviction that Konoye would accept whatever terms Roosevelt proposed at a meeting is echoed in Shigemitsu's memoir. *See Japan and Her Destiny*, pp. 243, 250 (Konoye "gave me some inkling of his thinking" and "appeared to be thinking that there was nothing for it but to make this the turning point, to make such concessions at the meeting as would bring the talks to a satisfactory ending" and that, "if he and President Roosevelt could meet and talk matters over, he was convinced that he could restrain the fighting services")

"I told"—*Id.*, p. 6.

341-42   "of which"—*Id.*, p. 7.

342   "any encouragement"—*Id.*, p. 8.

"a clear conception"—*Id.*, p. 10.

"inevitably"—*Id.*, pp. 11-12.

343   "half threw"—*Fearey*, p. 36.

"the Secretary"—*Id.*, p. 37.

"The Ambassador had in fact"—The first page of the August 14, 1942   Roosevelt Letter in Grew's papers includes a handwritten notation, "not sent." The reference to the report on page 7 of the Roosevelt Letter includes another handwritten notation, "destroyed at Mr. Hull's request." The notations appear to be in Grew's handwriting. The file in Grew's papers at Harvard's Houghton Library includes a separate 12-page cover letter to Hull, dated February 19, 1942 and written in Tokyo, with a 264-page attachment. However, a notation states that "pages 13-146 inclusive are eliminated." Those pages presumably constituted the report. The remaining pages consist of telegrams and other documents provided to the State Department and Roosevelt before the Pearl Harbor attack.

344   "was pretty"—Interview with Barbara Fearey West (May 13, 2017).

345   "Never before"—Quoted in *At Dawn We Slept*, pp. 675-76.

346   "report in writing"—PHA, Part 12, p. 698.

"Everything"—*Id.*, pp. 698-99.

"You said"—*Id.*, p. 699.

"Did you suggest"—*Id.*

347   "correct"—*Id.*, p. 709.

"Well"—*Id.*

"reports made"—*Id.*

347-48   "the documents"—Letter from Grew to Walter Johnson (November 23, 1950) (Peter Moffat Papers). Grew's letter references "despatches," which was a common spelling among diplomats at the time. That spelling has been changed to "dispatches." In that letter, Grew did tell Johnson that he wanted to see the documents that Johnson proposed to use in his book, saying, "If those documents turn out to be identical with the actual text of the dispatch which I undertook to destroy and did destroy, I may wish to tell the Konoye story in my own present words...." Grew's letter does not explain how Johnson could have had access to a report which the former ambassador destroyed. Grew may have had in mind the possibility that Johnson had found a copy of the report (perhaps from one of those Embassy employees who carried it out of Tokyo) that Grew had not destroyed.

348   "everything"—Interview with Peter Moffat (September 12, 2016).

SELECT BIBLIOGRAPHY

Acheson, Dean, *Present at the Creation: My Years in the State Department* (W.W. Norton & Co., Inc.: New York, 1969).

Adams, Peter Alexander, "Eugene H. Dooman, 'A Penny a Dozen Expert': The Tribulations of a Japan Specialist in the American Foreign Service, 1912-1945" (University of Maryland Masters Thesis: College Park, MD, 1976).

Barnhart, Michael A., *Japan Prepares for Total War: The Search for Economic Security*, 1919- 1941 (Cornell University Press: Ithaca, New York, 1987).

Beschloss, Michael, *Presidents of War* (Crown: New York, 2018).

Bix, Herbert P. , *Hirohito and the Making of Modern Japan* (HarperCollins: New York, 2000).

Bullitt, Orville (ed.), *For the President: Personal and Secret* (Houghton Mifflin Co.: Boston, 1972).

Burns, James MacGregor, *Roosevelt: The Lion and the Fox* (Harcourt Brace & Jovanovich, Inc.: New York, 1956).

Burns, James MacGregor, *Roosevelt: The Soldier of Freedom* 1940-1945 (Harcourt Brace & Jovanovich, Inc.: New York, 1970).

Butow, R.J.C. , *The John Doe Associates: Backdoor Diplomacy for Peace, 1941* (Stanford University Press: Stanford, CA, 1974).

Butow, Robert J. C. , *Tojo and the Coming of the War* (Stanford University Press: Stanford, CA, 1961).

Byas, Hugh, *Government Assassination* (Alfred A. Knopf: New York, 1942).

Chace, James, *Acheson: The Secretary of State Who Created the American World* (Simon & Schuster: New York, 1998).

Clifford, J. Garry & Masako R. Okura (eds.), *The Desperate Diplomat: Saburo Kurusu's Memoir of the Weeks before Pearl Harbor* (University of Missouri Press: Columbia, MO., 2016).

Conroy, Hilary & Harry Wray (eds.), *Pearl Harbor Reexamined: Prologue to the Pacific War* (University of Hawaii Press: Honolulu, 1990).

Craigie, Sir Robert, *Behind the Japanese Mask* (Hutchinson & Co.: London, 1945).

Dallek, Robert, *Franklin D. Roosevelt and American Foreign Policy 1932-1945* (Oxford University Press, Second Ed.: New York, 1995).

Davis, Kenneth S., *FDR: The War President* 1940-1943 (Random House: New York, 2000).

Dunn, Susan, *1940: FDR, Willkie, Lindbergh, Hitler—*

the Election Amid the Storm (Yale University Press: New Haven, CT, 2013).

Emmerson, John K., *The Japanese Thread: A Life in the U.S. Foreign Service* (Holt, Rinehart & Winston: New York, 1978).

Feis, Herbert, *The Road to Pearl Harbor* (Princeton University Press: Princeton, NJ, 1950).

Fleischer, Wilfred, *Our Enemy Japan* (Doubleday, Doran & Co., Inc.: Garden City, NY, 1942).

Gellman, Irwin F., *Secret Affairs: FDR, Cordell Hull, and Sumner Welles* (Johns Hopkins University Press: Baltimore, 1995).

Gillon, Steven M., *Pearl Harbor: FDR Leads the Nation into War* (Basic Books: New York, 2011).

Goldstein, Donald M. & Katherine V. Dillon, *The Pacific War Papers: Japanese Documents of World War II* (Potomac Books, Inc.: Washington, DC, 2004).

Goodwin, Doris Kearns, *Leadership in Turbulent Times* (Simon & Schuster: New York, 2018).

Goodwin, Doris Kearns, *No Ordinary Time: Franklin and Eleanor Roosevelt: The Home Front in World War II* (Simon & Schuster: New York, 1994).

Green, Lispenard, *A Foreign Service Marriage* (Privately Published: Washington, DC 1985).

Grew, Joseph C., *Report from Tokyo* (Simon and Schuster: New York, 1942).

Grew, J. C., *Sport and Travel in the Far East* (Houghton Mifflin Co.: Boston, 1910).

Grew, Joseph C., *Ten Years in Japan: A Contemporary Record Drawn from the Diaries and Private and Official Papers of Joseph C. Grew* (Simon & Schuster: New York, 1944).

Grew, Joseph C., *Turbulent Era: A Diplomatic Record of Forty Years 1904-1945, Vol. I & II* (Houghton Mifflin Co.: Boston, 1952).

Heinrichs, Waldo H., Jr., *American Ambassador: Joseph Grew and the Development of the United States Diplomatic Tradition* (Little, Brown and Co.: Boston, 1966).

Heinrichs, Waldo, *Threshold of War: Franklin D. Roosevelt and American Entry into World War II* (Oxford University Press: New York, 1988).

Hill, Max, *Exchange Ship* (Farrar & Rinehart, Inc.: New York, 1942).

Hodgson, Godfrey, *The Colonel: The Life and Wars of Henry Stimson 1867-1950* (Alfred A. Knopf: New York, 1990).

Hooker, Nancy Harvison, *The Moffat Papers: Selections from the Diplomatic Journals of Jay Pierrepont Moffat 1919-1943* (Harvard University Press: Cambridge, MA, 1956).

Hotta, Eri, *Japan 1941: Countdown to Infamy* (Alfred A. Knopf: New York, 2013).

Hoyt, Edwin P., *Warlord: Tojo Against the World* (Cooper Square Press: New York, 2001).

Hull, Cordell, *The Memoirs of Cordell Hull, Vols. I & II* (MacMillan Co.: New York, 1948).

Ickes, Harold L., *The Secret Diary of Harold L. Ickes, Vol. II, 1936-1939; The Inside Struggle* (Simon and Schuster: New York, 1954).

Ickes, Harold. L., *The Secret Diary of Harold L. Ickes, Vol. III, The Lowering Clouds 1939-1941* (Simon and Schuster: New York, 1955).

Ike, Nobutaka (ed. & translator), *Japan's Decision for War: Records of the 1941 Policy Conferences* (Stanford University Press: Stanford, CA 1967).

Israel, Fred L. (ed.), *The War Diary of Breckinridge Long: Selections from the Years 1939- 1944* (University of Nebraska Press: Lincoln, NE, 1966).

Jackson, Robert H., *That Man: An Insider's Portrait of Franklin D. Roosevelt* (Oxford University Press: New York, 2003).

Kase, Toshikazu, *Journey to the Missouri* (Yale University Press: New Haven, CT, 1950).

Kawamura, Noriko, *Emperor Hirohito and the Pacific War* (University of Washington Press: Seattle, WA, 2015).

Koster, John, *Operation Snow: How a Soviet Mole in FDR's White House Triggered Pearl Harbor* (Regnery History: Washington, DC, 2012).

Krock, Arthur, *Memoirs: Sixty Years on the Firing Line* (Alfred A. Knopf: New York, 1968).

Langer, William & S. Everett Gleason, *The Challenge to Isolation 1937-1940* (Harper & Bros. Publishers: New York, 1952).

Langer, William & S. Everett Gleason, *The Undeclared War 1940-1941* (Harper & Bros. Publishers: New York, 1953).

Lash, Joseph P., *Eleanor and Franklin: The Story of Their Relationship* (W.W. Norton & Co.: New York 1971).

Lomazow, Steven & Eric Fettmann, *FDR's Deadly Secret* (Public Affairs: New York, 2009).

Lu, David J., *Agony of Choice: Matsuoka Yosuke and the Rise and Fall of the Japanese Empire, 1880-1946* (Lexington Books: Lanham, MD, 2003).

Mauch, Peter, *Sailor Diplomat: Nomura Kichisaburo and the Japanese-American War* (Harvard University Asia Center: Cambridge, MA, 2011).

McCarty, Kenneth G., Jr., "Stanley K. Hornbeck and the Far East, 1931-1941" (Duke University Ph.D. Dissertation: Raleigh, NC, 1970).

McIntire, Ross T., *White House Physician* (G.P. Putnam's Sons: New York, 1946).

Meacham, Jon, *Franklin and Winston: An Intimate Portrait of an Epic Friendship* (Random House: New York, 2003).

Miller, Edward S., *Bankrupting the Enemy: The U.S. Financial Siege of Japan Before Pearl Harbor* (Naval Institute Press: Annapolis, MD 2007).

Mitchell, Richard H., *Thought Control in Prewar Japan* (Cornell University Press: Ithaca, NY, 1976).

Moe, Richard, *Roosevelt's Second Act: The Election of 1940 and the Politics of War* (Oxford University Press: New York, 2013).

Morley, James William (ed.) & David A. Titus (translator), *Japan's Road to the Pacific War: The Final Confrontation: Japan's Negotiation with the United States, 1941* (Columbia University Press: New York, 1994).

Najita, Tetsuo, *Japan: The Intellectual Foundations of Modern Japanese Politics* (University of Chicago Press: Chicago, 1974).

Nelson, Craig, *Pearl Harbor: From Infamy to Greatness* (Scribner: New York, 2016).

Nesbitt, Henrietta, *White House Diary* (Doubleday & Co.: Garden City, NY 1948).

Olson, Lynn, *Those Angry Days: Roosevelt, Lindbergh, and America's Fight Over World War II 1939-1941* (Random House: New York, 2014).

Overby, David Hoien, "The Diplomatic Stalemate of Japan and the United States: 1941" (Portland State University Masters Thesis: Portland, OR, 1973).

Pash, Sidney, *The Currents of War: A New History of American-Japanese Relations, 1899- 1941* (University Press of Kentucky: Lexington, KY, 2014).

Perkins, Frances, *The Roosevelt I Knew* (Viking Press: New York, 1946).

Persico, Joseph E., *Franklin & Lucy: President Roosevelt, Mrs. Rutherford, and the Other Remarkable Women in His Life* (Random House: New York, 2008).

Pipkin, J. and C. Lewis (eds.), *The Metropolitan Club of Washington: The First 150 Years* (Metropolitan Club: Washington, DC, 2012).

Prange, Gordon W. with Donald M. Goldstein & Katherine V. Dillon, *At Dawn We Slept: The Untold Story of Pearl Harbor* (Penguin Group: New York, 1981).

Prange, Gordon W. with Donald M. Goldstein & Katherine V. Dillion, *December 7, 1941: The Day the Japanese Attacked Pearl Harbor* (Penguin Group: New York, 1988).

Prange, Gordon W. with Donald M. Goldstein & Katherine V. Dillion, *Pearl Harbor: The Verdict of History* (Penguin Group: New York, 1986).

Pratt, Julius W., *Cordell Hull, 1933-1944, Vols. I & II* (Cooper Square Press: New York, 1964).

Rosenman, Samuel, *Working with Roosevelt* (Harper & Bros.: New York, 1952).

Seidensticker, Edward, *Tokyo Rising: The City since the Great Earthquake* (Harvard University Press: Cambridge, MA, 1991).

Schlesinger, Arthur M., Jr., *The Age of Roosevelt: The Coming of the New Deal* (Houghton Mifflin Co.: Boston, 1959).

Schlesinger, Arthur M., Jr., *The Age of Roosevelt: The Crisis of the Old Order: 1919-1933* (Houghton Mifflin Co.: Boston, 1957).

Schlesinger, Arthur M., Jr., *The Age of Roosevelt: The Politics of Upheaval* (Houghton Mifflin Co.: Boston, 1960).

Sherwood, Robert E., *Roosevelt and Hopkins: An Intimate History* (Harper & Bros. Co.: New York, 1948).

Shigemitsu, Mamuro, *Japan and Her Destiny: My Struggle for Peace* (E.F. Dutton & Co.: New York, 1958).

Shinsato, Douglas T & Tadanori Urabe (translators), *For That One Day: The Memoirs of Mitsuo Fuchida, Commander of the Attack on Pearl Harbor* (eXperience, Inc.: Lexington, KY, 2011).

Smith, Jean Edward, *FDR* (Random House: New York, 2007).

Smith, Kathryn, *The Gatekeeper: Missy LeHand, FDR, and the Untold Story of the Partnership that Defined a Presidency* (Simon & Schuster: New York, 2016).

Staff of Asahi Shimbun, *The Pacific Rivals: A Japanese View of Japanese American Relations* (John Weatherhill, Inc: New York, 1972).

Stimson, Henry L. and McGeorge Bundy, *On Active Service in Peace and War* (Harper & Bros.: New York, 1948).

Stinnett, Robert, *Day of Deceit: The Truth about FDR and Pearl Harbor* (Free Press: New York, 2000).

Summers, Anthony & Robbyn Swan, *A Matter of Honor: Pearl Harbor: Betrayal, Blame, and a Family's Quest for Justice* (HarperCollins: New York, 2016).

Terasaki, Gwen, *Bridge to the Sun: A Memoir of Love and War* (University of North Carolina Press: Chapple Hill, NC, 1957).

Thomas, Gordon and Max Morgan-Witts, *Voyage of the Damned: A Shocking True Story of Hope, Betrayal, and Nazi Terror* (Stein and Day: New York, 1974).

Togo, Shigenori, *The Cause of Japan* (Simon and Schuster: New York, 1956).

Toland, John, *Infamy: Pearl Harbor and Its Aftermath* (Doubleday: New York, 1982).

Toland, John, *The Rising Sun: The Decline and Fall of the Japanese Empire 1936-1945* (Random House: New York, 1970).

Tolischus, Otto D., *Tokyo Record* (Reynal & Hitchcock: New York, 1943).

Tully, Grace, *F.D.R. My Boss* (Scribner's Sons: New York, 1949).

Twomey, Steve, *Countdown to Pearl Harbor: The Twelve Days to the Attack* (Simon & Schuster: New York, 2016).

United States Naval Institute, *The Reminiscences of Capt. Henri Smith-Hutton, USN (Ret.)* (USNI: Annapolis, MD, 1976).

Utley, Jonathan G., *Going to War with Japan 1937-1941* (University of Tennessee Press: Knoxville, TN, 1985).

Ward, Geoffrey C. (ed.), *Closest Companion: The Unknown Story of the Intimate Friendship between Franklin Roosevelt and Margaret Suckley* (Houghton Mifflin: Boston, 1995).

Weintraub, Stanley, *Long Day's Journey into War: Pearl Harbor and a World at War December 7, 1941* (E.P. Dutton: New York, 1991).

Weil, Martin, *A Pretty Good Club: The Founding Fathers of the U.S. Foreign Service* (W.W. Norton & Co.: New York, 1978).

Welles, Benjamin *Sumner, Welles: FDR's Global Strategist* (St. Martin's Press: New York, 1997).

Welles, Sumner, *The Time for Decision* (Harper & Bros.: New York, 1944).

Wohlstetter, Roberta, *Pearl Harbor: Warning and Decision* (Stanford University Press: Stanford, CA, 1962).

Yagami, Kazuo, *Konoe Fumimaro and the Failure of Peace in Japan 1937-1941: A Critical Appraisal of the Three-Time Prime Minister* (McFarland & Co.: Jefferson, NC, 2006).

INDEX

BIOGRAPHY

Lew Paper is the author of five previous books, including *John F. Kennedy: The Promise and the Performance*, *Brandeis: An Intimate Biography*, and *Empire: William S. Paley and the Making of CBS*. Lew's articles and book reviews have appeared in a variety of newspapers and magazines, including the *New York Times*, the *Washington Post*, *The New Republic*, and *The American Scholar*.

Lew is a former Adjunct Professor at Georgetown University Law Center and a former Teaching Fellow in Government at Harvard College.

You can contact Lew and view descriptions and reviews of his books at lewpaper.com.